Collins
tracing your
family history

Collins
tracing your
family history

Anthony Adolph

Collins

'who begot whom is a most amusing kind of hunting' Horace Walpole

For our friends' daughter Kim Van Trier, who completed her journey from conception to birth in marginally less time and with considerably less fuss than the writing of this book, and for Scott Crowley, whose quiet support and encouragement throughout have been unfaltering.

First published in 2004 by
Collins, an imprint of
HarperCollinsPublishers
77–85 Fulham Palace Road
London W6 8JB

This edition published 2007 for Index Books Ltd

The Collins website address is www.collins.co.uk
Collins is a registered trademark of HarperCollins Publishers Ltd

11	10	09	08	07	06
7	6	5	4	3	2

Text © 2004, 2005 Anthony Adolph

Editor: Emma Callery
Art Editor: Ruth Prentice
Design: Hannah Attwell
Picture Research: Suzanne Bosman

A catalogue record for this book is available
from the British Library

ISBN 13 978-0-00-721483-9
ISBN 10 0-00-721483-9

Colour reproduction by Dot Gradations
Printed and bound in Great Britain by Butler and Tanner

CONTENTS

INTRODUCTION

Long before there were computer programmers and engineers, blacksmiths or even farmers, our ancestors told each other stories of who they were and where they came from. Over time, as other subjects became more important (or at least seemed to be), our ancestral tales began to take a back-burner, the older ones blurring into creation myths but the more recent ones remaining important to their tellers and listeners.

> ❛ *The rise of written records heralded a gradual erosion of oral traditions.* ❜

▽ My great-great-grandparents, Albert Joseph Adolph and his wife Emily Lydia, née Watson. When I started my research, they were as far back as my grandfather's memory stretched.

When memories started to be written down, one of the first things to be recorded were ancient genealogies, linking the living to their ancient roots. It is for that reason that we can trace the Queen's ancestry back through the Saxon royal family to their mythological ancestor, the god Woden. Yet for most, the rise of written records heralded a gradual erosion of oral traditions and, in medieval England, memories tended to grow shorter in proportion to the proliferating rolls of vellum and parchment recording our forebears' deeds, dues and misdemeanours. And then, just as it became apparent to our ancestors that they were losing touch with the past, it crossed people's minds that these self-same documents, compiled for no better reason than to record land transfer, court cases or tax liability, could help us retrace our past and discover the identities of our forgotten forebears.

This, the act of tracing family roots through both remembered stories and written records, is genealogy, the subject that has preoccupied most of my life, first as an amateur and later as a professional ever since, as a child, I encountered the pedigrees of elves and hobbits at the back of *The Lord of the Rings*. And it has been my good fortune that the past few decades have been ones of exceptional growth in genealogy as a pastime across the world, from a minority interest with snobby overtones in the 1960s to a mainstream activity, contributing significantly to the tourist industry and constituting one of the principal uses of the Internet. In recent decades, it has broken through, too, into the media.

▽ Genealogy hits TV: the publicity postcard for *Extraordinary Ancestors*, 2000, showing the author and co-presenter Shilpa Mehta.

Extraordinary
ANCESTORS

Thursday 12th October @ 8:00pm

Thursday 19th October @ 8:00pm

Thursday 26th October @ 8:00pm

NEW EDITION

FAMILY HISTORY is enjoying an extraordinarily dynamic phase and much is changing. In the last few years, internet companies have realised the profits to be made by setting up pay-to-view websites, especially covering the two great building blocks of 19th-century family trees, General Registration and census records. The small amounts paid by users fund further indexing work, thus bringing yet more records within far easier reach of more people than ever before.

These sites have truly revolutionised searching. When I wrote the first edition of this book, I would only have sought people in the 1871 census (for example) if I had a precise address, or had no alternative choice. Now, I can search the entire 1871 census online in seconds. I would make one plea, though: if you are new to this, please don't take these new developments for granted, or grumble at the relatively very small amounts of money being charged. You are at a vast advantage over genealogists in previous generations. Equally, however, pre-Internet genealogists did have to get to grips with and understand how these records worked in far more detail, and this tended to make them very good researchers. So, why not use the time you are saving by getting instant access to records on the Internet to read the relevant chapters in this book, so you can start getting a more rounded picture of how those records were created, and where the originals are to be found? This edition is as up-to-date as it can be – yet improvements in accessibility occur almost monthly. These are exciting times indeed.

△ My mother's great-grandfather, Rev. Patrick Henry Kilduff – one of a treasure trove of old photographs I was given by a distant cousin whom I had traced in the course of my research.

❛Millions of people are now actively investigating their origins, or at least thinking about doing so.❜

The first year of this millennium saw two series appearing on national television, BBC 2's *Blood Ties* and my own series, *Extraordinary Ancestors*, on Channel 4. These were followed by further series with which I have been privileged to be involved, particularly Living TV's *Antiques Ghostshow* and Radio 4's *Meet the Descendants*, which have continued to tell stories of genealogical investigation and discovery.

Millions of people, including you, are now actively investigating their origins, or at least thinking about doing so. This complete guide is intended to cover all the topics you will need to know about to trace your family tree. You can start at the beginning, letting it guide you through the process of getting started and working back through the different types of records which should, given time and patience, enable you to trace your family tree back for hundreds of years. Or, if you are already a genealogist, you can use it as a reference book to identify and learn more about the vast array of different types of source that may be available for your research.

In some respects, this book follows the standards already set out by its predecessors, and I fully acknowledge my enormous debts to genealogical writers who blazed the trail before me, not least Sir Anthony Wagner, Mark Herber, Terrick FitzHugh, George Pelling, Don Steel, John Titford and Susan Lumas. In other respects, and within the parameters set by what is expected of genealogical reference books, I have tried to add to this my personal perspective, not least by drawing on my experiences in translating genealogy into radio and television.

A NEW BOOK FOR A CHANGING WORLD

In this book, I have tried to reflect the extraordinary changes that have recently injected new life into this most ancient of subjects.

DNA technology

DNA technology has escaped the confines of the laboratory and become readily available to anyone with even a modest research budget. Do not be deceived by the relative brevity of my chapter on the subject; its implications for genealogy are vast.

Multi-cultural roots

Although Britain has always been a multi-cultural nation, a barrage of prejudices and phobias meant that we have only recently started to uncover the full extent of our global roots. Only in the last two decades have the many white families with black or Asian ancestors been able to start investigating such connections. Only recently have they been permitted by society and, in some cases, their own attitudes, to look on their connections with other continents with fascination rather than shame. Equally, thanks to the post-war mass immigration of black and Asian families, there are now a very great number of British families with roots exclusively from overseas. But by far the greatest trend, resulting from relationships between the different ethnic communities in Britain, is the rise of generations with roots both in indigenous white Britain and in other continents.

Other genealogical writers have not ignored this fact, but nor have they addressed the issue in any depth. I felt that, in writing a book for genealogists in modern Britain, it was appropriate to broaden its scope to acknowledge the vast number of readers whose ethnic English blood – if they have any at all – is only a small proportion of their total ancestral mix. I have not attempted to write a worldwide guide to tracing family trees but, while the focus of the book is on research in England, I have tried to show and remind readers how the same or similar sources can be located and used in the rest of the British Isles and in countries all around the world. Please note that, when I refer to records outside Britain, I do so by way of example: the absence of a reference to a type of record in a certain country does not mean that records are not there. The volume of material available for America requires a separate book and has therefore been omitted almost entirely.

△ Shilpa Mehta (on the right) with her father, Shailendra, and brother, Shayur, in Zambia before her family settled permanently in England (see page 248).

▽ The GenesReunited website home page: www.GenesReunited.co.uk

The Internet

The Internet has changed genealogy by making different types of records more easily searchable and by creating new resources that never existed before, such as the GenesReunited website. If you are serious about tracing your family tree, I recommend you either acquire a computer, find a good library or café providing Internet access, or are very, very nice to someone who is already connected to the web. While you should never trust anything on the Internet without checking it in original

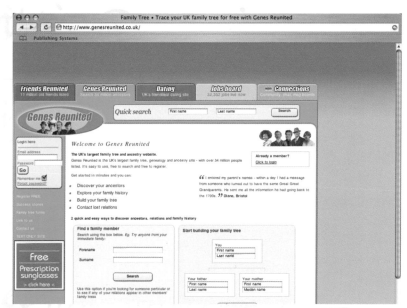

sources, the amount of time you can save using the resources available online is enormous.

On a daily basis, new indexes and resources appear, change, grow or, in some cases, disappear from the great information super-highway that is the worldwide web. Website addresses are so helpful and important that I have provided the ones that are most useful at the time of writing, and made them an integral part of the text. However, the rate of change inevitably means that, by the time you read this book, some things will have changed and proposed new legislation even threatens to restrict access to some of the records described here. In most cases, though, change will only have been for the better in terms of more records becoming more easily accessible via index and databases.

PROFESSIONAL HELP

I became a professional genealogist in 1992 after several years studying at the Institute of Heraldic and Genealogical Studies. During most of my career, first working for a well-known firm of genealogists and latterly with my own freelance business, I have spent more time establishing what sources are available to solve particular problems and commissioning record agents to search them, than actually being in archives myself.

This is a course of action I wholeheartedly recommend to all readers of this book. Many people say, 'But I want to do it all myself.' Fair enough – and use this book to acquire a detailed knowledge of the sources and their whereabouts. But there are many cases where paying a record searcher in a different county (or on the other side of the world) for a couple of hours' work can save a vast amount of time, travel and accommodation costs, especially if the source you identified turns out to have been the wrong one. Receiving positive results by post (or email) may not be quite as exciting as turning over a dusty page and finding an ancestor's name but, frankly, most records

▽ **Connections between the past and present. My great-great-aunt Louisa Havers (1832–1937) at Ingatestone Hall, Essex, in 1917, with her young cousin Philip Coverdale who, as an old man, took me under his wing and taught me how to trace family trees.**

are now searchable only by microfiche in record offices anyway. The time you will have saved having the search done can then be spent visiting the place where you have discovered your ancestor once lived. If you really want to do it yourself, though, don't let me stop you. I merely offer a piece of personal advice.

GETTING TO KNOW YOUR ANCESTORS

Throughout this introduction, I have referred to genealogy. There's also a subject called family history. Essentially, genealogy is tracing who was who – the nuts and bolts of the family tree – while family history is more about finding out about the ancestors themselves, exploring their lives and working out how they came to do what they did and be who they were. That in itself then merges into the subject of biography. Once you have researched your family history in depth you will, in effect, have researched mini (or not so mini) biographies of your ancestors. Most, if not actually all, of the sources used by biographers are described in this book. Getting to know your ancestors can be a fascinating experience even if you do not (as people who have seen me in *Antiques Ghostshow* will know) want to roam into the world of psychics.

But, in investigating your family tree, please bear in mind there is a real distinction between your ancestors and the records in which they appear. I have known people to cherish birth certificates as if they were the spiritual embodiments of their forebears. They are not. Think of when you last looked at yours and what a nuisance it is when you generate records similar to those you use for tracing ancestry. Obtaining passports and driving licences is a chore: dealing with banks, lawyers, the Inland Revenue and social services is tiring and invariably annoying. Often, when you encounter an ancestor in a record, they, too, were probably vexed and annoyed through the making of it. Equally, useful though they are, many modern genealogy programs and charts require you to focus so much on dates of birth, marriage and death that you can easily forget that the people concerned actually had lives in the intervening years. The real ancestors stand back behind the dates and records they generated: bear that in mind and you won't go far wrong in learning to understand them.

△ **Filming the story of *EastEnders'* convoluted family tree on location at Elstree, 2000.**

PART ONE

Tracing family trees is mainly about seeking records, but before you do that, there's a great deal you may be able to learn from your own family – close as well as distant relatives. And whatever you find out, don't forget to write it down. Start properly and avoid tears later!

CHAPTER ONE
ASK THE FAMILY

With very few exceptions, nobody knows more about your immediate family than your immediate family. Yet the first steps in tracing a family tree are often ignored or skipped over in the headlong dash for illustrious roots and unclaimed fortunes.

Most people reading this will probably have made at least some sort of start at researching their family tree. This chapter gives structure to your first steps and, I hope, to all your research over years to come.

STARTING OFF

However old you are, the very best way to start research is by writing down your own essential details, which are:

➤ Date and place of birth
➤ Your education, occupations and where you have lived
➤ Religious denomination
➤ Anything interesting about yourself, which future generations may be glad you took the trouble to record
➤ Date and place of marriage, and to whom (if applicable)
➤ Date and place of children's births and marriages (if applicable)

Then repeat the same process for your siblings, parents, their siblings, your grandparents and so on, adding details of when and where people died, if applicable.

One of the key elements here is write it all down because all this work will be to little avail if you do not record your findings.

Besides information on the living, you will soon start to record information on the deceased, as recalled by their children, grandchildren and so on. This is oral history – things known from memory rather than written records.

THE ORAL TRADITION

Originally, all family trees were known orally. In Britain, there are a handful of pedigrees of the ancient rulers of the Anglo-Saxons, Vikings, Celts and Picts, which stretch far back into the past, and which are known now because they were later written down. They contain some palpable mistakes and grey areas, but they are greatly valued because they are pretty much all we have left. Sadly, cultures such as Britain that adopted widespread use of written records tend very quickly to lose

△ Family papers: a letter to my great-great-grandmother from her husband's cousin, Mrs Dorthea Boulger (1908), concerning their family history.

LIFETIMES: A RICH ORAL TRADITION

JUST BECAUSE very few written records were made in pre-colonial Africa does not mean that family trees cannot be traced. Benhilda Chisveto of Edinburgh knew her father was Thomas Majuru, born in 1953, and that his mother was Edith, but that was all. She then made enquiries about her family from older relatives still living in her native Zimbabwe, and was told the following family tree, dictated orally and perhaps never recorded on paper before.

Thomas Majuru was son of Mubaiwa, son of Majuru (hence the modern surname), who lived near Harare, and who was apparently the only survivor of his area when British forces invaded in 1897. He buried the dead and then sought refuge in Murehwa, where the family now live. He was son of Mukombingo. Before Mukombingo, the line runs back, son to father, thus: Kakonzo; Mudavanhu; Mbari; Taizivei; Barahanga; Jengera; Zimunwe; Katowa; Mhangare; Maneru; Dambaneshure; Chihoka; Chiumbe; Musiwaro; Mukwashahuue; Makutiodora; Diriro; Gweru; Makaya; Chamutso; Guru; Waziva; Misi; Chitedza otherwise called Chibwe Chitedza; Nyavira also called Nyabira; Mukunti-Muora.

A FEW FACTS

The only dates in the oral history were for Mbari, who was chief of his tribe from 1795 to 1797, and Katowa, who was chief 1450–97. The earliest ancestor, Mukunti-Muora, supposedly lived 4000 years ago. One thousand would be more realistic, and to get back from 1795 to 1450 in five generations is stretching it. There may, then, be some omissions of generations, or misremembered facts, but that makes this no different to the earliest oral pedigrees of the British Isles, which stretch back to Arthur, Brutus of Troy and the god Woden. This does not detract from their immense value because they undoubtedly do record the names of ancestors who really lived, and who are not recorded in any other fashion. Lose the oral history and you lose them irrevocably.

the oral history that has been accumulated over the centuries. For much of the Third World, and the native cultures of the Americas and Australasia, this invasion of literacy has happened much more recently, and oral traditions are still strong. With the spread of literacy, though, oral history is under threat and will probably disappear altogether very soon; hence the need to write it down.

Such traditions should be treated with the greatest respect, but it is unrealistic to imagine that they can be strictly accurate. When using oral history as the basis for original, record-based research, you mustn't be surprised if you find names, dates or places are given slightly (or sometimes wildly) inaccurately. I sometimes get my own age wrong by a year (I certainly can't remember my telephone number all the time), so you should be prepared for this and, if you do not find what

on the 20th February by the Rev. J.Y.Bramston, Godfather Matthew Mason, Godmother, Julia Mason.

Michael John Mason born 26th March 1823 baptized by the Rev. J.Y.Bramston 31st March 1823. Godfather John Morgan Godmother, Rebecca Jackson, died 27th March 1824, buried in Vault at Moorfields Chapel.

Roma Frances Mason born 12th November 1824 by the Rev. Thos. Doyle. Godfather John Morgan, Godmother Frances Rolph.

Michael Furney Mason born 12th March 1825 baptized by the Rev. Thos. Doyle, Godfather, Furney Rolph, Surgeon Godmother Anna Mason

Certificates of Baptisms may be obtained at St George's Catholic Chapel, London Road, Southwark Surrey

△ **Family papers: lists of children's dates of birth and baptism were often kept by families, especially before the start of General Registration in 1837.**

you are looking for under Thompson in 1897, see if what you want isn't listed under Thomson in 1898 instead.

In fact, you can't trace a record-based family tree properly without developing a healthy scepticism for anything you are told, or indeed anything you read. There are deceptions and lies, of course. One family I helped, who were called Newman, discovered their ancestor had faked his own suicide and started a new life – as a 'new man', his original name having been something completely different. More often, though, discrepancies and inaccuracies arise through simple mistakes or lapses of memory. 'Granny would never lie,' said one client of mine, 'so that birth certificate must be wrong.' No, Granny didn't lie, she just got her age slightly wrong. There's a real difference.

Indeed, recording oral history often relies on interviewing the elderly. Sometimes, it's the only time very old people have any proper attention paid to them, so be indulgent if they don't reel out exactly what you want in ten minutes flat. Letter, telephone and email can all help you gain valuable information from your relatives, but if you can visit them, so much the better. It may seem a bind, but it's often worth it and will become part of your store of memories to pass on to later generations. I once went all the way to Tours in France to visit Lydia Renault, a cousin of my mother's. I arrived at 11am and, whereas her English relations would have offered me tea and some ghastly old biscuits, Lydia suggested whisky and Coca-Cola, which we drank on her balcony, overlooking the Loire, while she regaled me with tales of her family at the start of the 20th century.

ELICITING THE PAST

That was an exception. If you get tea and stale biscuits, receive them with as great a semblance of delight as you can muster. If you are approaching someone you haven't met before, make every effort to write and telephone in advance and make it absolutely clear you are after their invaluable knowledge, rather than their (usually less valuable) purse. Write down (or tape record) everything they say, as the seemingly irrelevant may later turn out to be the main clue that cracks the case. If they have difficulty remembering facts, ask them to talk you through any old photographs they may have – that often stimulates the synapses – and sometimes you may get more from them if you allow them to contradict you.

> *Write down everything your interviewee says, as the seemingly irrelevant may later turn out to be the main clue that cracks the case.*

FOR EXAMPLE:

'What was your grandfather's mother called?'

'Oh, I don't know.'

'I think it was Doris.'

'No, no, Doris was his sister. His mother was Milly!'

Another tip: if they can't remember a date of, say, when someone died, try to get them to narrow down the period in which it could have happened.

'When did your great-grandmother die?'

'I don't know.'

'Well, do you remember her?'

'Oh yes, she was at my wedding.'

'So she was alive in 1935. And was she at your first child's christening in 1937?'

'Oh no, she died before then.'

Be sensitive, too, to changing social attitudes. Fascinating though it may be to you, the very elderly may not want to talk about their parents' bigamous marriage, so if you want any information from them you must tread very carefully. One man's black sheep, after all, is another's hero.

THE POWER OF PAPER

Don't forget, though, that younger relations of yours may have been told things by much older relations who are now dead. Equally – and here we leave the realms of oral history and move on a step – they, like the elderly, may have family papers and heirlooms. These come in so many forms: letters, school reports, memorial cards, passports, vaccination and ration cards, and so on, all crowned by the queen of all family papers, the family bible.

▽ My grandfather's air raid warden card. Note that he had been appointed before the war, in 1938.

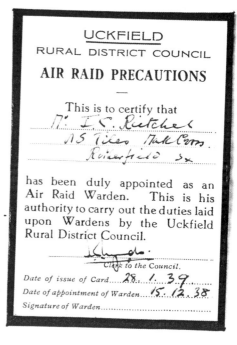

△ **Pages from the Fairfax family bible, which even includes an extra newspaper cutting.**

▽ **Family reunions: a family photograph showing the Adolph, Mitchiner and Gale families celebrating the 80th birthday of my grandfather Joseph Adolph in 1990.**

Some bibles can be centuries old, faithfully recording the births, marriages and deaths of each member of the family. The tip to finding family bibles is to trace down the female-to-female line of the family, as they are often passed from mother to daughter. Lost or unwanted ones (how can anybody not want a family bible?) often end up at car boot sales and genealogical magazines have been known to publish letters from well wishers who have found such a bible, describing its contents and volunteering to return it to the right family.

Whether it's a family bible or a 70-year-old funeral bill, write down all the salient details (or, better still, photocopy everything) because such papers may contain clues that will only become useful to you long afterwards. Ignore such advice at your peril and, if you have to go back all the way to Wigan to have another look at your cousin's grandmother's address book you didn't bother with ten years ago, don't blame me.

Actually, the real prize transcends even that, because sometimes you will find that an ancestor will already have tried to trace the family tree. One of the things that really encouraged me to pursue my own was

PRELIMINARY RESEARCH

☑ Make notes on what you know
☑ Constantly update your notes
☑ Ask immediate family
☑ Network with remoter family
☑ Register with www.genesreunited.co.uk
(see page 31) and other 'contact' websites
☑ Update your entries as you learn more

BASIC RESEARCH

☑ General Registration (from 1837) (see page 44)
☑ Censuses (1841–1901, especially those indexed online) (see page 66)
☑ Wills and administrations from 1858 (see page 124)

MORE IN-DEPTH RESEARCH

☑ Unindexed censuses, using directories (see page 82)
☑ Parish registers (from 1538) (see page 96)
☑ Bishops' transcripts (from 1598) (see page 114)
☑ Manorial records (see page 118)
☑ Wills and letters of administration (before 1858) (see page 124)
☑ Gravestones (mainly from 17th century) (see page 138)
☑ Newpapers for obituaries, etc. (Mainly from 18th century) (see page 144)
☑ Electoral registers (see page 164), etc. to find addresses

△ www.genesreunited.co.uk

☑ Parish chest and poor law material (mainly from 17th century) (see page 166)
☑ Occupation records (especially army and navy, mainly from 18th century) (see pages 179 and 190)
☑ Legal records (see page 224)
☑ Education records (see page 236)
☑ Printed pedigrees, heraldic records, etc. (see pages 290 and 298)

AND, IF ALL GOES EXCEPTIONALLY WELL ...

☑ Medieval tax lists and land records (from 1086) (see page 212)
☑ Early university and school records from Middle Ages (see page 236)
☑ Ancient oral pedigrees now in print

being given a Harrods' carrier bag full of 'the family papers', which turned out to be my great-great grandmother's notes, showing her attempts to trace her family tree between 1880 and 1920. Sadly there was no sign of her finished family trees – if there ever were any – and nor have they ever turned up. However, the bag did include replies to letters she had written to her second and third cousins, thus filling out my own family tree before I had ever set foot outside my front door.

CHAPTER TWO
WRITING IT ALL DOWN

The rest of this book is about how to trace your ancestry, but this chapter focuses on how to record your findings, from getting all your notes written down on computer or paper and moving onto understanding the family tree conventions.

Some people can get bogged down in choosing computer packages, filing systems and so on. Frankly, if you enjoy computer programs, then you'll love family history, as there is a vast array to chose from, reviewed and advertised in the genealogical magazines like *Your Family Tree* and *Family History Monthly*, with an excellent comparative chart at **www.My-history.co.uk**. Everyone has a preference. Personally, I don't rate very highly the packages that invite you to fill in forms about all your ancestors. I feel it de-humanises them and encourages some people to become obsessed simply with the act of form filling with completing forms that can't be. Me? I keep a cardboard file for each family I am tracing, containing photographs, documents, notes and so on, and a rough family tree on paper, and then maintain a narrative pedigree on my word processor. Once I feel satisfied with what I have done, I may also write up a summarised version of the family story, including the best pictures and documents, either to circulate among the family or to submit to a relevant family history journal (see pages 24–5).

GETTING IT ON PAPER

The main point at this stage is to write everything down. Be they oral or written, quote your sources precisely. Later, you can interpret the sources, but if you do this initially and discard the original information, and then find that your interpretation of the sources had been wrong, you (or someone else trying to help you – and, believe me, I've been there!) may have a terrible time disentangling what is correct from what is not. This applies just as much to interviewing people as to record-based research. In addition, *always* write down exactly what records you were searching, for what periods and for what you searched. If you do, and later you find that you are stuck, you may rely on your notes to tell you, say, that you looked under Thompson and also Thomson, thus potentially saving yourself a repeat journey to a record office to perform a search you had, in fact, already carried out but forgotten about.

THE BASIC FAMILY TREE

There are several different types of family tree. These are:

➤ **'Family trees' and 'pedigrees',** sometimes prefixed with the term 'dropline' (a chart with the earliest ancestor at the top and each subsequent generation connected by dropping lines), are one and the same – charts depicting a line or lines of ancestry.

➤ **'Narrative pedigrees',** which are family trees written down in paragraphs, a style that is used by *Burke's Peerage* and which is a highly effective way of recording a lot of information in a small space, but which isn't so good for easily seeing who's related to who. It is not much use for conducting original research, when only a family tree will make everything clear.

➤ **Seize quartiers,** which spread out either like trees or in concentric circles, to show both parents, all four grandparents, the eight great-grandparents and – if you can manage it – all 16 great-greats. The original purpose of seize quartiers was snobbish, as you had to prove that all 16 were noble if you wanted to join foreign orders of knighthood like the Golden Fleece. Now, however, they are a good way of showing you have traced your family exhaustively. But don't feel obliged and become exhausted, this is supposed to be fun and you can aim to trace as much or as little as you want.

CRANE PRINTS

OLD FAMILY TREES were drawn with the names of parents in circles and their children radiating out below them. This arrangement was thought to resemble the footprints of Cranes in the soft mud of river banks, hence their name 'Crane's foot' – 'pied de Cru' – pedigree!

▽ Part of my mother's family tree, showing how Germans printed pedigrees in the 1930s.

CHARTING CONVENTIONS

=   Indicates a marriage, accompanied by 'm.' and the date and place

—   Solid lines indicate definite connections

…   Dotted lines indicate probable but unproven ones

∿   Wiggly lines are for illegitimacy and 'x' for a union out of wedlock – important on old pedigrees but less relevant today

⌐⌐   Loops are used if two unconnected lines need to cross over

⊠   Wives usually go on the right of husbands, though only if that doesn't interfere with the overall layout of the chart

⊠   Conventionally, surnames are put after men's but not women's names, but again this is becoming a bit old fashioned

COMMONLY USED ABBREVIATIONS

b. born
bpt or c. baptised or christened (same thing)
bach. bachelor
bur. or sep. buried
coh. coheir(ess)
d. or ob./obit. died
d.s.p. or o.s.p. died without children

d.v.p. or o.v.p. died before father
ed. educated
fl. lived ('floreat')
inft infant
k.i.a. killed in action
lic. marriage licence
m. or = married
m. diss. by div. marriage dissolved by divorce

m.i.w. 'mentioned in the will of followed by f. for father, gf. for grandfather and so on
MI monumental inscription
spin. spinster
temp. in the time of
unm. unmarried
wid. widow or widower (as appropriate)
w.wr./pr. will written/proved

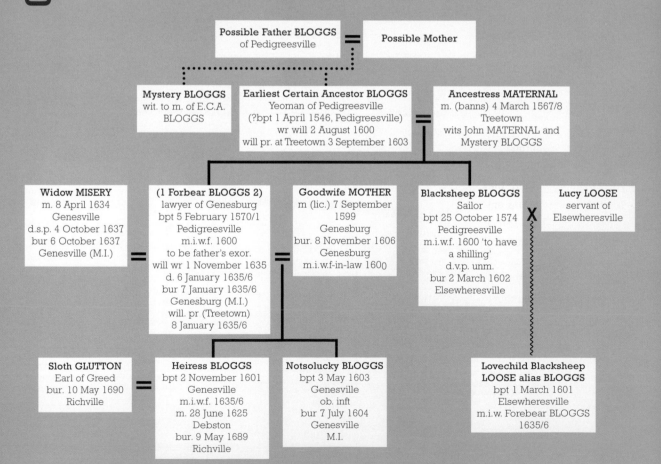

Equally, there are no rules about what you can or can't include on a family tree. Put in as much or as little as you want and include as many families as you want, though beware of cluttering. I would recommend a minimum of full names, dates of birth or baptism, marriage and death or burial, where those events took place, and occupations. If your chart lacks any of these, it will be of little use to other researchers and, more importantly, it will be boring. If you know someone was crushed to death by a bear or invented the casserole dish, for goodness sake put it on the chart!

There are some sensible conventions and abbreviations, which you'll need to know both for compiling your own charts and understanding other peoples'. These are outlined opposite.

EXPANDING ON THE BASICS

When it comes to writing up the family history, you can, again, decide what to say and how to say it, and you can get ideas from the examples in this book and the many published family histories and articles in family history journals and magazines.

It's a good idea to try to relate the events in the family to the world around them:

➤ Who was on the throne
➤ What wars and plagues would have concerned or affected them
➤ What the places where they lived were like at the time
➤ What their occupations entailed.

This is a valuable exercise, which might actually help you find out more about them, or highlight inaccuracies or even mistakes in the family tree. It is also a good reminder that these were real, breathing people who existed in the world, not as pale shadows on old, dusty records. Indeed, if you think your ancestors only existed within the confines of parish register entries and, now, the forms generated by genealogical computer programs, it's unlikely you will gain very much from family history, or that other people will enjoy and benefit from your hard work. The more you can think of and convey the idea of your ancestors as real human beings, the more fun – and success – you're likely to have.

△ Marriage bond for John Nursey, surgeon of Coddenham, Suffolk.

KNOW all Men by these Presents, That We William Kevil of Coddenham in ye County of Suffolk, Surgeon, & John Nursey of ye same place, Surgeon ——

are holden and firmly bound to the Worshipful FRANCIS FRANK, Batchelor of Laws Commissary in and throughout the Arch-deaconry of Suffolk lawfully appointed: in the Sum of Two Hundred Pounds of good and lawful Money of Great-Britain, to be paid to the said FRANCIS FRANK, or his certain Attorney, Successors or Assigns: To which Payment well and truly to be made, we bind ourselves, and each of us by himself for the whole, our and each of our Heirs Executors and Administrators, firmly by these Presents. Sealed with our Seals, Dated the twelfth —— in the Year of our Lord One Thou-

HERE IS THE SAME information about the Fairfax family, presented as a narrative pedigree, a prose account and a traditional family tree.

NARRATIVE PEDIGREE

John Fairfax, born about 1710, married Mary Hayward on 16 September 1735 at Framlingham, Suffolk. He was a draper and grocer of Coddenham and wrote his will in 1751, naming his executors as his wife Mary and brother-in-law John Hayward. It was proved 2 June 1758 (Suffolk Record Office IC/AA1/184/49). His children (details of which are recorded in the family bible) included:

1 Frances, born 24 May 1736, baptised 25 May and died 31 May, Stowmarket.

2 Mary, born 9 June 1738, baptised 26 June at Stowmarket.

3 John Fairfax, born 30 June 1739, died 15 weeks old, buried at Stowmarket.

4 John Fairfax, born 30 August 1741. Left a watch by his father. Married Penelope Wright at St James's, Bury St Edmund's, on 5 May 1770. Elected freeman of Bury St Edmunds, 1802. Death recorded in *Gentleman's Magazine* as being in a fit on 12 February 1805 while visiting 'a friend [sic], Mr P. Nursey, at Little Bealings'. He had two children:

    1 Penelope, born on 17 April and baptised on 31 May 1771 at St James's, buried on 30 June 1787 at Bury St Edmunds.

    2 Catherine, born on 6 November 1772 and baptised on 3 December 1790 at Bury St Edmunds by Rev. Mr Sharp, as is recorded in the family bible.

5 Catherine Fairfax, born 7 September 1742 and baptised by Mr Meadows. Inherited share of a messuage in Kettleburgh from cousin Katherine Fairfax in 1747/50. Married John Nursey by licence on 4 April 1764 at Coddenham, before witnesses John and Mary Fairfax; he was described as a surgeon of Coddenham and she as daughter of John Fairfax of Coddenham, a draper. Died at Wickham Market on 13 April 1827, aged 85. No will has been found in Suffolk. They had children, including the landscape artist Perry Nursey (baptised on 25 June 1771 at Stonham Aspall).

△ Catherine Nursey, née Fairfax, mother of the Suffolk landscape painter Perry Nursey. Picture owned by her descendant Mrs Nancy Bedwell

PRESENTING YOUR RESULTS

PROSE ACCOUNT

THE LIFE OF JOHN FAIRFAX

JOHN FAIRFAX was born in 1710, four years before the death of Queen Anne ushered in the reign of George I and the start of the Hanoverian period. Growing up in rural Suffolk, he was variously described as a grocer and draper in the village of Coddenham, indicating either an enterprising mind or (less likely in view of the relative prosperity of his children) an inability to find the right niche in life. He married Mary Hayward on 16 September 1735 at Framlingham, a market town some ten miles from Coddenham, and, indeed, going to market there may have been how he met her. He wrote his will in 1751, making her and her brother John his executors, and it was proved, indicating he had died by then, in 1758, two years before the death of King George II.

John's children included Frances, Mary, two Johns and Catherine, of whom Frances and the first John died young. To his surviving son JOHN FAIRFAX he left his watch 'that was my cousin Smith's' and £63 to apprentice him 'to some proper business at a fit age'. This younger John married Penelope Wright at St James's, Bury St Edmund's, on 5 May 1770 and obviously benefited from his apprenticeship, as he became a freeman of Bury St Edmunds in 1802. He died in a fit on 12 February 1805 while visiting his nephew, the artist Perry Nursey, at Little Bealings. He had two children, Penelope and Catherine.

John senior's daughter Catherine, born 7 September 1742, received a bequest of land from her father's cousin Catherine Fairfax in 1750 and, perhaps as a result of this, made a good marriage to the local surgeon, John Nursey of Coddenham. They married there by licence on 4 April 1764. She was mother of the artist Perry Nursey (baptised on 25 June 1771 at Stonham Aspall), at whose house her brother died in 1805.

FAMILY TREE

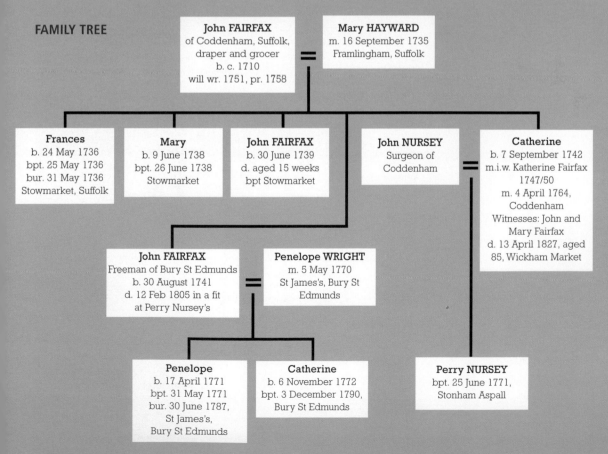

John FAIRFAX
of Coddenham, Suffolk,
draper and grocer
b. c. 1710
will wr. 1751, pr. 1758

Mary HAYWARD
m. 16 September 1735
Framlingham, Suffolk

Frances
b. 24 May 1736
bpt. 25 May 1736
bur. 31 May 1736
Stowmarket, Suffolk

Mary
b. 9 June 1738
bpt. 26 June 1738
Stowmarket

John FAIRFAX
b. 30 June 1739
d. aged 15 weeks
bpt Stowmarket

John NURSEY
Surgeon of
Coddenham

Catherine
b. 7 September 1742
m.i.w. Katherine Fairfax
1747/50
m. 4 April 1764,
Coddenham
Witnesses: John and
Mary Fairfax
d. 13 April 1827, aged
85, Wickham Market

John FAIRFAX
Freeman of Bury St Edmunds
b. 30 August 1741
d. 12 Feb 1805 in a fit
at Perry Nursey's

Penelope WRIGHT
m. 5 May 1770
St James's, Bury St
Edmunds

Penelope
b. 17 April 1771
bpt. 31 May 1771
bur. 30 June 1787,
St James's,
Bury St Edmunds

Catherine
b. 6 November 1772
bpt. 3 December 1790,
Bury St Edmunds

Perry NURSEY
bpt. 25 June 1771,
Stonham Aspall

CHAPTER THREE
ANCESTRAL PICTURES

Most of this book is about finding records of ancestors. Pictures can be records, too; even a photographer's address on the back of an old snap could provide a clue as to where the depicted ancestor came from. But they are also valuable in their own right as a fantastic way of bringing your family history to life.

Before the invention of photography in the 19th century, some of our ancestors were depicted in paintings, sketches, silhouettes and even busts and sculptures. From grand Van Dycks to amateur scribbles, such pictures are always worth seeking out, for, especially in family history, a picture really can be worth a thousand words.

WHERE TO SEARCH

PAINTERS AND PAINTINGS

⌨ For painters and paintings, look to M. Bryan's *Dictionary of Painters and Engravers* (London, 1903–4) and F. Spalding's *20th-century Painters and Sculptors* (Antique Collectors Club, 1991).

⌨ The best places to make searches are in London at **Westminster Central Reference Library**, the **National Portrait Gallery** (which has a database of over 500,000 portraits and engravings), and the **National Art Library** at the Victoria and Albert Museum.

⌨ Of course, many 'painters' in the past were no more than jobbing artisans and many, such as engravers, herald painters and so on, appear in routine apprenticeship records. A detailed article on sources for artists and their subjects is in *Family History Monthly*, March 2003.

QUICK REFERENCE

WESTMINSTER CENTRAL REFERENCE LIBRARY
35 St Martin's Street
London WC2H 7HP
☎ 020 7641 4636
www.westminster.gov.uk/libraries/westref

NATIONAL PORTRAIT GALLERY
St Martin's Place
London WC2H 0HE
☎ 020 7306 0055
www.npg.org.uk/search

NATIONAL ART LIBRARY
Victoria and Albert Museum
Cromwell Road
London SW7 2RL
☎ 020 7938 8315
www.nal.vam.ac.uk

△ My cousin Ernest Rietschel of Dresden, a renowned German sculptor, who was born in Pulsnitz in 1804 and died in Dresden in 1861.

◁ Gainsborough's famous family portrait of Mr and Mrs Andrews, c.1748-9.

PHOTOGRAPHERS AND PHOTOGRAPHS

Photography began in earnest in the 1850s and portrait photographs of people who became our ancestors took off in the 1870s. Collections of photographs are at county record offices, libraries and elsewhere, often enabling you to see what places where your ancestors lived looked like and, if you are very lucky, you might even find a picture of your ancestor.

WHERE TO SEARCH

PHOTOGRAPHERS AND PHOTOGRAPHS

▢ The largest collection in Europe is the **Hulton Getty Collection** with a staggering 12 million pictures. The **National Monuments Record Centre** has 6.5 million pictures, mostly of buildings around the time of the Second World War, indexed by parish.

▢ There are many commercial outlets for old photographs and reprints from old negatives, such as the **Francis Frith Collection**. There will often be a book of old photographs of the places where your ancestors lived.

▢ There are also several excellent guides to dating old pictures, including R. Pol's *Dating Old Photographs* (FFHS, 1998). Many other sources for pictures are listed in J. Foster and J. Sheppard's *British Archives: A Guide to Archive Resources in the United Kingdom* (Palgrave, 2002). Another guide to collections is R. Eakins' *Picture Sources UK* (Macdonald, 1985).

QUICK REFERENCE

HULTON GETTY COLLECTION
Unique House
21–31 Woodfield Road
London W9 2BA
☎ 020 7579 5777
www.hultongetty.com

**NATIONAL MONUMENTS
RECORD CENTRE**
Kemble Drive
Churchland
Swindon
☎ 01793 414600
www.swindon.gov.uk/nmro

FRANCIS FRITH COLLECTION
Frith's Barn
Teffont, Salisbury
Wiltshire SP3 5QP
☎ 01722 716376
www.francisfrith.co.uk

CHAPTER FOUR
BEFORE YOU BEGIN

Before starting with the main sources for tracing ancestry it is important to understand a little about how and where records are kept, starting with the main archives, and the different ways of gaining access to them. Reading this chapter now may save you a great deal of head-scratching and wasted time later on.

USING THE NATIONAL ARCHIVES

GETTING HOLD of material from the NA couldn't be easier:

⊠ You can establish what documents you want to see on **www.catalogue.national archives.gov.uk** and pre-order them so they will be ready when you arrive.

⊠ You can also have photocopies made on the spot or take a digital camera with you and photograph the records you want while you are there.

⊠ Finally, you can also order documents once you are there for delivery to your home address.

ARCHIVES

There are many organisations that hold archives of records. Be aware that most exist to preserve records, and not primarily to let you finger them. Most of the help you will receive from such organisations will be provided out of kindness, not obligation. Courtesy and thanks never go amiss, whoever you are dealing with.

If you are thinking of visiting an archive to undertake some research, always make sure it will be open, find out if you need to book and also do your best to establish that the records you want to see are actually there. Remember that sometimes records are temporarily removed from their permanent homes for restoration, rebinding and other reasons. Most are free but require a reader's ticket, so if you do not have one, take some identification, preferably a passport.

THE NATIONAL ARCHIVES (formerly Public Record Office)

In 2003, the Public Record Office announced it was merging with the **Historic Manuscripts Commission (HMC)** to become the **National Archives (NA)**. The NA is the principal repository for British national records, which are referred to constantly in this book. Among those records that are used the most by family historians are censuses and Prerogative Court of Canterbury (see page 120) wills and records relating to soldiers and sailors.

The main task of the HMC, also called the Royal Commission on Historical Manuscripts, is to catalogue collections of records outside the NA. Its published reports cover a vast array of manuscripts in public and private hands, from the House of Lords to Longleat, and including businesses, solicitors' papers, county record offices and so on.

The indexes to the printed reports can make surprising and rewarding 'lucky dip' searches, and the HMC's on-going work is indexed centrally in the **National Register of Archives**, accessible via the NA's website. This includes a search facility for those personal names and topics that have been indexed within the records and leads direct to contact details for the relevant archive.

The NA's website provides a great deal of information about how to get to and use the archives and its records, and also enables you to download any of its many very informative information leaflets which will tell you more about many of the most commonly used records. Look at the website before you go to the NA, not least because you can pre-order the documents and have them ready and waiting for you when you walk in. The website also contains some very useful databases, particularly the main catalogue, **www.nationalarchives.gov.uk**, which you can use as a short cut for specific searches or as a general trawl for references to the names that interest you. You are highly likely to find them cropping up in categories of documents you never expected, or even categories of documents you had never heard of before. An article by Amanda Bevan on how to use PROCAT appears in *Ancestors*, December 2002/January 2003.

The NA also maintains **Access to Archives**, an online catalogue to material held in many British archives, including the county record offices. Once you have found material that interests you it also provides links to the **Archon Directory**, to give you full contact details for the archive concerned.

Under the NA's wing too is the **Family Records Centre (FRC)**, jointly run by the NA and the **General Register Office (GRO)** (see page 44). The FRC (which used to be known by its former locations, Somerset House and then St Catherine's House), holds the original indexes to General Registration of births, marriages and deaths in England and Wales from July 1837 (see page 44). It also holds microfilm copies of the censuses from 1841 to 1901 and has a library containing many useful genealogical finding aids.

OTHER ARCHIVES

Wales: Wales was officially subsumed by England in 1536, but it has its own archives in the **National Library of Wales**.

Scotland: Scotland's archives are at the **National Archives of Scotland (NAS)**, formerly the Scottish Record Office. The catalogues of this and most other Scottish archives are available at **www.scan.org.uk**.

Ireland: Both Eire and Northern Ireland have central archives, the **National Archives of Ireland** and the **Public Record Office of Northern Ireland (PRONI)**. (Contact details for these addresses in Ireland are given in the Quick Reference panel overleaf.)

QUICK REFERENCE

HISTORIC MANUSCRIPTS COMMISSION (HMC)
Ruskin Avenue
Kew, Richmond
Surrey TW9 4DU
☎ 020 8876 3444
www.archon.nationalarchives.gov.uk/hmc

NATIONAL ARCHIVES (NA)
Ruskin Avenue
Kew, Richmond
Surrey TW9 4DU
☎ 020 8876 3444
www.nationalarchives.gov.uk

NATIONAL REGISTER OF ARCHIVES
www.archon.nationalarchives.gov.uk/nra

ACCESS TO ARCHIVES
www.A2A.org.uk

ARCHON DIRECTORY
www.archon.nationalarchives.gov.uk/archon

FAMILY RECORDS CENTRE (FRC)
1 Myddleton Street
London EC1R 1UW
☎ 020 8392 5300
www.familyrecords.gov.uk/frc

GENERAL REGISTER OFFICE (GRO)
Smedley Hydro
Trafalgar Road
Southport
Merseyside PR8 2HH
☎ 0151 471 4200
www.statistics.gov.uk/registration

NATIONAL LIBRARY OF WALES (LLYFRGELL GENEDLAETHOL CYMRU)
Panglais
Aberystwyth SY23 3BU
☎ 01970 632800
www.llgc.org.uk

NATIONAL ARCHIVES OF SCOTLAND (NAS)
HM General Register House
2 Princes Street

QUICK REFERENCE

NATIONAL ARCHIVES OF IRELAND
Bishop Street
Dublin 8
Eire
☎ 00 353 1 407 2300
www.nationalarchives.ie

PUBLIC RECORD OFFICE OF NORTHERN IRELAND (PRONI)
66 Balmoral Avenue
Belfast BT9 6NY
Northern Ireland
☎ 028 9025 5905
http://proni.nics.gov.uk

ACCESS TO ARCHIVES
www.A2A.org.uk

BRITISH LIBRARY
96 Euston Road
London NW1 2DB
☎ 020 7412 7676
http://blpc.bl.uk

MORMON FAMILY HISTORY CENTRES
Hyde Park Family History Centre
64/68 Exhibition Road
South Kensington
London SW7 2PA
☎ 020 7589 8561
(Main centre – see website for other locations)
www.familysearch.org

❝As with the rest of this book, I use English and Welsh records as the main example, but the general principle of how to use the records can be applied to many other countries, from Jamaica to India.❞

COUNTY RECORD OFFICES

Unlike the NA, county record offices are a relatively new innovation, starting from the archiving work of George Herbert Fowler in 1913. The county record offices grew out of the old diocesan record offices and their main achievement was bringing together many of each county's public records under one roof, and it was this that helped fuel the first boom in family history research in the 1970s. Most county record office catalogues are now accessible through **Access to Archives**. Offline, an excellent guide to the county record offices is J. Gibson and P. Peskett's *Record Offices: How to find them* (FFHS, 1996).

OTHER ARCHIVES

The best guide to specialist archives is J. Foster and J. Sheppard's *British Archives: A Guide to Archive Resources in the United Kingdom* (Palgrave, 2002). One page alone gives details of the Carpenters' Company archives in the City of London, which date from the Middle Ages; the Carlton Club, with registers of members from 1832; and Camden Local Studies Centre, whose holdings include records of the Manor of Hampstead 1742–1843 and the papers of George Bernard Shaw.

MUSEUMS AND LIBRARIES

Both are excellent for background information on what places were like when your ancestors lived there, but they can also hold extraordinary collections that may include information on your families. Foremost is the **British Library**, whose website includes its catalogue to manuscripts and printed books, enabling you to search for what you want and order it before you go.

Local museums and libraries, especially local studies libraries, hold photographic collections for the locality, and the librarians themselves are often very knowledgeable about the area, electoral registers, local maps, and so on.

MORMON WEBSITE AND FAMILY HISTORY CENTRES

With its world HQ at the Family History Library, the Mormon church, officially the Church of Jesus Christ of Latter-day Saints, maintains about 100 **Mormon Family History Centres** around the UK, freely open to the public and containing many useful genealogical resources. The church's interest in family history is religious – its aim ultimately is to identify as many people as possible, living and dead, in the context of their family relationships. To this end, they have amassed a vast collection of microfilms of original records from all over the world, including many British archives and many records described in this book. Any of these can be ordered to your local centre. The timorous should be reassured that visitors are entirely safe from any attempt to convert them – far from it: Mormons have made an immense contribution to this field, accessed for free. The Mormons' free website, **www.familysearch.org**, is described in detail on pages 110–13. Another Salt Lake-based organisation, **MyFamily.Com**, which owns **Ancestry.Com**, has a pay-to-view website (**www.ancestry.com**), which contains a great and growing number of records, especially drawn from censuses.

OTHER WEBSITES

SCOTLANDSPEOPLE

Much of Scotland's General Registration and censuses and indexes to all its old parochial registers are now on-line on a pay-to-view basis at **www.scotlandspeople.gov.uk**.

GENESCONNECTED

There are a number of websites that aim to link up family trees, but the most exciting is **www.GenesReunited.co.uk**, the sister site to **www.FriendsReunited.co.uk**. The site allows you to enter details of your family (or upload a family tree already typed in 'Gedcom' format), building an online family tree, which is easily altered and amended. A number of search tools then enable you to find out if surnames on your tree appear on other trees on the site. In return for a £7.50 a year membership fee, you can email the contributors of other possibly relevant names and work out if you do indeed have ancestors in common, and if so create a link between the two trees. Those with common surnames will be relieved to know that the searches can be honed, by personal name, year of birth and by place of birth.

The site was launched in November 2002 and at the time of writing has a million members worldwide (though mostly so far in Britain and the English-speaking world) and over 6 million names. It is therefore becoming a formidable research tool, which can already be used to localise where people with particular surnames were born and communicate with people actively researching them.

OTHER GENERAL WEBSITES

The Internet, as everyone knows, contains a great many websites of use to genealogists. There is no official central portal for these, but there is

△ **Access to Archives website home page: www.A2A.org.**

△ **Scotland's very own research website home page: www.scotlandspeople.gov.uk.**

‘ *The Internet, as everyone knows, contains a very great many websites of use to genealogists.* ’

an unofficial one, **www.cyndislist.com**, which has assumed this role and contains categorised links to pretty much everything that's out there.

A British version of this is **www.genuki.org.uk**, containing links to many useful websites for the whole British Isles, from a list of people executed for witchcraft to Methodist church websites, civilian internees in Japanese-occupied Singapore to a Latin dictionary and grammar aid, archives to newspaper holdings, population statistics to cemeteries, correctional institutions to Jewish records.

SOCIETIES

Many countries have societies formed by genealogists to help each other. The main one in Britain is the **Society of Genealogists (SoG)**. Its library is the finest of its kind, including the Great Card Index (3.5 million slips from a vast array of sources) and a huge collection of pedigrees submitted by members, varying enormously in quality but including many of very high standard. The contents of its library together with many searchable databases are on its website. It publishes the *Genealogists' Magazine*.

A curiosity in English genealogy is the **Institute of Heraldic and Genealogical Studies (IHGS)**. It organises a graded series of courses and qualifications in genealogy. It also has a library that is open to the public for a fee and produces a journal, *Family History*.

Most counties (sometimes even parts of counties) and some specialist areas such as Catholic and Anglo-German have family history societies. They come under the umbrella of the **Federation of Family History Societies (FFHS)**. Membership includes many Commonwealth and United States societies too, and it publishes *Family History News and Digest* biannually, summarising the contents of the different journals. Family History Societies have membership worldwide and their journals include articles on relevant sources and case studies, lists of members' interests and ancestral names. Many also have their own libraries and organise projects to index records such as gravestones and censuses. It is often a good idea to join your nearest Family History Society even if you do not have any local ancestors, because many of the talks will be of more general application, and many organise reciprocal research via other societies.

MAGAZINES

There are a number of family history magazines on the market, publishing 'how to' articles, items on general and specialist sources and

ONE-NAME SOCIETIES

THESE SOCIETIES concern those interested in specific names, such as the Fairfax Society. Many are members of the **FFHS** and **Guild of One-Name Studies ('GOONS'!)**. Many produce journals or newsletters, and besides collecting and tracing individual family trees for a name, many systematically extract all references to the name from categories of records such as General Registration indexes, so are well worth consulting.

Large libraries, such as the **SoG**, have collections of journals from societies outside Britain. The FFHS and **www.cyndislist. com** can put you in touch with relevant societies abroad.

specific family stories, and usually including book, software and website reviews, question-and-answer pages, letters, news and contact details for both professional and private researchers. The main ones in Britain are *Family History Monthly*, *Family Tree Magazine*, *Practical Family History*, *Your Family Tree* and *Ancestors*, the latter produced by the NA. In a similar category is the *Genealogical Services Directory*, which provides up-to-date contact details for all British Isles record offices, family history societies, organisations and professional record searchers and genealogists.

BIBLIOGRAPHIES

Much research has already been published and it is always worth checking to see if your family tree is included. The main British genealogical bibliography is G. W. Marshall's *The Genealogist's Guide* (GPC, reprinted 1973); supplemented by J. B. Whitmore's *A Genealogical Guide: An Index to British Pedigrees in Continuation of Marshall's Genealogist's Guide* (J. B. Whitmore, 1953). Besides the well-known Burke's publications, heralds' visitations (see page 302) and much else, these books encompass the rich veins of material ranging from transcripts of pedigrees in Close Rolls (see page 150) to copies of memorial inscriptions in overseas cemeteries, published in Victorian and early 20th-century antiquarian journals.

QUICK REFERENCE

SOCIETY OF GENEALOGISTS (SoG)
14 Charterhouse Buildings
Goswell Road
London EC1M 7BA
☎ 020 7251 8799
www.sog.org.uk

INSTITUTE OF HERALDIC AND GENEALOGICAL STUDIES (IHGS)
79–82 Northgate
Canterbury
Kent CT1 1BA
☎ 01227 768664
www.ihgs.ac.uk

FEDERATION OF FAMILY HISTORY SOCIETIES (FFHS)
PO Box 2425
Coventry CV5 6YX
☎ 024 7667 7798
www.ffhs.org.uk

GUILD OF ONE-NAME STUDIES (GOONS)
C/o Society of Genealogists
Box G
14 Charterhouse Buildings
Goswell Road
London EC1M 7BA
www.one-name.org

❝*Bibliographies encompass the rich veins of material ranging from transcripts of pedigrees to copies of memorial inscriptions.*❞

Coming closer to the present, there is G. B. Barrow's *The Genealogists' Guide: An Index to Printed British Pedigrees and Family Histories 1950–75* (Research Publishing Co., 1977), followed by T. R. Thompson's *A Catalogue of British Family Histories* (Research Publishing Co and SoG, 1980). Incredibly useful too are Stuart Raymond's *County Bibliographies* (S. A. and M. J. Raymond). These books reference published material (including family history journals) in terms of family histories and local histories, newspapers, county histories and published records of all sorts, particularly providing an overview of the publications of the county and national record societies and publications.

For Scotland there are M. Stuart's *Scottish Family History* (GPC, 1978), supplemented by P. S. Ferguson's *Scottish Family Histories* (National Library of Scotland, 1986), and for Ireland, W. Clare's *A Simple Guide to Irish Genealogy, First Compiled by the Rev. Wallace Clare* (Irish Genealogical Research Society, revised R. Ffolliott, 1966).

Most published genealogies also appear in the SoG's library catalogue **www.sog.org.uk/sogcat/index.html**.

BIOGRAPHICAL DICTIONARIES

Many countries have biographical dictionaries. Britain has led the way with L. Stephen and S. Lee's *Dictionary of National Biography* (Smith, Elder & Co., 1885), which was kept up to date by a series of supplements and completely revised and re-edited to create the *Oxford Dictionary of National Biography* (OUP, 2004). It is available in print and can be searched on-line on a subscription basis at **www.oup.com/oxforddnb**, though it should also be available at good libraries. You can search not just under the names of the subjects, but also under any other names (such as wives, sons-in-law, and so on) appearing in the articles and also by topic. So if you want to find any biographies mentioning something like ice cream, you can.

The DNB has been fully updated by a huge team of writers, including me, and the biographies include, where known, dates and places of birth, death, marriage and burial and any known details of parents, family origins, spouses, and offspring and is thus a formidable genealogical as well as biographical source.

Many people were important or well known in their time but are not considered so by posterity. There have been many biographical dictionaries past and present, not least *Who's Who* (OUP), which has been published annually since 1897, and its accompanying *Who Was*

△ **From hip to history: Linda McCartney's tragically early death means she has joined Princess Diana in the** *Oxford Dictionary of National Biography.*

Who (OUP), concerning the deceased, both of which are combined on a CD-Rom version. Here you will find the great and the good, from holders of public office to captains of industry, the top brass in the armed forces, the upper echelons of the clergy, and also writers, artists, editors and a host of others. Brief details are provided of dates of birth, marriage, death, parents and offspring. It is more useful for providing a date of birth so you can seek a birth certificate than in actually providing adequate genealogical details in its own right – but, of course, the biographical information it contains is marvellous.

Besides these, there are many further biographical dictionaries relating to specific groups in society, like the armed forces or religious groups, which are discussed in the appropriate chapters.

RECORD SOCIETY PUBLICATIONS

Many county record offices and archives have published indexed volumes transcribing some of their original records. The Lancashire and Cheshire Record Society, for example, has published many of its counties' wills, royalist composition papers, freemen records and much else. Trawling through these can throw up all sorts of treasures.

The easiest way of finding out what has been published is through E. L. C. Mullins' *Texts and Calendars: An Analytical Guide to Serial Publications, Vol. I* (RHS, 1958) and *Vol. II, 1957–1982* (RHS, 1983), D. and W. B. Stevenson's *Scottish Texts & Calendars: An Analytical Guide to Serial Publications* (Royal Historical Society, London) and *Scottish Royal Historical Society* (Edinburgh, 1987). These may save you very lengthy searches through original records.

SPECIALIST INDEXES

A catch-all to the many weird and wonderful indexes out there is J. Gibson and E. Hampson's *Specialist Indexes for Family Historians* (FFHS, 1998). This covers topics as diverse as Congregational and Baptist ministers at Dr William's Library, London (see page 260); multiple births worldwide; memorial cards (1846–1980); criminal registers in NA class HO 27 (1805–92); members of the Ancient Order of Foresters; and much else.

RESEARCH DIRECTORIES

Besides magazines, journals and an increasingly huge number of websites, many private researchers are also listed in special directories and for a small fee you can be listed too, with your name, address and the names you are interested in, with specific periods and countries, if

THE SOCIETY OF GENEALOGISTS

MANY PUBLISHED and even manuscript family histories have been deposited at the **Society of Genealogists**. Their catalogue is therefore a sort of super-bibliography of work done previously. As of 2005, the catalogue can be searched online at **www.sog.org.uk/sogcat/index.html**. Many family histories can also be seen online at **www.lib.byu.edu/fhc**.

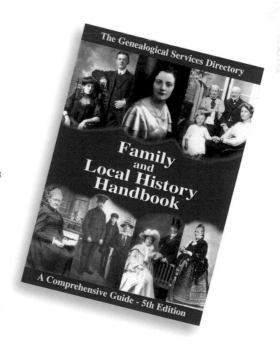

EXAMPLES OF ARCHIVES IN OTHER COUNTRIES

Many people living in Britain were born abroad and many more have ancestry from overseas. Most have national archives or equivalents. To find them, you can consult **www.cyndislist.com** or T. F. Beard with D. Demong's *How to Find your Family Roots* (McGraw-Hill Book Company, 1977). Besides Europe, these are countries that will contribute most significantly to the ancestry of people living in Britain over the next few generations, and their archive details are given here.

INDIA

Much of India belonged to the Mogul Empire, which was founded in India in 1526. Various European states, starting with the Portuguese, established trading bases in India but the Honourable East India Company (HEIC) had become the dominant power by 1691. The British Empire in India was recognised by the Treaty of Paris in 1763.

In 1947, the records of the HEIC were transferred to the British Library's Oriental and India Office Collections, known as the **India Office Library**, whose records are comprehensively described in M. Moir's *A General Guide to the India Office Library* (British Library, 1988). The library's vast collections are very well indexed and has a biographical index, which brings together details on individuals from many of its sources, including records of birth, baptism and so on. Records include ships' passenger lists for those coming and going – and a vast many did, either with the army or in some civil capacity.

In addition to the wealth of material at the India Office, the **SoG** has a formidable collection relating to the British in India, not least the India index, containing much biographical data. *The Indiaman*, a magazine covering the British in India, has launched a wesbite **www.indiaman.com**. In India the main archives are the **National Archives of India**.

PAKISTAN AND BANGLADESH

Pakistan was created in 1947 out of two distinct parts of India as a separate state for Muslims. It was a British dominion and became a republic in 1956, and a federal Islamic republic in 1973. In 1971, the eastern part of Pakistan achieved its own independence, as the state of Bangladesh. The main archives are the **Pakistan National Archives**. Bangladesh's main archive is the **Directorate of Archives and Libraries**.

KENYA

The British established a protectorate over the region in 1895 and white settlers arrived from South Africa and Britain, with many Indian immigrants arriving also. Many Kenyan Indians were subsequently forced to leave due to the 'Kenyanisation' of business and commerce in 1968 at which point they moved to Britain. The archives are at **Kenya National Archives**.

JAMAICA

The national archives for Jamaica are the **Registrar General's Department** Island Record Office.

QUICK REFERENCE

INDIA OFFICE LIBRARY
British Library
96 Euston Road
London NW1 2DB
☎ 020 7412 7513
www.bl.uk/collections/orientalandindian.html

NATIONAL ARCHIVES OF INDIA
Janpath
New Delhi 110001
India

PAKISTAN NATIONAL ARCHIVES
National Archives
Block N
Pakistan Secretariat
Islamabad
Pakistan

DIRECTORATE OF ARCHIVES AND LIBRARIES
103 Elephant Road
Dhaka 5
Bangladesh

KENYA NATIONAL ARCHIVES
Jogoo House
PO Box 30520
Nairobi
Kenya

REGISTRAR GENERAL'S DEPARTMENT
Island Record Office
Spanish Town
Jamaica

applicable. The best known directories are the *Genealogical Research Directory* and the Federation of Family History Societies' *British Isles Genealogical Research Directory*, commonly known as the 'Big R', which is now available on CD-Rom. If making contact by post, be aware of the widely practised code of conduct: always to enclose SAEs. Some people will not reply to correspondents who do not do so, even if they are offering valuable information or are long-lost cousins. Online equivalents to these directories are the many websites that put people in touch with those with similar interests, particularly **www.genesreunited.co.uk** (see page 31).

PROFESSIONAL GENEALOGISTS AND RECORD AGENTS

An increasing number of people and small firms are advertising their services as researchers in genealogical magazines such as *Family History Monthly*, in the *Genealogical Services Directory* and similar publications, and in the lists of independent searchers maintained by many record offices. They come in two categories – professional genealogists like me who plan, implement, direct and report on projects investigating family trees; or record agents, who are hired to undertake very specific pieces of research at their client's instructions. It is best to hire those who are qualified under educational systems such as the **IHGS** or who have a proven track record of experience and professionalism. Many belong to organisations such as the **Association of Genealogists and Researchers in Archives (AGRA)**, but be aware that membership often means just that and does not imply very stringent tests of ability.

There are very few dishonest researchers in the field, but a great many incompetent ones. If someone's initial response to your enquiry is in any manner unprofessional (badly typed or not typed at all), throw it away. Very few professionals worth their salt are without email. Whoever you hire, make sure that they understand exactly what you want to know before you part with your money.

Be equally understanding, though, that professionals must charge for their time and effort regardless of whether they find exactly what they and you were hoping for. Negative results must be paid for too and it is not always entirely negative to know where an ancestor was *not*.

QUICK REFERENCE

INSTITUTE OF HERALDIC AND GENEALOGICAL STUDIES (IHGS)
79–82 Northgate
Canterbury
Kent CT1 1BA
☎ 01227 768664
www.ihgs.ac.uk

ASSOCIATION OF GENEALOGISTS AND RESEARCHERS IN ARCHIVES (AGRA)
29 Badgers Close
Horsham
West Sussex RH12 5RU
www.agra.org.uk

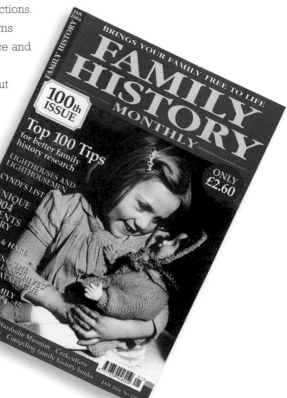

THESE PAGES contains various miscellaneous but also very useful facts to help you in your research.

ENGLISH WORDS

⊠ You will come across lots of old-fashioned expressions and phrases, which is half the fun of exploring the past. There are some specialist dictionaries like R. Milward's *A Glossary of Household, Farming and Trade Terms from Probate Inventories* (Derbyshire Record Society, occasional paper 1). A stalwart source, however, remains the *Oxford English Dictionary*, the older the edition the better.

OLD HANDWRITING

Reading old handwriting is called palaeography. There are two sorts of problems:

1 In the past, some letters were written differently to the way they are now, so are extremely unfamiliar.

Examples of the different styles of letters are given to the right.

⊠ Be aware, too, that writers often abbreviated words using apostrophes, or sometimes apostrophes followed by the last letter or two – and sometimes the apostrophes were just missed out. 'William' was often written 'Will'm' or Wm, James as 'Jas', 'Majesty' as Maty' and so on.

⊠ Two excellent guides to old scripts are H. E. P. Grieve's *Examples of English Handwriting 1150–1750* (Essex Record Office, 1949) and L. Mumby's *Reading Tudor and Stuart Handwriting* (Phillimore for BALH, 1988).

2 Bad handwriting. However, like cracking codes, you can often work out what an incomprehensible letter is by studying its companions. For example, if you can read 'Ed-ard' then you can surmise the other letter is a 'w' – but look for the letter elsewhere to make sure you have it right: never go with an unsupported guess.

⊠ You can also see how letters are written in phrases or words where you know what the letters should be. Many wills, for example, start 'In the name of God Amen', so you can see how the scribe wrote his 'I's, 'n's, 't's and so on before tackling the will itself.

⊠ Don't be daunted by age. Sometimes a 16th-century document can be so beautifully written as to be easier to read than some modern scribble.

Letter		Letter	
A	*(handwriting examples)*	S	*(handwriting examples)*
B		T	
C		U, V	
D		W	
E		X	
F		Y	
G		Z	
H			
I, J			
K			
L			
M			
N			
O			
P			
Q			
R			

MONEY

⊠ Besides being a 60s' drug, LSD was also the acronym for pre-decimal currency of pounds (livres), shillings and pence (dinarii). This was written in a number of different ways; for example, four pounds, two shillings and three pence ('thruppence') could be written £4-2-3 or £4 2s 3d or 4l 2s 3d or using Roman numerals – ivl iis iiid or even iiijl ijs iijd.

⊠ It is very difficult to find out how much money was worth relative to what it is today. The Bank of England has a ready reckoner and you can also study C. R. Chapman's *How Heavy, How Much and How Long? Weights, Money and Other Measures Used by our Ancestors* (Lochin Publishing, 1995) and L. Mumby's *How Much is that Worth?* (Phillimore for BALH, 1996).

DATES

⊠ Years and days haven't always been recorded the same way in every country. C. R. Cheney's *Handbook of Dates for Students of English History* (CUP, 2000) lists all old forms of dating, including by saints' days and popes' and kings' regnal years.

⊠ Years were often counted from the date of a sovereign's accession, so, for example, the first day of the first year of the reign of Elizabeth II started on 6 February 1952, the day she succeeded her father.

⊠ The book also provides a calendar for looking up which day of the week fell in what date in a given year. So, if someone wrote a letter dated 25 May 1657 saying their father died 'last Monday' you can find out that 25 May 1657 was a Friday, so 'last Monday' must have been 20 May.

OLD STYLE AND NEW STYLE

⊠ Britain and Europe used to use the old-style Julian calendar, whereby the year began on Lady Day, 25 March, not the new-style Gregorian calendar, which starts the year on 1 January. The Julian calendar started to die out among lay people in the Tudor period, and by the 18th century it is often hard to tell whether a date is being given in old style or new style.

⊠ Different countries changed to the Gregorian calendar at different times. Most of Western Europe changed in 1582, Scotland in 1600, England and Wales in 1752 and Russia and the Balkans in the 20th century. Therefore, a letter written in France on 1 February 1610 was likely to have been written just under a year before one dated 25 January 1610 in England.

⊠ It also means that dates appearing in old records need adjusting to make sense in modern terms. A baptism recorded in a PR on 24 January 1722 would, in modern terms, have taken place on 24 January 1723 because, under the old calendar, New Year's Day (25 March) had not yet arrived.

⊠ To avoid confusion, researchers tend to record the

△ A member of Pope Gregory's commission on the calendar pointing out the backslide of the Julian calendar.

date using 'double dating', recording the old-style year followed by the new-style year, i.e. 24 January 1722/3. Never, when you see this, strip out the 'old' date and just write 24 January 1723, because someone else may come along, realise that 23 January is before 25 March, not realise that you've already adjusted for double dating and write 24 January 1724 instead.

⊠ On the International Genealogical and Vital Records indexes (see page 110), dates are allegedly adjusted but without double dating. Non-conformist registers were using new-style dating well in advance of 1752.

⊠ Another difference between the Julian and Gregorian calendars was that the latter used leap years and the former didn't. By the time Pope Gregory introduced the new calendar in 1582 the lack of leap years had already caused the old-style date to lapse ten days behind the solar year, so he simply ordered ten days to be cut out off 1582, between 4 and 15 October. Because England persisted with the old calendar, it sunk increasingly behind Europe, and was 11 days behind by the 17th century. Therefore, events that share the same dates in different countries, such as the deaths of Shakespeare and Cervantes on 23 April 1616 in England and Spain respectively, actually took place 11 days apart. England and Wales cancelled the days between 2 and 14 September 1752 to catch up with Europe.

COMMON ABBREVIATIONS AND ACRONYMNS

Someone in AGRA or the SoG will know how to work back from GRO records at the FRC and PPR and maybe stuff in class WO 97 at the NA (the old PRO) back via the IGI to CMBs taken from PRs or BTs on mf at CROs. I have tried to keep acronymns and abbreviations to a minimum in this book, but here are the main ones I have used together with some additional acronymns you will encounter in the outside world.

AGRA	Association of Genealogists and Researchers in Archives
BT	bishop's transcript
CMB	baptisms, marriages and burials
CRO	county record office
FFHS	Federation of Family History Societies
FHS	Family History Society
FRC	Family Records Centre
GRO	General Register Office (records are searchable at the FRC)
HMC	Historic Manuscripts Commission (now NA)
IGI	International Genealogical Index
IHGS	Institute of Heraldic and Genealogical Studies
NA	National Archives (ex-PRO and HMC)
NAS	National Archives of Scotland
PCC/PCY	Prerogative Court of Canterbury/York
PPR	principal probate registry
PR	parish register
PRO	Public Records Office (now NA)
PRONI	Public Record Office of Northern Ireland
SoG	Society of Genealogists

LATIN

⊗ Few things terrify genealogists as much as the use of Latin in old records. Sorry, but that's the way things were and we've got to live with it. If you really can't cope with basic Latin there are some very good, modestly priced translators, but often you should be able to manage, however poor or non-existent your school-book Latin. Remember, you were not alone and many of the compilers of the records had only the most tenuous grasp of the language, and therefore used it very basically and often with English rather than Latin word orders and plenty of stock phrases.

⊗ Especially in parish records, Latin is scarcely an impediment to understanding. That 'Petrus filius Ricardus et Gracia Smith' means 'Peter son of Richard and Grace Smith' will surprise few. However, just because ancestors' names were recorded in Latin does not mean they ever used them thus: when Ricardus Smith went to the pub in the evening he was plain Dick and should appear on the family tree as Richard.

⊗ Good guides to Latin include E. A. Gooder's *Latin for Local History: An Introduction* (Longmann, 1978) and R. A. Latham's *Revised Medieval Latin Word-list from British and Irish Sources* (OUP, 1965). There is also one online at **www.genuki.org.uk**.

SOME COMMONLY USED LATIN WORDS

annus	year
dies	day
est	is
filia	daughter
filius	son
matrimonium	marriage
mater	mother
mensis	month
mortuus	dead
natus	born
nuptium	married
obit	died
parochia	parish
pater	father
sepultat	buried
uxor	wife
vidua	widow

▷ The beginning of St Luke's Gospel, Lindisfarne Gospels, c.698.

PART TWO

This section covers the big records in genealogy – birth, marriage and death records, censuses, and so on. These form the backbone of your family tree and should provide you with a vastly increased knowledge of your family history.

CHAPTER FIVE
GENERAL REGISTRATION

For most people tracing ancestors in Britain and overseas, record-based research often starts with General Registration records of birth, marriage and death. These records are increasingly accessible via the Internet, and also held both centrally and regionally.

△ **Mary Ann Collingwood Paterson, before her wedding to Rev. Patrick Henry Kilduff in 1879.**

FRC INDEXES

FROM 1984 THE INDEXES are annual rather than quarterly. Marriages are indexed in the quarters in which they took place but births can be registered up to six weeks after they took place, so may appear in the next quarter, and death registration can be held up by lengthy inquests or post mortems.

The main use of these records to genealogists is that birth records usually provide parents' names; marriage records usually provide at least the father's name and death certificates provide ages, and those for some countries provide details of place of birth and parentage. They provide names of the next generation back, which is exactly what you want.

USING GENERAL REGISTRATION

General Registration was introduced in England and Wales on 1 July 1837 as part of the government's attempts to find out how many people lived in the country, how quickly they were breeding, what was killing them – and, of course, how much they could be conscripted and taxed in the intervening time. The country was divided into registration districts, each split into sub-districts under a local registrar. These local registrars were responsible to the registrar general at the **General Register Office (GRO)**, now part of the Office of National Statistics. Births and deaths were to be reported to the local registrar, who reported them to his superintendent registrar, who in turn sent copies to the registrar general in London. Marriages could be performed by Anglican clergy or local registrars in their own offices or in Catholic or non-conformist chapels. From 1898, non-Anglican marriages could be performed in the presence of an authorised person (usually a clergyman) without the local registrar needing to be present. In all cases, copies of the resulting certificates were sent to the registrar general.

The registrar general's clerks then compiled separate alphabetical indexes to births, marriages and deaths, each divided into four quarters of each year: January–March, April–June, July–September and October–December, known as the March, June, September and December quarters respectively. These are all housed at the **Family Records Centre (FRC)** (see box, opposite).

FINDING A CERTIFICATE

AN IDEAL CASE INVOLVING MANUAL GENERAL REGISTRATION WOULD WORK AS FOLLOWS:

☒ You approach the indexes with a certain piece of information – let's say the names of your maternal grandparents.

☒ You know that your mother was married in November 1956, so start with the General Registration marriage indexes for the December quarter, which covers marriages registered in October, November and December that year, and make a note that you have done so.

☒ Choose the least common of your grandparents' surnames and look it up, note down each instance of it, and cross-reference each to the other name.

☒ If you do not find a record of the marriage, take the preceding volume (for the September quarter) and repeat the process.

☒ Work your way back quarter by quarter until you find a pair of names that cross-reference. If the names are right, and the registration district and reference numbers match, you have probably found the right entry. Order the certificate.

☒ If you know something else about either parties, such as their fathers' names, or a middle name where only an initial is given in the indexes, ask for a check to be made by filling in appropriate details on the back of the application form.

☒ The resulting marriage certificate should provide your grandparents' ages and your father's names and occupations. You can then calculate the rough time when they would have been born. If your grandfather said he was 23 when he married on 2 May 1923, then you can calculate that he would have been born between 2 May 1900 and 3 May 1899.

△ Birth record of Mary Ann Collingwood Paterson, 1854.
Her father was then a railway agent.

QUICK REFERENCE

FAMILY RECORDS CENTRE (FRC)
1 Myddleton Street
London EC1R 1UW
☎ 020 8392 5300
www.familyrecords.gov.uk/frc

GENERAL REGISTER OFFICE (GRO)
PO Box 2
Southport
Merseyside PR8 2JD
☎ 0151 471 4200
www.statistics.gov.uk/registration

Certified Copy of an Entry of Birth.

Pursuant to the Births and Deaths Registration Acts 1836 to 1874.

Registration District of ROCHFORD.

191.2   Birth in the Sub-District of PRITTLEWELL, in the County of ESSEX.

No.	When and Where Born.	Name (if any).	Sex.	Name and Surname of Father.	Name and Maiden Surname of Mother.	Rank or Profession of Father.	Signature, Description, and Residence of Informant.	When Registered.	Signature of Registrar.	Baptismal Name if added after Registration of Birth.
31	Twenty second September 1912 34 Argyll Rd Southend U.D.	Beryl Ivy	Girl	William Thomas Waters	Winifred Adeline Emily Waters formerly Coleman	Commercial Traveller	W. T. Waters Father 34 Argyll Road Southend	Second November 1912	A. J. Ball Registrar.	Th A.

I, Albert James Ball Registrar of Births and Deaths for the Sub-District of PRITTLEWELL, in the County of ESSEX, Do hereby Certify that this is a True Copy of the Entry No. 31 in the Register Book of Births, for the said Sub-District, and that such Register Book is now legally in my custody.

Witness my Hand this 2nd day of Nov. 1912

Ball Registrar.

The Statutory Fees payable for an ordinary certified copy of an entry in a Register of Births, Deaths, or Marriages, if taken at time of registration, are 2s. 7d. (including 1d. for the stamp); but if taken at any time afterwards an additional fee of 1s. is chargeable for a search

BIRTHS

There is no point seeking records unless you know in advance that they are likely to provide you with information you actually want. Here is a summary of what is on General Registration records.

The indexes give:
> **The name (with initials instead of middle names)**
> **The registration district where the birth was registered**
> **A reference number**
> **From September 1911, the mother's maiden name**

While births had to be registered, parents sometimes waited until later to decide their baby's names. If you cannot find a birth you are sure should be there, try looking at the end of the list of people of the same surname for children entered simply as 'male' or 'female'.

Birth certificates record the following:
> **Date and place of birth.** If the exact time of birth is given, the child probably belonged to a set of twins. Look in the General Registration index for other children born in the same quarter and district who could be your ancestor's twin.
> **Child's name.** Names can be added to or altered on birth certificates for up to a year after registration, unless a baptism has occurred. The child will appear

△ An original birth certificate of my grandmother Beryl Ivy Waters, 1912.

▷ A page from a General Registration index.

in the indexes under both the original name (or lack of it) and changed or added one, so this is unlikely to cause problems for the searcher.
> **Name and occupation of father.** Be cautious of occupational status: there are many instances of tailors' clerks saying they were tailors, cottagers claiming to be farmers and so on.
> **Name and maiden name of mother.** Former married names are usually given in the form; for example, 'Rose Smith late Jones formerly Evans'. This means that Rose was born Rose Evans, married Mr Jones, was widowed or divorced and then married Mr Smith.
> **Signature or mark and address of informant.** This was usually a parent. Signing with a mark usually indicated illiteracy but, of course, the signatory might merely have injured their hand. Sometimes registrars incorrectly assumed that poor people could not sign their own names and invited them to make their marks instead, and the signatories were simply too deferential to speak up.

⊠ First calculate your ancestor's birth date:

EXAMPLE: MY ANCESTOR'S AGE WAS GIVEN AS 23 ON 2 MAY 1923.

DEDUCT AGE FROM YEAR: 1923 − 23 = 1900

THEREFORE, THAT ANCESTOR WAS BORN BETWEEN 2 MAY 1900 AND 3 MAY 1899

⊠ This means that his birth should appear in the indexes covering the June, September and December quarters of 1899, or the March, June and (remembering that births could be registered up to six weeks after the event, taking us into the month of July) September quarters of 1900.

⊠ Write down the period you have searched and the possibilities encountered. If you are searching for a very popular combination of names, like Mary Smith, it is sensible to limit yourself at first to entries in the registration districts surrounding the area where the birth might have taken place.

⊠ If your search fails, widen the geographical area. Do not under any circumstances stop at the first possibility you find, but cover the period fully. There are plenty of instances of two children being born into the same family with the same forenames. For example, a child might die very young and its name

be given to the next child born into the family. Alternatively, two children might be born to very close relations and each given the same 'family' names. You can work out the most likely entries from the geographical locations of the registration districts: ask for a check to be made for the right father's name.

⊠ If the birth certificate does not appear in the period, assume that the age at marriage was slightly inaccurate and widen the search to cover a year or two either side.

⊠ The birth certificate will provide you with the full names of your great-grandparents, enabling you to search back for their marriage – and an earlier generation of your family tree.

⊠ It is often useful to know the registration district in which your ancestors lived. These originally corresponded to the old Poor Law Unions. http://tiger.iso.port.ac.uk:7778/pls/nfp/prog.core.home provides this date for each parish, or you can look in a trade directory (see page 82). The IHGS publishes two maps showing the location of the registration districts for 1837–51 and 1852–1946. For details after 1946 you can consult J. A. Newport's *An Index to the Civil Registration Districts of England & Wales, 1837 to date* (Pledger, 1989).

LIFETIMES: MARGARET DUNCAN WILSON

EDINBURGH PHYSIOTHERAPIST Lorna Barbour's ancestor has an interesting birth record. Margaret Duncan Wilson was the first child to be registered in Lerwick once General Registration began in 1855. The exceptionally detailed birth certificate (of the type issued in the year alone) states she was born at Chromate Lane, Lerwick at 5.30am on 6 January, 7th child of James McAllum Wilson, a superintendent of police at Lerwick, aged 34 and born in Fraserburgh, and his wife Jane Wilson formerly Smart. The couple had married in Stonehaven in June 1840 and had two other girls and four boys, of whom one had died.

The 19th-century Shetlands may conjure up images of weather-beaten crofters knitting chunky sweaters, the warm glow of their cosy peat fires flicking across the picturesque wrinkles of their weather-beaten faces. Far from it. Plunged into semi-darkness half the year and with little to warm them save whisky the islanders, whose Viking blood has recently been confirmed through extensive DNA testing, seem to have been an exceptionally unruly mob. The local papers report almost continuous drunken disorder, not least at their drinking extravaganza, Upheliar, including running gun battles and once the nail bombing of the chief magistrate's house. And when the American whaling boats put in and drunken sailors filled the streets and bars of the town, things really hotted up.

POLICE RECORDS

The Shetland Islands Council has the records of the Lerwick Police Commissioners (see page 182), who invited James, then a member of the Aberdeen Police Establishment, to become their police constable on 6 April 1852. He had asked for 20s a week but accepted their offer of 18s and a suit of clothes yearly, provided he could act as sheriff officer as well. In June they agreed to pay him an extra £2 'for the freight of himself and his family and furniture from Aberdeen to Lerwick'.

On 15 July the next year he was granted leave of absence to take his sick child to Aberdeen. But in March 1854 we find that 'objections had been made by many people to [Wilson's] leaving the town on the fiscal business of the county, he stated he would engage not leave town for any greater distance than such as he might be able to return from in the course of the following night'. Reading between the lines, the criminally inclined part of the populace had been rubbing their hands with delight whenever they saw the policeman departing on a boat, and the law-abiding section of the population had had enough of it!

Wilson appears in the archives giving lengthy statements about various crimes, thefts and breaches of the peace he had to deal with. But then, in December 1854, Wilson, James Angus a joiner and Andrew Nicholson, spirit dealer, were attacked by two sailors from a ship from Boston and Angus and Nicholson were knifed. Wilson had probably saved their lives, but he had had enough. In May 1855 he asked the commissioners for a certificate of good character and leave to 'go south with the view of looking after some situation'. The commissioners regretfully obliged, commending his work in 'repressing breaches of the peace' and off he went, to work in Edinburgh first as a policeman and then as a cooper, leaving it to his wife to write to the commissioners chasing them for his arrears in salary. It seems that anything by then seemed preferable to being policeman in Lerwick.

18 79. Marriage solemnized at *the Parish Church* in the *Parish* of *Stoke Newington* in the County of *Middlesex*

No.	When Married.	Name and Surname.	Age.	Condition.	Rank or Profession.	Residence at the time of Marriage.	Father's Name and Surname.	Rank or Profession of Father.
246	April 29 1879	Patrick Henry Kilduff	40	Bachelor	Clerk in Holy Orders	Tottenham	Michael Kilduff (deceased)	Farmer
		Mary Ann Collingwood Paterson	25	Spinster	-	Stoke Newington	James Paterson	Carrier

Married in the *Church* according to the Rites and Ceremonies of the Established Church, by *Banns* or after *Banns* by me, *Thomas Jackson*

Kate Paterson

This Marriage was solemnized between us, { *Patrick Henry Kilduff* *Mary Ann Collingwood Paterson* } in the Presence of us, { *Alex. Henry Smith* *J. Paterson* *Laura T. Knott* }

CERTIFIED to be a true copy of an entry in the certified copy of a register of Marriages in the Registration District of *Hackney*
Given at the GENERAL REGISTER OFFICE, LONDON, under the Seal of the said Office, the *28th* day of *April* 19 *90*

△ Marriage certificate of Patrick Henry Kilduff and Mary Ann Collingwood Paterson, 1879.

MARRIAGES

The indexes give:
> The names of the parties marrying
> The registration district where the event took place
> A reference number

The best way of searching is to choose the most unusual of the two surnames and, when you find a possible reference to one party, see if there is a corresponding reference for the other, with an identical registration district and reference number. However, as the reference numbers prior to 1912 relate to pages containing two marriage entries, there may be a few unlucky cases in which John Smith and Mary Brown do indeed appear on the same page but as the groom and bride respectively of two completely different people! In such cases, you will simply have to continue the search once your application for the certificate has been returned.

From March 1912, the name of the other spouse appears next to the index entries, avoiding this problem and making searches much more straightforward.

Marriage certificates record the following:
> Date and place of the marriage. Marriages often took place at Christmas, because this was one of the very few times of the year – if not the only time – when poor families had enough time off work to come together. The parish was usually the home parish of the bride.
> Names of bride and groom. If the bride was a widow, she will be recorded (and therefore indexed) under her last married name, not her maiden name. If you are unaware that an ancestor had been married before, you may run into problems, although the maiden name should have been stated in the birth certificate of any children of the marriage.
> Marital condition: bachelor or spinster, widower or widow. If divorced, the name of the previous spouse may be recorded.
> Ages. Ages on marriage certificates are notoriously vague or inaccurate. In many cases the bride and groom will simply state either 'full age' or 'minor'. 'Minor' means under 21. Until 1929, provided they had parental consent, boys could marry at 14 and girls at 12, and after 1929 the minimum age was 16. Marriages between such young persons were rare, but they did happen and many marriage searches fail simply because people

do not search back before their ancestors would have been 18. 'Full age' means 21 or over, or under 21 but lying to avoid the need for parental consent. If ages are given, they may be inaccurate: boys who upped their age to join the army might say they were older than they really were, while the opposite was often true for older women wanting to marry nice young soldiers. If you suspect an ancestor was not being entirely truthful, it is worth checking a later census to see if they gave more accurate information later in life.

➢**Occupations.** Until the mid-20th century, even if she worked 18-hour days at a coal mine or scrubbing other peoples' doorsteps, the bride's occupation was very seldom deemed worthy of recording.

➢**Place of residence.** These are often misleading. Generally, the bride's address is likely to have been her normal address, but grooms often took up temporary residence in the parish, usually for a minimum of four weeks, in order to be allowed to marry in the parish church. Sometimes the bride and groom will give the same address, but this is unlikely to mean they were openly sleeping together. More likely, he was her father's apprentice or lodger, or his family and hers were renting different sets of rooms in the same building.

➢**Names and occupations of fathers.** Mothers' names were not recorded. If fathers were retired, they might be rather grandly entitled 'gentleman'. Dead fathers were very often given a posthumous promotion by their proud children, such as boatswain to captain. It was normal, but sadly not universal, to state whether the fathers were alive or dead at the time of the marriage: generally, assume that the father was alive unless otherwise stated, but do not take this as absolute fact.

➢**Whether the marriage was by banns or licence.** These terms are explained more fully on page 99.

➢**Signatures or marks of bride, groom and a minimum of two witnesses.** As we have seen, marks did not always denote illiteracy. Remember that although signatures of the bride, groom and witnesses will

▽ **An Adolph family wedding in Hove, 1915.**

▷ *The Wedding Breakfast* by George Elgar Hicks (1824–1914).

appear on the original certificate, the certificates issued by the GRO are copies in the registrars' handwriting. You can apply to the relevant superintendent registrar if you want to see the originals. This is especially useful if you wish to identify someone by their signature. Witnesses were often siblings of the bride or groom; but do not make the mistake of thinking that because a favoured sibling did not witness a marriage they cannot have been present.

➤**Name of clergyman.** If the bride or groom were related to a clergyman, he might have come to their local church to perform the ceremony for them.

Many people fail to find marriage records because they assume their ancestors practised the rule of 'no sex before marriage'. After several years as a full-time genealogist I have serious doubts as to whether many people have ever heeded that maxim, as a great deal of couples registered the first child's birth less than nine months after their wedding day. Nor was it unknown for couples to say they were married when they registered their first child, but not walk up the aisle until a year or two later. If you cannot find the marriage before their first child was born, try looking afterwards. Equally, some people forget how large families could be in the past, and give up far too soon. It is not unusual, especially in the 19th century, to find a marriage taking place 15 or 20 years before an ancestor's birth. Sometimes, you will find out that your ancestor was older than their youngest aunts and uncles.

Genealogists were universally disconcerted by M.W. Foster's *A Comedy of Errors, or the Marriage Records of England and Wales 1837–99* (M.W. Foster, 1999), which revealed that up to 5% of marriages recorded by local registrars never made it to the registrar general's records. So if you cannot find the marriage you want in the GRO indexes and suspect you know where it took place, try the local registrar.

LIFETIMES: JULIA LITTLE

THE DEATH CERTIFICATE of Julia Little is reasonably typical in the sort of information it contains. She died on 17 May 1876 at 17 Stockdale Street, in the sub-district of Howard Street and registration district of Liverpool. She was a female, aged 32, wife of Thomas Little, a shoemaker, and died of:

'excessive drinking, 12 months, certificate received from Clarke Aspinall, coroner for Liverpool, Inquest held 20th and 29th May 1876.'

DEATHS

The indexes give:
> **The deceased's name**
> **The district in which they died**
> **A reference number**
> **Age.** For the early decades they do not include ages, so a reference to someone who you thought was your 90-year-old great-great-grandfather might turn out to have been a day-old baby. Between June 1866 and March 1969, they include the deceased's age, and after then the date of birth is given.

Most people tended to marry around their twenties, so it is often easy to guess very roughly when people's marriage and births might have taken place. The same is not true of deaths and this, coupled with the sparse information given in the indexes before 1866, tend to make death searches difficult. Here are some pointers:
> **A marriage certificate will often state whether the bride and groom's fathers were alive at the time.**
> **You can get an idea of when someone might have died** by their appearance or non-appearance in some of the fully indexed census returns, such as those of 1881 and 1901 (see pages 66–70).
> **Elderly relatives can give you an idea of when someone might have died** simply by virtue of whether they can remember them or not, so if 87-year-old great-aunty can remember someone, you know that person must have died less than 87 years ago.

Because death indexes are so uninformative, it can sometimes be easier to look for the person in the indexes to wills first (see pages 127 and 128). This will give you a date of death, and you can then buy the death certificate to learn their age.

Death certificates record the following:
> **Name**
> **Date and place of death.** This will usually be the deceased's house. However, hospitals were usually recorded simply by their postal address too.
> **Cause of death.** As you work back into the past, you

CERTIFIED COPY OF AN ENTRY OF DEATH

GIVEN AT THE GENERAL REGISTER OFFICE, LONDON

Application Number Y 118534

REGISTRATION DISTRICT	Hendon							
1917. DEATH in the Sub-district of	Harrow			in the county of Middlesex				

Columns:— 1	2	3	4	5	6	7	8	9
No. When and Where died	Name and surname	Sex	Age	Occupation	Cause of death	Signature, description and residence of informant	When registered	Signature of registrar
177 Twenty-second December 1917 Bryanstead Ealing Road Wembley	Patrick Henry Kilduff	Male	79 Years	of 5 Lyon Park Wembley and Clerk in Holy Orders Pensioned Chaplain of Poor Law union	(1) Senile decay (2) Heart failure Syncope no PM Certified by Wm D.T. Thompson MB	J. Rietchel Son-in-law Braeside Slades Hill Enfield	Twenty-fourth December 1917	Arthur Bone Registrar.

CERTIFIED to be a true copy of an entry in the certified copy of a Register of Deaths in the District above mentioned.
Given at the GENERAL REGISTER OFFICE, LONDON, under the Seal of the said Office, the 2nd day of May 1990.

This certificate is issued in pursuance of the Births and Deaths Registration Act 1953. Section 34 provides that any certified copy of an entry purporting to be sealed or stamped with the seal of the General Register Office shall be received as evidence of the birth or death to which it relates without any further or other proof of the entry, and no certified copy purporting to have been given in the said Office shall be of any force or effect unless it is sealed or stamped as aforesaid.

DX 501233

CAUTION:—It is an offence to falsify a certificate or to make or knowingly use a false certificate or a copy of a false certificate intending it to be accepted as genuine to the prejudice of any person, or to possess a certificate knowing it to be false without lawful authority.

Form A504M Dd 8098446 8640959 25M 1/90 Mcr(230313)

will find these becoming less informative. Many old people died in the 19th century of 'decay of nature'.

➤**Age.** From June 1969, the date of birth is given.

➤**Occupation.** Married women and widows were sometimes described as 'wife' or 'widow' of their husband. Death certificates do not provide parents' names, except in the cases of young children, for whom the 'occupation' box was often used to name the child's father. Very occasionally I have come across older people being described in terms of who their father was, such as the death of Robert Hugill, which took place on 2 March 1842 at Stockton in Co. Durham. Although he was 42, he was described as 'son of Jonathan Hugill, corn miller'. Not only was this a fascinating find in its own right but, because Robert was born long before General Registration began, this co-ordinate on his origins was especially useful.

➤**Name, address and signature or mark of the informant.** The informant was often a child of the deceased or other close relative, so this section is very useful if you are trying to find the deceased's living descendants. However, informants were sometimes doctors, especially after 1874, when a doctor's certificate was required before a death certificate could be issued.

△ **Death certificate of Rev. Patrick Henry Kilduff, 1917.**

▽ **Detail from a Catholic memorial card (see page 140).**

VIE D'UNION A MARIE

MIROIR DE JUSTICE

Je prends pour miroir
le saint cœur de MARIE.

GENERAL REGISTRATION

If you know the exact name, date and place of the birth, marriage or death you want from 1900 onwards, you can place an order with the Registrar General at **www.gro.gov.uk** without needing to look up the index reference. Usually, though, you will need to search for the event you want.

At the time of writing, General Registration searching has undergone a partial revolution. The pay-to-view website **www.familyrelatives.org** (see below right) has a full index to all General Registration births, marriages and deaths for the periods 1866–1920 and 1984–1983. The period 1867–1983 can be searched but by surname only, though the site plans to extend its coverage to cover the whole of General Registration. By the time you read this, they may well have achieved their goals, and good luck to them.

The site **www.BMDIndex.co.uk** is a pay-to-view site currently providing a full index to births, marriages and deaths 1984-2003.

You may also find what you want in **www.freebmd.org.uk**, which is an index to a vast number of privately submitted entries up to 1983 – a lucky dip, but quite often worth the effort.

Some counties' local registrars' records have been computerized. These can be sought on **www.ukbmd.org.uk** and certificates ordered from the relevant registrar. However, this will only work if the entry you want was actually in the relevant registrar's area. Often, when searching for events, you cannot know this for certain, making the national indexes a safer bet. Also, restricting your search to one area may lead to you plumping for the 'only possible' yet actually wrong entry – yet missing the right one just over the border in the next district.

To find the entry you want in these sites, simply key in the name and any other relevant details you know, and hopefully the right entry will pop up.

These represents a massive step forward. However, they presumably all contain errors and omissions, do not yet cover all the entries, and you may, in any case, want to use a different route.

You can search the original Registrar General's quarterly indexes (January–March, April–June, etc., for each year) online at **www.1837online.com**). Offline, you can search fiche copies of the indexes in dedicated

genealogical libraries, many good libraries and record offices and all **Mormon Family History Centres**.

You can go to the **FRC** in Islington and search the big, heavy original volumes (though even there the entries from 1984 are on computer). Newcomers to genealogy ought to go there while they still can and experience what we all had to go through once – heaving one's way through a succession of 25lb volumes in a crowded search room full of fervent ancestor hunters not afraid to use their elbows to get at the volume they want!

Alternatively, you can pay £17.50 and visit a superintendent registrar's office to search the indexes for that district, or request a search by post, but my comments on the drawbacks of not searching nationally apply.

Many one-name societies and individuals interested in single surnames have produced exhaustive lists of General Registration references to that name. See General Register Office one-name lists in the library of the **SoG**, SoG, 1997).

Local family history societies and archives often collect certificates and others are published as 'Unwanted Certificates' in *Family Tree Magazine*, but the chances of these collections containing the very certificate you want are always going to be slim.

QUICK REFERENCE
See main sources in Useful Addresses, page 306

PURCHASING CERTIFICATES

You can search the indexes to births, marriages and deaths (see page 57), but to see the records themselves you must purchase certificates, costing £7 each. There are strong arguments against paying for this as they are, after all, public records and things may change, but not yet.

LIFETIMES: DEATH IN A FENCE

THE DEATH CERTIFICATE of Samuel Blain showed that he died on 19 April 1899, aged 88, and was a retired roadman. His place of death was unusual, 'The Forest, Delamere', and the cause of death was 'exhaustion the result of being suspended in a wire fence – accidental'. The certificate tells us an inquest was held by the Chester coroner on 21 April.

The local Cheshire newspaper, the *Chronicle* (examined at the British Library's newspaper library at Colindale), for 22 April gave the following report:

Mr J. C. Bate, coroner, held an inquiry to-day (Friday) at the Tiger's Head Inn into the circumstances attending the death of Samuel Blain, labourer, aged 86 [sic], who was found dead in Delamere Forest on Wednesday night. It appeared from the evidence of the widow that her husband had not been able to work for several years, but it had been his habit to go out for a walk into the Forest every morning and to come back with a few sticks for fire lighting. On the morning in question he left home but did not return.- Samuel Blain, son of the deceased said that when he came home from work on Wednesday evening his mother told him that his father had been out all day and had not returned. In consequence of this he went to search for him in the Forest, and found him fast in a wire fence, quite dead. He went for assistance and the deceased was taken home.- Having heard the evidence the jury returned a verdict in conformity therewith.

Besides the terribly sad story, note that a different age (86 rather than 88) is given for Samuel, and we learn he had a widow who survived him, and a son, also named Samuel.

△ **The Family Records Centre in Myddleton Road, London EC1, home of the General Registration indexes.**

Once you have found the entry you suspect is the right one, you can order a certificate using the Registration Online Ordering Service (ROLO) at www.gro.gov.uk or ring 0845 603 7788. Alternatively you can order a certificate by filling in a form and handing it in to the cashier at the FRC. The cost is £7 and there is usually a delay of four working days before you can collect the certificate or have it posted to you. If you want next-day results, you can pay £23 for a priority service.

A checking process is available for all GRO certificates. It is a system whereby you can provide additional information on the back of the application form about what you hope will appear on the certificate. If the information does not appear on the certificate, the certificate will not be issued and you will be refunded £4 of the £7 you paid for it. This means that if you have four possible references to an ancestor's birth, you do not have to buy all four (at a cost of £28) but you can have them checked: three negative results and one correct certificate will cost you only £19. However, the fact that you are unsure which reference is likely to be right emphasises how little you really know about the people concerned, so be very careful about what information you use as a checking point.

Occupations and addresses changed a lot, so avoid using these as checking points. The best ones to use are rough ages or parents' names but, again, be careful because the registrar general's staff have been known to be somewhat over-punctilious.

If you are seeking the marriage of someone with a father called John, and the certificate actually gives the father as John Edward, the checkers may return your application with a negative result, so make your search criteria broader by requesting a check for a father called 'John plus or minus any other names'. Equally, instead of stating the exact age that you think someone should have been, give yourself a little leeway. Instead of 'age 20', say 'age 18–22'.

Beware false economies

Because of the fees involved, some people may be reluctant to buy certificates, but not to do so is invariably a false economy. When I started tracing my ancestry, I had a rough idea of my great-great-grandmother's age, and found an index reference to someone of the right age in Shepton Mallet. I decided to save money by not buying the certificate and wasted ages searching through other Shepton Mallet records looking for her family, without success. In the end I bought the certificate only to find that the certificate belonged to somebody completely different. Faced with this frustration, it was only then that I broadened my search and managed to find the right reference, but this time it was in London. Even if the Shepton Mallet entry had been right, I still would have benefited by having bought the certificate at once. Many people are in similar situations and will often say 'I've hit a brick wall' when all they actually need to do is to fork out for a certificate.

OTHER USEFUL POINTERS

Until 1874, stillborn children did not have to be registered. When children died very young, you will sometimes find their death but not their birth has been registered.

Like other certificates, information recorded on death certificates will often be slightly unreliable, but none more so than on elderly peoples' death certificates, because the informant was invariably of a younger generation and unlikely to know all the facts for certain. Doctors, care-home workers or friends can register deaths and they may scarcely have known the deceased, but bereaved children are equally unlikely to get all the facts straight.

Do not forget that death certificates can provide information on people born long before General Registration began. The death certificate of an elderly ancestor in 1837 will provide co-ordinates on your family history back in the 18th century.

If a coroner's inquest took place, this will be noted on the death certificate. Coroners' records are closed to access for 75 years after the event and many have been destroyed. Those over 75 years old and which have survived are usually to be found in the relevant county record office, and their whereabouts is detailed in J. Gibson and C. Rogers' *Coroners' Records in England and Wales* (FFHS, 1997). A much better way of finding details of an inquest, however, is to look in the local newspaper (see page 144).

Death certificates seldom provide much useful information in themselves, but they can be helpful if you are stuck.

OVERCOMING PROBLEMS

➤**Clerical errors.** The General Registration indexes were compiled by the registrar general's clerks from copies of certificates sent in by the superintendent registrars, who in turn were receiving information from the local registrars: at each stage of the process, errors could and did creep in. If you receive a certificate that does not say exactly what you expected,

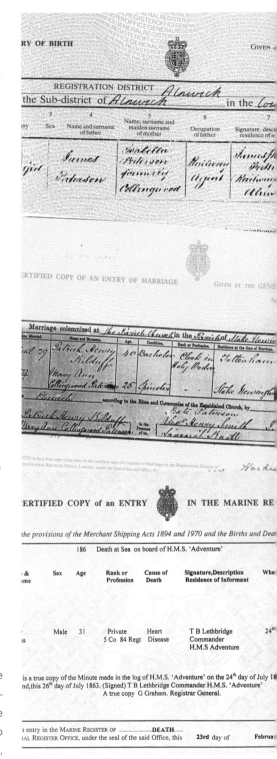

this may be due to a clerical error somewhere along the line, although you would be most unwise to assume this was the case without good evidence.

➤**Human errors.** Equally, while the GRO staff do a splendid job, they are not all highly trained and can be prone to human error. If a search you requested from the Registrar General's office comes back negative, the entry may simply have been missed. Also, although some certificates are photocopied from the original Registrar General's copy, many more are copied out or typed and may thus contain mistranscriptions. This is seldom a problem, but it is always worth bearing the possibility in mind. If you think a certificate contains a transcription error, send it back and ask for it to be checked.

➤**Misreading of information.** Another source of trouble is that the General Registration indexes themselves contain errors. One reason for not finding what you wanted may be that a surname was misread, and thus misindexed. Write down the surname you are searching for in the worst handwriting you can manage, and then ask someone else to try to read it. If they suggest a different name, try searching under that one instead.

NON-RECORDING OF EVENTS

Sadly, not all events were recorded. Although most people voluntarily registered their children's births, they were only legally obliged to before 1875 if specifically told to do so by a registrar. It is thought that up to 15% of births escaped registration in this period.

➤**If you cannot find a birth,** it could be because you are looking in the wrong year or the birth was indexed under a variant. But if you keep failing, you may have to accept that you are descended from ancestors who, knowingly or not, made life harder for their genealogist descendants by not registering their child's birth.

➤**Missing the deadline.** In 1875, parents became legally obliged to register their children's births within six weeks, and were fined if caught not doing so. This greatly reduced the number of non-registered births, but did not eradicate the problem. Also, if parents missed the six-week deadline, they might register the birth but lie about the date of birth to avoid paying the fine.

➤**Incorrect logging of marriages.** It used to be thought that almost all marriages were correctly registered, but recently studies are showing that a great deal were never properly logged by the registrar general. However, most deaths were registered.

➤**Unregistered babies** do not stand out in the crowd, but decomposing corpses certainly would and, in any case, death certificates have been required since 1837 before burial can take place.

➤**If you cannot find an ancestor's birth record** but you know the names and years of birth of siblings (for example, from a census return – see page 66), seek the births of siblings instead. Their birth records will tell you what you need to know about your ancestor's parents. If your ancestor was born before 1837 but had siblings born after, seek their birth records instead.

➤**Parish registers** (see page 96) are a poor substitute for General Registration records, but if you cannot find an event and have a pretty good idea where it would have taken place, try seeking a baptism, marriage or burial record instead, either in the original register or using parish register indexes such as the International Genealogical Index (see page 110).

DIFFERENT LOCATIONS, DIFFERENT NAMES

➤**A mobile population.** Never forget that an ancestor may have been born, married or died far from their normal home. Some areas, such as the naval bases of Portsmouth and the Thames-side dockyards, contain many births, marriages and deaths of people from all over the world. Also, remember how mobile our ancestors were – the English and Welsh registration records cover those two countries alone. If someone died on a day-trip to France or was born while their parents were stationed with the army in Ireland – or India – the event will not appear in the English and Welsh indexes.

➤**Nicknames.** A problem searchers sometimes encounter is that an ancestor was known under one name but has been officially registered under another one. Sometimes you simply cannot guess that Uncle Tom was registered as Arthur, but there are many nicknames which relate to proper names, such as Jack for James or John, Bill for William, Frank for Francis, Nancy for Anne, Ann or Hannah and so on.

➤**Middle names.** It is not always the case that people stated their middle names when they married, or indeed had them quoted when they died. Your William Frederick Smith might be registered as plain William Smith, and equally the man known all his life as Jim Hanson might have been registered at birth as James Frederick Augustus Timothy Hanson. By the same token, if you find a certificate with an absence or addition of middle names that surprises you, seek further evidence that it is the right person before you start seeking the next generation back.

GENERAL REGISTRATION OUTSIDE ENGLAND

A good general guide to General Registration world-wide is T. J. Kemp's *International Vital Records Handbook* (Genealogical Publishing Co., 2001), which includes details of general registration worldwide with copies of application forms and fees.

SCOTLAND

Scottish General Registration records date from 1 January 1855 and are kept by the **Registrar General of Scotland** at New Register House, Edinburgh. Booking is advisable, and you will be charged a fee of £16 per day or £60 per week for access to Civil Registration, census and parish records. You can search the General Registration indexes by computer, note down the reference number of entries that seem relevant and then examine them on microfiche. The computer does not pick up variant spellings, so if your ancestor John McDonald was indexed as John MacDonall, then you will miss him unless you search under that spelling. You can check the original records at once, at no extra cost, and it is often possible to trace back to 1855 in a day. A certificate costs £6 while a photocopy of an event between 1855 and 1891 costs £1.50.

www.scotlandspeople.gov.uk is a major development in Scottish genealogy. It includes indexes to Scottish General Registration of births, marriages and deaths from 1855 to 1904, 1929 and 1954 respectively. You can see basic details of an entry for 30p or download images of the original records for £1.20.

Microfiche copies of the records 1855–1920 are available at **Mormon Family History Centres** and the **SoG**.

You can also commission a search from the register office staff.

The **Registrar General of Scotland** also has indexes to:
- Consular returns of birth and death from 1914 and marriages from 1917.
- Army births, marriages and deaths of Scots in British bases worldwide from 1881.
- Deaths of Scots in the armed forces for the Boer War and the First and Second World Wars.
- Births and deaths of Scots or children of Scottish fathers in British aircraft from 1948.

IRELAND

Civil registration for Protestant marriages started on 1 April 1845 and on 1 January 1864 for all births, marriages and deaths. The records and registration districts were organised as in England. The public searchroom is at Joyce House, Dublin. You can pay €1.90 for a search of five consecutive years or €15.24 for six hours unlimited searching. Births are indexed quarterly. Between 1903 and 1927 and from 1966 to 1995 they are indexed annually and include the child's date of birth as well. Mothers' maiden names are included from 1903. Marriages and deaths are indexed quarterly right up to 1965. Indexes to marriages and deaths from 1966-1995 are in alphabetical order and with precise date and surname of spouse for marriages, and precise date, age and marital status for deaths. All post 1995 records are indexed on computer and can be checked by the staff: it is believed that all indexes will soon be computerised. The Registrar General in Dublin also holds:
- Births at sea from 1864 and deaths at sea up to 1921
- British consular returns for Irish abroad 1864–1921.

Civil records for Northern Ireland from 1922 are kept by the **Registrar General of Northern Ireland**, which also has microfiche copies of the Irish birth indexes from 1864. Mothers maiden names are given in the birth indexes from' 1903. You can search the indexes for a fee of £8/day with extra charges depending on how many records you would like to see. Book in advance.

The Registrar General in Belfast also holds:
- Births and deaths at sea from 1922.
- British consular returns for Northern Irish people abroad from 1922.
- War deaths 1939–48.
- If you know when the event took place you can order certificates online at **www.groni.gov.uk**. It is important to remember variant spellings, not least because many Irish names are English renderings (and sometimes quite arbitrary ones) of Gaelic names. Surnames may appear with or without the prefixes O', Mc or Mac.
- Irish civil registration for births 1865–74 and Protestant marriages 1847–64 are indexed on the Vital Records index (see page 111) on **www.familysearch.org**.

CHANNEL ISLANDS

Alderney and Sark: Births and deaths from 1925 and marriages from 1919 are kept by the **Clerk of the Court** (Alderney) and the **General Registrar** (Sark). All other records are held on Guernsey.

Guernsey: Births and deaths from 1840 and marriages from 1919 are held by at **Her Majesty's Greffier**. The indexes and records are available for public searching. Up to 1949, married women's deaths were recorded under their maiden names. Occasionally, death certificates will give the maiden name of the mother. Copies of the 19th-century records are also at the **Priaulx Library**. Copies of the birth and death registers 1840–1907 and marriages 1840–1911, and indexes for births and marriages to 1966 and deaths to 1963 are at the **SoG**. During the German occupation 1940–45 a separate set of records was kept, and is now held at the General Register Office with copies at the SoG.

Jersey: Births, marriages and deaths from 1842 are kept by the **Judicial Greffe**. Only postal searches are possible, although copies of the indexes 1842–1900 are at the library of the **Société Jersiaise** and the Channel Islands Family History Society. Marriage certificates often give the spouses' birthplaces.

A general-purpose Channel Islands research site is **ttp://user.itl.net/~glen-not**.

ISLE OF MAN

Civil Registration of births and marriages started in 1849 and deaths in 1878, and was compulsory for births and deaths from 1878 and marriages from 1884. The records are kept by the **Chief Registrar** at the General Registry, where you can search in the original registers and obtain certificates. Copies of the indexes up to 1964 are at the **SoG**.

QUICK REFERENCE

See also main sources in Useful Addresses, page 306

REGISTRAR GENERAL OF SCOTLAND
New Register House
Charlotte Square
Edinburgh EH1 3YT
☎ 0131 334 0380
www.gro–scotland.gov.uk

REGISTRAR GENERAL OF NORTHERN IRELAND
Oxford House
49–55 Chichester Street
Belfast BT1 4HL
Northern Ireland
☎ 028 9025 2000
www.groni.gov.uk

REGISTRAR GENERAL OF EIRE
Public Searchroom
Joyce House
8–11 Lombard Street
Dublin 2
Eire
☎ 00 353 1 635 4000

REGISTRAR GENERAL OF EIRE
Headquarters (for correspondence)
Convent Road
Roscommon
Ireland
☎ 00 353 90 663 2900
www.groireland.ie

For Channel Island and Isle of Man addresses, see page 311

SCOTTISH CERTIFICATES

ALTHOUGH THEY WERE SLOW to follow the English by introducing General Registration, the Scots made up for the lost time by introducing much more detailed certificates in 1855 (see page 105). Sadly, these were so complicated that the amount of information required was reduced the next year, though the ensuing documents are still more detailed than those found south of the border.

Births. Mothers' maiden names are given in the birth indexes from 1929. Certificates for 1855 and from 1861 onwards have the addition of the date and place of the parents' marriage. Those for 1855 alone also record the ages and places of birth of the parents and details of the child's older siblings.

Marriages. Married women are indexed under both their maiden and married names. Certificates include the names of both parties' mothers and fathers, and mothers' maiden names.

Deaths. Ages are given in the death indexes from 1868 and dates of birth from 1969. The mother's maiden name is given in the death indexes from 1974. Certificates for 1855 and since 1861 provide the name of the spouse and of the deceased's parents, including the father's occupation and mother's maiden name. For 1855 alone the names of offspring were recorded, and from 1855 to 1861 so was the place of burial.

WHEN MARK CURTIS and his son Daniel started having their family tree traced three years ago, they could never have predicted what a complicated story would emerge.

Mark's great-grandfather Frank was born in India in about 1884/5, son of a soldier called George Curtis, though by the time of Frank's Lancashire marriage in 1909, George had become a postman. Frank's birth and baptism were recorded twice in the Army Register Book of births, marriages and deaths, a copy of which is at the FRC, once by George's regiment and secondly by the Royal Army Service Corps, and showed he was born in Bangalore on 15 June 1885, son of George Curtis, a sergeant in the 8th Hussars, and his wife Mary Richards.

George, son of William Curtis, a labourer, and Mary married in church at Trinulghery, Secunderabad on 30 July 1884 and the marriage record showed George was 30, so born about 1853–4. However, searches for his birth or baptism either in the army birth/baptism records at the FRC, the English and Welsh General Registration records or elsewhere all drew complete blanks. A record of George's birth simply was not to be found.

FURTHERING THE SEARCH

We knew George became a postman. Postmen's records are at the Post Office Archives (see page 182) and the pension records showed only one likely candidate, whose pension started in 1919. His application told us he had joined the Royal Mail in 1899 and had served with 'diligence and fidelity'. His date of birth was stated to be 22 June 1855, a year later than the age suggested on the marriage record. But even with this new information, a record of the birth was still not to be found.

We therefore tried his army records, finding his service papers in the NA, in class WO 97. These told us masses about George, including that he was 5' 8" tall with a chest measuring 3¼' and that he had a sallow complexion, brown hair, brown eyes, a good physique and a pulse of 64 beats per minute. We learned of his travels to India and South Africa, and back, the diseases he had suffered there: like most soldiers, he caught both hepatitis and syphilis, but he continued to serve. In the end he was posted back to England, to Canterbury, not far from the Royal Dragoons pub on the appropriately named Military Road. He later suffered a riding accident while serving in Ireland, leaving the army there in 1898; his conduct had been 'exemplary' and 'temperate', which means he did not drink too heavily. For the record, his death certificate shows that he died of pneumonia and a fractured bone on 18 November 1939, aged 84, at 41 Elswick Row, Newcastle.

FURTHER DELVING

But where was he born? His army discharge papers (see page 197) stated he was born on 22 June 1855 at St Mary's, Reading. However, no birth record could be found there, nor a corresponding baptism, and neither he nor his father William Curtis, the labourer, were in the 1861 census. It turns out Reading was not his birthplace, and we still do not know why he said it was.

In fact, the 1901 census (see page 69) states his birthplace as 'Barnby', Suffolk, but in this record he is mis-entered as George Carter and, in any case, at the time the research was being undertaken, the 1901 census had not yet been released. However, his army papers also gave his next of kin as Mary and, before his marriage, as 'Mother, Harriet------ Barnaby near Beccles [Suffolk]'.

Although it is most useful for events before General Registration began in 1837, the International Genealogical Index on **www.familysearch.org** can sometimes be helpful solving mysteries after then (see page 110). There was no George Curtis entry, which was obviously right, but further searching revealed a William Curtis, son of

William and Harriet, baptised on 24 June 1860 at Barnby, Suffolk. This certainly seemed to indicate the right family – and the original entry confirmed that the father, William, was indeed a labourer.

As George was supposedly born around 1853–5, the 1861 census of Barnby was the next stop. This revealed William Curtis the labourer at Back Lane, Barnby, with his wife Harriet and children, including William's step-son George Moore, aged eight.

FOUND!

Taken aback, yet very excited, we sought a birth certificate. George Moore was born on 22 June 1852, at Barnby, as George, son of Harriet Moore, an unmarried woman from Barnby. And to seal the case we found the marriage of William Curtis and Harriet Moore taking place on 12 April 1855.

I cannot explain why George said he was born in Reading, but it seems that sometime after the 1861 census was taken, William and Harriet decided to alter George's surname and year of birth to make it fall within the year of their wedding. This made George seem like their legitimate son, or else George decided to do this himself. Illegitimacy carried some stigma at that time, and perhaps it was considered best all round if the matter was glossed over.

The moral of the story, as Mark and Daniel discovered, is that the answer to a family mystery can be found, but you must keep on seeking new information about the person you are after: eventually, with sufficient persistence, you may well succeed.

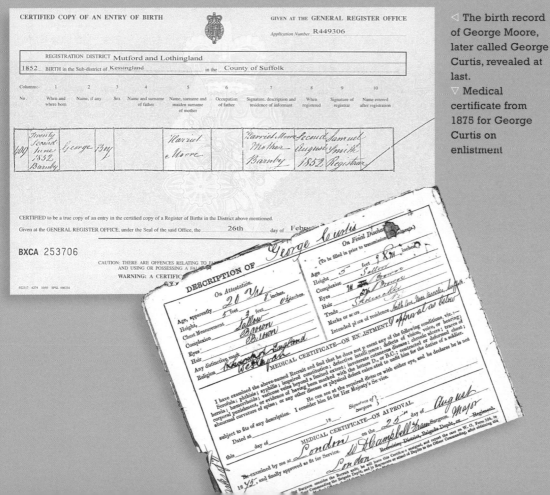

◁ The birth record of George Moore, later called George Curtis, revealed at last.
▽ Medical certificate from 1875 for George Curtis on enlistment

LIFETIMES: THE TALE OF THE NEARLY LOST SOLDIER

EXAMPLES OF GENERAL REGISTRATION IN OTHER COUNTRIES

Most countries around the world have General Registration, although relatively few have had such a system for anything like as long as Britain. Below are some details of General Registration in countries where British people may wish to do research. In all cases, you can obtain up-to-date information and advice from the relevant country's embassy in London, usually from the embassy's cultural section. Bear in mind that the primary duty of an embassy is not to help you trace your family tree, and the average receptionist is unlikely to be an expert on genealogy, so a considerable degree of polite persistence is often required to ensure you are passed on to someone who will be able to help. But, invariably, your efforts will pay off.

AUSTRALIA
Civil registration started at different times in the different states, beginning with Tasmania in 1838. Many of the records for different states are being published on CD-Rom by the Latter Day Saints in the form of pioneers' indexes: contact them on **www.familysearch.org.** Records tend to be fairly detailed, e.g. including parents' names on death certificates.

BANGLADESH
Modern civil registration started in 1960. What little has been recorded can be accessed via the **Bangladesh Demographic Survey and Vital Registration System**.

INDIA
Contact the **Registrar General's Office** or address enquiries to the 'Chief Registrar of Births, Deaths and Marriages' of the capital city of the relevant state, union or territory. Civil registration of births and deaths was introduced in Bengal in 1873 and throughout India in 1886 but outside major towns and cities compliance was very low. Registration of marriages became compulsory for some faiths by special Acts: for Christians (1872 and 1955), Parsees (1936) and Hindus (1955). In practice, the best way of finding out about a marriage is to contact the place of worship where the event is thought to have taken place.

JAMAICA
Compulsory civil registration of births, marriages and deaths started on 1 January 1878. Records are kept at the **Registrar General's Department**. Much can be accessed on microfiche through the **Mormon Family History Centres**.

KENYA
Modern civil registration of births and deaths for whites began in 1904, available to Asians from 1906, compulsory for Asians from 1928 and compulsory for blacks from 1963 (and in other states from years up to 1971). Contact the **Principal Civil Registrar** or the local district registry. White marriages have been registered since 1902 but few black marriages have been recorded. Islamic marriages are registered by the **Minister of Mohammedan Marriages**.

NEW ZEALAND
Civil registration started in 1848, first for whites only, but Maoris soon started to use the system voluntarily until it became compulsory in 1911 for marriages, and 1913 for births and deaths. Copies of the indexes to 1920 are at the **SoG** in London.

PAKISTAN
Modern Pakistan has required the registration of all over 18, and all foreigners, since 1973. Birth, marriage, death and divorce records kept by the Directorate of General Registration, which you can contact via the **Pakistan Embassy**.

SIERRA LEONE
Civil registration began in Freetown in 1801 but has never been truly comprehensive. Information is held at the **Office of the Chief Registrar**.

SOUTH AFRICA
Civil registration started piecemeal in its constituent provinces, beginning with the Cape of Good Hope (1820), while national civil registration started in 1923, with records held by the Department of Home Affairs, which you can contact via the **South African High Commission**.

QUICK REFERENCE

See also main sources in Useful
Addresses, page 306

**BANGLADESH DEMOGRAPHIC SURVEY
AND VITAL REGISTRATION SYSTEM**
Bangladesh Bureau of Statistics
Gana Bhavan Extension Block-1
Sher-A-Bangla Nagar
Dhaka 7
Bangladesh

REGISTRAR GENERAL'S OFFICE
West Block 1
P. K. Puram
New Delhi 110066
India

REGISTRAR GENERAL'S DEPARTMENT
Island Record Office
Spanish Town
Jamaica

PRINCIPAL CIVIL REGISTRAR
PO Box 30031
Nairobi
Kenya

**MINISTER OF MOHAMMEDAN
MARRIAGES**
PO Box 45687
Nairobi
Kenya

PAKISTAN EMBASSY
Community Directorate
36 Londes Square
London SW1X 9JN
☎ 020 7664 9246

OFFICE OF THE CHIEF REGISTRAR
Births and Deaths Office
Ministry of Health
3 Wilberforce Street, Freetown
Sierra Leone

SOUTH AFRICAN HIGH COMMISSION
South Africa House
Trafalgar Square
London WC2N 5DP
☎ 0870 005 6974
www.southafricahouse.com

OTHER GENERAL REGISTRATION RECORDS

The FRC holds a number of civil registration records besides those for
England and Wales. They contain broadly similar types of information
and are indexed at the FRC and on **www.1837online.com**.

➤**Consular records:** records of birth, marriage and death of British
subjects kept by British consuls from 1 July 1849.

➤**Birth and death at sea:** from 1 July 1837.

➤**Forces deaths:** for Boer (1899–1902) and First and Second World Wars.

➤**Forces births, baptisms, marriages and deaths** (except foregoing):
regimental returns (1761–1924), forces chaplains (1796–1880) and
returns (1881–1965).

➤**Indian service deaths:** 1939–42.

➤**Deaths in the air and missing persons:** 1947–65.

➤**Births, marriages and deaths:** in Ionian Islands (1818–64).

▽ **A record of death at sea.**

CERTIFIED COPY of an ENTRY   IN THE MARINE REGISTER

NA 006432

Application Number Y548992

Pursuant to the provisions of the Merchant Shipping Acts 1894 and 1970 and the Births and Deaths Registration Act 1953.

186   Death at Sea on board of H.M.S. 'Adventure'

When Died	Name & Surname	Sex	Age	Rank or Profession	Cause of Death	Signature,Description Residence of Informant	When Registered	Signature of Registrar
24 July 1/63	Henry Collins	Male	31	Private 5 Co 84 Regt	Heart Disease	T B Lethbridge Commander H.M.S Adventure	24th July 1/63	T B Lethbridge Commander

I hereby certify that this is a true copy of the Minute made in the log of H.M.S. 'Adventure' on the 24th day of July 1863.
Witness my hand,this 26th day of July 1863. (Signed) T B Lethbridge Commander H.M.S. 'Adventure'
A true copy G Graham. Registrar General.

TIFIED to be a true copy of an entry in the MARINE REGISTER OF ....DEATH........
Given at the GENERAL REGISTER OFFICE, under the seal of the said Office, this   **23rd** day of   **February** , **2004** .

CHAPTER SIX
CENSUSES

The first mention of censuses is familiar to many from the Christmas story. Sadly, Caesar's census will not help many modern family historians, but more recent ones will. Those for 19th-century Britain can provide ages and places of birth, essential information for seeking births and so identifying earlier generations.

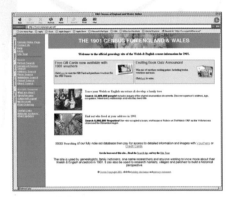

△ An increasing number of censuses can be searched on websites (see Where to Search on page 68 for details). This is the homepage of the 1901 census (www.census.pro.gov.uk).

Census returns used to be regarded as the second port-of-call after General Registration records. Now, with the 1901, 1891, 1881 and 1871 censuses full indexed on-line, and those for 1861, 1851 and 1841 following rapidly behind, they can often represent the first and easiest way of tracing a family tree back into the 19th century.

From 1851 to 1901, census returns provide ancestors' names, relationships to others in the same household, ages and places of birth. With good fortune, you may be able to find your grandparent or great-grandparent with their parents in the 1901 census, then seek the same family in the preceding censuses, using the on-line indexes or through manual searching of the original returns. At that point (and with good fortune still attending), you will find the names of your forebears who were born in the early 19th or even late 18th centuries, whose baptisms can be sought in parish registers.

In practice, you are unlikely to be able to perform these genealogical gymnastics using censuses in isolation. To be sure you have traced the right line, you will need General Registration records as well. Both categories of records complement each other to help you build up details of your ancestors' lives. Used together, they can enable you trace a fully proven family tree back to the early 19th century.

THE RECORDS

Each enumeration book (see opposite) starts with a brief description of the area covered, usually street by street, and also always includes details of the parish, town or borough. Censuses provide a splendid snap-shot of your family on a specific evening in the past showing your ancestors in the context of their family, extended family and neighbourhood. But do remember that the records are just that. If someone was away from the household, even for just that one night, they were supposed to be enumerated where they actually were, not where they normally lived.

IN ENGLAND, various population counts have taken place since the Domesday survey of 1086, but thereafter only on a local basis, such as the censuses for parts of the City of London for 1638 and 1695, held at the Corporation of London Record Office. The first national census taken in England, Scotland and Wales was in 1801. It was made in response to the threat of invasion by Napoleon and was designed mainly to ascertain how many men were available for conscription into the army. A debate had also been raging on and off for half a century as to whether the population was declining or, on the other hand, whether it could rise to an unsustainable level. The results showed a population of 8,893,000 in England and Wales. In 1811, largely because of more efficient enumeration, the number was much greater – 10,164,000 in England and Wales – triggering a genuine panic of a population explosion which would rapidly overwhelm the country.

Censuses have been taken every decade since then, except for 1941, when everyone was busy with the all-too-real threat of invasion from Germany. However, until 1841, in almost every instance, they remained mere head counts, although in some 750 happy cases enumerators chose to write down the names and sometimes even occupations (see overleaf). From 1841 onwards, when the Registrar General was placed in charge of the system, Britain has had proper censuses listing everyone together by address, with ages and occupations. Because of secrecy legislation, they are not available for public searching for 100 years, so the most recent records available now are those of the 1901 census.

COMPILING CENSUSES

To compile censuses, the General Registration sub-districts were divided into enumeration districts, which were basically the areas that a single enumerator could cover in foot on an evening. Just as now, forms were distributed in advance of census night, to be completed by each household on the appointed evening or, if everyone in the household was illiterate, by the enumerator. The enumerators copied the resulting information into enumeration books and sent them to the Registrar General for statistical analysis. This was done by clerks with blue pencils, ticking or crossing off entries as they were counted, something which newcomers to census returns sometimes find confusing. Equally, the clerks sometimes wrote general descriptions against occupations – but once you know this, the clerks' notes are easy to spot and ignore.

The original householders' forms were destroyed but, more by luck than judgement, almost all the books were kept, but scarcely very well – the returns for 1841 and 1861 were found in the roof of the Houses of Parliament, and sections of the former, particularly for parts of Kent, Essex and London (Paddington, Kensington, Golden Lane and Whitecross), have never been located. They were transferred to the Public Record Office by 1912 and it was not until much later that their immense value for family history was realised. The microfilmed copies of the books are what we use now for census searching and formed the basis for the increasing number of census indexes.

▽ Detail from *The Census at Bethlehem* by Brueghel (1525–69).

THE STORY OF CENSUSES

△ A page from an 1841 census return.

1821 CENSUS

A few returns include more than mere head-counts (see box, opposite). Shropshire Record Office also has partial returns for Shrewsbury, including names of occupiers listed street by street.

Hendon's quite detailed censuses for 1801–21 are at Barnet Borough archives and on CD *The Parish of Hendon, 1801, 1811 & 1821* from **www.archivecdbooks. co.uk**. The 1821 Hackney returns were found in a cupboard in St John's church, Hackney and have been published by the East of London FHS as *Parish Returns Series no. 2 part 1, Hackney 1821*. The returns list heads of households only, even if several households were in one house.

1831 CENSUS

The 1831 returns for Hackney survive as well and have been indexed in J. Chaudhuri's *Hackney Street Directory 1831* (East of London FHS, 2001), listing head of household by name, with their occupation and the occupations but not names of the other inhabitants. Originals for both are in the Hackney Borough Archives. For details of other surviving early censuses, see Where to Search, overleaf. An enumerator's notebook survives for Saxmundham, Suffolk, including names of people being counted.

1841 CENSUS

Most of these returns survive. They give:

➤**Address.** This may be precise, or simply a street name or even just the name of the village, with each house numbered sequentially as the enumerator walked around.

➤**Name of each person in the household.** Middle names or initials were not to be recorded.

➤**Age.** The ages of those under 16 were recorded precisely, and the ages of those over 16 were rounded down to the nearest round five years. Thus, people aged from 50 to 54 were all to be recorded as 50. Luckily, some enumerators failed to heed this and wrote down the exact ages.

➤**Occupation.**

➤**Whether the person was born in the same county.** Usually 'Y' for yes and 'N' for no, or 'NK' for not known. If the birth was outside England and Wales, the abbreviations were 'S' for Scotland, 'I' for Ireland or 'F' for 'foreign parts' – the rest of the world! Relationships were not stated, and should not be assumed: two 50-year-olds of opposite sex and a 20-

year-old could be husband, wife and child, or otherwise brother, sister and a child of one of their cousins – or one of many other possible permutations.

1851–1901 CENSUSES

These are broadly similar in their detail and survive almost complete. They give:

➤ **Address**. As 1841. In 1891 and 1901, the number of rooms occupied, if less than five, was recorded. Double dashes indicate the break between buildings; single dashes indicate the break between different households in the same building.

➤**Name of each person in the household.** Initials of middle names could be and often were recorded.

➤**Relationship to the head of household.** Usually wife, son or daughter, but also step-child, in-laws, servants and, if you are very lucky, parents or grandparents. Sometimes the terms 'in-law' and 'step-' were used differently to nowadays: a son-in-law today means the daughter's husband, but then it was sometimes used for the wife's son by a previous marriage, what we would now term a 'step-son', and vice versa.

➤**Marital condition.** Married, single or widowed.

➤**Age.** Ages were recorded precisely.

➤**Occupation.** In 1891 and 1901, the census notes whether the person was an employee or employer and, if the latter, how many people, if any, they employed. The acreage of farms was also noted.

➤**If working at home.** This was a new column added in 1901.

➤**Place of birth.** Recorded by parish and county. If the person was born outside England and Wales, usually only the country would be given, although sometimes you may be lucky and find the parish or nearby town stated too. If luck does not strike with the first census return you examine, try another.

➤**Physical and mental condition.** This was a column for those who were blind, deaf and dumb. Further categories, 'imbecile or idiot; lunatic' were added in 1871, subsequently changed to 'lunatic, imbecile, feeble-minded' in 1901.

1911 CENSUS

This census should be released at the NA and FRC in 2012 and cannot be searched in advance under any circumstances.

1821 CENSUS EXAMPLES

THREE CONSECUTIVE ENTRIES from the Hackney 1821 index show:

'Rossers, James, Jolly Butchers Yard, [Stoke] Newington, 2 males, 2 females, total 4/4' [meaning four people in Rosser's household, and another three families in the same building, p. 173]

'Rossomond, Joseph, Aldermans Walk, tailor, 5 males, 2 females, total 7' [p. 30]

'Rothschild, Mr [Nathan Mayer], Stamford Hill, gent, 3 males, 7 females, total 10' [p. 162]

DATES OF BIRTH

ONCE YOU HAVE located a person's census return, you will be able to see his or her age at the time of the census. From this you can deduce an approximate time of birth – see table on pages 78–81.

CENSUS RETURNS

⊞ Census returns 1941–1901 can be searched on microfilm at the **FRC** and at **Mormon Family History Centres** (by appointment). Many libraries and record offices hold sets of fiche, usually just for their own area or county. Full details are in J. Gibson and E. Hampson's *Census returns 1841-1891* in microform; a directory to local holdings in Great Britain, Channel islands, Isle of Man (FFHS, 6th ed., 1994).

⊞ Increasingly large amounts of census returns are also indexed on the Internet. The 1901 census is at **www.1901census.nationalarchives.gov.uk**. The index search is free and pages can be viewed or printed for a small fee, payable by credit card online or by purchasing a voucher from record offices and local libraries.

⊞ Indexed transcriptions of the 1881 census are freely available at **www.familysearch.org**.

⊞ From April 2006, all the available censuses, from 1901 to 1841, are fully indexed on **www.ancestry.co.uk**, a pay-to-view site allowing you to search by name, occupation or address and download images of the original returns. Access costs £9.95 per month or £69.95 per year. Cheaper access is also available through **www.nationalarchives.gov.uk/census** (£7.05 to view 20 images).

⊞ The 1861 census is available at **www.1837online.com**. Parts of the 1871 and 1841 censuses can also be seen at **www.britishorigins.com**.

⊞ Many searchable sections of the census returns can be bought on CD-Rom, though their advantage over the websites is questionable. Companies supplying CDs include **www.genealogysupplies.com**.

⊞ Even when the foregoing do not cover what you want, help may be at hand. **www.familyhistoryonline.net** includes a substantial collection of census indexes, some of which include full transcriptions of entries – 1851 is particularly well covered. Some sections of censuses are available freely – **www.freecen.org.uk** is focused on the 1891 census returns. A directory of free census records is at **http://www.censusfinder.com**. For example, the 1891 census for Cornwall is now available free at **http://freepages.genealogyrootsweb. com/~kayhin/ukocp.html**.

⊞ For sections of censuses that are not online, or where you have not been able to use their sometimes not very good indexing system to locate a family you are sure should be there, there are many older, off-line census indexes. J. Gibson and E. Hampson's *Marriage and Census Indexes for Family Historians* (FFHS, 2000) remains a good guide to these, many of which were labours of love by local volunteers, compiled decades before the Internet or pay-to-view sites had been heard of. Some give fairly full details and others are just surname indexes, giving references to pages on which entries appear.

⊞ There are fiche indexes, compiled by the Mormons, to the 1881 census, and some counties in the 1851 census. These have certain advantages over online versions (the 1851 indexes in many cases have yet to be superceded by anything online) in that they are indexed in a number of creative ways. You can scan through the index of everyone in with your surname. You can also search by birthplace, enabling you (for example) to easily pick out all the Smiths who were born in a certain village.

⊞ Such indexes can save hours of precious time or help solve previously unsolvable problems. Using the 1881 and 1901 censuses especially, I have been able to find children who were away from home at boarding school or working as servants, men who were away on census night on business (or so they presumably claimed) or in hospital or prison, and many other strays, not to mention families who were simply staying somewhere completely unexpected, including the workhouse.

QUICK REFERENCE

See main sources in Useful Addresses, page 306

HOW TO SEARCH THE ORIGINAL RETURNS

In many cases, you will be able to use an index to obtain the exact reference to where your ancestors were. However, this may not be the case and you will have to search the originals. If the family lived in a small village, you can simply look through the village records and, besides finding your ancestors, you will probably see (and be able to note down) others of the same name who will probably be members of your extended family.

If the family lived in a town, you could be faced with a very lengthy search. However, as the NA provides street indexes for all towns of over 40,000 inhabitants (and many held locally for smaller towns), you can save much time by finding an address where your ancestors lived from another source (see left), and then using the street index to go straight to the right place.

SIMPLIFYING MATTERS

Finding a village on microfilm or fiche and searching through it is quite easy. However, searching through a large town, which may span several piece numbers (and possibly several whole microfilms), can be extremely time-consuming, running the risk that you may become so exhausted by the work that you may quite simply miss the entry for your ancestors. Fortunately, the NA generally provides street indexes for places with populations of over 40,000. Having found an ancestor's

DATES OF CENSUSES

NA REFERENCE NUMBERS FROM 1841

10 March 1801	(no records at NA)
27 May 1811	(no records at NA)
28 May 1821	(no records at NA)
30 May 1831	HO 71
6 June 1841	HO 107
30 March 1851	HO 107
7 April 1861	RG 9
2 April 1871	RG 10
3 April 1881	RG 11
5 April 1891	RG 12
31 March 1901	RG 13
2 April 1911	RG 14

FINDING A PLACE

TO FIND THE TOWN OR VILLAGE YOU WANT, follow this procedure:

❶ Use the Place Name indexes provided for each census in the FRC search room and most county record offices and libraries that hold local census returns. These will give you a page number for the corresponding Reference Book to learn the 'piece number' covering that place.

❷ Find the relevant microfilm or, for 1901, microfiche, which are arranged by piece number.

❸ Locate the relevant place on the microfilm or fiche. Each piece contains numbered Enumeration Districts (EDs) or, in the case of the 1841 census, Enumeration Books. The Reference Books also provide the number(s) of the Book(s) or ED(s) covering the place you want (a large town will be covered by a number of EDs, while in rural areas an ED may cover a number of small villages). This leads you to the right section of the film, enabling you to start searching through the pages covering the relevant place, looking for your ancestor.

FINDING ADDRESSES

THE MAIN SOURCES for finding addresses are directories (see page 82) and General Registration certificates (see page 44). It is sometimes worth buying the birth certificate of a child who was born near a census year just to gain the family's home address at the time. Many of the other records described in this book may give addresses for census searching as well.

address, look it up in the street index to learn the folio numbers covering the street. Each page of the Enumeration Books has a folio number, printed in the top right-hand corner of each right-hand page (not to be confused with the page numbers). A folio is a page printed on both sides, so the first page of a book is 'folio 1 recto' or fo.1.r, and the back of the page is 'folio 1 verso', or fo.1.v. If the street was a long one, parts of it might appear in different Enumeration Books, but this will be indicated by the street index.

Once you find the entry you want, obtain a photocopy or write down everything, including the reference numbers, details of the parish, sub-district and so on at the top of the page, and all the information about the household. It is also worth noting the immediate neighbours: even if they have different surnames, they might turn out to be close relatives. Equally, if your search fails, write down exactly what you searched so that the work can be continued another time and, of course, a negative search will at least tell you where your ancestors did not live.

OVERCOMING PROBLEMS
IN THE INDEXES

➢**If you do not find that you are looking for, consider variant spellings.** In census indexes, names are recorded and indexed exactly as they appeared. Thus, after hosts of William Smiths come the William A. Smiths, William Anthony Smiths, and so on, followed by the Will Smiths and then the Wm Smiths. So too are birthplaces: 'Kent, Canterbury' is indexed in the birthplace index under K, a long way away from plain 'Canterbury'. There are no magic answers here: just think of as many permutations to look up as you can, and if you do not find the direct ancestors you are seeking, look up other family members and see if their entries lead you to your forebears.

➢**All indexes are subject to mistakes.** One reason for not being able to find an ancestor in an index is that the index might be wrong. If you are sure an ancestor should have been at a certain address, and they do not appear in a census index, check the original returns for that address anyway. The 1881 census index was compiled fairly rigorously and is usually accurate.

➤**The 1901 census appears to have been less carefully compiled** and many omissions or mistakes have been discovered. It is only indexed online and is not always straightforward to use. The index gives names, age, county and parish where born, county and parish of residence and occupation. Once you have spotted the right person, you can download a transcription or digitised image of the relevant page. The trouble is that certain information has been deliberately left out (such as middle names and middle initials, precise address and names of other people in the household) so it is seldom entirely clear which of several possible entries may be correct. This may necessitate having to download several pages, which will immediately turn out to be irrelevant. If you know where the family lived but cannot find them in the index, you can still search the original returns at the FRC, where limited place and street indexes are now available.

➤**Surnames are also indexed as they appear.** If you cannot find your ancestor under the spelling you thought, make a search using forename, age or place of birth and see if the right person comes up under a variant spelling of the surname. For example, if 'James Dinnie' age 24, born in Kirkintilloch does not appear, type in James, 24, Kirkintilloch and possibilities may appear including (say) James Dinny, who would probably be your man.

➤**Equally, beware variants in place names.** If the county of birth was transcribed as Cambridge, it will not appear if you type in Cambridgeshire, nor will 'Leighton' appear if you type 'Leyton', or 'Oxon' for 'Oxfordshire': be prepared to try as many possible variants as you can think of.

IN THE ORIGINAL RETURNS

➤**There will be times when you do not know the exact address,** although you will know or suspect roughly where in a town an ancestor lived. This can be especially true when working without the aid of indexes. If this happens to you, use a contemporary map to find the names of the streets, locate each one using street indexes, and search them thoroughly.

➤**Once you have found the entry you want,** you may still experience some problems. Almost all records used in family history are likely to be inaccurate, but censuses are among the worst. The reason for this is simple: if you ask people a number of fairly intrusive questions, they

---

LIFETIMES: EVEN OFFICIALS MAKE MISTAKES

CHARLES TOWNER was listed in 3 April 1881 census returns for Hastings Union Workhouse as a 50-year-old basketmaker born in Lydd. The census form would have been filled in by an official, so you would expect it to have been accurate. And you would expect the same of a death certificate filled in by John Pearce, master of the Union Workhouse, two days later. It related to the death in the workhouse, on 5 April, of Charles Towner, a 51-year-old cooper of Hastings! It just shows — discrepancies occurred and ultimately (and most unfortunately), the officials may not have cared less.

WHERE TO SEARCH

CENSUS RETURNS OUTSIDE ENGLAND & WALES

An extraordinary guide to census returns around the world is published in the somewhat unlikely guise of G. Johnson's *Census Records for Scottish Families at Home and Abroad* (Aberdeen and North East Scotland FHS, 1997).

SCOTLAND

The foregoing applies to Scotland as well as England and Wales. The records are kept by the **Registrar General of Scotland** and are covered by the same £16 search fee as for General Registration records. The returns are almost identical, except that, from 1861 onwards, they state the number of rooms with one or more windows, whether people were employers and, if so, how many people they employed. The Scottish censuses are already indexed on-line for 1901, 1891, 1881, 1871, 1861 and 1851 on **www.scotlandspeople.gov.uk**; those for 1841 will appear soon. This site also includes downloadable images.

IRELAND

Censuses were taken every decade from 1821, but 1861–91 were destroyed by the Government and most of 1821–51 burned when the Four Courts were bombed in 1922. The surviving sections, which list all occupants, are at the National Archives of Ireland and details are given, county by county, in J. G. Ryan's *Irish Records – Sources for Family and Local History* (Ancestry, rev. ed., 1997).

The 1901 and 1911 returns, which were filled in by the householders (or enumerators on their behalf), have survived and are on open access, arranged by Poor Law Union and then by district, parish and townland, which are indexed. They list names, age, gender, religious denomination, marital status and relationship to the head of the household, but the place of birth is no more precise than the county or city, or country if born outside Ireland. The 1911 returns state how long women had been married and how many surviving children they had.

For Eire, only the 1901 censuses of Kerry and Longford have been indexed. Otherwise, if you know a general location, you can check the heads-of-households lists, which accompany the census forms, for a townland or street name. The other approach is to seek an address from a **GRO** certificate first. Some **heritage centres** have their own indexes, which can be searched for a fee.

You can also check applications for old age pensions made between 1908 and 1921 where, as proof of age, extracts from the later-destroyed census returns could be submitted. The applications are indexed; copies are at the **NA**, **PRONI** and the **SoG** and **www.pensear.org**.

▷ **A census enumerator collects a completed census form.**

QUICK REFERENCE

See also main sources in Useful
Addresses, page 306

REGISTRAR GENERAL OF SCOTLAND
New Register House
Charlotte Square
Edinburgh EH1 3YT
Scotland
☎ 0131 334 0380
www.gro-scotland.gov.uk

For the Channel Islands and Isle of Man
addresses, see page 311

NORTHERN IRELAND

As Ireland. Copies of the relevant section of the Irish census are at the **PRONI**. An index to the 1901 census of Fermanagh is L. K. Kuchenbach Meehan's *1901 Irish Census Index, Vol. 1, County Fermanagh* (Largy Books, 1992).

CHANNEL ISLANDS

As England and Wales. Copies of the returns for Guernsey are held by **Her Majesty's Greffier** at the General Register Office, and for Jersey at the St Helier Public Library and **Société Jersiaise**: all returns for 1841–91 have been indexed by Jersey Library. There are also (indexed) censuses for 1806 and 1815, called 'General Don's muster rolls'. Those for 1806 list some 4000 heads of households with the numbers of people in their families, whilst those for 1816 list all men aged 17–80, with the numbers of women, boys and girls in their households.

ISLE OF MAN

As England and Wales. Copies of returns for the island are at the **Manx Museum**. The 1851, 1881, 1891 and 1901 returns are fully indexed.

EXAMPLES OF CENSUS RETURNS IN OTHER COUNTRIES

AUSTRALIA

Although musters were kept of men in Australia from 1788, proper Australian censuses kicked off with the 1828 census of New South Wales and Tasmania, giving ages, occupations, where people lived, and whether they were born in Australia or, if not, when they landed. There is a surname index at the SoG and a microfilm copy at the **NA** in class HO 10. The first national census was made in 1881, but few returns have survived.

CARIBBEAN

A guide to censuses in the NA is in G. Grannum's *Tracing your West Indian Ancestors; Sources at the PRO* (PRO Publications, 1995). Most early ones focus on the white population. There are returns of Maroons of Mooretown, Charlestown, Scot's Hall and Accompanying, giving name, age, colour and some notes on the father's name, and slaves belonging to Maroons. Jamaica's own censuses are at the Department of Statistics.

INDIA AND PAKISTAN

The first all-India census was taken in 1871–2 and have been taken regularly every ten years from 1881. However, these record nothing of any help to genealogists. Equally, although Pakistan has taken census decennially since 1951, including names and relationships, only the other two categories, ages and occupations, are available to the public, making them virtually useless for our purposes.

KENYA

Censuses were taken in 1911, 1921, 1926 and 1931, but these did not include Africans. The first complete census was in 1948 followed by one in 1969. These are at the **Central Bureau of Statistics**.

NEW ZEALAND

The few preserved census records for this country are at the **New Zealand National Archives**.

SIERRA LEONE

The **NA** have a Sierra Leone census for 30 June 1831 in class CO 267/111, which includes the whole population with ages and occupation of the head of household. There is also an 1833 census in CO 267/127.

SOUTH AFRICA

Censuses date back to 1865 for the Cape, and 1904 for the rest of the country, but they were later destroyed.

QUICK REFERENCE

See also main sources in Useful
Addresses, page 306

CENTRAL BUREAU OF STATISTICS
PO Box 30266
Nairobi
Kenya

NEW ZEALAND NATIONAL ARCHIVES
10 Mulgrave Street
Thorndon
Wellington

ONCE YOU HAVE LOCATED a person's census return, you will usually be able to see his or her age at the time of the census. From this you can deduce an approximate time of birth. **Example:** My ancestor's age was given as 34 in the 1861 census. Age from year = 1861 – 34 = 1827. Therefore, she was born between (check date of census) 7 April 1827 and 8 April 1826.

Year of birth	Date of census	1841	1851	1861	1871	1881	1891	1901
1901	[31 March]							0
1900								1
1899								2
1898								3
1897								4
1896								5
1895								6
1894								7
1893								8
1892								9
1891	[6 April]						0	10
1890							1	11
1889							2	12
1888							3	13
1887							4	14
1886							5	15
1885							6	16
1884							7	17
1883							8	18
1882							9	19
1881	[4 April]					0	10	20
1880						1	11	21
1879						2	12	22
1878						3	13	23
1877						4	14	24
1876						5	15	25
1875						6	16	26
1874						7	17	27
1873						8	18	28
1872						9	19	29
1871	[3 April]				0	10	29	39
1870					1	11	21	31
1869					2	12	22	32
1868					3	13	23	33
1867					4	14	24	34
1866					5	15	25	35
1865					6	16	26	36

Year of birth	Date of census	1841*	1851	1861	1871	1881	1891	1901
1864					7	17	27	37
1863					8	18	28	38
1862					9	19	29	39
1861	[7 April]			0	10	20	30	40
1860				1	11	21	31	41
1859				2	12	22	32	42
1858				3	13	23	33	43
1857				4	14	24	34	44
1856				5	15	25	35	45
1855				6	16	26	36	46
1854				7	17	27	37	47
1853				8	18	28	38	48
1852				9	19	29	39	49
1851	[31 March]		0	10	20	30	40	50
1850			1	11	21	31	41	51
1849			2	12	22	32	42	52
1848			3	13	23	33	43	53
1847			4	14	24	34	44	54
1846			5	15	25	35	45	55
1845			6	16	26	36	46	56
1844			7	17	27	37	47	57
1843			8	18	28	38	48	58
1842			9	19	29	39	49	59
1841	[7 June]	0	10	20	30	40	50	60
1840		1	11	21	31	41	51	61
1839		2	12	22	32	42	52	62
1838		3	13	23	33	43	53	63
1837		4	14	24	34	44	54	64
1836		5	15	25	35	45	55	65
1835		6	16	26	36	46	56	66
1834		7	17	27	37	47	57	67
1833		8	18	28	38	48	58	68
1832		9	19	29	39	49	59	69
1831		10	20	30	40	50	60	70
1830		11	21	31	41	51	61	71
1829		12	22	32	42	52	62	72
1828		13	23	33	43	53	63	73
1827		14	24	34	44	54	64	74
1826		15	25	35	45	55	65	75
1825		16	26	36	46	56	66	76
1824		17	27	37	47	57	67	77

Note Ages of adults in the 1841 census were usually rounded down to the nearest 5 years. Someone aged '45' could have been aged between 45 and 41 etc.

CALCULATING AGES FROM CENSUS RETURNS/1

Year of birth	1841	1851	1861	1871	1881	1891	1901
1823	18	28	38	48	58	68	78
1822	19	29	39	49	59	69	79
1821	20	30	40	50	60	70	80
1820	21	32	41	51	61	71	81
1819	22	32	42	52	62	72	82
1818	23	33	43	53	63	73	83
1817	24	34	44	54	64	74	84
1816	25	35	45	55	65	75	85
1815	26	36	46	56	66	76	86
1814	27	37	47	57	67	77	87
1813	28	38	48	58	68	78	88
1812	29	39	49	59	69	79	89
1811	30	40	50	60	70	80	90
1810	31	41	51	61	71	81	91
1809	32	42	52	62	72	82	92
1808	33	43	53	63	73	83	93
1807	34	44	54	64	74	84	94
1806	35	45	55	65	75	85	95
1805	36	46	56	66	76	86	96
1804	37	47	57	67	77	87	97
1803	38	48	58	68	78	88	98
1802	39	49	59	69	79	89	99
1801	40	50	60	70	80	90	100
1800	41	51	61	71	81	91	
1799	42	52	62	72	82	92	
1798	43	53	63	73	83	93	
1797	44	54	64	74	84	94	
1796	45	55	65	75	85	95	
1795	46	56	66	76	86	96	
1794	47	57	67	77	87	97	
1793	48	58	68	78	88	98	
1792	49	59	69	79	89	99	
1791	50	60	70	80	90		
1790	51	61	71	81	91		
1789	52	62	72	82	92		
1788	53	63	73	83	93		
1787	54	64	74	84	94		
1786	55	65	75	85	95		
1785	56	66	76	86	96		
1784	57	67	77	87	97		
1783	58	68	78	88	98		

Year of birth	1841	1851	1861	1871	1881	1891	1901
1782	59	69	79	89	99		
1781	60	70	80	90			
1780	61	71	81	91			
1779	62	72	82	92			
1778	63	73	83	93			
1777	64	74	84	94			
1776	65	75	85	95			
1775	66	76	86	96			
1774	67	77	87	97			
1773	68	78	88	98			
1772	69	79	89	99			
1771	70	80	90				
1770	71	81	91				
1769	72	82	92				
1768	73	83	93				
1767	74	84	94				
1766	75	85	95				
1765	76	86	96				
1764	77	87	97				
1763	78	88	98				
1762	79	89	99				
1761	80	90					
1760	81	91					
1759	82	92					
1758	83	93					
1757	84	94					
1756	85	95					
1755	86	96					
1754	87	97					
1753	88	98					
1752	89	99					
1751	90						
1750	91						
1749	92						
1748	93						
1747	94						
1746	95						
1745	96						
1744	97						
1743	98						
1742	99						

CALCULATING AGES FROM CENSUS RETURNS/2

CHAPTER SEVEN
DIRECTORIES & ALMANACS

Directories are published lists of peoples' addresses and occupations, which in the 18th, 19th and early–mid-20th centuries fulfilled broadly the same role as telephone directories do today. They are useful for gaining a snapshot of the communities in which ancestors lived. By searching a series of directories, they can give an idea of when our forebears lived and died. Their main genealogical use, however, is to learn where ancestors lived so as to facilitate census searches.

DIRECTORIES

With the exception of a merchant's directory for London published in 1677, directories started to appear in the 18th century. Those for London were published annually from 1734; Dublin's first appeared in the mid-18th century; Birmingham's earliest directory appeared in 1763; Edinburgh's in 1773 and Glasgow's in 1783. The earliest known English county directory was for Hampshire and was published in 1784. There were some national directories, such as the Universal British Directory 1793–98, although its coverage of people was limited to the most important residents and businessmen.

Directories started to appear in much more significant numbers for town and county alike in the early 19th century. They were produced by competing firms so some counties may have several directories for one year, but equally there may be gaps in coverage with some years not covered at all. Directories generally listed tradesmen, craftsmen, merchants, professionals, farmers, clergy, gentry and nobility, but as the 19th century progressed, the number of people listed increased as directories included many private residents, rich and poor alike.

A BIRD'S EYE VIEW

Directories provided short descriptions of the parishes, towns and cities they covered, combining practical details of population and geography; soil types and the main forms of agriculture and industry; schools and hospitals, with more antiquarian information on local history. These descriptions provide marvellous detail of the world our forebears inhabited. You may even find an advertisement placed by your ancestor to promote his business.

Directories can also help explain your family history. If an ancestor became a coal miner, a directory might tell you that a mine had been

DIRECTORY

The 1677 London Merchant's directory can be found online at http://freepages.history. rootsweb.com/~frpayments/ LM1677

opened in his home parish about the same time. If he came from a poor background yet became highly literate, you might learn from a directory that a free school had been opened in their village.

Directories stated which poor law unions and thus which workhouses covered the place concerned. As poor law unions equated to General Registration districts, you can use directories to establish the parameters for General Registration index searching (see page 57). They also indicate which manors covered the parish, and where the local burial grounds and non-conformist chapels were.

Furthermore, directories provided details of roads, canals and railways and the whereabouts of local markets. When trying to work out where an ancestor came from, it is helpful to know the lines of communication on which their place of residence lay. Many couples met at the local market, so if you know where one ancestor came from and want to work out the origins of their spouse, find out which the local market town was and then work out which other villages were in its catchment area.

WHAT DIRECTORIES CONTAIN

From the mid-19th century onwards, directories tended to be divided into the following sections:

➤**Commercial:** traders, professionals, farmers and suchlike, in an alphabetical list.

➤**Trades:** individual alphabetical lists of the foregoing arranged under each trade or profession.

➤**Streets:** lists of tradesmen and private residents listed house by house, street by street.

➤**Court:** originally these were the heads of wealthier households, but this rapidly became simply an alphabetical listing of the heads of all families save the poor.

By following your ancestors forward through a series of directories, you may be able to watch their careers developing – opening a new shop, expanding an existing one, changing occupations and finally handing over to their children. Finding out when an ancestor disappears from directories can provide a clue to when they might have died.

Directories may also introduce you to other relatives you had not encountered before. If you cannot find your ancestor listed, but there were other people with the same surname in the area, look them up in census returns as you may find your ancestor was living with them.

WHERE TO SEARCH

DIRECTORIES

⊟ Substantial collections of directories covering the British Isles are held by the **SoG** at the **Guildhall Library** and a smaller collection by the **IHGS**. **County record offices** and many **libraries**, especially local studies libraries and museums, hold collections for the area.

⊟ Original directories are sold in antiquarian bookshops and even car boot sales, and some have been reproduced on microfiche, such as much of the 1830 Pigot county series, available from the **SoG**.

⊟ There is no comprehensive guide to all directories, but G. Shaw & A Tipper's *British Directories: A Bibliography and Guide to Directories Published in England & Wales (1850–1950) and Scotland (1773–1950)* (Leicester University Press, 1997) is useful.

⊟ Leicester University has a national collection of directories online at **www.historicaldirectories.org**. Some are also available on CD, as advertised in the family history magazines. Electronic versions of directories have the advantage of being easily searched.

⊟ Many other countries have directories. For example, **www.rootsweb.com/~ttowgw/research/almanacs.htm** provides a catalogue of Trinidad directories held in Britain. Many Jamaican almanacs, listing mainly white inhabitants from 1811 onwards are on **www.jamaicafamilysearch.com.**

QUICK REFERENCE
See also main sources in Useful Addresses, page 306

GUILDHALL LIBRARY
Aldermanbury
London EC2P 2EJ
☎ 020 7332 1868
www.cityoflondon.gov.uk

TELEPHONE DIRECTORIES

Telephone directories are available in **local libraries** and **county record offices**, with a national collection viewable by appointment at **British Telecom Archives**.

They are also available for many countries on the Internet with services such as **www.192.com** and **www.infobel.com**, which have telephone directories for Britain, much of Europe, USA, Canada and others.

QUICK REFERENCE

BRITISH TELECOM ARCHIVES
3rd Floor, Holborn Telephone Exchange
268–270 High Holborn
London WC1V 7EE
☎ **020 7492 8792**
www.btplc.com/archives

OVERCOMING PROBLEMS

➤**Directories were commercial ventures,** usually compiled in the year prior to publication but not always fully updated between editions. It is best, therefore, to think of an entry for an ancestor in an 1874 directory as an indication of what their state of play may have been in 1873.

➤**The information provided was so scant** – name, address and/or trade – that numerous possibilities exist for confusing people with the same name, so be very careful before making the assumption that you have definitely found the right person. The descriptions may be inaccurate; for example, a man with several occupations, such as farmer and butcher, may be listed under only one. Continuity of name and trade, such as listings each year for John Smith, butcher, may mask the death of John Smith senior and the succession of John Smith junior to the business.

➤**Directories did not list the majority of the poor,** and were never intended to be in any sense complete, so if an ancestor is not listed where you expect them to be, this is no indication that they were not there. Obviously, however, if it is feasible, it is worth seeking them elsewhere, in other years or in neighbouring towns or counties.

➤**When searching in London,** do not forget that the city grew so big that from 1799 separate directories were published for the suburbs.

TELEPHONE DIRECTORIES

Telephone directories date from the 1880s and eventually took over from trade and street directories after the Second World War. They can fulfil a similar role to that of the older directories but bear in mind for research purposes that they may be out of date as soon as they are published.

Be aware, too, that telephone directories are very incomplete in their coverage; only about 70% of households have telephones and the directories usually only list the main householder. They exclude all those who wish to be ex-directory (about 70% in London) or who have opted for mobile phones rather than landlines.

Because of data protection, directory enquiries are very limited in the information they will supply.

SIXTH EDITION:

THE UNITED TELEPHONE COMPANY, LIMITED.

Head Offices:
OXFORD COURT, CANNON STREET, LONDON E.C.

BOARD OF DIRECTORS.

Chairman:
JAMES BRAND, Esq.

Vice-Chairman:
JAMES STAATS FORBES, Esq.
DILLWYN PARRISH, Esq.
JOHN W. BATTEN, Esq.
W. CUTHBERT QUILTER, Esq.

Managing Director:
JOSEPH B. MORGAN, Esq.

Secretary:
THOMAS BLAIKIE, Esq.

LIST OF SUBSCRIBERS
TO THE EXCHANGE SYSTEM.
UNDER LICENSE FROM THE POSTMASTER-GENERAL.
CLASSIFIED INTO

PROFESSIONS & TRADES.

Subscribers are requested to notify any mistake in their Names, Addresses, Classifications, or Exchange Numbers; and it is most particularly desired that gratuities be not, under any circumstances, offered to the Servants of the Company. All Communications to be addressed to the Secretary.

September, 1885.

DIRECTORIES proved both informative and useful in solving the mystery of the origins of George John Stewart. I knew that his son was supposed to have been born in St George's, Southwark in about 1827, and that when the son married in 1856 he described his father as a coffeehouse keeper, but all further searches for him failed, so I decided to seek the father in directories.

I was delighted to find a listing for a George Stewart in the commercial section of an 1856 directory as coffeehouse keeper, 183 Union Street, Borough, which was in St George's, Southwark. I was fairly sure this was the right entry, so I followed him forwards, checking each year until he disappeared after 1861. However, in 1860 and 1867 there were also entries for a George Stewart owning coffee rooms, 44 High Street, Bow.

This provided addresses for searching in the 1851 and 1861 censuses, but sadly he was not at either address. However, by searching the census returns for the streets around Bow High Street, I located George John R. Stewart, a married 53-year-old listed as a house proprietor, born in Bromley. So here was George with his correct middle name, John, and it seems that he had indeed had a coffeehouse in Southwark, and then opened coffee rooms in Bow, and finally ended up living there.

▽ Mixed company patronise a popular London coffee shop near the 'Olympic' theatre, Wych Street, Strand by Robert & George Cruikshank from *Life in London*, 1820.

CHAPTER EIGHT
LIVES LESS ORDINARY

If all your family were born within wedlock, married once and stayed happily and faithfully married, you are likely to find tracing your ancestry quite easy – and probably quite boring. Events such as illegitimacy cause great problems to genealogists, but can also prove the most interesting overall.

△ *Forgiven* by Thomas Faed (1826–1900).

FOUNDLINGS

MANY SINGLE or destitute mothers abandoned babies in places where they could be found and cared for. These children often received the Christian name of the parish's patron saint, or the location where they were found, such as Church and Porch. Parish registers may identify foundling children as such. Sadly, you will have little hope of tracing their parentage, but at least you will know you have reached the beginning of the line.

ILLEGITIMACY

People think of illegitimacy as a modern phenomenon, but between 1837 and 1965, some 5–7% of all children born in England and Wales were born out of wedlock and the situation was little different over the preceding centuries. But while illegitimacy no longer carries a social stigma, and we can celebrate the diverse lives of our forebears, it does pose problems for genealogists. If the mother subsequently married, her illegitimate child would often informally adopt the surname of the new husband, whether or not this was its father. This can place you in a Catch-22 situation, looking for the birth of a child whose original surname was that of its mother before her marriage, but you can't find the marriage record because you may not know what the mother's original name was! The solution: to seek other co-ordinates on the family from some of the other sources suggested in this book.

Another problem is that illegitimate children either make up or do not state at all their father's name when asked later in life, such as on General Registration marriage certificates. If the father's name is left blank, you are almost certainly dealing with an illegitimate child. In many cases, however, the illegitimate person did not wish to admit to this fact, and would give inaccurate information. Sometimes they would give the name of a man with the same surname as their own but say the man was dead, or an accountant, lawyer or auctioneer – popular occupations, it seems, for our ancestors' fictitious fathers. Alternatively, they might state the true forename and occupation of the father, but give the man their own surname. These cases offer researchers a ray of hope as other sources can then be searched for men with the right forename and occupation, and then evidence sought to prove they were the true father.

DISCOVERING ILLEGITIMACY

Most illegitimacies come to light from birth certificates, where the father's name is left blank, and the mother is recorded with just her

△ *The Consequences of the Seduction* by Antoine Beranger (1785–1867).

maiden surname and without a married name. This may mean that the natural father's identity will never be known, but there is always hope. For one reason or another, registrars (and before them, clergymen) would often ask the mother who the real father was, and then suggest (or insist on) giving the baby its father's surname as a middle name. Thus, Herbert Schofield Langan, illegitimate son of Emma Langan, was almost certainly the son of a Mr Schofield, and probably of a man called Herbert Schofield.

Parish clerks were often better able to record the truth than registrars and were more likely to record that a child was illegitimate, 'baseborn' or a 'bastard', sometimes even noting the father's name.

Parish chests (see page 166) may contain bastardy bonds whereby men indemnified the parish against the expense of supporting their illegitimate offspring. From 1576, Justices of the Peace could root out illegitimate children's fathers and issue bastardy orders, which will be in the Quarter Session records (see page 232), requiring them to marry the mother or pay for her child, and if he refused, they could issue maintenance orders to force him to reach into his pocket. Sometimes arguments ensued, with women (or their enraged fathers) pointing the finger, and men – guilty or not – flatly denying any responsibility. These records provide essential information on ancestors' paternity and, in many cases, colourful episodes of family history.

RECTIFYING ILLEGITIMACY

IN THE INSULAR COMMUNITY of manor and parish, direct action was often taken to rectify illegitimacy. Mothers might be locked up or whipped, and fathers forced to marry their pregnant lovers or pay money to the overseers (and this would be recorded in the overseers' accounts) towards the support of their offspring.

TRACING NATURAL PARENTS

IF YOU WERE ADOPTED, The first step in tracing natural parents or relations is to obtain a copy of your original birth certificate. Unlike the one you were given when you were adopted, this will provide information about your natural parents. If you have been told your original name, you can seek the certificate through the normal means as described on page 47. If you do not, contact the Registrar General's office at the Office for National Statistics, who will issue you with an application form.

If you were adopted before 12 November 1975, you will need to attend a birth records counselling interview. Ironically, if you were adopted after that date, you will not, though these sessions can be useful in preparing you for the possible traumas of finding unpleasant information and advising you how to proceed should you wish to trace your birth family. Counselling can be obtained locally to where you live and British social services also make it available abroad for those living overseas.

WHAT HAPPENS NEXT

The counsellor will give you a form (CAS 5/6) with which to apply for your original birth certificate and also tell you which court authorised your adoption order as well as giving you a form enabling you to ask the court to tell you which adoption agency or local authority handled your case. Sadly, many court records before 1946 have been thrown away. The court should also have a special report on your adoption, called a *Guardian ad Litem* report. If the court proves unwilling to release this, your counsellor may be able to persuade them to do so by contacting the Lord Chancellor's department.

A number of organisations may have been involved in your case: an adoption society, a local education officer (up to 1948), a children's department (1948–71) or a social services department (1971–84), or even a private individual (up to but not beyond February 1982). Although many adoption societies (and the Mother and Baby Homes which usually referred cases to them) have closed or merged, the records can be traced through G. Stafford's *Where to find Adoption Records*, copies of which are held by NORCAP (see page 93).

Be sure to ask the counsellor if she has any further personal information about your origins or whether any members of your natural family have enquired about you. If your adoption was arranged by the agency from whom you receive the counselling, they should have your complete file (although some were lost in the Second World War). If not, ask the counsellor to contact the organisation that arranged your adoption and ask for your file to be made available to you. If you do not specifically ask for this information, the counsellor may not volunteer it.

The file will be important because it should give you extra clues about your origins, such as your mother's date of birth and normal occupation. If you are lucky, the file will also contain letters and photographs from your birth relatives (ask whether these can be photocopied for the file so you can take away the originals). Remember that you might not learn anything useful from the file or that, if the circumstances leading to your adoption were very traumatic, the counsellor might decide you would be better off not seeing the file at all.

NEW DEVELOPMENTS

An increasing number of adopted children and parents who gave their children up for adoption are being reunited through **www.GenesReunited.co.uk**.

contacted, will put you in touch. Even if the adopted person does not want to be contacted, you can still do so under some circumstances. The FRC holds the Adopted Children Register, to which access is open, and birth certificates can be bought by any who choose. The register states that the child's adopted name but not the original name. It does, however, state the date of birth, the names and address of the adoptive parents, the date of the adoption order and the name of the court that issued it. Therefore, if you are trying to find out what happened to a child who was adopted, and know their date of birth, you can pay to have every possible entry for the appropriate gender checked for a child with the right birth date. This could cost you a great deal of money but, hopefully, you will only find one, or perhaps a small number of possibilities, to follow up on. A considerable amount of detective work would then be required to determine which, if any, really is the right person – and frankly anybody wanting to do this should think very long and hard about the distress it would very likely cause to the adopted persons and their adoptive families – but that, at any rate, is the method. (See also Where to Search, overleaf.)

MISSING PEOPLE

Attempting to trace a missing person is almost impossible without knowing their name. If this is not known, searches in the General Registration indexes may help or, alternatively, if you are adopted, follow the procedure described overleaf. It also helps to have some idea of how old they were. This section applies equally to seeking birth parents if you are adopted, a distant relation, or an old friend.

CHANGE OF NAME

Except during the Second World War, British subjects have always been able to call themselves anything they want, and change their names as often as their socks, provided there is no intent to commit fraud. However, most people who change their name need proof they have done so and create a deed poll, enrolled in the High Court of Justice and recorded in class J 18 at the NA. Those made before 1903 are in the Close Rolls at the NA. From 1914 it was obligatory to publish deed polls in the *London Gazette*. Many notices were published in newspapers, particularly *The Times* (see page 144). It is also worth consulting W. P. Phillimore and E. A. Fry's *An Index to Changes of Name under Authority of Act of Parliament or Royal Licence and Including Irregular Changes from 1760 to 1901* (GPC, 1968).

(see page 144)

YOUR BIRTH CERTIFICATE

AS A TOOL for starting research your birth certificate on its own might be relatively unhelpful. It will give your original name and date and place or birth, and it should also provide your mother's name, address and occupation. Be aware, though, that in many cases the reason for adoption was illegitimacy, and women giving birth to illegitimate children often purposely went somewhere where they were not known in order to give birth, so the place of birth and mother's address might very well bear no relation to her normal home. Also, do not be too surprised if no details of your father are given on the certificate. Since 1875, mothers were not allowed to register the name of their natural child's father without his consent. Equally, little if any information about the father may appear in your adoption file. There are many cases, after all, such as rapes or one night-stands, when mothers would not even know the forename of the men who made them pregnant. Equally, however, the absence of the father's name from a birth certificate is often because a mother might not have had the name of the father recorded unless she was married to him, or he was present in person to give his consent.

Church baptism records can be an excellent solution – just because the father's name is not on a birth certificate does not mean it will not be on a baptism certificate.

SEEKING A BIRTH RELATIVE

- The first step to take is an easy one and may result in immediate success. Since 1991, the Registrar General has maintained an **Adoption Contact Register** for England and Wales. For a fee of £15, adopted people can register their wish to be put in touch with a birth relative, and birth relatives can register for a fee of £30. If two such people match, the adopted person will be given the name and address (or post box address) of the birth relative.

- A subsidiary register, which has been running for a longer period, is run by the charity **NORCAP**.

- Also contact the other places where birth relatives may already have tried to obtain information about you – the **adoption society** or **local authority** that arranged your adoption and the address given on your original birth certificate (check the electoral roll to see who is now living there before visiting or telephoning).

- Armed with the name of your mother and perhaps of your father too, you are now ready to start searching in earnest (see Missing People, right). If your original birth certificate has been annotated with a Statutory Declaration, this will usually indicate that the husband named on the certificate was not the baby's father, in which case, seek a divorce record.

SCOTLAND

- Adoption records from 1930 are with the **Registrar General of Scotland**.

IRELAND

- The records from 1953 are held at the **General Register Office** and the **Adoption Board**.

For Eire only non-identifying information will be released and original birth certificates are not released. The **Federation of Services for Unmarried Parents and their Children** maintains an unofficial Adoption Contact Register.

NORTHERN IRELAND

- Adoption records from 1931 are on the **Adoption Contact Register** at the General Register Office.

CHANNEL ISLANDS

- The Jersey **Superintendent Registrar** keeps an adoption contact register and will release the original birth certificate after counselling by the Children's Service, who can be contacted via Social Services. For Guernsey, apply for your original birth certificate from **Her Majesty's Greffier** at the General Register Office, which also keeps an Adoption Contact Register.

ISLE OF MAN

- Adoption records are with the **Chief Registrar**.

SEEKING AN ADOPTED PERSON

- Birth relatives can register with the **Adoption Contact Register** and make themselves known to the other organisations listed above.

- The Children's Society will give birth mothers selected information provided it does not enable the children to be traced. They can be contacted at the **Children's Society**'s Post Adoption and Care Project. There is also a society called the **Natural Parents' Network**.

- Other useful organisations are **British Agencies for Adoption & Fostering (BAAF)** and the **Salvation Army**.

MISSING PEOPLE

- The most direct way is to seek missing people in telephone directories and electoral registers (see pages 82 and 164). If you are seeking a woman who might have married, you may be able to guess the year of the wedding by her disappearance from the registers or, if she stayed at the same address, to be sure about the year of her marriage by her change of name.

- If you do not find what you want, then by working back from the present (or forward from the past) you should be able to establish when the person or family you are seeking left. If they only moved a short distance away, a search through the electoral registers may establish a current or more recent address. Note the names of any long-term neighbours; they might be able to tell you what happened to the family you are seeking. If the streets you are searching turn out to be council houses, the local council might allow you access to their re-housing records.

- Try typing the missing persons' name into an Internet search engine. **www.tracesmart.co.uk** is a subscription-based website for tracing lost relatives, containing the electoral register and 'millions of additional records' and births and deaths from 1984 to 2002.

- General Registration records of birth, marriage and death (see pages 44) can be a valuable tool. There are limits, of course, the most important being that if the person you are tracing was born outside the country, and has neither married or died, they will not appear in them. Equally, they only cover set areas, and if someone decided, say, to get married on holiday abroad, they will not appear in the indexes. However, they can usually be used very effectively.

The most obvious searches to undertake for a missing person are to see if they married (see page 49), or whether they have died (see page 52). Sometimes such searches end in failure. The person you want may have changed their name, or emigrated. You may not be able to find the person you want, but there is no reason why you should not try to find someone else who already knows.

If you know when the person was born, or can make a guess, look through the birth indexes (see page 46). You may find the right entry, or at least a couple of possibilities. These will give you the names of the person's parents, and an address where they lived at the time. They may be alive and still living at the same address.

If not, you could seek their death records and contact the informants, or seek the records of the birth of other children born to the same couple and work forward, seeking their whereabouts. Indeed, the very reason why someone is missing in the first place suggests they may have been restless, or otherwise keen to move or change their lives, whereas their siblings could very well have been the stay-at-home type.

Other sources to consider are wills, old newspapers and medical records, which GPs and Family Health Service authorities will occasionally be persuaded to use on behalf of adopted people trying to find birth parents.

For those who have gone abroad, the Passport Office may hold a forwarding address and foreign embassies hold electoral registers of whose who have emigrated, which can occasionally be useful.

QUICK REFERENCE

ADOPTION CONTACT REGISTER
(England and Wales)
Smedley Hydro
Trafalgar Road
Southport
Merseyside PR8 2HH
☎ 0151 471 4830
www.statistics.gov.uk/registration

NORCAP
112 Church Road
Wheatley
Oxford OX33 1LU
☎ 01865 875000
www.norcap.org.uk

REGISTRAR GENERAL OF SCOTLAND
New Register House
Charlotte Square
Edinburgh EH1 3YT
☎ 0131 334 0380
www.gro-scotland.gov.uk

GENERAL REGISTER OFFICE
Joyce House
8–11 Lombard Street East
Dublin 2
Eire
☎ 00 353 1 635 4000
www.groireland.ie

ADOPTION BOARD
Shelbourne House
Shelbourne Road
Ballsbridge
Dublin 4
Eire
☎ 00 353 1 667 1392
www.adoptionboard.ie

FEDERATION OF SERVICES FOR UNMARRIED PARENTS AND THEIR CHILDREN
The Adopted Peoples Association
27 Templeview Green
Clare Hall
Dublin 13
Eire
☎ 00 353 1 868 3020
www.adoptionireland.com

ADOPTION CONTACT REGISTER
(Northern Ireland)
General Register Office
Oxford House
49–55 Chichester Street
Belfast BT1 4HL
Northern Ireland
☎ 028 9025 2000
www.groni.gov.uk

For Channel Islands and Isle of Man addresses, see page 311

CHILDREN'S SOCIETY
Post Adoption and Care Project
91–93 Queen's Road
Peckham
London SE15 2EZ
☎ 020 7732 9089
www.the-childrens-society.org.uk

NATURAL PARENTS' NETWORK
Garden Suburb
Oldham
Lancashire OL8 3AY
☎ 01273 307597
www.n-p-n.fsnet.co.uk

BRITISH AGENCIES FOR ADOPTION & FOSTERING (BAAF)
Skyline House
200 Union Street
London SE1 0LY
☎ 020 7593 2000
www.baaf.org.uk

SALVATION ARMY
Social Work Department
101 Newington Causeway
London SE1 6BN
☎ 0845 634 0101
www.salvationarmy.org.uk

LIFETIMES: REVEALING ALL

IT WAS KNOWN that Peter Critchley left his wife and children in Warrington, Lancashire, and emigrated to America. He was at last located in www.ancestry.com's index of the 1920 census of Manhattan, which shows Peter Crotzly, engineer, 69, married, who immigrated in 1878 and was naturalised in 1890: both he and his parents were born in England. This entry corresponds with an entry in the 1900 census for Manhattan for Peter Critchley, engineer, 50, who immigrated in 1879. Meanwhile, his abandoned wife Eunice remarried, in 1883 – saying she was a widow!

QUICK REFERENCE

See also main sources in Useful Addresses, page 306

PRINCIPAL REGISTRY OF THE FAMILY DIVISION
First Avenue House
42–49 High Holborn
London WC1V 6NP
☎ 020 7947 6980
www.courtservice.gov.uk

LAMBETH PALACE LIBRARY
Lambeth Palace Road
London SE1 7JU
☎ 020 7898 1400
www.lambethpalacelibrary.org

DIVORCE ...

Until 1858, divorce could only be obtained by a private act of Parliament. Records of the 318 successful cases prior to 1858 are at the House of Lords Record Office and NA. The process was way beyond most people, but quarrelling couples could go to church courts to seek annulment on the grounds that one party was a bigamist or (from 1754) had married below 21 years of age without parental consent. They could also grant a decree of separation *a mensa et thoro*, which released a spouse from the obligation to live with a violent or adulterous partner. Usually, a couple wishing to separate simply did so unofficially, and if one of them wished to remarry, they went elsewhere and hoped their bigamous union would not be found out. In 1858 divorces became much more easily obtainable, through the Court for Divorce and Matrimonial Causes, but it was not until 1923 that women were accorded equal rights with men.

Wife selling, whereby a cuckolded husband sold his wife to her lover at the local market, was without legal basis, but because it was done so publicly it had the effect of protecting the first husband from his wife's debts, and the new 'husband' from any further action from the original one. There are only a few hundred recorded cases but newspapers can provide a useful source for many such shenanigans.

In Scotland, church courts could dissolve marriages as in England and Wales, but divorces were much easier to obtain, on grounds of adultery or desertion, through the Commissary Court of Edinburgh from 1536 to 1830 and thereafter from the Court of Sessions.

... AND BIGAMY

It is impossible to tell how widespread bigamy, the illegal marriage of a person while their spouse is still alive, ever was. It is, however, something that may crop up from time to time in your research. When discovered, bigamy was punished in ecclesiastical (see page 231) and, latterly, civil courts (see page 226), and may appear in local newspapers (see page 144).

DIVORCE

⊡ The only divorces available before 1858 were by private Act of Parliament. These (and all Acts of Parliament) are searchable on **www.a2a.org.uk**).

⊡ Records for 1858–1943 are at the **NA** (class J 77), and searchable through **www.catalogue.nationalarchives. gov.uk**, although few for 1937–43 survive. Those after 1943 are held by the **Principal Registry of the Family Division**, who will search them for a fee: see L. Stone's *Road to Divorce – England 1530–1987* (OUP, 1990). Access to the files themselves is closed for the last 75 years except to either party concerned. You can apply for a form or turn up in person and have the search done immediately.

⊡ The Court of Arches, whose records are at **Lambeth Palace Library** (and indexed in J. Houston's *Cases in the Court of Arches 1660–1913* (BRS 85, 1972)), contains 1400 cases of marital squabbling, which may include your ancestor.

⊡ Divorce records for 1858–1903 are indexed at **www.nationalarchivist.com**.

SCOTLAND

⊡ Scottish divorce records from 1560 are with the **National Archives of Scotland**.

IRELAND

⊡ In Ireland, separations were granted through the church courts until 1870, then responsibility passed to the Irish High Court. Divorce proper still had to be sought though Act of Parliament until 1939, when British divorce law was first applied to Northern Ireland. Civil divorce was forbidden in Southern Ireland until 1995: records are only available to the parties themselves.

LIFETIMES: DIVORCED CATHOLICS

PERHAPS THE MOST EXTRAORDINARY CASE of tracing a missing person with which I have been involved was a request that came to me from a private detective, who phoned me at lunchtime on 20 March 1996. A Catholic knight had been legally married to an English Catholic divorcee for many long and happy years, but now she was dying. A friend of his, a very high-ranking Catholic clergyman, reminded him that unless the couple were married in a Catholic church they would not be regarded as husband and wife in the eyes of the Almighty. The only way to do this was if the woman's first husband was dead, making her (in Catholic eyes) a widow. The trouble was, they had no idea what had happened to the first husband: he could have gone anywhere in the world in the last 50 years.

The woman's first marriage record gave the age of her first husband and his father's name . A search for his birth certificate in England and Wales failed to reveal it, so we looked in Scotland and there it was. Now we knew his date of birth and parents' names, we could proceed with confidence to seek his death certificate, in Scotland. We started in the year of the divorce, and worked forwards, on and on, until we came so close to the present we were beginning to think he was probably alive and that the hopes of the elderly Catholic couple would be dashed. But then, when hope had almost faded to nothing, we found a reference and obtained a certificate that included details of the parents' names, which corresponded exactly with what we had already found about the first husband. And then I noticed the date and time of death – lunchtime on 20 March 1996.

CHAPTER NINE
PARISH RECORDS

The first generally useful census was taken in 1841 and General Registration began in 1837. To trace information from before these years, family historians rely on different sorts of records, mostly based around the church and many kept by parishes and manors.

▽ *The Christening* by Francis Wheatley (1747–1801).

In the early Middles Ages, manorial lords would keep a priest in their household, and usually ended up building a separate chapel for them to say Mass. Out of the lord's manorial landholdings grew the parishes, and from the private chapels developed parish churches.

Many parish registers were kept during the Middle Ages, but sadly none survive outside the Vatican Archives, whence many were sent by anxious priests during the Reformation. Very few of these registers are identified by place and access to them is not allowed so, for our purposes, parish registers date from 1538.

Before 1830 there were some 11,000 parishes in England and Wales. Since then, many new parishes have been created out of older, larger ones, with former 'chapels of ease' (built to save parishioners' lengthy journeys to the parish church) becoming parish churches in their own right. The parish was run by a clergyman, or incumbent, either a vicar, rector or parson. When clergymen had more than one parish, they either neglected their duties in one or paid a curate to undertake the work on their behalf. The clergyman or curate's work of baptising, marrying and burying resulted in one of the most important genealogical tools, parish registers (PRs).

Below the clergyman was a council called the vestry and also a staff of parish officials, who performed many of the functions that had been performed before the Reformation by manorial officials. They generated a wealth of records relating to our ancestors, known by their traditional place of storage, the parish chest (see page 166).

PARISH REGISTERS

Parish registers to which access is permitted date from 1538 and consist of baptisms, marriages and burials. We normally turn to PRs once we have gone as far back as we can through General Registration records and census returns, and indeed the latter will indicate in which parish you will need to search. Baptism records provide parents'

△ *Thomas Cromwell, Earl of Essex* by Hans Holbein (1497/8–1543). Cromwell was the creator of the parish register and thus a posthumous hero of family historians.

names, which lead back to searches for marriages. Marriage records do not provide ages or parents' names, so we use the ages usually recorded in burial registers to ascertain when our ancestors would have been baptised. By working back step by step, it is sometimes possible to trace back to the 16th century unaided by any other categories of records. But because PRs are not always very informative, genealogists end up seeking further co-ordinates on their ancestors from sources such as manorial records, wills and so on.

It was Thomas Cromwell, Vicar-General to Henry VIII, who inadvertently laid the foundations of modern English genealogy by issuing orders to all parish clergy to keep registers of baptisms, marriages and burials. Unfortunately, most were kept on paper and have been lost to damp, rats, fire or flood, so only a small proportion of registers date from 1538. In 1558, orders were issued for registers to be kept on parchment, and the survival rate increases rapidly, though in general terms relatively few have survived from before 1600.

While the Anglican church was a religious institution, it was also a branch of the state and if anyone, except Quakers and Jews, wanted

WHERE TO SEARCH

PARISH REGISTERS

🖶 The location of the registers of all parishes that existed up to 1832 is given in *The Phillimore Atlas and Index of Parish Registers* (Phillimore, 2003) together with details of their coverage (or lack of it) by indexes, including the IGI (see page 110). Most are in **county record offices**, but some are still at the **parish churches** to which they relate, so you will need to write to the incumbent and ask for a search, or make an appointment to do so yourself. Much more detailed coverage is given in the county record offices' own catalogues, now available on **www.A2A.org.uk**.

🖶 The alternative is to use bishops' transcripts (see page 114) instead. Most registers are now in county or city record offices, which will also hold many of the records described in the rest of this book. Before visiting a record office, telephone or check its website, as in most cases it is necessary to book, sometimes well in advance.

🖶 It can, however, be easier and cheaper to pay a record searcher to examine a PR instead of visiting the record office yourself.

🖶 Many new parishes were created by dividing up old ones after 1832, five years before General Registration began. The **SoG**'s *National Index of Parish Registers* series provides in-depth details of all PRs, including the post-1832 parishes.

🖶 Many PRs have been indexed in the IGI, available on the Internet at **www.familysearch.org** (see page 110) or studied on microfilm or fiche at a Mormon Family History Centre.

🖶 Many PRs have been transcribed. Brief details of coverage are in the *Phillimore Atlas* (Phillimore, 2003) with more detail in the *National Index of Parish Registers*: collections for each county will be in the relevant **county record offices**. Many transcriptions have the advantage of an index. Remember that these are finding aids, not primary sources and are subject to the same shortcomings as any non-original document – transcriber and indexer-error.

🖶 **http://freereg.rootsweb.com/** is a growing free database of parish register entries 1538–1837.

QUICK REFERENCE
See main sources in Useful Addresses, page 306

BIRTHS AND BAPTISMS

PLEASE REMEMBER that baptisms are not the same as births (nor are burials), deaths and you should record them as such in family trees, i.e.:

'John Smith, bpt. [or chr.] 2 April 1790, Dawlish, Devon'.

If you see a family tree showing people born before 1837, be aware that it could have been compiled by someone with very little knowledge of the subject.

legal proof of their marriages and their children's ages and legitimacy, they had no choice but to have Anglican marriages and baptisms. Equally, until relatively recently, there were very few places to bury a body except for the ancient, consecrated ground of parish churches, so most people, Anglican, atheist, agnostic and non-conformist alike, lie buried in parish church yards. It is often helpful, therefore, to think of PRs not so much as religious records, but as civil ones.

BAPTISMS

These provide the date of baptism, name of the child and the father's full name. In the 16th and early 17th centuries, parents' names were sometimes not recorded, reducing genealogical research to a guessing-game, although hopefully other sources such as manorial records (see page 118) will have survived to provide further co-ordinates. Mothers' Christian names usually appear from the 17th century. Between 1780 and 1812, mothers' maiden names appear fairly often and, as the 18th century progressed, it became more usual to record the child's date of birth as well. Fathers' occupations and places of residence within the parish were often recorded.

In 1812, Rose's Act introduced printed registers with spaces requiring:

➤ **Date of baptism**
➤ **Name of child**

WHERE TO SEARCH

BAPTISMS

See Where to Search: Parish registers, page 97

▽ An original baptism certificate issued by the incumbent of St Mary, Newington. Such documents sometimes turn up in family papers.

Page 74

BAPTISMS in the Parish of St. Mary. Newington, in the County of Surrey, in the Year 1787.

When Baptized.	Child's Christian Name.	Parents' Name.		Abode.	Quality, Trade, or Profession.	By whom the Ceremony was performed.
		Christian	Surname.			
1787 Nov. 26. Born Oct. 25. 1787 No.	William S. of	Richard & Margaret	Goodwin	—		

The above is a true Copy of the Baptism Register of the Parish aforesaid, extracted this *13* Day of *July* in the Year One Thousand Eight Hundred and *Twenty five*

> **Name, residence and occupation of father and Christian name of mother,** all of which are excellent for genealogy, but removed most of the optional extra information, which many clergymen had been recording.

If the child was too ill to be bought to church, it might be privately baptised at home. The register entry may record this as 'P' or 'Priv', and when the child was finally brought to church for a public ceremony, the register entry might be annotated 'rec'd' or 'received into the church'.

MARRIAGES

Marriages before 1754 gave the date of marriage and the Christian and surnames of both parties. Additional information was sometimes given, such as groom's occupation, bride's father's name and whether the marriage was by banns or licence. Marriages usually took place in the bride's parish, but those by licence might take place in the town where the licence was issued.

On 25 March 1754, Hardwicke's Marriage Act came into force and remained so until 1837. Marriages had now to take place (with certain exceptions) in the bride or groom's parish by an Anglican clergyman, either after banns had been read in both parties' home parishes for three Sundays running, or on production of a marriage licence. Jews and Quakers were not obliged to comply, but everyone else had to, regardless of denomination. Boys could still marry at 14 and girls at 12, but parental consent was required for all under 21. Marriages were now to be recorded in a separate register (until then they were usually listed with the baptisms and burials, sometimes neatly separated, other times jumbled up together), with a form requiring:

> **Date**
> **Names of both parties**
> **Whether they had been married before** ('bach[elor]', 'spin[ster]', 'wid[ow/er]').
> **Whether married by banns or licence**
> **Parish of residence** ('otp' means 'of this parish', 'soj[ourner]' meant someone who had only recently settled there).
> **Signatures or marks of both parties**
> **Names and signatures of two witnesses,** who would usually be siblings of the bride and groom.

Generally, the printed forms prevented any extra comments which clergy might have been tempted to make – but some still did: the registers of St Mary, Lewisham, around 1803, for example, contain many marriages of people not from that parish. To satisfy the law they had

SOME CLERGYMEN made their own rules, such as Rev. Thomas Patten, Vicar of Seasalter, Kent, from Cote, Somerset, who served as Vicar of Seasalter and Curate of Whitstable from 1712 until his death on 9 October 1764. When Edward Tried and Mary Aeres married at Seasalter on 12 November 1737(?) we learn that:

'a Bowl of Punch was made almost as big as the Caspian.'

Another of his gems was:

'Little Osiah Oakham and Sarah Slater, both of Seasalter, were married by License, September 27 1744. Sarah was his first wife's sister… and now very pregnant.'

LIFETIMES: LITTLE GEMS

△ An original marriage certificate showing the wedding of my 4 x great-grandparents William Hammond and Emma Ayres, on 10 June 1815, only eight days before the Battle of Waterloo.

been resident there for three weeks – or so they claimed – and were officially 'of this parish'. But next to their signatures or marks the incumbent wrote their real parishes of residence – from as far afield as Sussex and Birmingham. As someone who hates filling in forms, I say hurrah for the incumbent of Lewisham!

Ancestors also appear in marriage registers as witnesses. If they do, there is a good chance they may be related to one of the two parties, indicating wider family connections than you suspected. Such references may also provide useful evidence that an ancestor was alive on that date. Be aware, though, that some people were regular witnesses – if you see them witnessing several marriages on the same day, they probably were not related to either party at all.

From July 1837, civil registration marriage certificates were used both in and outside of parish churches.

Marriage licences, allegations and bonds

Marriage licences, which originated in the 14th century, enabled marriages to take place immediately – especially if the girl was pregnant – but were more usually obtained as status symbols for those who thought it above their dignity to have banns read out in front of the hoi polloi.

Apart from some issued by the Archbishop of Canterbury, which allowed the marriage to take place anywhere, marriage licences would specify one of two places, theoretically the parties' home parishes. But in practice at least one was often the parish in which the couple were staying at the time for a minimum of four weeks (after 1753) or 15 days (after 1823).

Licences may be found in family papers but were more often handed in to the officiating priest. What survive in record offices are more usually the associated bonds (until 1823) and allegations. An allegation was a statement made by the prospective groom swearing that both parties were free to marry, usually stating names, ages, places of residence, marital status, groom's occupation, where the couple intended to get married and name of consenting parent of either party under 21. Be aware that, between September 1822 and March 1823 only, both couples had to produce evidence of baptism or an equivalent certificate proving their age: these will be found with the allegation and are well worth seeking.

A bond was made stating a sum of money to be forfeited should the information on the allegation (especially regarding the parties' freedom to marry) be found to be incorrect. There were two bondsmen, one of

BANNS OF MARRIAGE

THE READING or 'calling' of banns was a means of preventing bigamous or clandestine marriages, dating back to 1215. They were either recorded in the same register or in a separate banns book. These may state the parishes of residence of both parties, so they can lead you from the groom's parish to the one in which he married, or from the parish of marriage back to the groom's original parish.

WHERE TO SEARCH

MARRIAGES

⊟ *See also* Where to Search: Parish registers, page 97.

⊟ Licences were issued by broadly the same ecclesiastical authorities that proved wills (see page 124) and are generally found in **county record offices**. Their whereabouts are outlined in detail in J. Gibson's *Bishops' Transcripts and Marriage Licences, Bonds and Allegations: A Guide to their Location and Indexes* (FFHS, 1997). This also lists the many indexes and calendars available

⊟ If the bride and groom lived in different dioceses within the same archdiocese, licences were issued by the relevant Vicar-General. Those for York are at the **Borthwick Institute** and those for Canterbury are at **Lambeth Palace Library** and indexed (surnames only) 1694–1850 on **www.englishorigins.com**, along with Faculty Office licences 1701–1850.

⊟ York Faculty Office marriage allegations from 1567, the originals of which have been lost, were copied by Paver, published by the Yorkshire Archaeological Society and are included in Boyd's marriage index (see page 114).

⊟ If the two parties lived in different dioceses they were issued by the Archbishop of Canterbury's Faculty Office. These are especially useful because of the wide range of people and places they cover, and are partially covered by published indexes. None for the Isle of Man.

⊟ Most licences have been thrown away, but some collections of original licences survive, notably those collected by Frederick Crisp from some 20,000 London parish churches and held at the **IHGS** and some at the **SoG**.

⊟ **www.englishorigins.net** has an index to marriage licence allegations 1694–1850 containing some 670,000 names.

⊟ Although many Irish marriage licences were blown up in 1922, the **NA** in Kew hold indexes made before that date, which provide names and dates of bonds for most of Ireland except for Derry, and it also holds abstracts of licences collected together after the bombing.

⊟ Marriage licences that concern landed families are often found in family papers, record offices and there are also many in the manuscripts section of the **British Library**, and more still collected and abstracted by Frederick Crisp in *Fragmenta Genealogica, Vol. 11*. They are sometimes referred to and abstracted in family wills ('whereas by a deed of settlement dated ...').

⊟ Many irregular marriages were not recorded at all, and many that were have been lost. For those London ones that have survived, see T. Benton's *Irregular Marriages in London before 1754* (SoG, 1993). Many (for London and elsewhere) will be recorded perfectly normally in PRs but, unlike the angry parents or guardians of the parties concerned, you have access to marriage indexes which in many cases will reveal the unexpected location of the event.

⊟ The location of elopement records is detailed in *Family Tree Magazine*, December 1981, updated in March 1994, since when the **IHGS** acquired four registers from Lang's house at Springfield near Gretna Green.

QUICK REFERENCE
See also main sources in Useful Addresses, page 306

BORTHWICK INSTITUTE FOR ARCHIVES
University of York
Heslington
York YO10 5DD
☎ 01904 321166
www.york.ac.uk/inst/bihr

LAMBETH PALACE LIBRARY
Lambeth Palace Road
London SE1 7JU
☎ 020 7898 1400
www.lambethpalacelibrary.org

them usually the groom, the other often a relative (perhaps the bride's father) or a good friend, and provided similar information to the allegation.

Remember that licences were issued to facilitate marriages but are not evidence that a marriage took place: the couple may have had a last-minute change of heart, or one or both may have dropped dead.

Marriage settlements

These were deeds signed before weddings arranging for the future ownership of property. Parents might settle property or income on one of the two parties marrying (often as a dowry); grooms (or their families) would guarantee property or income for their brides. They provide excellent details not only of who was getting married and when, but also names of relatives on both sides, family friends and the location and nature of lands held.

Irregular and clandestine marriages

Before Hardwicke's Marriage Act (1753), and despite the Anglican church's disapproval, unions between two parties were regarded as legal under Common Law provided both parties consented and exchanged vows, regardless of whether witnesses, priests or anybody else were present. Sadly, these generated no records for genealogists.

Before 1754 there were also clandestine or irregular marriages. Irregular marriages took place by banns or licence, but away from one of the spouses' home parishes, or in private houses, or at times of the year when marriages were not supposed to take place, such as Lent.

Clandestine marriages were those conducted in secret, away from the parties' home parishes. This happened for many reasons, such as an apprentice wishing to marry without waiting until his seven-year term of apprenticeship had expired; an heir or heiress desirous of marrying without their guardian's consent; widows wishing to receive income from their deceased husband's estate yet have a new husband into the bargain; couples in a very great hurry to have sex – and, of course, aspiring bigamists. Both would be conducted by priests on receipt of a backhander, often on production of a corruptly obtained marriage licence.

These practises were brought to a halt by Hardwicke's Marriage Act. However, the Act did not apply to Scotland and the Channel Islands, whither many of the English couples who might have tried the Fleet Prison (see box, opposite) now eloped. Scotland's Gretna Green was the most popular, although this was only one of many such marriage houses. An Act of 1856, declaring such run-away marriages illegal unless the couple had resided in Scotland for at least three weeks, led to a great decline in the popularity of Gretna Green and its neighbours.

△ **Many couples opted for less conventional forms of marriage as depicted in *The Elopement* by George Morland (1763–1804).**

THE FLEET PRISON

IN LONDON, many clandestine marriages took place around the Fleet Prison; St James, Dukes Place; Holy Trinity, Minories; St Pancras; St Botolph, Aldgate; St Katherine by the Tower; St Dunstan, Stepney and May Fair Chapel. In the decades leading up to 1754, increasing numbers of marriages were taking place in and around the Fleet Prison, a debtors' prison which claimed to be exempt from ecclesiastical law, and which numbered many corrupt priests among its inmates and visitors.

The marriages were recorded in numerous registers and notebooks, one of which is at the Bodleian Library, Oxford, with the others at the NA in class RG 7. They have been partly transcribed, indexed and published in M. Herber's *Clandestine Marriages in the Chapel and Rules of the Fleet Prison 1680–1754* (Francis Boutle Publishers). These often-neglected sources should always be borne in mind, for families from London and all over the country. Be aware that some of the entries may be partial forgeries indicating, for example, that a marriage took place before it really did, or even a complete fabrication paid for by fortune-seekers wishing to claim they were married to heiresses they had never even met.

BURIALS

Burial entries can help in seeking wills, but their main use is in providing ages, which in turn indicate a year of birth and thus an indication of when a baptism might have taken place. The records provide the names of the deceased and date of burial. As the 17th century progressed, it became more usual than before to add extra details, such as age, place of residence and occupation. Married women were often described as 'wife of X' and widows were described as such, with or without the deceased husband's name. The father's name was usually provided in cases of deceased children. 'P' denoted a pauper.

From 1666 we have burials in wool. To revive the flagging English wool industry, Charles II ordered that all corpses be wrapped in woollen shrouds, hence the notes 'buried in wool', 'P' – paupers were exempt – or 'aff[idavit]' next to burial entries, the latter denoting an affidavit sworn before a JP that a woollen shroud had indeed been used. Some survive, usually providing a close relative's name. There was a £5 fine for disobedience and it became a status symbol to pay the fine and use a

WHERE TO SEARCH

BURIALS

See Where to Search: Parish registers, page 97

LIFETIMES: QUACKS AND TRAMMELLERS

BESIDES OR INSTEAD OF what they were supposed to record, parish clergy and clerks sometimes made comments of their own. These can be wonderful finds, and remind us too how essential it is to check original register entries of events found through indexes.

Leek, Staffordshire, marriage 10 February 1707/8
 '*Thomas Bowler of Ashbourne, Quack Pharmachopolar to Ellin Thorpe of Leek a widow.*'
This a man who made drugs, the term coming from the book he used, a pharmacopoeia.

Manuden, Essex, 31 December 1847
 '*John Bush farmer of Manuden aged 48 hung himself on Friday Dec 24th.*'
A sad story for Christmas.

Eglingham, Northumberland
 '*John Morpeth, W[est] Lilburn, South Sheds, Baptised 26 August 1803, born 15 August 2nd but 1st in Wedlock of John & Eleanor Morpeth Farmers there under N. Collingwood Esq. Her maiden name was Ormston.*'
The detailed northeastern entries for this period can be highly informative.

 '*John Housdon, widower, a young gape-mouth'd lazy fellow and Hannah Matthews, Hotupont, an old toothless wriggling Hagg, both of Faversham, were trammel'd by licence at the cathedral of Seasalter, June 6th, 1744.*'
NB: It was not a cathedral: the incumbent was delightfully short of his marbles.

These entries from the Walloon or Stranger's church in Canterbury clearly map the migration of Gervais Despagne from Lisle to Canterbury after the birth of Andre and before the birth of Marie:
 '*Août 14 1603 Andre Despagne, filz de fue Geruois, natif de Lisle, et Marie Pancouq, fille de fue Noel, natifue de Ypres*' and '*Jan 10 1607/8 Michel le Clerc, vefu, natif de Ham, et Marie d,Espanne, fille de fue Geruoys, natifue de Canturbery,*'

silk shroud instead. The Act was generally ignored after the 1770s. Rose's Act of 1812 provided forms requiring:

➤ **Date**
➤ **Name**
➤ **Residence**
➤ **Age**

This is all useful information, but again we lose the odd extra notes, which could bring colour to earlier entries.

PR TRANSCRIPTS

Transcripts of PRs, made at any time from the last century to the present day (but more so before the advent of the Internet), can be found in county record offices. They are often a compilation of the original register and the bishops' transcripts, so what the transcript says might not be a verbatim quote from either of the original sources, and of course, like anything else, errors and omissions can creep in. An advantage of the PR transcripts is that they are often indexed, enabling speedy searches.

PARISH RECORDS OUTSIDE ENGLAND AND WALES

SCOTLAND

The vast majority of Scottish PRs are at New Register House, with a few others and copies of many local ones at the regional register offices. Maps showing the location of the approximately 900 Scottish PRs are included in the *Phillimore Atlas and Index* (Phillimore, 2003).

One of the great problems of Scottish research is that registers tend to start more recently than English ones and, even when they survive, they are easily as incomplete as their counterparts south of the border. A few survive from the 16th century but most have only survived from the very late 17th century or early–mid-18th century, and one down-side of having no bishops was that there are no bishops' transcripts (see page 114).

A plus is that the registers are usually slightly more detailed. Women did not automatically change their names on marriage, so their maiden names tend to appear in the registers. Births were often recorded instead of baptisms, but where baptisms appear, you may well find godparents recorded too.

A catalogue of all Scottish registers of all denominations is at Utah. In Scotland, married women kept their maiden names by law. Until the 20th century, most marriages took place at the bride's house or the local manse in a ceremony called *hamfesting*, or *handfasting*, after the proclamation of banns. It is the proclamations, rather than the marriage itself, that you will often find recorded in the registers of *both* parties' parishes. If the marriage did not then take place, the forfeit of the cautionary bond may appear in the Kirk Sessions.

IRELAND

Ireland originally consisted of the four provinces of Connaught, Leinster, Munster and Ulster. These were divided into 32 counties, 325 baronies,

THE PARISH REGISTERS of Rushbrooke, Suffolk, include the burial of one of the most influential, yet little-known, statesmen of the 17th century, the probable secret second husband of Queen Henrietta Maria and maybe even the real father of Charles II. The entry reads:

'*The Right Honorble Henry Jermyn Earle of St Alban was Buried in the South side of the Chancel Janry 10 1683. because he was Buried in Linnen contrary to an Act for Burying in woolen only therefore by Order of A warrant from a Justice of the Peace fifty shillings as Paid to the Informer and fifty shillings to the Poor of the Parish upon the Sunday next following.*'

Our loopy friend Rev. Patten of Seasalter (see page 99) couldn't resist a few comments in his burial register. One is of an old man who: '*Lived 40 years in a little cottage near the sea-side. He was 78 years old. And, when he was happy, always sung.*' And another is about Martha Chamber, '*the most accomplish'd woman that ever liv'd in a Country Hole*'. That was the last time he bothered to record a burial – thereafter he simply noted the death of the odd aristocrat from the newspapers.

PARISH RECORDS OUTSIDE ENGLAND AND WALES

SCOTLAND

🖸 Many baptism and marriage registers have been included in the IGI (see page 110) but a much more complete index is the microfiche *Old Parochial Register Index*, with a three-fiche addenda, covering baptisms and marriages separately for each county enables you to order copies of original entries. **www.scotlandspeople.gov.uk** indexes these and enables you to order copies of original entries.

🖸 Few parishes kept burial registers but many **kirk session records** include 'mort cloth' dues, the renting out of the parish's black pall to cover the coffin, and these records will give you the date and deceased's name: the accounts may also record fees for digging the person's grave.

IRELAND

🖸 Surviving PRs for Eire are mostly at the **Representative Church Body Library**, while those for Northern Ireland are best accessible on microfiche at the **PRONI**. The IGI contains some 2 million entries from surviving registers.

🖸 Most Catholic registers are still with the parish priest but most of those up to 1880 are microfilmed at the **National Library of Ireland**.

🖸 Increasingly, Irish registers are being housed in local and county **heritage centres**, a list of which is on **www.scripts.ireland.com/ancestor/browse/addresses/major.htm**. The centres hold a wealth of local material, and many have also indexed, or are indexing, their local registers. Be aware, though, that they will not always tell you if there is more than one possibility for an ancestor's baptism. If you are unsure you have been given all that is available, ask.

CHANNEL ISLANDS

🖸 Registers are held by the parishes or you can commission a search from closed copies held at the **Judicial Greffe** on Jersey. Those for Guernsey are at the **Priaulx Library** and copies of some are at the **SoG**.

ISLE OF MAN

🖸 PRs, which generally date from the 17th century, are mostly still in their parishes, but microfilm copies of them all are at the **Manx Museum** library. Marriages are apparently fully indexed by the **IGI**, which also contains many Manx baptisms.

🖸 From 1849 onwards, copies of the registers were sent to the island's **Chief Registrar**, where entries are indexed parish by parish (with microfilm copies of these indexes at the **Manx Museum**). Copies of some are at the **SoG**.

🖸 Manx bishops' transcripts (see page 114) for 1734–67 and 1786 onwards are at the **House of Keys and Registry Office** with copies at the **Manx Museum**.

EXAMPLES OF PARISH RECORDS IN OTHER COUNTRIES

AUSTRALIA

🖸 Most Australian PRs are held by the state civil registrars and some are indexed in the **IGI**.

INDIA

🖸 Christian PRs kept by Europeans in India can date back to the 17th century. For Europeans, there are returns of the Indian Catholic and Anglican churches in India; Singapore; St Helena; Aden; Whampoa (Canton); Macao; Malaysia; Burma and Kuwait, fully indexed, at the **India Office Library** in the British Library.

JAMAICA

🖸 PRs were kept by the Church of England. Many have been microfilmed but few yet indexed by the Mormons. Slaves' baptisms and burials may be in church registers but many slave owners prevented their chattels from attending church: in such cases, you might find records in plantation records instead.

KENYA

🖸 Church registers were kept under British rule and have continued to the present.

NEW ZEALAND

🖸 Registers start from about 1820 and most are still with the churches.

about 2450 parishes and some 64,000 townlands. Townlands were originally family plots, ranging from large tracts of land to virtually nothing. An essential tool is the *General Alphabetical Index to the Townlands and Towns, Parishes and Baronies of Ireland* (GPC, 1984).

The Anglican Church of Ireland, which was the established church until 1869, divided Ireland into some 1600 parishes, divided into 31 dioceses. Registers were required to be kept in 1634 although few have survived from before the mid-18th century, and more than half of them were destroyed when the IRA bombed the Four Courts in 1922.

Most southern Irish people were Catholic. Besides Church of Ireland parishes, there were also Catholic ones, sometimes both using the same names, sometimes not. Catholicism was not fully legalised in Ireland until 1829 and, although many Catholic priests operated in the country, few dared keep registers and, of those that were kept, few survive. From the 1830s onwards, the number of Catholic parishes proliferated and many registers started to be kept, usually just of baptisms and marriages, though the former usually noted mother's maiden names and also the names of godparents, which would usually have been close relations, so in this small respect they have the edge on standard Anglican PRs.

OVERCOMING PROBLEMS

➤It is sometimes very hard to distinguish between different people of the same name because PR entries generally contain relatively little information. Clergymen sometimes made an effort (by suffixing 'senior' or 'junior', or recording different places of abode), but not always. Sometimes a listing of children of John Smith may go on decade after decade, until you realise with a sinking heart that there were two or possibly even more John Smiths having children baptised. In such cases, the burial registers can be used to try to eliminate possibilities, but you may need to turn to other sources, such as wills and manorial records, to get a true picture.

➤Finding what appears to be an ancestor's baptism is not in itself proof of a pedigree. With infant mortality at roughly 150 deaths for every 1000 live births (now infant deaths are only 1% of all deaths), it is also important to try to establish that the child you have found did not die young. The absence of such a burial from the PR is not, of course, proof that the child survived (it could have been buried somewhere else), but it adds greatly to the balance of probability that it survived.

➤Some events were recorded in registers termed non-parochial registers,

QUICK REFERENCE

See also main sources in Useful Addresses, page 306

REPRESENTATIVE CHURCH BODY LIBRARY
Braemor Park
Rathgar
Dublin
Eire
☎ 00 353 1 492 3979
www.ireland.anglican.org/library

NATIONAL LIBRARY OF IRELAND
Kildare Street
Dublin 2
Eire
☎ 00 353 1 603 0200
www.nli.ie

For Channel Islands and the Isle of Man, see page 311

INDIA OFFICE LIBRARY
British Library
96 Euston Road
London NW1 2DB
☎ 020 7412 7513
www.bl.uk/collections/orientaland indian.html

because they related to places such as hospitals, workhouses, chapels of institutions such as the Greenwich Hospital and Sheerness Dockyard. These are always worth considering if you simply cannot find what you want. They are not listed in the *Phillimore Atlas and Index* but are in the *National Index of Parish Registers* and you can also find out about them from the catalogues of the relevant county record office.

➤ **Whilst most baptisms took place soon after children were born, this was not always the case.** Parents might wait weeks or months to have the child baptised, or even save up several children and have them all baptised at once (cheaper, after all, for the post-christening party). So two people baptised the same day were not necessarily twins. Some people were not baptised until they were grown up. If you cannot find the baptism you want in the year of birth, search forwards.

➤ **As well as the Commonwealth Gap (see opposite), a later cause for missing entries was the Stamp Duty Act,** which levied tax on baptism, marriage and burial entries between 1783 and 1794. Only paupers were let off (often denoted by a 'P' against entries), so not surprisingly the number of so-called paupers shot up in this period. Marriages tended to happen anyway, and you could not very well avoid having a body buried, but couples certainly could and did put off having their children baptised. If you cannot find your

FINDING A PARISH

IF YOU CANNOT FIND the entry you want in a particular parish (and indexes do not help) there are a number of methods you can adopt.

➤ Use *The Phillimore Atlas and Index* (Phillimore, 2003) to discover the parishes neighbouring the one where you thought your ancestor was born (bearing in mind too that someone might be born in one parish but baptised in another) and search in them instead, working outwards in a radius.

➤ Use indexes to wills, marriage licences and so on to learn the names of nearby parishes where people of the same surname lived, and where your ancestors' baptism might therefore be found.

➤ Do not be blinkered by county boundaries, either. They seem formidable when you look at a county map, but meant little or nothing to our roving forebears. Much more relevant to their movements were rivers, canals and roads, so use old maps to see where these were and where they lead: they may, literally, lead you to the parish in whose registers your ancestors will be found.

ancestor's baptism in these periods, look in the registers immediately after 1794, when there was a spate of late baptisms. However, the Act had aggravated a general trend towards non-conformity, which left many Anglican churches half empty, and their registers sparsely filled until the first six months of 1837. Before General Registration started that July, many children and adults were baptised, presumably due to a misapprehension that the new system meant the permanent end of the old one, so it is always worth searching this period for the late baptism of an ancestor.

➤**Burials were usually well recorded except in times of plague or similar epidemics,** when bodies might be buried without ceremony or record. Bear in mind that many were buried not in the parish church yard, but in workhouse and hospital graveyards, whose records will be in either the county record office or the NA.

THE COMMONWEALTH GAP

IN 1642, THE DISPUTE between Charles I and his Parliament, which had been simmering for several years, erupted in civil war. Among the issues at stake was the nature of the established church. Many Anglican clergymen in Parliamentarian areas were quickly ejected from their parishes and in 1647 Presbyterianism became the official faith of England and Wales. Not surprisingly, most PRs have a gap from some point in the 1640s up to the re-establishment of the Church of England when Charles II was restored in 1660, though it took some years after that for all parishes to be refilled with Anglican clergy. There are instances of Anglican clergy remaining in their parishes and conducting ceremonies furtively, and then writing them up in the PR after 1660. In such fortunate cases, a gap may not be noticeable at all.

In 1653, Cromwell instituted a system of Civil Registration whereby births, marriages (or more usually intentions to marry) and deaths were recorded by clerks called 'parish registers'. Some of these records have survived although in 1660 some returning Anglican clergy destroyed the civil records on the grounds of their being godless. Most clerks used their own notebooks, and most of these were similarly destroyed after 1660. Those that survived are listed in Record Office catalogues and can be very informative.

FILLING THE GAP

In most cases, it is an awkward gap, not least because the Civil War was a time of much migration within the country, and many family trees will end up with an ancestor born around the 1640s or 50s whose baptism date and parentage are unknown, even if there is a clear line of people with the same surname who are highly likely to have been ancestors, going back through the earlier registers for another century before. The answer is to seek other documents, such as manorial records and wills (see pages 118 and 124), to bridge the hiatus. If the family appear in a parish in the 1660s but were not there by the 1640s, examine the county's Protestation Returns and similar records (page 220), to see where people of the surname lived before the disruption of the war.

FAMILYSEARCH

⊟ Log on to **www.familysearch.org** and search within seconds the 58 million English and Welsh PR entries (240 worldwide, including entries from similar records) indexed in the Mormons' IGI (see opposite)

⊟ If you do not have access to the Internet, you can search the IGI on CD-Rom or microfiche in **county record offices**, institutions such as the **SoG**, good local libraries and **Mormon Family History Centres**. At the latter, you can use the reference numbers connected to each entry to order the microfilm of the original record from which the entry was taken, so that you can check the original register yourself. Bear in mind that the CD-Rom version appeared in 1993 and the fiche was updated periodically over several decades, so will not contain nearly as many entries as the Internet version.

QUICK REFERENCE
See main sources in Useful Addresses, page 306

FAMILYSEARCH AND THE IGI

Parish register indexes help genealogists determine which original registers they should search for their ancestors.

The indexing of PRs and their subsequent appearance on the Internet of PRs has done more to change genealogy from an exclusive activity to a massively popular pastime than any other single development. Within living memory, someone wishing to trace their ancestry to before 1837, having struggled through the then dusty bundles of unindexed census forms at the old Public Record Office, had no choice but to write polite letters to parish clergy requesting PR searches. A response from a vicar stating he had no time to undertake a search for a baptism (or, worse, stating the baptism was not there when in fact it was) might take several weeks or months, after which you would write another polite letter, disguising your frustration, to the incumbent of the next-nearest church, and so on. The expensive alternative was to take a week off work and travel from parish to parish yourself, sitting in vestries for days on end, freezing cold and squinting hard because of the poor light, compiling listings from the original parchment register books taken from the iron-bound parish chests.

OVERCOMING PROBLEMS ON THE IGI

The IGI (see box, opposite) is a massive index, but it does not cover all PRs, and covers others only partially. It used to be possible to discover exactly what the IGI covered, but no longer. *The Phillimore Atlas and Index* (Phillimore, 2003) has a column providing details of the broad coverage for each parish as it stood in 1994, and this is still a good general guide. This column also shows you whether a particular county is well covered or not: Kent and Norfolk, for example, are very poorly covered, while County Durham is (dare one say it) almost complete.

➤ *The Phillimore Atlas* **coverage column does not, however, alert you to gaps in coverage:** it may tell you a parish is covered from 1610 to 1850, but what it will not tell you is that there are gaps from 1645 to 1662, five illegible years in the 1760s, and the coverage of marriages stops entirely in 1801. More detail is given in the volumes of the National Index of Parish Registers.

➤ **However, do not waste too much time worrying about what the IGI does and does not cover.** If there is an entry in the index that you believe is relevant, check it in the original registers. If the entry you want is not there, search the original registers of the parishes where you think it is most likely to have been, regardless of whether those parishes are

TO SEARCH www.familysearch.org, simply key in the name you want, with or without places or dates, and the website searches through a number of indexes.

➤ **Ancestral file.** A compilation from unverified family history information submitted to the Mormons since 1978. Entries include contact details for the submitters for more information.

➤ **Vital records index.** An index of over 4 million PR entries not on the IGI and also the majority of births recorded at Dr William's Library (see page 260) and Wesleyan Methodist Registry (see page 267), Irish Quaker births and marriages 1850–75 (see page 265) and Irish civil registration for births 1865–74 and Protestant marriages 1847–64.

➤ **US 1880 census.**

➤ **British and Canadian 1881 census.**

➤ **Pedigree resource file.** Contains names, family relationships, birth, marriage and death information for millions of people, appearing as it was originally submitted and not formatted or merged with information submitted by others.

➤ **US social security death index.**

➤ **Genealogical websites** linked to Familysearch, including links to a vast number of Internet resources, including surname histories, heraldry and nobility records, archives, libraries, software vendors and so on, but not researchers.

➤ **The IGI.** (See below.)

THE INTERNATIONAL GENEALOGICAL INDEX (IGI) is the undisputed Leviathan of genealogical indexes. It mainly covers baptism and marriage registers from the earliest date up to varying dates in the 19th century (there are even some early 20th-century entries). Besides Anglican PRs, there are entries from bishops' transcripts, Commonwealth civil registration records and other reliable sources. The main abbreviations used are:

➤ **C = christening**

➤ **M = marriage**

➤ **S = spouse** (probably denoting an entry taken from one of the Phillimore series of marriage register transcripts)

➤ **A = an adult baptism**

➤ **Infant = infant burial** (indicating the indexer's assumption that the burial of an infant recorded in the registers relates to a particular baptism entry).

Original entries in the IGI are accompanied by batch, source, call and printout call numbers. You can click on these to see the full details and, if you wish, to order a copy of the relevant entry or microfilm to your nearest Family History Centre, which you can seek simply by clicking on the hyperlink on the 'Advice' page.

SOME TYPICAL ENTRIES FROM THE IGI

GENERALLY, AN ENTRY from an original entry will be as follows:

DAVID BEECHAM

Male	Death:
Event(s):	Burial:
Birth:	Parents:
Christening: 27 MAR 1842	Father: THOMAS BEECHAM
Kirton In Holland, Lincoln,	Mother: ANN
England	

Messages: Extracted birth or christening record for locality listed in the record. The source records are usually arranged chronologically by the birth or christening date.

These will probably be derived from original sources but remember that they may be inaccurate and will almost certainly not contain all the information (occupations, previous marital status and so on) in the original register. In contrast to the foregoing are entries from private submitters, which should always set alarm bells ringing, such as:

SILVESTER SALISBURY

Male	Christening:
Event(s):	Death: About 1690
Birth: About 1629, England	Burial:

Messages: Record submitted after 1991 by a member of the LDS Church. No additional information is available. Ancestral File may list the same family and the submitter.

'About' is generally a euphemism for 'I don't know', and the idea that someone thought Sylvester (the spelling of his Christian name varies, as we can see) was probably born around 1629 in England is scarcely going to help you. But that's not the only entry for him in the IGI. Here is another:

SYLVESTER SALISBURY

Male	
Event(s):	Christening:
Birth: 1629 Albany, Albany,	Death: About 1680
New York	Burial:

Messages: Record submitted after 1991 by a member of the LDS Church. No additional information is available. Ancestral File may list the same family and the submitter.

Equally unimpressive and, as we shall see, a complete shot in the dark. Here is yet another entry:

SILVESTER SALISBURY

Male	Death:
Event(s):	Burial:
Birth:	Parents:
Christening: 07 SEP 1631	Father: ROBERT SALISBURY
Swepstone, Leicester,	Family
England	Mother: MARY

Messages: Record submitted after 1991 by a member of the LDS Church. No additional information is available. Ancestral File may list the same family and the submitter.

That looks much more reliable, doesn't it? But beware, it is still a private submission and it turns out that it is actually an entry for what the submitter thought the original register ought to say. In fact, Sylvester is clearly stated in the original register to be 'the supposed and reputed sonn of Robert Burgeland and Mary Salisbury'.

So, the IGI helped by directing us to Swepstone, but it would have been a disaster if the entry had been accepted without checking the original.

However, do not dismiss the false entries entirely. Through the website you may be able to order copies of the original submission or contact the submitter: in some cases the information may turn out to be highly accurate and derived from a rare source, such as original family papers. Even if the information turns out to be wrong, though, you may still end up contacting a long-lost (if a little misguided) cousin as a result!

➢ **The IGI** has various criteria for searching. You can seek all references to a surname in a certain country (Great Britain and the whole of Ireland can be searched in one go) but, if the surname is a very popular one, you can 'filter' your search on the CD version to cover only one county, although bear in mind that if an event took place just over a county border, you will miss it.

theoretically covered by the IGI or not. If you base any decisions or any aspects of your family tree solely on the presence or absence of entries in the IGI, you are almost certainly to come a cropper.

➤ **The IGI is helpful in grouping variant spellings of surnames together,** but be aware that the groupings are ultimately random and the variant under which your ancestor was recorded might not have been picked up by the indexers, so will appear on its own under its own individual spelling. Be creative when entering possible variants: scribble the name down and then think of ways it could be misread, or mumble it to someone and ask them to say what they thought you said. The surname Coldbreath, for example, exists in Sussex, and puzzled me for ages, so I started going around mumbling it to people in various different accents and then asking them what they thought I had said. Finally, someone said 'Galbraith?'. I looked up the Scottish surname Galbraith and, to my delight, found that Coldbreath was indeed listed as a recognised variant.

➤ **As with all indexes, the entries are only as good as the people who copied them,** and there are many omissions and mistranscriptions (such as John Thomas baptised at Hexham being indexed as John Thomas Hexham, and so on). To make matters worse, in a somewhat misguided move in 1992, the Mormons allowed private researchers to submit their own information, some based on accurate sources, such as family bibles, and some derived from pure fantasy (see box, opposite).

➤ **Until recently, Wales was like many Scandinavian, Eastern European and non-European countries for its continued use of patronymics that changed with each generation** (see page 285). The IGI on CD enables you to search a region and time frame for the birth of anyone with a particular forename. Say your Welsh ancestor was Evan Jones, born about 1850. His father might have been called Jones as well, or Evan could literally have been 'son of John', so his father would have had a different patronymic surname, according to his father's name, such as John Thomas, resulting in Evan's baptism being entered as 'Evan son of John Thomas'. Without knowing in advance who John's father was, you would not know that you had to look under Thomas, not Jones. With the IGI's help, though, you can see a list of possible baptisms for boys called Evan, which you can then explore in the original records.

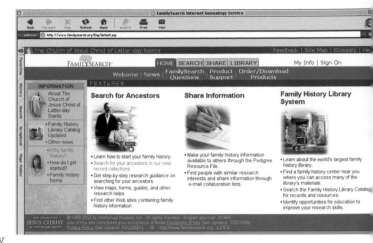

△ The familysearch website home page: www.familysearch.org.

YOU CAN FIND all the IGI entries for a surname from a particular parish using the website **http://tinyurl.com/8dkr.** Click on the county; find the parish you want; select the batch you want, and click on it. Then enter the surname you want in the top right-hand box and press 'submit query'. All the entries will appear. Fantastic!

A NEW TRICK

'Remember that the absence of an entry from an index does not necessarily mean that it is not in the original record, and that entries you do find should always be checked in the original register.'

1			ABB
1776	ABBOTT	Tho & Han Birch	Lamarsh
1782		Tho & An Eve	Dunmow Gt
1788		Jos & Mary An Crush	Roxwell
1788		Jn & Mary Right	Chelmsford
1788		Jn & Kitty Tomson	Walthamstow
1789		Jn & Marth Flint	Chelmsford
1789		Ric & Mary Pool	Dunmow Gt
1790		Jn & Sar Cadman	Bradwell on Sea
1791		Wm & Mary Pitch	Wrkittle
1791		Tho & Bridg Metcalf	Braintree
1796		Jas & Els Frier	Walthamstow
1797		Jn & Judith Burgess	Chelmsford BANNS
1797		Abr & Mary Sanders	Dedham
1778	ABEL	Pet & Elz Broadhurst	Westham
1795	ABBLWHITE	Tho & Jemime Southernwood	Boxted
1791	ABERDEEN	Adam & An Burton	Woodford
1778	ABERY	Sam & An Heard	Springfield
1779		Sam & Elz Allen	Springfield
1776	ASLEY	Jn & Lidia Scarff	Frittlewell
1777	ABRAHAM	Geo & An Saggers	Stanstead Montf
1778		Jn & Marth Ilett	Clavering
1780		Jn & An Martin	do
1780		Jos & Sara Doniah	Bocking
1780		Jn & An Perry	Loughton
1782		Jn & Sar Finch	Sible Hedingham
1784		Hen & Sus Perrin	Elmdon
1786		Isaac & Amy Watson	Chrishall
1788		Wm & Elz Markwell	Loughton
1791		Jas & Rachel Hawkins	Halstead
1793		Jn & An Perry	Loughton
1798		Tho & Mary Dieny	Sible Hedingham
1799		Isaac & Amy Button	Chrishall
1799		Tho & An Galloway	Westham
1779	ABRAHAMS	Jas & Han Lay	Pebmarsh
1784		Jn & An Searl	Littlebury
1785		Jn & Sara King	Dunmow Lit
1794		Jas & Amy Kinsey	Clavering
1798		Sam & An Carter	Pebmarsh
1798		Tho & Han Bush	do
1788	ACKER	Jn & Mary Chapman	Radwinter
1776	ACKERS	Matt & Elz Saunders	Bradfield
1778		Jas & Sara Archer	Dunmow Gt
1785		Ben & Mary Shonk	do
1793		Abr & Elz Scotcher	do
1795		Tho & Mary Swallow	Chelmsford
1796		Cavey & Elz Hoy	Dunmow Gt
1775	ADAMS	Jn & Sus Beavers	Bocking
1776		Rob & Lidia Davey	Chelmsford BANNS
1776		Jn & Elz Bates	do
1776		Rob & Lidia Davy	Sible Hedingham
1776		Jn & An Speed	Haydon
1778		Tho & Ruth Osborn	Bocking
1778		Philip & Elz Crash	Burnham
1780		Jn & Sara Willis	Chishall Gt

△ **A page from Boyd's Marriage Index.**

OTHER INDEXES AND BISHOPS' TRANSCRIPTS (BTs)

Here some other indexes to help you search for original entries in PRs.

BOYD'S MARRIAGE INDEX

This index was compiled by Percival Boyd and his clerks in the 19th century. It gives brief details of spouses' names, parish and year, indexed by bride and groom, usually divided into 25-year batches arranged by English county, with two series of miscellaneous indexes with entries from all over the country.

Boyd's sources were mainly PRs but bishops' transcripts, marriage licences and banns registers were also used. Not all counties are covered by any means, and some parishes are only partially covered, but with coverage of about 15% of all English marriages from 1837 back to 1538, it is always worth a search if the entry you want is not in the IGI. Some indexing was phonetic, so surnames starting Kn … are indexed under N, and so on.

COUNTY INDEXES

Many counties have marriage indexes – see Where to Search, opposite.

PALLOT MARRIAGE AND BAPTISM INDEX

Held at the IHGS, the index covers the period 1780–1837. It focuses on London marriages, including some such as at Christchurch, Southwark, that were later destroyed in the Blitz, and many from Kent, Surrey, Essex and Middlesex. There are also entries from further afield, mainly from the published Phillimore marriage series. Sadly, all but 100,000 entries in the baptism index were also destroyed in wartime bombing.

BISHOPS' TRANSCRIPTS (BTs)

Bishops transcripts are contemporaneous copies of PRs, which help genealogists bridge gaps in the original registers and which may sometimes provide extra information. In 1598, in a law entirely beneficial to later generations of genealogists, most parishes were told to send in copies of each year's registers to their local bishop. In some areas these are called register bills or in counties such as Suffolk, where the annual returns were sent to the local archdeacon, archdeacons' transcripts.

If you encounter a gap or illegible patch in the PR you are using, you may be able to turn to the BTs instead. Generally, they contain only bare details minus the extra notes and comments clergymen sometimes inserted into original registers. However, sometimes the clergyman or parish clerk might add a comment to the transcript, or even insert an entry he had forgotten to put in the original register. Therefore, it will sometimes repay you to examine the transcripts as well as the PRs, even if the latter seem complete. Sometimes looking at both a PR and BT will give you two different pieces of information, in which case you will have to use your judgement or look further to establish which is correct. In some cases, the transcripts from each parish in a deanery were bound into annual volumes. These make for easy searching for a given year across a spread of adjoining parishes.

WHERE TO SEARCH

OTHER INDEXES AND BTs

BOYD'S MARRIAGE INDEX
The index can be searched on microfiche at some **county record offices**, **libraries**, **Mormon Family History Centres** and so on. The index can be searched online at **www.englishorigins.net**.

COUNTY INDEXES
The *Phillimore Atlas and Index* (Phillimore, 2003) indicates coverage, but the most useful and detailed guide is J. Gibson and E. Hampson's *Marriage and Census Indexes for Family Historians* (FFHS, 2000), which also tells you how you can search them: most are held by societies or individuals who charge a small fee for a postal search.

There are also some baptism indexes, but these rarely compete with the IGI's coverage.

There are also some county burial indexes, especially Boyd's London Burials with some 250,000 burials of adult males from London churches and cemeteries from 1538 to 1853, held at the **SoG** with a copy on film. The National Burial Index, available at many **libraries** and from the **FFHS** on CD-Rom, has growing coverage, currently mainly focused on the northeast, Midlands, East Anglia and home counties, although London, Kent and Hampshire are poorly covered and Sussex not at all.

PALLOT MARRIAGE AND BAPTISM INDEX
Coverage is given in the *Phillimore Atlas and Index* (Phillimore, 2003). The index can be searched at **www.ancestry.com** or bought on CD-Rom from Ancestry.com for £60 for marriages and £30 for baptisms.

BISHOPS' TRANSCRIPTS
BTs are usually held at **county record offices**. This is not necessarily the record office for the county concerned, but the one holding the records for the relevant diocese or archdiocese.

The *Phillimore Atlas and Index of Parish Registers* (Phillimore, 2003) will tell you which diocese covered the parish you are interested in, and a complete guide to what is where is given in J. Gibson's *Bishops' Transcripts and Marriage Licence Bonds and Allegations; A Guide to their Location and Indexes* (FFHS, 1997). These records are not complete: none were made during the Commonwealth Gap (see page 109), while those for Dorset and Durham do not start until 1731 and 1760 respectively, and those for Middlesex, the City and Essex generally only survive for the 19th century.

Few Welsh transcripts survive from before 1700.

There are no BTs in Scotland as there are no bishops!

Most Irish bishops' transcripts were destroyed in 1922. Those that survive are noted in J.G. Ryan's *Irish Records – Sources for Family and Local History* (Ancestry, 1997).

QUICK REFERENCE
See main sources in Useful Addresses, page 306

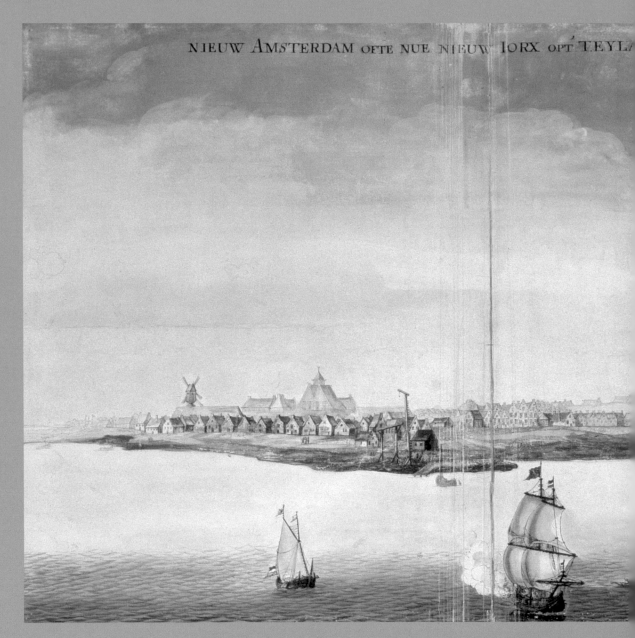

NIEUW AMSTERDAM OFTE NUE NIEUW IORX OP' TEYLA

CAPTAIN SYLVESTER SALISBURY was a 17th-century soldier who went to America in 1664 to help capture New Amsterdam from the Dutch and turn it into New York. Sylvester settled nearby at Albany, leaving a son, Francis, who subsequently produced many descendants, still living there today.

But who was he? American descendants enthusiastically tried to turn him into a younger son of Cadwalladr Salisbury of Llyweni, the scion of an extraordinary and very well-documented family claiming descent from Adam de Salzberg, grandson of Eberhard, the deposed duke of Eastern Bavaria, who came to England with William the Conqueror. However, no amount of searching among the wills and muniments of the Salisburys of Llyweni

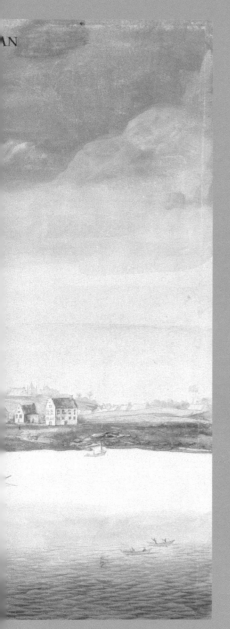

△ New Amsterdam, now New York, destination of the intrepid Sylvester.

produced even the slightest mention of him – and no wonder. His baptism, albeit inaccurately entered, finally turned up in a routine search of the IGI (see page 111) and the original register entry told us that he was baptised on 7 September 1631 at Swepstone, Leicestershire, 'the supposed and reputed sonn of Robert Burgeland and Mary Salisbury'. Mary was herself baptised there on 9 March 1602. Mary later married John Robinson on 16 July 1634.

SYLVESTER'S SIRES

Mary may have been promiscuous, but she was not from an un-privileged background. Her parents were William Salisbury of Newton and Cornelia, daughter and heiress of John Benrye of Bocheston. In fact, the family were gentry and appear on a pedigree in Jonathan Nichols' *History and Antiquities of Leicestershire*, which then was taken from the Heralds' visitation pedigrees of 1619 and 1682 (see page 302). It turns out that Mary was the fourth of five daughters (perhaps significantly her marriage to John Robinson is not shown) and had seven brothers too, including a brother Richard who married another member of the Burgoland family.

The pedigree traces back to Mary's great-great-grandfather Richard Salisbury of Newton Burgoland. It does not go any further back, but it is significant that no less a herald and antiquary than William Camden allowed the family to continue using its coat of arms, which were exactly the same as those of the Salisburys of Llyweni. In other words, they believed the Salisburys of Newton were a younger branch of the Welsh Salisburys, meaning Sylvester was descended from Duke Eberhard after all.

IF THE FACE FITS

Why had the American researchers plumped for Cadwalladr? The simple truth is that undertaking research in America before the advent of the Internet meant many researchers were confined to libraries of printed sources. If they found a printed pedigree – in this case that of the Welsh Salisburys – they might tend to forget or not even realise that there could be other families of the same name. Add an illustrious noble descent and the temptation was often too great: 'Sylvester must have been a younger son of, hmm let's see, which generation would fit best …?'

CHAPTER TEN
MANORIAL RECORDS

Manorial records can be a marvellous complement to or substitute for parish records. They record our ancestors inheriting land, from large farms to tiny rented cottages and vegetable patches, generation by generation, often providing more detail and going much further back than parish records. Their slight drawback is that they can be harder to use, but they will often repay your trouble handsomely.

Manorial documents record the proceedings of courts attended by the local community, at which people had to make statements and give evidence in front of the people they had lived and worked with all their lives. Accidental mistakes could be contradicted by those listening, and hoodwinking others was virtually impossible. Manorial records are more likely to be accurate than practically any other records you will encounter in your research.

Manors arose in the Middle Ages as units of land held by lords from the Crown, and by tenants from the lord. Besides thus controlling most

▽ *Richmond Castle*, Yorkshire by Alexander Keirincx (1600–c.52). Until 1922, all of England's green and pleasant land was subdivided into manors.

English land tenure, the medieval manor also exercised many of the administrative functions later carried out by the post-Reformation parishes. Yet the manorial system remained the basis under which most of our ancestors lived until its abolition in 1922 (the final pieces of copyhold land being turned into freehold in 1926) and the records they generated from 1066 onwards forms one of the cornerstones of English genealogy.

As manors evolved, some were subdivided into what ended up as tiny lordships, while others consumed neighbouring ones and grew vast – the largest was the manor of Wakefield, covering over 150 square miles. Nobody knows how many manors there were – estimates vary between 25,000 and 65,000. Each was administered by the lord's steward, who managed the manor, with a bailiff to collect rents, a reeve to collect fines, a hayward to maintain the infrastructure of fences, barns and so forth, and a constable to keep law and order and see off vermin.

Excellent accounts are given in J. West's *Village Records* (Phillimore, 1997). For genealogical purposes, however, the records and their uses are fairly straightforward.

There were many sorts of manorial court but the three main types were:

➤**Court Leets.** These evolved from the Saxon View of Frankpledge, which reviewed the grouping of men into bands of ten or twelve, each man held communally responsible for the others' behaviour. It became a court to maintain order within the manor, a function that was largely superseded by the parish constable and Justics of the Peace by the 17th century.

➤**Court Customaries.** These were technically for customary rather than freehold tenants but in practice it was usually absorbed within the Court Baron.

➤**Court Baron (or Halmote).** These dealt with the management of the manor and, very importantly for genealogists, the transfer and inheritance of land. If your ancestors held copyhold land – and very many did – the Court Baron records should tell you from whom he inherited it, and from whom that person inherited it, and so on – the very backbone of the family tree.

Manorial tenants had obligations to fulfil, either by labour or surrender of produce or money, but possession of their ancestral tenancies was guaranteed by inviolable rights. These obligations and rights were recorded in Court Rolls. When someone became a tenant, whether by inheritance or purchase, they would be given a copy of these obligations and rights, and were thus known as copyholders.

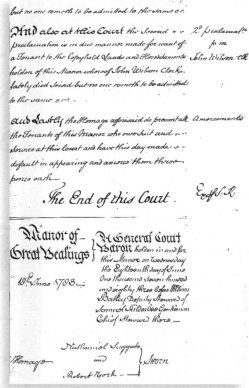

△ **Manorial records from Great Bealings, Suffolk.**

When a tenant died, the heir would appear at the next Court Baron and state their right to inherit the tenancy. They would then have their right acknowledged, thus being 'admitted' to the tenancy, and paying a forfeit to do so. The forfeit was traditionally a 'heriot', the tenant's best beast, but after the Restoration (1660) a money payment was made instead.

COPYHOLD TENANCIES

Copyhold tenancies were hereditary and could not technically be sold. Of course, in reality they were, all the time, both to neighbours and incomers. This involved a little pantomime, by which the vendor would attend the Court Baron and surrender their holdings to the lord, who would then admit the purchaser, while cash changed hands behind the scenes.

Copyhold land fell into two categories, heritable copyhold and copyhold for lives. Heritable copyhold passed to the holder's heir, according to the custom of the manor. The heir was usually the eldest son, but manors in some areas practised 'gavelkind' (dividing the land between all sons, with the hearth – the family home – going to the youngest) or 'borough English' (which allowed the youngest son to inherit). Copyholders sometimes managed to overcome these strict rules by attending the manorial court to surrender the holding 'to the use of his will', and then bequeathing the land to whomever they wanted. Copyhold 'for lives' allowed the holding to remain in the family during the lives of a set number of people, usually three – holder, wife and son – and when all three had died the land reverted to the lord, though the custom of 'free bench' allowed the widow of the last 'life' to keep her deceased husband's holding for life. Copyhold for lives often altered over time to become straightforward leasehold land.

OTHER RECORDS

Manors generated other sorts of records too, such as:
➢ **Surveys** (also called extents) of the lord's holdings, which can include the tenants' names and obligations of rents.
➢ **Custumals** setting out the manor's customs and sometimes naming tenants.
➢ **Relief rolls** recording freeholders paying what was usually the equivalent of a year's rent to inherit freehold land within the manor.
➢ **Rent rolls,** which came in as paying of rent started to replace performance of services.

When you examine these records, you may notice that, for his own ease of searching, the steward had written the names of those concerned in the margin.

▷ *Landscape with Harvesters Returning Home* by Henry Peacham (c.1576–1643).

MANORIAL ROLLS (or, later, books) can survive from the 13th century. Before 1732 (except for the Commonwealth period, 1653–60) they were often compiled in Latin. Most of the records are formulaic and therefore relatively easy to decipher. Good guides are P. Palgrave-Moore's *How to Locate and use Manorial Records* (Elvery Dowers, 1985), which contains examples of these formulae and D. Stuart's *Manorial Records: An Introduction to their Transcription and Translation* (Phillimore, 1992), which explains many of the terms you may encounter. On a basic level, you only need to know that John was son of Tom, and if you discover a record that definitely relates to your ancestor and appears to contain some interesting text, you can always pay a translator, and many translators charge very reasonable rates.

A TYPICAL COURT BARON WILL PROVIDE NAMES OF POTENTIAL ANCESTORS IN SEVERAL CATEGORIES:

➤**Names of the lord and steward.** Lords of manors are usually well documented in heraldic records and wills and it is unusual to need to track them down through manorial records, unless you are studying their lives in depth. Stewards tended to be quite well-off but you may not even realise an ancestor was one until you encounter him holding a series of Court Barons for his master. Their jobs were often unofficially hereditary.

➤**Amercements and misericorda.** These are fines for tenants without a good excuse for non-attendance – useful evidence that an ancestor was alive at a particular date. These were sometimes recorded in separate estreat rolls.

➤**Essoins.** Fines for those with a good excuse for being absent.

➤**Swearing in of jurors.** Jurors were normal tenants and their job was to arbitrate disputes and make sure that everyone who appeared was telling the truth.

➤**Proceedings before the jury.** Here we have the business of the court, in which your ancestor might appear for breaking the rules of the manor, not paying his rent, disputing a boundary with a neighbour or a host of other interesting things, which will add colour to your family tree. Most importantly, you should find the inheritance or transfer of copyhold or, if you are really lucky, a jolly good row over which of several members of the family were to inherit a holding. Argumentative families are usually much better documented than compliant ones. Those inheriting or otherwise acquiring a landholding paid a fine called a heriot, payment of which was sometimes recorded separately in estreat rolls.

MANORIAL RECORDS

Many manorial records have been deposited in their relevant **county record offices**. However, many manors were owned by people and institutions from other counties – the Oxford and Cambridge colleges, for example, owned manors all over England – and are now deposited in the archive or record office most local to the owner's residence.

A large number of manorial records are in the hands of private owners in Britain and abroad. A vast number of documents was thrown out and burned after the abolition of the manorial system in 1922, and yet more have been sold to document collectors, especially in America, and cut up, framed, misused or lost.

Finding the surviving records' is usually a matter of consulting the Manorial Documents Register of the **Historic Manuscripts Commission (HMC)**, now part of the **NA**. This will tell you which manors covered a particular parish, and what surviving records have been reported to the HMC. It is slowly being computerised – see **www.nationalarchives.gov.uk/mdr**.

△ *Month of October: Sowing*, from 'Breviarium Grimani' (Italian School, 16th century).

If no records are listed for the manor you want, try to trace the present lord or lady of the manor and see if they have records which they have not reported to the **HMC**.

Lists of manorial lords in 1925 are in the **NA** in class HMC 5. The volumes of the *Victoria County History* series often indicate the most recent known lord, as will directories (see page 127) published up to the mid-20th century. You can then trace forwards to try to locate the present lord and write a very polite letter asking if he has any records which might help you.

Although the manorial system was abolished in the 1920s, the lordships were not. They are now a saleable commodity, sometimes conveying some practical rights (over fishing, gravel extraction and so on), but more usually valued simply for their perceived social caché. Being the lord of a manor, though, is just that: buying a manorial lordship does not make one 'Lord Bloggs'. For more information about manorial titles, contact the **Manorial Society of Great Britain**.

QUICK REFERENCE
See also main sources in Useful Addresses, page 306

MANORIAL SOCIETY OF GREAT BRITAIN
104 Kennington Road
London SE11 6RE
☎ 020 7735 6633
www.msgb.co.uk

WHERE TO SEARCH

HAVING TRACED THE ELLIOTT FAMILY back from London to the Sussex village of Tillington, I decided to examine the records of the local manor, Petworth. Here I found the earliest known Thomas, who is the second Thomas mentioned in the record:

Capital Court, 3 September 1822

DEATH OF THOMAS ELLIOTT A FREEHOLDER

Also the homage present that Thomas Elliott late of Tillington, Sussex, yeoman ... who held a freehold tenement Barn Stable Orchard and Croft and several new built tenements thereon near the Church in Tillington and formerly called the Roebuck (late copyhold and enfranchised to the Lord to the said Thomas Elliott deceased) ... died ... (no heriot, as no living beast) now at this Court comes Thomas Elliott only son and heir ... and acknowledges to hold ... by the said yearly rent of two shillings and six pence heriot Relief ffealty suit of court and other services And thereupon pays to the Lord for a Relief two shillings and six pence and doth to the Lord his ffealty.

So now I knew that Thomas's father was another Thomas. There were several other Elliott references in the records, including this one:

Capital Court, 8 September 1789

DEATH OF SARAH DAY

Also the homage presents that Sarah Day widow who held of the Lord all that Copyhold or Customary Messuage or tenement Barn Garden Orchard Land and Premises with their appurtenances frmerly called the Roebuck lying in Tillington the yearly rent of two shillings and sixpence since the last court [26 August 1788] died thereof seized (no heriot as no living beast) NOW ... comes Hannah wife of Thomas Elliott of Tillington shopkeeper ... and produces the will of Sarah Day bearing date 29 December 1788- wherein she devises said premises to her niece Hannah Elliott wife of Thomas Elliott and her Heirs for ever. She is admitted. Fine £10-00-00.

Thus, it was possible to add a new maternal aunt to the family tree, who might never have been discovered otherwise. Later, the will of Sarah, proved in 1787, was discovered, and this confirmed the manorial record:

whereas I have surrendered all my customary tenement, garden, barn, stables and orchard with croft of land of the same formerly called the Roebuck in Tillington held of the manor of Petworth to the use of my will now I devise the sd copyhold or customary premises and all the rest of my real estate to my niece Hannah Elliott the wife of Thomas Elliott and her heirs forever.

In other words, Sarah had taken the steps necessary to bequeath her copyhold land to whoever she wanted, in this case, her niece.

CHAPTER ELEVEN
WILLS

Wills are written by people to express how they wish their property and money to be inherited when they die. Because people usually leave legacies to close family, they are immensely useful to genealogists wishing to learn about, and prove, family relationships.

▽ *A Dying Man Dictating his Will* (14th century). Many deaths, even from the Middle Ages, were followed by the proving of wills.

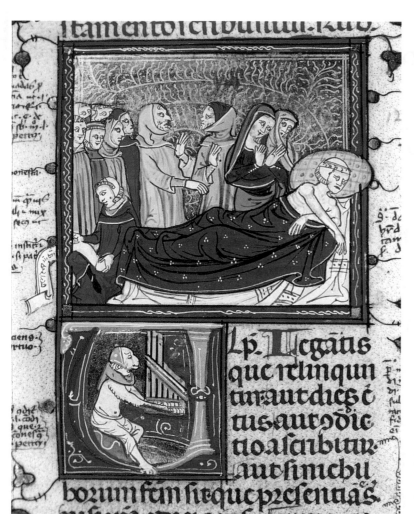

WHAT WILLS ARE

While wills can sometimes enable us to trace family trees in their own right, they are most often used to clarify and prove pedigrees constructed from General Registration records, censuses and parish registers. They can also add colour to family trees, detailing unusual belongings, eccentric desires and suggesting how members of the family felt about each other.

HOW WILLS DEVELOPED

In the Middle Ages, there were very strict rules governing the inheritance of land and property ('real estate'), which usually went to the eldest son, although in parts of England real estate was divided between all children, with the youngest receiving the hearth ('gavelkind', found particularly in Kent), or went to the youngest son ('borough English'). The wife would customarily receive a third for life (or half under gavelkind). Personal estate could be bequeathed, but a third had to go to the widow and at least a third to the children. To get around the rules, people passed land to trustees who held the land under the terms specified in a deed or a will, and in practice allowed it to be used by the person to whom the original holder would have bequeathed it had he been free to do so.

The Statute of Wills of 1540, followed by the Wills Act of 1837, laid down the rules under which most wills you will encounter were made. From 1540, men aged 14 or more and women aged 12 or more could write wills, until 1837 when the age for both sexes was raised to 21. Those who were excommunicated, mad, or prisoners could not write wills and, while spinsters and widows often wrote wills, married women seldom did until 1882, because until the Married Women's Property Act of 1882 they could not legally own anything.

WRITING A WILL

In a will, the writer ('testator', or 'testatrix' if female) nominated executors to distribute their property after their death. The executors would take the will to a court to 'prove' it, by swearing that it was authentic and represented the deceased's last wishes and undertaking to fulfil the instructions expressed.

Wills were usually written by lawyers following their clients' instructions but sometimes they were dictated by testators, usually on their death beds. These were called nuncupative wills and, when they were proved, they were often accompanied by statements from a couple of people who had been present. After 1837, nuncupative wills were only valid if made by members of the armed forces prior to being killed in action.

Original wills are held in public archives, unless they were never proved – if there was no likelihood of a dispute, families often decided to avoid the cost of going to probate – in which case they may be in family or solicitors' papers. Some were taken to church courts but the process of probate was never seen through. Family papers may often, however, contain probate copies, kept by the executors to enable them to do their jobs properly.

FINDING A WILL

The wealthier a family was, the more likelihood there is of them having left wills. However, some very rich people never left wills and, although many poor people did not either, plenty did. If you are tracing a family of labourers, it is unlikely you will find wills for them, but you should never assume this, because some did and you could miss out on a very great deal of interesting and useful information if you never look. Equally, you may have traced a family tree perfectly well using other

---

LIFETIMES: DRUNK INTO DEBT

A SAD STORY involving creditors emerges from the administration documents of William Hercomb of Chisbury, Little Bedwin, Wiltshire, in 1838, and is recorded in the records of the Dean of Sarum in Wiltshire Record Office. His brother and next of kin, Reuben, renounced the right to administer William's estate in favour of Henry Neale, a brewer of Great Bedwin. William's death certificate shows his cause of death as 'suffocation occasioned by drinking'. The awful truth seems to be that he drank himself to death, and left nothing but the debts he owed the brewer.

▽ **A late 17th-century will, complete with signatures and marks.**

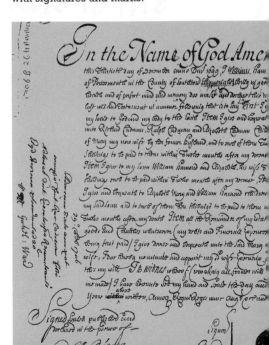

ARCHDIOSESAN DIVISIONS

THE ARCHDIOCESES were divided into individual dioceses presided over by bishops, and if the deceased had property within only one diocese, then it was usually easier and cheaper (especially in terms of saving on travel expenses) to have a will proved or administration granted through the Bishop's Consistory Court.

Dioceses were divided into archdeaconries and, if the deceased's property all lay within one archdeaconry, their will could be proved in the archdeacon's court unless a bishop's visitation was in progress, in which the will would be proved within the Bishop's Commissary Court.

Archdeaconries were composed of deaneries, which were made up of parishes, and there were some deaneries and parishes, not to say some manors and institutions like Cambridge University, which could prove wills in their own right.

records and decide you do not need to look for wills. Again, you might just as well not have bothered starting the exercise at all, as wills often provide far more colour and interest than most of the other documents genealogists use.

Up to 1898, the value of the estate would be recorded in the probate details. This was the value of the personal estate (not freehold land, unless it had been rented out for a fixed term of years) before deduction of funeral expenses and debts. After 1898 real estate was included unless it was held in trust. Up to 1881 the value was usually quoted as 'under' a round sum, such as 'under £700', after which the exact sum was stated.

LETTERS OF ADMINISTRATION

If someone dies without leaving a will, they are said to be intestate. Close relatives, often the deceased's husband or wife, or sometimes creditors or close friends, could, and indeed still can, apply for authority to allow them to settle the estate. The resulting letters of administration provide details of who died and when, and where they lived, and the person or people (with places of residence and usually their relationship to the deceased) to whom power of administration was granted, and the date of the grant. They are not nearly as useful as wills, but usually provide a little information that can still be very helpful in tracing a family tree.

There have always been strict laws as to how intestates' property is to be distributed. Widows were entitled to a third of their husband's estate, with the remainder going equally to the children, although under gavelkind in Kent they received half if there were children and, since 1926 this rule has applied to the whole country. After the spouse, the children inherit, or if any of them are dead their own offspring inherit their parent's share. If there is no spouse, children or other descendants, the estate passes to the deceased's parents, or if they are deceased to the deceased's siblings or descendants of deceased siblings. This is followed then by grandparents, and failing them siblings or descendants of siblings of the parents, or failing that siblings or descendants of the siblings of the grandparents (and so on), always in equal shares.

WILLS FROM 1858 ONWARDS

From 12 January 1858, all wills were proved and administrations granted by local probate offices and the records collated by the Principal Probate Registry (PPR), now termed the Principal Registry of the Family

WILLS FROM 1858

The indexes can be searched at the **Principal Registry of the Family Division**, 1858 to the present, or on microfilm or fiche up to 1943 at many record offices and organisations such as the **SoG** and **IHGS**. Although access to these indexes is free, you must now pay £5 at the Principal Registry to be shown a will or have it photocopied and posted to you. You can see wills 1858–1903 for free if you obtain a Literary Enquirer's Permit. Postal searches cost £5 for a four-year search and a copy of the will, with £3 for each extra four-year period you want searched. Postal applications should be sent to the **Postal Searches and Copies Department**.

If you know when your ancestor died, you can turn straight to the index volume for that year. Remember that wills were sometimes proved a year or even a number of years after the person died (you will occasionally find the will of the first spouse who died being proved at the same time as that of the second), so do not give up if you do not find what you want immediately.

If you do not know when someone died, but think they may have left a will, a search in the will indexes is often a lot easier than one in the General Registration death indexes, so you will find a date of death and a will to boot. You will then, however, have to look up the entry in the death indexes (after March 1866) or buy a copy of the death certificate (before March 1866) to learn the deceased's age.

QUICK REFERENCE

See also main sources in Useful Addresses, page 306

PRINCIPAL REGISTRY OF THE FAMILY DIVISION
First Avenue House
42–49 High Holborn
London WC1V 6NP
☎ 020 7947 6980
www.courtservice.gov.uk/cms/
wills.htm

POSTAL SEARCHES AND COPIES DEPARTMENT FOR WILLS AFTER 1858
The Probate Registry
Castle Chambers
Clifford Street
York YO1 9RG
☎ 01904 666777

Division. Wills and administrations were indexed in separate annual, alphabetical volumes up to 1870, after which both were indexed together in the same annual alphabetical volumes. The volumes are easy to search, providing sufficient detail in almost all cases to determine whether you have found the right person. The annual indexes state:

➢**Name and residence** of deceased.

➢**Date of death**

➢**Where the will was proved** or letters of administration granted.

➢**Names or executors** or administrators.

➢**Value** of deceased's estate.

➢**Occupations** of deceased and executors or administrators are often stated.

➢**Residence** of executors or administrators and, between 1858 and 1892, their relationship (if any) to the deceased.

WILLS BEFORE 1858

Before 1858, wills were proved by church courts, also called ecclesiastical courts, and, unfortunately, even if you know where your ancestor lived it is not always obvious which church court would have proved their will.

WILLS BEFORE 1858

⊟ Archdioceses were divided in very complicated ways (see page 126), so start looking for your ancestor's will or administration in the most local court. If you don't find it there, search in the calendars and indexes of each court, working up to the most senior, the PCC (see right).

⊟ Records of the PCY are at the **Borthwick Institute**. Those for the dioceses and archdeaconries will be in the **county record office** covering the location of the court concerned, and bear in mind that these do not coincide with county boundaries.

⊟ Finding out the layers of jurisdiction under which your ancestral parish lay could not be simpler. *The Phillimore Atlas and Index* (Phillimore, 2003) marks out the different areas of ecclesiastical jurisdiction in different colours, while J. Gibson and E. Churchill's *Probate Jurisdictions: Where to Look for Wills* (FFHS, 2002) will tell you exactly which record office holds wills for the parishes you want.

⊟ All pre-1858 wills for Wales are at the **National Library of Wales**. Some Welsh wills will be found in neighbouring English courts.

⊟ Some probate records have only been calendared, a form of index arranged annually but within which surnames are grouped together by initial letter rather than strict alphabetical order. Most, fortunately, have been indexed, and all indexes and other finding aids are listed in J. Gibson and E. Churchill's *Probate Jurisdictions, Where to Look for Wills* (FFHS, 2002). Indexes may be published or

they may exist as card indexes in the relevant record office. There are also privately held probate indexes, not least some record offices, such as Cheshire's and **David Wright**'s index covering the patchwork courts that covered London, complete for 1750–1800 and 1820–58.

⊟ Some will indexes are now on the Internet, such as **www.englishorigins.net**, which has indexes to the Archdeaconry Court of London 1700–1807, and the PCC 1750–1800.

⊟ If you are lucky, you will find that the wills you want to examine have been transcribed or abstracted, and printed. Many county record societies have done this for early PCC wills relating to their counties. Gibson and Churchill's guide, cited above, indicates what is available, and where.

⊟ For the period 1796–1903, many wills were abstracted in estate (or death) duty registers, at the **NA** in class IR 26, indexed in IR 27, with copies available to the **FRC** and fully indexed on a pay-to-view site, **www.national archivist.com**. The Government's aim was to tax deceased peoples' estates. Up to 1805 about 25% of wills were abstracted and details noted of who received what, and what tax was due, the figure rising to almost 100% after 1815. The indexes are not in strictly alphabetical order, but these national records can be very helpful if you are not sure where a will might have been proved. They can tell you the state of the family when the will was written and also when it was proved. They may indicate, for example,

that the testator's wife had died in the interim or that daughters had married (and thus give their married names). They can also tell you what the testator was actually worth, as opposed to what he fancied he was worth.

⊟ Similar abstracts for estates including government stocks, 1717–1845, are held in the **Bank of England Archives** and indexed in **www.Englishorigins.net**.

WILLS AT THE PCC

⊟ Wills proved at the PCC are at the **NA**. Probate copies are in class PROB 11, original wills in PROB 10 and administrations in PROB 6 and 7; all can also be seen on microfilm at the **FRC** except for the original wills, which you can see at the **NA**, although it is advisable to order the documents in advance.

⊟ PCC wills, which are likely be relevant at some point to anyone with English or Welsh ancestry, are almost fully indexed from 1383 to 1857. Indexes are printed up to 1800 at **www. documentsonline.nationalarchives. gov.uk**. Digital images of wills can be downloaded for £3. You can also search by word, e.g. an occupation or place, as well as a name, making this a very useful research tool. The indexes to 1700 are quite detailed, those from 1801 onwards less so but still give names, years of probate and counties of residence. If the person died on or beyond the seas, they are denoted 'pts' or 'parts', meaning 'foreign parts'. The printed indexes are available at the **NA** and **FRC**, many **record offices** and **libraries** such as the **SoG** and **IHGS**.

England and Wales, and all English and Welsh subjects dying abroad, not least soldiers and sailors, fell under the jurisdiction if the Archbishop of Canterbury. Anyone who wished could take a will to the Archbishop's court, the Prerogative Court of Canterbury (PCC), which (somewhat confusingly) was at Doctor's Commons near St Paul's Cathedral, London. This was often the option of the wealthy, for whom the PCC had a certain caché. During the Cromwellian Commonwealth (1653–60) it was renamed the Court of Probate of Wills and Granting of Administrations and was the only place where these activities could take place.

The Archbishop's own archbishopric itself only extended as far north of the River Trent, beyond which probate jurisdiction fell to the Archbishop of York. If someone had property worth more than £5 in both archbishoprics, their will had to be proved at the PCC. Because government stock held at the Bank of England was deemed to be property in London, Bank of England clients from all over the country had to have their wills proved at the PCC, and after 1812 the Bank of England did not recognise any wills not proved there. However, if the person's property was only within Cheshire, Cumberland, Durham, Northumberland, Westmoreland and Yorkshire, it could be proved at the Prerogative Court of the Archbishop of York (PCY) or, before 1577, at his Exchequer Court.

OVERCOMING PROBLEMS

➤ **Remember that wills are arranged by date of probate, not date of death,** so if your ancestor died in 1720 but their will was not proved until 1740, then that is the year in which the will appears in the index. Generally, the broad periods of time covered by the indexes make them easy to search and it is usually straightforward to find both the person you want and also to note others of the same name who could be relatives. It is not uncommon to search for an ancestor's will and to end up finding wills for their parents and grandparents in the same index.

➤ **Indexes seldom take variant spellings into account,** and sometimes indexers may have mistranscribed a testator's name, so you must be as alert to these problems, as when conducting any other searches.

➤ **If you are lucky, you will find wills and associated documentation relating to your direct ancestors.** You can then enjoy obtaining photocopies or even photographs of the records, and seeing how much they will tell you about your ancestors' lives. Do not forget, however, that much of the wording itself was usually imposed on the testator by lawyers and clerks. When the will of your farmer ancestor states, 'I devise and bequeath unto my eldest son Thomas my black coat', he probably said something much

BECAUSE ONE OF THE problems of dealing with old wills is trying to decipher difficult handwriting, it is helpful to know the sort of phrases you might expect to encounter in a will written in or around the 17th century.

In the name of God Amen,
Wills were religious documents and almost always started thus, until the 18th century when this opening was often dropped and a more secular style adopted.

I John Havers of Winfarthinge in the Countie of Norff[olk] gent[leman].
You can usually expect to find the place of residence and occupation stated. Women will usually give their 'occupation' either as widow or spinster: wives very rarely wrote in their husbands' lifetimes.

beinge sick of bodie but of sounde memorye and perfecte remembrance
Well or ill, it was important to emphasise that the testator was indeed of sound mind, so as to lessen the chance of the will being challenged later.

Make this my last will and testament in manner and forme followinge
Technically, property is divided into land and buildings, 'real estate', which is 'devised' by a testament and movable goods and money, 'personal estate', which is bequeathed by a will. However, because both were contained in the same document, these terms have come to be used interchangeably.

And my body to be buried in the churche of Winfarthinge aforesaid or in the chappell of the same
Church as close as maybe to the grave of Agnes my firste wife.
People often stated where they wished to be buried and sometimes, as here, gave incidental genealogical information about the burial places of other members of the family. If the place of burial was a different parish to the parish of residence, it will almost certainly be the person's parish of origin.

I desire after the payment of my just debts and funerall expenses
This was standard and did not necessarily mean the testator was in debt.

I bequeathe to the parish church of ... and the poore of the parish of ...
When such bequests mentioned parishes other than the parish of residence they usually denoted where the testator held other property or had ancestral connections.

I will and bequeathe unto Charles Havers my eldest son xxxli vs 2d of lawful money of Englande to
be paid unto him when he attain the age of twentie one yeares

Wills will often name all the children, either in age order or specifically numbered 'second son', 'third son' and so on, and give a clue as to their ages. The bequest here, made in Latin and followed by abbreviated words, is for 30 pounds (livres), 5 shillings and 2 pence (denarii).

I bequeathe my tenements, hereditaments and messuages situate within the parish of...
A tenement was any sort of property held by one person from another; an hereditament was any property which may be inherited; and a messuage was a dwelling house with the land around it including outbuildings. These phrases together, then, covered any sort of building the testator might own or be likely to own.

I bequeathe my sylver and gilte cupp in the lyttle parlour and the bedd and cupborde standeing in the great parlour
Sometimes the testator takes you on a written tour of their house.

I appointe my said wife Anne and my said son Thomas Havers.... to be executrix and executors of this my said will
Men were executors and women executrixes. Testators might appoint one or several of these, usually spouses, very close relations, trusted friends or family lawyers. Their task was to have the will proved once the testator was deceased and ensure that the instructions in the will were carried out.

And I therefore set my hande and seale
The testator's signature will appear on an original will but not on a probate copy. The seal will usually be a standard lawyer's seal, with a pattern or simple picture on it, but if the testator had a coat of arms the seal may well be from his own sealing ring and will show you his arms or crest. If a record office issues you with a probate copy but you want to see the original signature or seal, ask for this specifically.

In the presence of Henrye Abbott and Joseph Horne...
Witnesses were often friends or relations. Their names may not be immediately familiar to you but they may turn up later as you extend the family tree upwards and sideways, so always note them.

a codicil
If the testator wanted to alter a small part of their will, rather than have the whole thing drawn up again (and thus incurring lawyers' and scriveners' fees), they might add a codicil, revoking or altering a bequest. This might be done months or years after the will was written.

LIFETIMES: CURIOSITIES

WILLS CONTAIN ALL SORTS OF CURIOSITIES. HERE ARE SOME FAVOURITES:

Christopher Dowlinge, a husbandman of Stowey, Somerset, wrote his will in 1571, itemising his animals by name. His oxen Martin and Pike were left to his daughters Juliana and Alice respectively, while his cows Filpaile, Chirrie, Violet and Cople went to his wife and three of his daughters. Some other oxen and cows lacked names, and his sheep seem to have been anonymous too.

Benjamin Smart, a lawyer of the Middle Temple in London, had other things on his mind when he wrote his will in 1760 (which was proved in the PCC), specifying that 'in order to avoid some very ill practises in making skeletons of deceased persons

... I do most especially make it my Earnest Request not to be buried from any Undertakers or public Hal l... but from my Chambers ... and that some of my ffriends or servants may see me immediately before my coffin shall be ffastened ... and as I have Reason to think that several persons have inadvertently been buried alive I do hereby make it my earnest request that my coffin may not be fastened up till full forty-eight Hours after my decease (if it can be avoided) and if it can be kept open longer without inconvenience I desire it may be so kept open and not ffastened up till it become necessary'.

The following is from the will of Thomas Jefferies of Draycott Foliat, Wiltshire (1872): presumably Thomas senior did not like his nephew's prospective wife very much.

And in case my nephew Thomas Jefferies shall marry Elizabeth Waldron of Draycott.. in the Lifetime of his mother then I leave his share to her to dispose of as she shall think proper

WILLS OUTSIDE ENGLAND AND WALES

SCOTLAND

Until 1868, the inheritance of land was rigidly fixed, going automatically to the eldest surviving son (or his heir), or if there were no sons to the eldest surviving daughter, so technically there were no wills (which bequeath land), but only testaments, whereby people could bequeath their movable goods to whomever they liked. The equivalent of letters of administration, appointing an administrator to distribute the goods of someone who had died intestate, was known as a testament dative.

Probate matters were dealt with in church courts until 1560 when, unlike England and Wales, probate was handed over to secular commissary courts or commissariots under the overall jurisdiction of the Principal Commissariot of Edinburgh, which also dealt with Scots who had goods in Scotland but who had died elsewhere.

In Scotland there are also services to heirs (also called retours). Most heritable land simply passed from father to eldest son, but in cases

MANY FAMILIES HAVE STORIES that they are entitled to great wealth from a distant ancestor or relative's will, or that their forebear would have come into a great deal of money but was 'cut off with/without a shilling'. Most of these stories are mere pie-in-the-sky, excuses made by daydreamers or people embarrassed by lack of money. In many cases, it turns out that the 'cut off' ancestor received their legacy after all, and promptly spent it. In other cases, such notions arise because parents sometimes made generous provision for a particular child while they were alive, and left them a shilling in their will to preclude them or their heirs from claiming anything further.

Family stories are sometimes started by missing kin notices. In 1950, say, Mr Evans sees a missing kin notice for heirs of the late millionaire Miss Agnes Evans, and remarks fancifully that it would be a fine thing if she turned out to be a relation. In 1975, Mr Evans's son Tom recalls the remark and tells his own daughter, *'my father used to say we were related to Miss Evans, the millionairess.'* By 2000, Tom's daughter is convinced her grandfather was the heir to millions but never claimed it, and ruins the rest of her life in a wild-goose chase to try to locate what she by now regards as her rightful inheritance.

Sometimes such stories arise due to contact from a Chancery agent. Chancery agents often trace and contact 'missing' heirs and offer to reunite them with their legacies if they will sign a percentage over to them. If this happens to you, think carefully. If you have no idea where the money came from, there is no harm in signing up and rewarding the Chancery agent for their hard work. However, if you have the slightest inkling of who might have left the money, do not sign anything, because if you can find the deceased relative's will you can establish who the executors were or contact the Treasury solicitor (who has ultimate responsibility for unclaimed funds) and claim your share yourself. You may gain useful clues as to which side of the family the deceased relative was on by finding out which of your other relatives has also been contacted. If your cousin on your mother's mother's side has also been contacted, you will know that the deceased relation was someone on that side of the family, and by a process of elimination you may successfully identify who the deceased relative was.

WHERE TO SEARCH

WILLS OUTSIDE ENGLAND AND WALES

SCOTLAND

🗐 *The Phillimore Atlas and Index* (Phillimore, 2003) will show you which court had jurisdiction over your ancestors' home parishes, and more detail is given in J. Gibson and E. Churchill's *Probate Jurisdictions: Where to Look for Wills* (FFHS, 2002).

🗐 Testaments from 1824 were proved in the county sheriff's court, most of whose records – save for the most recent – are at the **NAS**, indexed 1824–75 with annual national indexes thereafter to 1959, called calendars of confirmations and inventories.

🗐 An index to Scottish wills for 1513-1901, with downloadable images, is at **www.scotlandspeople.gov.uk**. Estate duty records, similar to those for England, are at the **NAS**.

🗐 Services to Heirs or Retours for 1700–1859 are clearly indexed in printed volumes and now on CD-Rom from the **Scottish Genealogical Society**.

IRELAND

🗐 Wills proved from 1922 are safe and well, at the **National Archives of Ireland** and the **PRONI**.

🗐 Most pre-1922 wills were destroyed, but the situation is not all doom and gloom. From 1858 onwards, the wills sent to the PPR had first been copied by the local registries where they were proved. These copies are now at the **National Archives of Ireland** and those for Northern Ireland are at the **PRONI**.

🗐 For further research, there are also collections at the **Genealogical Office**, **Trinity College** and the Land Commission records are at the **NA** (up to 1858).

🗐 See also Phillimore's *Irish Wills, a typescript at the IHGS and the Deeds Registry* (1708–1832), indexed by P. B. Eustace's *Registry of Deeds, Dublin, Abstracts of Wills* (Irish Manuscripts Commission, 1954–84).

🗐 Many Irish landowners and merchants who had financial interests in England had their wills proved at the PCC (see page 129).

CHANNEL ISLANDS

🗐 Wills up on Jersey to 1949 are held at the **Judicial Greffe**, except for those concerned with real estate since 1851, which are at the land registry.

🗐 On Guernsey, some wills concerned with real estate are with **Her Majesty's Greffier**.

🗐 Some Channel Island wills may be found in the PCC up to 1858 and thereafter in the PPR (see page 126).

ISLE OF MAN

🗐 Wills up to 1910 are at the **Manx Museum** and thereafter at the Deeds and Probate Office of the **Chief Registrar,** Douglas. If you cannot find what you want, you can look in the PCY or PCC, or the PPR after 1858 (see pages 126–9).

QUICK REFERENCE

See also main sources in Useful Addresses, page 306

SCOTTISH GENEALOGICAL SOCIETY
15 Victoria Terrace
Edinburgh EH1 2JL
Scotland
☎ 0131 220 3677
www.scotsgenealogy.com

GENEALOGICAL OFFICE
2–3 Kildare Street
Dublin 2
Eire
☎ 00 353 1 603 0200
www.nli.ie

TRINITY COLLEGE
Trinity College Library
College Street
Dublin 4
Eire
☎ 00 353 1 677 2941
www.tcd.ie/library

For the Channel Islands and Isle of Man, see page 311

where it did not (e.g. grandchildren inheriting from grandparents because their parents were dead, nephews inheriting from childless uncles and so on), it was common to record the right with a retour. Retours were also used to appoint 'tutors' or guardians for fatherless children ('pupils'). Those pre-1700 are in Latin and very awkward to use.

IRELAND

Irish probate worked in the same way as in England and Wales, with wills being proved in the consistory courts of the Church of Ireland bishops (there were no archdeaconry courts and very few peculiar courts), under the overall jurisdiction of the Prerogative Court of Armagh, the equivalent of the PCC. In 1858, a Principal Probate Registry was established in Dublin. As previously stated, the great disaster to Irish genealogy was the destruction of records during the IRA's bombing of the Four Courts in 1922.

The indexes to wills and administrations for all the courts before 1858 survive and at least give the names and addresses of testators, and the year of probate, so even if you cannot read the will you shall still know that someone of a certain name and residence died in or about a certain year. In fact, many wills had been abstracted by solicitors, family archivists and genealogists on an ad hoc basis and, after the disaster, about 20,000 of these were collected together at the NA, where they are indexed.

THE CHANNEL ISLANDS

In Jersey, wills up to 1949 were proved by the Ecclesiastical Court of the Dean of Jersey.

Guernsey wills are proved by the Ecclesiastical Court of the Bailiwick of Guernsey, St Peter Port.

ISLE OF MAN

Wills and administrations were proved in or granted through either the Consistitory Court of Sodor and Man or the Archdeaconry Court of the Isle of Man. Unlike the rest of Britain, the church did not relinquish control over wills until 1884, when probate was transferred to the Manx High Court of Justice.

WHERE TO SEARCH

EXAMPLES OF WILLS IN OTHER COUNTRIES

AUSTRALIA
Wills were proved by the state probate courts.

CARIBBEAN
Wills for British settlers were proved either in the local church or civil courts or at the PCC or PPR. Slaves are often mentioned, especially in inventories. The main archive for wills in Jamaica is the Island Record Office. Many are also abstracted on **www.jamaicanfamily search.com**.

INDIA
Wills of the British in India, dating back to 1618, are at the **India Office Library**, and very well indexed, although if property was also held in Britain, wills may have been proved in the relevant courts in Britain.

NEW ZEALAND
Wills were proved across the Tasman Sea in New South Wales, Australia, until 1842, and thereafter by the Supreme Court of New Zealand in its regional registries. Records are held by the registries, not centrally, and deceased estate accounts were published in the *Provincial Gazette*, which became the *New Zealand Gazette*.

SOUTH AFRICA
Wills and death notices, which will tell you name, dates of birth and death, parentage, spouse and offspring, and how much was distributed to which beneficiaries, are kept in deceased estate files by the Supreme Court registries of each province.

QUICK REFERENCE

INDIA OFFICE LIBRARY
British Library
96 Euston Road
London NW1 2DB
☎ 020 7412 7513
www.bl.uk/collections/
orientalandindian.html

CHAPTER TWELVE
GRAVESTONES & MEMORIALS

Gravestones found in churchyards and cemeteries (and sometimes called monumental inscriptions, 'MIs' for short), can provide detailed and often unique information on ancestors and their families and can be one of the most tangible remains of our forebears that we will ever encounter.

Most tools used for tracing family trees are written documents, but not all. Gravestones are, in fact, documents carved on stone rather than written on paper, but because of this they are sometimes overlooked by family historians working in warm, dry record offices. Besides the fascinating information gravestones can give us, they also provide a form of physical contact with the past. Ancestors who existed simply as names on a page suddenly seem much more real when you realise their bones lie beneath your feet, and you can reach out and touch the stone erected by their grieving kin. The graves of the rich can stir us with pride in our distinguished forebears, but we can be equally if not more moved by the humble graves of our poorer ancestors.

Besides the name and date of death of the deceased, you may also find occupation, age at death or dates, and even place of birth as well as the names and similar details of the spouse, children and other relatives sharing the same grave. By walking around the graveyard you may encounter graves of others with the same surname, which might turn out to have been those of relations.

You will not always find them – many poor people were buried in graves marked by wooden crosses, or nothing at all. The inscriptions may have been made years later, and consequently with inaccurate information. Many have now been worn away or the stones may have been stacked in a corner or moved

▽ A 19th-century photograph of the 19th-century grave of Catherine Maria Hammond at Ovington, Hampshire.

◁ The graveyard of St John the Evangelist, Westbourne, Sussex.

▽ The 20th-century grave of my great-grandfather Joseph Adolph and his wife Angela Maria at Sanderstead, Surrey.

entirely. Those for one London church have been moved to Yorkshire to become the graveyard of the made-up village of television's long-running soap *Emmerdale*.

Many burials took place in cemeteries rather than churchyards. Some have existed for centuries, such as Bunhill Fields non-conformist burial ground in London, founded in 1665 (with registers 1713–52 in the NA in class RG 4/3974–3987, 1713–94). Most cemeteries date from the 19th century, when graveyards were becoming full up. Highgate Cemetery in north London is probably the most famous one in London, but many Londoners were taken by train (from a special platform at Waterloo Station, whose entrance can still be seen today) to Brookwood Cemetery near Woking, Surrey.

CREMATIONS

Apart from a few amateur efforts, the first public cremation took place at Woking Crematorium in 1885. It became the most popular method of disposing of bodies in the mid-20th century.

LIFETIMES: JOHN YSTYMLLYN

IN THE TINY GRAVEYARD of Ynyscynhaiarn, near Criccieth in Gwynedd, North Wales, is the gravestone of a remarkable person. It reads:

Here lieth the Body of John Ystymllyn who Died July the 27th 1791 AGED 46 years
Yn India gynna'm ganwyd, – a nghamrau
Ynghymru'm bedyddiwyd;
Wele'r fan dan lechan lwyd,
Du-oeraidd y'm daiarwyd'.

The Welsh inscription states that John, who lies in the 'cold dark ground' below the stone, lived in Wales but was born in India. The Ynyscynhaiarn parish register only says:

1786: John Ystymllyn of Ynnhyrran; Gardener, July 2d.

As we can see, the stone gives the wrong date – it was actually erected many years later, but it does alert us to John's unusualness. It is wrong about where he was born. He was, in fact, a black African, kidnapped from his family and brought to Britain as a slave. He ended up as a gardener to the local landowner, happily married to a white girl, and apparently the first black man recorded to have lived in North Wales.

MEMORIAL CARDS

Another form of memorial, which you are most likely to find in family papers, is memorial cards. Besides being tangible evidence of a relative, they provide very useful information. The date of death may lead to a death certificate (and thus an address for census searching), will or obituary, and often other relatives will be mentioned, such as grieving parents, spouses, children and so on.

▷ The memorial card of my great-grandfather Joseph Aloysius Adolph (d.1966).

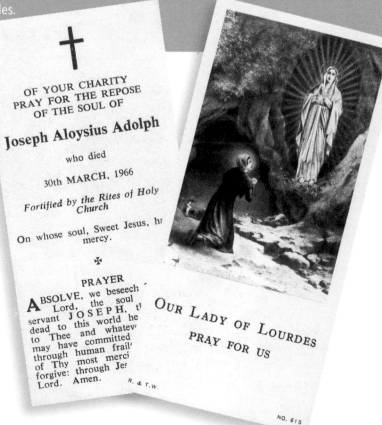

OF YOUR CHARITY
PRAY FOR THE REPOSE
OF THE SOUL OF

Joseph Aloysius Adolph

who died

30th MARCH, 1966

Fortified by the Rites of Holy Church

On whose soul, Sweet Jesus, h[?]
mercy.

✠

PRAYER

ABSOLVE, we beseech [?]
Lord, the soul [?]
servant JOSEPH, t[?]
dead to this world he [?]
to Thee and whatev[?]
may have committed [?]
through human frail[?]
of Thy most merc[?]
forgive: through Je[?]
Lord. Amen.

R. & T.W.

OUR LADY OF LOURDES
PRAY FOR US

NO. 615

GRAVESTONES

- There is no easy way of tracing where an ancestor was buried, unless you can find a newspaper announcement of a death or burial. If you have to resort to guessing, consult contemporary directories or even modern maps to find out what cemeteries were near where your ancestor died. If the death took place away from the original family home, consider the possibility that the body may have been taken back there for burial. Most cemeteries kept excellent records, which can be searched at **county record offices**, or by telephoning the local authority or, if the cemetery is still functioning, the cemetery office itself. Deeds for burial plots will often be found among family papers.

- Many parishes have had their gravestones transcribed and copies can be found in **county record offices** and in the **SoG**'s large collection for England, Wales and Scotland. These can enable you to gain the information from a gravestone without having to visit the graveyard (but do try to eventually, just for the experience).

- Sometimes a gravestone may have been moved or rendered illegible, but a transcription made years ago will provide details of what it said. There are some 170 transcripts of inscriptions of demolished graveyards at the **NA** (RG37).

- The graves, inscribed memorials and memorial brasses of the wealthy are often found inside churches. If you have well-to-do ancestors it is worth visiting or writing to their local church. Details of such memorials often appear in antiquarian county histories and there are a number of catalogues, such as M. Stephenson's *A List of Monumental Brasses in the British Isles* (Headley Brothers, 1926).

- Some English and Welsh counties have indexes of gravestones, and these are listed in J. Gibson and E. Hampson's *Specialist Indexes for Family Historians* (FFHS, 1998). Although you will usually be led to a gravestone by a death certificate or burial entry, these indexes can indicate where to seek a record of death or burial.

- Ancestors and relations who died in the two World Wars will probably be commemorated on local war memorials but may have been buried far afield, in the Great War graves of northern France and Belgium, for example. Details of all such graves can be found on the War Graves Commission's website **www.cwgc.org.uk**.

- Irish MIs have been extensively transcribed, and many have been published, especially in the *Memorials of the Dead in Ireland* series.

GRAVESTONES IN OTHER COUNTRIES

- Those for the British in India are at the **India Office Library** in London.

- Many MIs for white Caribbean families have been transcribed and published in V. L. Oliver's *The Monumental Inscriptions of the British West Indies* (F. G. Longman, 1927). There is an earlier version of this book and a list of monumental inscriptions in Scotland relating to the West Indies on **www.jamaicanfamilysearch.com**.

CREMATIONS

- The **Cremation Society of Great Britain** can help you work out which crematorium may have been used for your ancestors, or you can search on **www.savinggraves.co.uk**, a county-by county list of crematoria and cemeteries.

- An article by me on the history of cremation, 'Ashes to Ashes', is in *Family History Monthly*, March 2003.

- **www.londonburials. co.uk** is a guide to London burial grounds.

- **www.interment. net/uk/index.htm** contains assorted burial records and Memorial Inscriptions from cemeteries throughout Britain.

QUICK REFERENCE

See also main sources in Useful Addresses, page 306

INDIA OFFICE LIBRARY
British Library
96 Euston Road
London NW1 2DB
☎ 020 7412 7513
www.bl.uk/collections/
orientalandindian.html

CREMATION SOCIETY OF GREAT BRITAIN
Brecon House, 16 Albion Place
Maidstone
Kent ME14 5DZ
☎ 01622 688292
www.cremation.org.uk

PART THREE

Britain has an incredibly rich store of archives containing a vast amount of written records. This section covers the main areas, from feet of fines to freemen records, which will enable you to solve problems and add a huge amount of extra detail to your family's history.

CHAPTER THIRTEEN
NEWSPAPERS & MAGAZINES

Many of our ancestors appeared in newspapers and magazines, in birth, marriage and death announcements, advertising their services as tradesmen or professionals, as parties in lawsuits, attending public meetings, suing for damage, being tried as criminals and in a host of entirely unexpected ways, which can add amazing details to family histories.

△ Newspaper reports for the death of my great-grandmother in a car accident, and the funeral of her husband's cousin Walter Nursey.

Newspapers and magazines can be used either through focused searches to try to solve a specific problem, or simply by scanning them for local colour, seeing what events took place when your ancestors were alive.

THE BEST-KNOWN NEWSPAPERS

Newspapers and periodicals grew out of newsbooks, especially *Mercurius Britannicus* and *Mercurius Aulicus*, which the Parliamentarians and Cavaliers produced respectively to spread their propaganda during the Civil War. They include the most marvellously quirky woodcuts of characters and events and can best be examined in the pamphlets section of the British Library.

The *Oxford Gazette*, later to become the *London Gazette*, was founded in 1665, printing official announcements, from bankruptcies, granting of honours and medals, changes of name, naturalisations and official appointments in government, church and the armed forces.

The first daily newspaper was the *Daily Courant*, initially published in 1702. Many other titles appeared during the 18th century, fuelled in no small part by the growth of coffeehouses. The *Gentleman's Magazine* was published monthly from 1731 to 1868, with announcements of birth, marriage and death of members of the middle and upper classes (and those aspiring to be so). It also included information on the lower classes, noting things like exceptional longevity, and executions. Like the *London Gazette*, it also included information such as bankruptcy and appointments, essays, prices of commodities, and news items. The *Illustrated London News* was published from 1847 and contains many obituaries, often with engraved illustrations

The best-known newspaper of all, *The Times*, started life in 1785 as the *Daily Universal Register*. From the 19th century onwards, it provides a wonderful source of birth, marriage and death announcements for

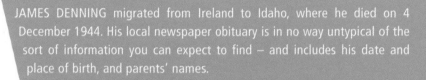

LIFETIMES: AN IDAHO PIONEER

JAMES DENNING migrated from Ireland to Idaho, where he died on 4 December 1944. His local newspaper obituary is in no way untypical of the sort of information you can expect to find – and includes his date and place of birth, and parents' names.

PIONEER LIVESTOCK MAN SUCCUMBS

James Denning, 81, prominent Idaho livestock man, died Monday at 10.25 a.m. at a local hospital following a lingering illness. A colorful figure of the west for nearly half a century, Mr Denning operated his ranch on Medicine Lodge river until December, 1943, when he sold his interests and retired, moving with his wife to Idaho Falls, where they have since made their home. He was born at Coothill, Cavin county, Ireland, June 15 1863, the son of James and Elizabeth Denning. At the age of 21 he came alone to the United States and remained in New York for about 10 years in the employ of Senator W.A. Clark. He then came west with Senator Clark to Butte, Mont., and after being there a short time came to Arco with one of the senator's sons and together they formed a partnership in the cattle business. Later he became affiliated with Frank Swauger in the livestock business at Arco. They then purchased a ranch at Medicine Lodge and started raising sheep. A few years later the partnership was dissolved and Mr Denning continued operating alone. In 1908 he returned to New York and on March 2 of that year he was united in marriage to Miss Elizabeth Agnes McCabe of the metropolis. They returned to the west and a few years later he combined his interests with those of Sam Clarke and sons and together they operated as the Denning and Clarke Livestock Company for several years. After Mr Clark's death, several years ago, Mr Denning took over the entire ranch property and livestock, operating it until he retired about a year ago. A member of the Catholic Church. Mr Denning was a fourth degree member of the Knights of St Columbus at Salt Lake City. He was also affiliated with the Elks lodge 1087 at Idaho Falls. Besides his widow, he is survived by one sister, Mrs Annie McMahon of New York City. The body is at the McHan and Buck Funeral Home. Services will be announced later. Funeral will be at New York.

middle and upper class families, together with much valuable information on bankruptcies, business partnerships, trials and events. Coming closer to the present are other broadsheets, and a host of local newspapers. Local papers can date from the 18th century (the earliest was the *Norwich Post*, founded in 1701) but can be disappointing because of their focus on national news. It is only from the mid-19th century that they really began to focus on local news and people, such as inquests, obituary notices and detailed accounts of the funerals of the more important inhabitants. For the 20th century local newspapers can include photographs of ancestors, especially their wedding photographs, often accompanied by detailed accounts of who gave which wedding presents.

△ Newspaper picture of the wedding of my grandparents, Jerome Collingwood Rietchel and Maureen Denning, in 1934.

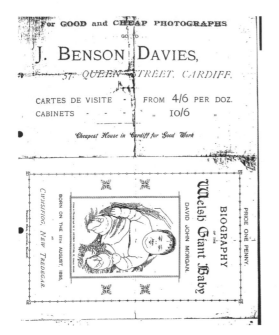

◁ Besides newspapers, specially printed pamphlets can provide some pretty weird family history information.

SCOTTISH AND IRISH NEWSPAPERS

Scottish newspapers appeared at the same time as English ones, with the *Edinburgh Evening Courant* published thrice weekly from 1718, followed by the *Glasgow Journal* in 1741 and *Aberdeen Journal* in 1748. The first daily paper was the *Conservative*, established in 1837. The equivalent of the *Gentleman's Magazine* was the *Edinburgh Magazine*, founded in 1739 and renamed the *Scots Magazine* in 1817, which is indexed annually for births, deaths and marriages.

Irish newspapers started appearing in the 17th century, first in Dublin and Belfast (though copies for the latter apparently do not survive before 1737), and then spreading to towns and cities such as Limerick and Waterford in the early 18th century.

'The Times *indexes contain a plethora of insights into our ancestors' lives. Under the surname Angel, for example, we have Charles, bankrupt in 1843; William, tried for stealing in 1865; Charles and David, drowned while bathing in 1879, and, weirdest of all, in 1887 'Death, Mysterious, of Rachel Angel, found poisoned by nitric acid in bed, and a man found lying under the bed, in Whitechapel'.*

LIFETIMES: MARRIAGE LINES

The following is an account of my grandfather's wedding, including all sorts of intimate details I would never have learned from other family sources – or even from him himself!

'Considerable interest was evinced in the wedding of Mr Jerome Collingwood Rietchel, son of Mr and Mrs J. Rietchel, of 10, Culverden Grange, Tunbridge Wells, and Miss Maureen Josephine Denning, daughter of the late Mr and Mrs W. Denning, of Knockatane, South-drive, Ruislip, which took place at the Church of the Sacred Heart, Ruislip, on Wednesday. The Rev. W. P. Denning, brother of the bride, came especially from Rome to conduct the service, and he was assisted by the Rev. A. E. S. Blount, and the Rev. J. J. Curtin ... Mr W. Hyde presided at the organ ... who played at the entrance of the bride, who was given away by Mr J. B. Dore. Her beautiful dress of dull parchment satin ... The bride defied superstition, for the colour of the bridesmaids' dresses was green. The bride and bridegroom left later in the day for their honeymoon, which is being spent in the South of France.'

WHERE TO SEARCH

NEWSPAPERS

The best place to search newspapers, national and local, for the entire British Isles, is the **British Library Newspaper Library**. A good bibliography of newspapers is the *Tercentenary Handlist of English & Welsh Newspapers, Magazines & Reviews, 1620–1919* (Dawsons, 1966), and you can also consult J. Gibson's *Local Newspapers 1750–1920, England and Wales, Channel Islands and Isle of Man: A Select Location List* (FFHS, 1991). Otherwise, ask at **local libraries**, **museums** and **archives**, as many hold good collections and may also have indexes to their holdings.

The Times is best searched by two CD-Rom indexes, 1785–1905 (incorporating the earlier index compiled by Palmer) and 1906–80 (using the official *Times* index) – both are at the **Guildhall Library**. Searches can be made under names or topics. For the periods 1785–1790 and 1906–present there is the more cumbersome *Official Index to the Times*, in quarterly volumes, which can also be searched at **Guildhall Library** (which also holds microfilm copies of the newspapers themselves). These and copies of the *Official Index* may also be found at other locations, such as some **university libraries**.

London Gazette: Complete sets are at the **NA**, **British Library** and **Guildhall Library**, with annual indexes from 1787.

The Gentleman's Magazine: There are indexes covering 1731–1810 and a complete typescript index exists at the **Family History Library** at Salt Lake City (942 B2g index V.26) – it costs very little to pay a searcher there to examine the index for you. Collections of the magazine itself are at the **British Library**, **NA** and a partial set at the **SoG**. Indexes to obituaries to 1855 are in a manuscript volume at **Guildhall Library** and those for the 16th–18th centuries are included in J. G. Armitage's *Obituary, Obituary Prior to 1800 (as far as relates to England, Scotland & Ireland) compiled by Sir William Musgrave* (Harleian Society, vols 44-49, 1899–1901).

The Scotsman newspaper, published since 1817, is now fully online up to 1900 at **www.archive.scotsman.com** at £7.95 a day.

Good collections of newspapers for their respective areas are at the **National Libraries of Wales and Scotland** and the **India Office Library**.

For Irish newspapers there are collections at the **British Library Newspaper Library** and also at the **National Library of Ireland** and the **PRONI**. Most include birth, marriage and death announcements, making excellent substitutes for the many destroyed parish registers.

EXAMPLES OF NEWSPAPERS IN OTHER COUNTRIES

A detailed list of Trinidad newspapers and where they are held of them in Britain and the USA is given in **www.rootsweb.com/~ttowgw/research/newspapers.htm**.

Some Jamaican newspapers, including extracts from the *Royal Gazeteer* and the *Gleaner*, are on **www.jamaicanfamilysearch.com**.

QUICK REFERENCE

See also main sources in
Useful Addresses, page 306

BRITISH LIBRARY NEWSPAPER LIBRARY
Colindale Avenue
Colindale
London NW9 5HE
☎ 020 7412 7353
www.bl.uk/collections/
newspapers.html

FAMILY HISTORY LIBRARY
35 North West Temple Street
Salt Lake City
Utah 84150, USA

NATIONAL LIBRARY OF SCOTLAND
George IV Bridge
Edinburgh EH1 1EW
Scotland
☎ 0131 466 2812
www.nls.uk

INDIA OFFICE LIBRARY
British Library
96 Euston Road
London NW1 2DB
☎ 020 7412 7513
www.bl.uk/collections/
orientalandindian.html

NATIONAL LIBRARY OF IRELAND
Kildare Street
Dublin 2, Eire
☎ 00 353 1 603 0200
www.nli.ie

CHAPTER FOURTEEN
LAND RECORDS

Records to do with land can frighten people because of their esoteric names and legal jargon, but in essence they tell you who lived where and what they did with their land. These are worth seeking and studying and, once you have mastered them, they can be absolutely fascinating. They're also one of the best sources to use if you want to trace your family back to the Middle Ages.

LAND MEASUREMENTS

Acre: This started as the area a team of oxen could plough in a morning but became fixed at 4480 square yards in England, 6100 square yards in Scotland and 7840 in Ireland.

English mile: 8 furlongs or 1760 yards.

Furlong: 40 rods or 220 yards.

Hide/carucate/ploughland: The area a team of oxen could plough in a year, which varied from 60 to 180 acres depending on the soil.

Rod/pole/perch: 16½ square feet or 5½ square yards.

Rood: 40 square rods.

Square mile: 640 acres.

THE MAIN RECORDS

English Public Record no. 1 is Domesday Book (no 'the' before it), compiled for William the Conqueror in 1086. William wanted to find out exactly how much tax he could raise from each village, and threatened to annihilate any settlement which provided inaccurate information. The people listed in Domesday Book are the tenants in chief, who held land direct from the Crown, and the sub-tenants, both after the Norman settlement and at the time of the Conquest, providing a ghostly record of the dispossessed Saxon nobility and their sub-tenants.

Below these levels, the numbers of freemen, slaves, villeins, cottars and sokemen are then stated – but not named – along with the mills and churches, and size and use of the landholdings. The whole country was included except for the areas that the Normans had devastated – Durham, London, Northumberland, northern Westmoreland and Winchester. A copy of this tome is in most good libraries.

INQUISITIONS POST MORTEM

These were taken from 1235 to 1649 and recorded the deaths of those who held land direct from the Crown, stating what land they held and under what terms, and who their heir was. In some cases, jurors and tenants may be listed.

TITLE DEEDS

Originally, land was transferred by the possessor by 'livery of seisin', the handing over of a lump of turf (or similar) to the incomer, who became literally the 'holder' of the land. In the Middle Ages, written records of these transactions began to be kept, called deeds, and these can provide key evidence of early generations of your family.

To be able to sell a property, the owner needed to prove his right to it by producing evidence of his inheritance or purchase of it, and all previous inheritances or purchases. This collection would often include an abstract of title summarising the transactions. In 1925 the law changed so that title only had to be proved for the preceding 30 years (it is now 15 years). Consequently, many old deeds and wills were thrown away but a great number found their way eventually to record offices and other local and national archives and libraries. Those not thrown out remain with the present owners, be they private individuals or corporations such as the Ministry of Defence.

After 1840, title deeds include maps of the property. They may also mention ancestors who were tenants of a freeholder, mortgagees or owners of abutting property. Bundles of documents relating to a property are also one of the main sources for tracing house histories.

Most deeds were indented, which means that the wording was written out twice on the same sheet, and the two copies were then cut apart by a wavy line, to deter subsequent forgery. They usually record, in this order:

➤ **Date**

➤ **Names of the vendor/leasor and purchaser/leasee**

➤ **Type of transaction and earlier relevant ones**

➤ **Name of vendor/leasor again**

➤ **Value of purchase/lease** (prefixed 'in consideration of the sum of ...').

➤ **Type of transaction again** (in terms of the vendor/leasor 'demising' to the purchaser or leasee).

➤ **Details of the property**

➤ **If a lease,** the length or type, how the rent would be paid and any obligations incumbent on either party.

➤ **Signatures of parties and witnesses**

N. W. Alcock's *Old Title Deeds: A Guide for Local and Family Historians* (Phillimore, 1986) provides valuable help on reading and understanding these documents.

FEET OF FINES

In the 12th century, problems were arising with purchase and sale of freehold because most landholders did so by custom but had no written records to prove their ownership. To try to guarantee future legal recognition of sales, therefore, lawyers devised a legal pantomime acted out in the Court of Common Pleas, whereby the purchaser ('plaintiff' or 'queriant') would claim he had always owned the land and that the vendor ('deforciant') was squatting in it. The two parties then agreed to settle the affair by the purchaser paying the vendor to go

---

WHERE TO SEARCH

INQUISITIONS POST MORTEM

At the **NA**, mainly in classes C 133–42 and E 149–50. Abstracts of many have been published by county record societies and similar works and can be identified through E. L. C. Mullins's *Texts and Calendars, an Analytical Guide to Serial Publications* (RHS, 1958) and *Vol. II, 1957–82* (RHS, 1983). Those for Ireland are at the **Genealogical Office**, Dublin (and on microfilm via **Mormon Family History Centres**).

QUICK REFERENCE

See also main sources in Useful Addresses, page 306

GENEALOGICAL OFFICE
2–3 Kildare Street
Dublin 2
Eire
☎ 00 353 1 603 0200
www.nli.ie

away and renounce any future claim to the land. Their final agreement of the case, also termed *finalis concordia* or 'fine', was written out three times on the same sheet and then cut with a jagged line. The top two were given to the two parties and the bottom part kept by the court.

Fines also came to be used extensively to break old encumbrances on property such as entails, to enable women to sell land and to create family settlements. Besides the names of the purchaser and vendor they will mention, where relevant, wives, heirs or people to whom they were heirs. The part kept by the court is the 'feet of fines'.

COMMON RECOVERIES

This type of property transfer developed in the 15th century. The purchaser ('demandant') would, of course, pay the vendor for the land, but to gain legal recognition for the sale, the purchaser then took the vendor to court. The vendor would not appear but would deputise the task of proving his right to the property to a vouchee, who would leave and not turn up again, thus allowing the court to rule in favour of the purchaser.

If the intention was to break an entail, the purchaser would claim he had owned the property but had been thrown out by a non-existant

TYPES OF LAND HOLDING

'FEE' MEANS A TENANCY or possession of land and came in four types:
Fee simple was land that could be transferred freely.

Fee tail or 'entail' was a lease to one person and their descendants, so long as there were any, after which the estate reverted to their heir of the grantor. The holders of fee tail could sub-lease the land but such leases became automatically void when the holder died. There were many cases when holders wished to end the entail and dispose of the land, for example to free property of charges such as providing widows' dowries or, of course, to be able to sell it.

For life or lives was a lease that expired on the death of one or several people. While the lease was running, the holder of the fee simple owned what was termed the 'reversion', which meant the estate would pass to them or their heirs once the life or lives had expired. The lives were usually a close family unit, such as a man, his wife and son. Often, the third person in the lease might pay the landlord to extend the lease for further lives, thus ensuring continued tenure for the family. Needless to say, such leases provide highly reliable material linking different generations of the family tree. Generally found in the West Country.

Term of years was a lease for a set term of years.

TITLE DEEDS

⊡ Your first encounter with deeds may be in family papers. Many of the described types of deed were enrolled at the local Quarter Sessions (page 232), whose records are now in **county record offices**, or with **borough courts** in towns. Many deeds are at the **NA** in the Close Rolls, Patent Rolls, Exchequer and other courts, Treasury papers, Charter Rolls, the Exchequer series of Ancient Deeds and so on, to which many indexes and calendars have been compiled. See the *Guide to the Contents of the Public Record Office* (HMSO, Vols 1 (1963), 2 (1963) and 3 (1968)) for details.

⊡ Sale catalogues were produced especially in the 19th and 20th centuries when businesses, farms or bankrupts' estates were sold, and may be found in **county record offices**.

⊡ Returns of owners of land were compiled in 1873 for England, 1874 for Scotland and 1876 for Ireland: London was omitted. They record all landowners with more than an acre, in alphabetical order with home addresses, acreage and rateable value, but not precise location of the land. They were published by **HMSO** and can be studied in **local libraries**.

⊡ Inland Revenue valuations were compiled between 1910 and 1920 and are held at the **NA** in IR 58 (field books) and IR 121–35 (maps) with comparable records for Scotland at the **NAS**. They list surveys and valuations of most buildings with the names of owners and leaseholders. They seldom include subletters, and besides being incomplete in the first place they also suffered some damage in Second World War bombing, but are still worth examining if you are researching the history of an ancestral property.

⊡ As with manorial records (see page 118), the record office holding the deposit may not be in the same county as the properties in the deeds, so look in all the counties where the family had interests. They are sometimes poorly catalogued, but increasingly they can be accessed through record offices' personal name indexes, and thus through the Access to Archives website: **www.A2A.org.uk**.

⊡ Published deeds may be identified through E. L. C. Mullins's *Texts and Calendars: An Analytical Guide to Serial Publications* (RHS, 1958) and *Vol. II 1957–82* (RHS, 1983). Many are catalogued in the HMC's National Register of Archives database, **www.hmc.gov.uk/nra**. They are always worth seeking as they can provide fascinating detail of an ancestor's inheritance, purchase or sale of property, with details of what the property was like.

FEET OF FINES

⊡ These are at the **NA**, and many have been published by **county record societies** and **HMSO**.

COMMON RECOVERIES

⊡ These provide similar genealogical details to feet of fines and are at the **NA** in the Recovery Rolls, Plea Rolls and records of the Palatine courts.

QUICK REFERENCE

See also main sources in Useful Addresses, page 306

HER MAJESTY'S STATIONERY OFFICE (NOW THE STATIONERY OFFICE LTD)
St Crispins
Duke Street
Norwich
Norfolk NR3 1PD
☎ **01603 622211**
www.thestationeryoffice.com

person called Hugh Hunt. The tenant who occupied the entailed property would not contradict the purchaser's claim, enabling the court to subsequently grant possession of the property to the purchaser. Sometimes the tenant 'in tail' would then purchase the land back off the purchaser, which meant that the whole rigmarole had been solely for the tenant in tail to keep the land – but under different conditions than the entail.

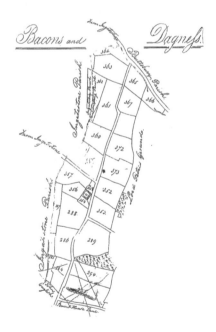

△ **A page from one of Lord Petre's account books, showing William Havers renting Bacons and Dagness Farm, Ingatestone, Essex from 1810 to 1812, including notes on what the land was used for. There is also a corresponding map and details of which fields Havers was renting.**

USES

These were a device to enable people to settle land on whom they wished, whereby they transferred the land to trustees who were to hold it but allow a third party to 'use', profit from and bequeath, it. The third party was often the original owner himself, who was now able to write a will leaving the use of the land to whomever he wanted. It was sometimes also used to avoid having to perform feudal service for the land, because neither the original holder nor the trustees were in full possession of the land. The state tried to prevent this practice with the Statute of Uses of 1535/6. However, this proved so unpopular that the state subsequently gave people the right to bequeath land to whomsoever they wished by the Statute of Wills of 1540. Uses remained, however, as trusts, whereby a landowner could ensure continuity of land ownership within the family (preventing profligate heirs from mortgaging or selling the land) by creating a settlement by will or deed specifying the descent of the land, usually to the landowner's wife, then their eldest son and his heirs or, failing any, the second son and his heirs, and so on. Such records of settlements can obviously provide a great deal of useful family history details.

BARGAIN AND SALE

Deeds of bargain and sale started to be made after the Statute of Uses of 1535/6, as secret transfers of land, or interest in land, from one person to another, in consideration for a sum of money. The sale created a use, which meant that the purchaser had the use of the land, but, because no 'enfeoffment' had taken place, the vendor still technically owned the land. The state responded in 1536 with the Statute of Enrolment, forcing bargain and sales to be enrolled at a court, so they were no longer secret.

LEASE AND RELEASE

This was the method that lawyers devised to get around the Statute of Enrolment, and it operated up to 1845. The vendor bargained and sold the six- or 12-month lease of a piece of land to the purchaser for a nominal rent. The purchaser thus acquired the use of the land, but as it was only by a lease, not a conveyance of freehold, it did not have to be enrolled. The following day, the vendor and anyone else with an interest in the property released their right to the reversion of the property once the lease had expired. As this was effectively the transfer of a right, not actually of a piece of land, it did not have to be enrolled either.

▷ Family photograph of my great-great-great-grandfather, William Joseph Havers (1813–77), who inherited his father's tenancy of Bacons, near Ingatestone, Essex.

MORTGAGES

A landowner in need of money might mortgage his land, remaining in occupation of it but granting a long lease of it to the lender of the money, who would gain possession of the land if the owner failed to pay the money back in full.

ESTATE RECORDS

Estate maps started to be made in the late 16th century, often showing and naming fields, woods and buildings with precise acreage and including names of neighbouring landowners.

They often accompanied rent rolls or rentals naming the tenants, and are especially useful when a series exists covering a specific period, allowing you to trace the succession of generations holding the same house or field. Irish and Scottish estate records are particularly useful when they pre-date surviving parish registers.

Most estate records remain in private muniment rooms or solicitors' offices, but there are plenty in national and county record offices, usually catalogued under the estate owners, be they private individuals, the church, corporations or the Crown. You can use directories (page 82) to find out who were the main landowers in your ancestral parish. Many are catalogued on the National Register of Archives, which can be viewed at **www.nra.nationalarchives.gov.uk/nra/**.

LAND REGISTRIES

Unlike such countries as America, Britain has never had a comprehensive system of recording who owns what land. Registration of all sales and leases of seven years or more became compulsory in the East Anglian Fens from 1663, and records are held at the Cambridge Record Office. From the 18th century, voluntary registration of title deeds became possible in Middlesex and Yorkshire. The Middlesex records comprise memorials (summaries of the original deeds), covering freehold and leases of 21 years or more and indexed annually by vendor or landlord. A national system of land registry was introduced in 1862, followed by the gradual introduction of compulsory registration of title deeds when property was bought and sold.

△ Elizabeth Anastasia (née Slaughter) (1808– 62), wife of William Joseph Havers, who was also Lord of the Manor of Shopland Hall, Essex.

LAND REGISTRIES

The Middlesex records are at the **London Metropolitan Archives** and cover the period 1709–1938.

The Deeds Registries for the Yorkshire Ridings, dating from 1704 (West), 1707 (East) and 1735 (North), up to 1970, are at the Northallerton, Beverley and Wakefield **county record offices** respectively.

HM Land Registry holds plans and associated records, which can be searched. Searches can be made for a property (you cannot search under owners' names) for a small cost by post with the relevant **district land registries**. If the property appears, you will learn the names of previous owners since the property was first registered, with notes of special rights or encumbrances, such as public footpaths or mortgages. However, some properties remain unregistered and many more have records dating back only a few decades, making these records moderately useful for house historians and of relatively little use for genealogists.

LAND DEEDS OUTSIDE ENGLAND & WALES

SCOTLAND

All land in Scotland was held from the Crown by grants known, north of the border, as 'feus', which could in turn be sublet by grant. Land could not be bequeathed by will as in England, but passed strictly to the next living heir who, in the case of those holding land from the Crown, had to prove their right at a Sheriff's inquest. The resulting decisions, or retours, recorded in Latin until 1847, survive from about 1530 and are at the **NAS**. These are indexed and abstracts of the records to 1699 are also in print.

The Scottish Land Registry is at the **Registers of Scotland Executive Agency**.

Scottish parish registers and testaments can often prove disappointing, so it is fortunate that land records are quite well preserved. The best guide to them is C. Sinclair's *Tracing your Scottish Ancestors: A Guide to Ancestry Research in the Scottish Record Office* (HMSO, 1997), which lists the sources available and accompanying abstracts and indexes.

Sale of land was conducted before witnesses in a public ceremony called a 'sasine', recorded in notaries' protocol books which can be found at the **NAS** and the **regional record offices**. Many have been published by record societies and are listed in D. and W. B. Stevenson's *Scottish Texts & Calendars, An Analytical Guide to Serial Publications* (Royal Historical Society, London, and Scottish Royal Historical Society, Edinburgh, 1987). They often name several members of the family and provide useful co-ordinates on the family in relation to its land holdings.

From the end of the 16th century until the 20th, when land registration gradually took over their role, sasines were also registered in 'General' or 'Particular' (i.e. local) registers, all of which are at the **NAS**, which can be searched in the original volumes or, from 1781, via indexed volumes of abstracts called 'abridgements'.

Deeds, for everything from land-transfer to marriage contracts, could be enrolled at any Scottish court, so unfortunately the variety of different courts sometimes makes searching complicated. From 1804, the power to do this was limited to the Royal Burgh, Sheriff and Sessions courts.

From 1854, land was valued annually and names of owners, tenants and occupiers paying £4 or more per annum were recorded. These records are at the **NAS**, as is a copy of the published *A Return of Owners of Land of One Acre and Upwards* (HMSO, 1972/3).

IRELAND

The **Deeds Registry** holds many deeds relating to marriages, businesses and mainly the transfer of land or tenancies of 21 years upwards from 1708, all of which are indexed by place and names of those disposing of (but not receiving) the land or tenancy. The surname and place-name indexes can also be seen on film at **Mormon Family History Centres**.

Irish estate records are of great importance because of the loss of so many other types in the 1922 bombing of the Four Courts. Many surviving estate records are at the **National Archives of Ireland** and **National Library of Ireland** and are listed in M. D. Falley's *Irish and Scots-Irish Ancestral Research, A Guide to the Genealogical Records, Methods and Sources in Ireland, Vols I and II* (GPC, 1989).

JERSEY

Jersey had a land registry from 1602, in which all transfers or mortgages of land were to be recorded, as were divisions of land between landowners' children, making for extremely interesting and useful genealogical records. Its records and indexes can be studied at **Mormon Family History Centres**.

THE ISLE OF MAN

Manx deeds up to 1910 are held at the **Manx Museum** and thereafter at the island's **General Registry**. Manx land records are described by J. Narasimham's *The Manx Family Tree, A Beginner's Guide to Records in the Isle of Man* (1994).

EXAMPLES OF LAND DEEDS IN OTHER COUNTRIES

Australian land was granted for free by the Crown to colonists until 1831, after which land was sold. Most records are in the relevant **state archive office** or **land title offices**.

Canadian land grants and transfers are generally recorded at land registry offices, often with microfilm copies at the **National Archives of Canada**.

New Zealand land records are at the **National Archives**, Wellington and local **land registries**. They record grants of land to very many of the original settlers, while the **deeds registries** and land registries record subsequent transfers from 1841 and 1870 respectively.

◁ Title deed

QUICK REFERENCE

See also main sources in Useful Addresses, page 306, and The Isle of Man, page 311

LONDON METROPOLITAN ARCHIVES
40 Northampton Road
London EC1R 0HB
☎ 020 7332 3820
www.cityoflondon.gov.uk

HM LAND REGISTRY
32 Lincoln's Inn Fields
London WC2A 3PH
☎ 020 7917 8888
www.landreg.gov.uk

REGISTERS OF SCOTLAND EXECUTIVE AGENCY
Erskine House
68 Queen Street
Edinburgh EH2 4NF
Scotland
☎ 0845 607 0161
www.ros.gov.uk

DEEDS REGISTRY
Kings Inn
Henrietta Street
Dublin 7
Eire
☎ 00 353 1 804 8412
www.landregistry.ie

NATIONAL LIBRARY OF IRELAND
Kildare Street
Dublin, Eire
☎ 00 353 1 603 0200
www.nli.ie

NATIONAL ARCHIVES OF CANADA
395 Wellington Street
Ottawa
Ontario K1A ON3
www.archives.ca

NATIONAL ARCHIVES OF NEW ZEALAND
10 Mulgrave Street
Thorndon
Wellington

LIFETIMES: GRAHAM EVELYN

ONE OF MY FAVOURITE *Extraordinary Ancestors* cases concerned the ancestry of Graham Evelyn, a young Bristolian descended from a mixed-race Jamaican family called Drummond.

The *Scots Magazine* for October 1754 contains a record of his ancestor: 'June 20, At Savannah la Mer, Jamaica, Dr John Drummond. He was killed in a duel, by one Donaldson, an Irishman.' It also records under deaths in 1804, 'April 14. In Westmorland, Jamaica, Dr John Drummond, who had practised 40 years in that parish with great reputation.' The second Dr John, who was son of the first, appears very briefly in the records of Edinburgh University, having come over from Jamaica for a year to attend a handful of lectures, after which he felt himself qualified to become a doctor back home. He appears in a slave owner's published diary, ministering to slaves, particularly with his home-made smallpox vaccine: 'inoculated 17 of my Negroes, on each arm between the elbow and shoulder; just raised the skin with a lancet, dipped in matter and let it dry' – a method that was apparently very successful.

JOHN DRUMMOND'S WILL

A copy of the second Dr John's will has survived in Edinburgh University library. In it he describes himself as John Drummond 'practitioner of physic and surgery, Westmorland, Jamaica', and leaves 'a free negro woman Mary Drummond [born] of slaves, an annuity of £50 current money', and also his furniture, horses and cows and the right to live at Drummond Lodge. He then left bequests to Thomas Drummond, whom he acknowledged as his son by Mary. He also left legacies to Peggy Bartlett, a free quadroon (i.e. a quarter black), and a mulatto slave, Hannah Browning, and provided for the manumission (freedom) of two other children he had had by slaves, who were currently Mary's property.

The freeing of Thomas, 'a mulatto', son of John, had, in fact, required a special Act in the Jamaican House of Assembly in 1793. In the 1840 *Jamaica Almanac* Thomas is recorded as holding a 1200-acre plantation in Westmoreland.

The returns of slaves for Westmoreland, made in 1817 to record which slaves were there and so prevent the acquisition of new ones by purchase from outside the island, show what happened next. The son Thomas Drummond, 'of colour', owned 86 slaves, while his mother Mary had 28. There was also William Drummond, also 'of colour' and probably another son of Dr John, with two slaves. Finally there was Bazillia or 'Bazzy' Drummond, a 'free black', who had two slaves in her capacity as guardian for John and Elizabeth Drummond.

This combination of records shows a clear line coming down from white Scotsmen to mixed-race Jamaicans.

◁ Illustration of a Slave Camp (French School, 18th century).

SLAVES

▣ Many records relating to British people in the Caribbean – and including somewhat incidental information about their slaves – are in Britain. Holdings at the **NA** are described in G. Grannum's *Tracing your West Indian Ancestors: Sources at the PRO* (PRO Publications, 1995). Published sources include the *Calendar of State Papers Colonial: America and West Indies 1574–1739* (HMSO).

▣ The **SoG**'s Smith collection of manuscript genealogies of British families in the Caribbean is worth consulting, and there are published works for many islands. The upper- and middle-class white families of Antigua, for example, are minutely recorded in V. L. Oliver's *The History of Antigua* (Mitchell and Hughes, 1899).

▣ There were no records of lists of slaves transported to the Caribbean until the trade was abolished, and only a few after that date when ships carrying slaves illegally were captured. There are plenty of records of the Mixed Commission Courts at the **NA**, particularly that in Sierra Leone (FO 313), concerning the capture of slave ships, but the Africans usually only appear as numbers, not names. There are some records of petitions and passenger lists for freed black people travelling from Sierra Leone to Jamaica in the 1840s in CO 267.

▣ Besides the sources (civil registration, census, parish registers and so on) listed in this book, slave ancestry can also sometimes be studied through slave registers 1812–34 in class T 71 in the **NA**. These recorded the slaves on each plantation (arranged alphabetically) to prevent the illegal import of more Africans. They name the slaves (though often only by a single name), with details of colour (i.e. black, mulatto, etc.) and their 'increase' (birth) and 'decrease' (death). However, after first registration in 1812, many islands just give numbers, not names. Others, though, retained the initial high level of detail, even giving mothers' names in some cases. Those for St Lucia are arranged by family with siblings and cousins, though fathers are rarely recorded.

▣ The records of the Slave Compensation Commission at the **NA** in class T 71 give statistical details of slaves to be freed when slavery was abolished in 1833, but little about the people themselves is recorded. Among other sources for slave ancestry are newspapers, which include rewards offered for slaves who had escaped.

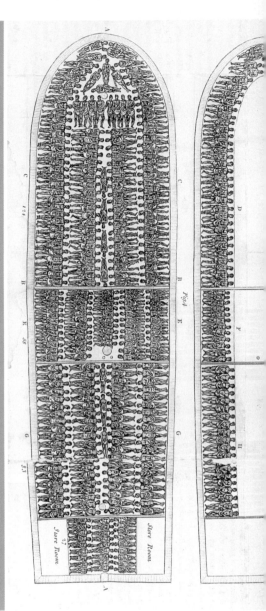

△ Engraving of a slave ship (American school, 18th century), showing just how closely packed was its unfortunate human cargo.

Most black Jamaicans therefore can trace their lines of ancestry back to Arawak Indians, African slaves, maybe some East Indians and Chinese, and very often to white slave owners. Indeed, because many slave owners had aristocratic connections, many modern Jamaicans are probably more closely related to British nobility than the majority of white Britons. One mixed race Jamaican immigrant to Oldham who I researched turned out to be a direct cousin of the Queen herself.

WHERE TO SEARCH

CHAPTER SIXTEEN
MAPS & LOCAL HISTORIES

When you research your family tree, you will discover not just who your ancestors were, but also where they lived. Places affected every aspect of our ancestors' lives, dictating what sort of jobs they did, how they fared and whom they met and married.

ORDNANCE SURVEY MAPS

THE FIRST SURVEYS started in 1784 in order to provide the army with effective maps to use in case of French invasion. The first maps were produced between 1817 and 1839, and included contour lines from 1847. The maps were reprinted up to 1870, with railways overlaid. Thus, the maps show things that may never have been exactly so, such as a village as it was in 1790 with a railway built in 1850 running past it. A second survey was started in 1840, with subsequent editions updated in the 20th century.

The more you find out about where your ancestors lived, the more fulfilling your research will be, and the easier it will become to work out the answer to that all-important question – 'Where did they come from?'

MAPS

The function of maps in genealogy is two-fold. Most records are arranged geographically, so it is important to know where your ancestors lived and what villages and towns were nearby. They are also a fabulous way of bringing your family history to life, helping you to get a feel for what the places where your ancestors lived were like at the time.

By examining a series of historical maps of the county in which your ancestors lived, you can trace forward and see how the towns grew, roads, canals, railways and bridges were built, estates were enclosed and forests diminished with the progress of the Industrial Revolution.

County maps, so familiar from the walls of many a pub and hotel, can date from the 16th century, especially those made by Christopher Saxton in the 1570s to benefit Lord Burghley's intelligence service.

Many maps were produced from the 17th century to show proposed routes of railways, turnpike roads or canals. Some of these show routes that were never built, and other maps can be misleading too: Burdell's map of Cheshire from the 1770s shows woods and roads accurately but, as far as can be told, the salt mines depicted were simply strewn about for general effect.

◁ Old Ordnance Survey map from 1913 of Camberwell and Stockwell in London.

△ The county of Norfolk, engraved by Jodocus Hondius (1563–1612).

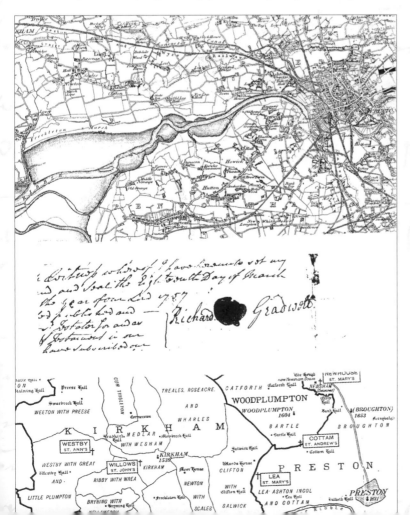

LIFETIMES: JAMES SIMPSON DINNIE

A PERSONAL FAVOURITE topographical dictionary entry is the one I found in Lewis's *Topographical Dictionary of Scotland* (see page 163) when I was researching the Dinnie family for the pilot of *Antiques Ghostshow*.

James Simpson Dinnie's birth was located at Ayr in 1892, with parents Agnes Smith Dinnie, née Wilson, and James Simpson Dinnie, a warder. In the 1891 census, the then unmarried James was found listed as a 22-year-old asylum attendant, born in Glenbervie, Kinkardineshire and indeed there he was in the 1881 census of Glenbervie, working as a 12-year-old farm servant. Lewis's dictionary devotes half a page to the parish, telling me that Glenbervie contained '1296 inhabitants, of whom 397 are in the village of Drumlithie'. It then went on to say: 'This parish, which obviously derives its name from the situation of its church in a small glen on the north-eastern bank of the river Bervie, is totally unconnected with any event of historical importance.' No wonder James went elsewhere to establish a new life for himself!

◁ Two maps of Preston, Lancashire, illustrate the different landscapes in which Catholic yeoman Richard Gradwell lived. One is physical and the other shows the location of Catholic chapels where he and his extended family could worship.

MAPS

⊡ Many 17th-century maps are in the **House of Lords Record Office**, while each **county record office** will hold collections relevant to their area.

⊡ The county maps from J. Bell's *A New and Comprehensive Gazeteer of England and Wales*, dated 1834, are reproduced in the *Phillimore Atlas and Index* (Phillimore, 2003) along with the maps showing the borders of parishes and ecclesiastical jurisdictions. They are tremendously useful, but they carry with them the danger of creating the mind-set that counties existed as self-contained islands. When searching for ancestors in parish registers, don't just blindly search every register for the county where the family ended up living, especially if they lived near the border of another county. They were as likely to have come across a nearby county border as they were to have come from the farthest reaches of the county they ended up in.

⊡ The original Ordnance Survey maps for the British Isles are fascinating to examine at local **libraries**, **museums** or **county record offices**. Full sets are held at the **British Library**, **IHGS** and so on, while replica copies are sold by David & Charles. The Ordnance Survey's excellent **www.getamap.ordnancesurvey.co.uk** includes the option 'search for', allowing you to type in the name of the place you want. You can see the relevant modern map on-screen, zoom in and out of it, and also compare it with the 1878 version.

⊡ **www.multimap.com** is another good map website, including travel information.

⊡ On a more local level, libraries and **county record offices** hold collections of town plans, sometimes dating back to the Tudor period, and Ordnance Survey town maps, both of which can be essential when seeking ancestors in census returns or understanding which church or chapel they were most likely to have attended.

⊡ There are 18th- and 19th-century fire insurance plans, covering many towns, held at the **British Library** and **Guildhall Library**. These include details of the materials used for the house, number of storeys and sometimes even names of the householders. Sun Insurance Company records 1816–24 are indexed on **www.A2A.org.uk** (the original records are at the Guildhall Library).

⊡ Parochial assessment maps at the **NA** date from the 18th and 19th centuries, and many were made following the Parochial Assessments Act of 1836, to enable the accurate levying of rates.

⊡ Old large-scale maps often depicted the houses standing in streets. I remember researching a family in 16th-century London and finding their very house, next to the old Bedlam Hospital in Aldgate, depicted in the Agas map, copies of which are in **Guildhall Library** and the **NA** and published in A. Prockter and R. Taylor's *The A–Z of Elizabethan London* (Harry Margary in association with the Guildhall Library, 1979)). Don't expect these drawings to be accurate, however.

⊡ For the county parishes there are tithe apportionment maps. These covered roughly three-quarters of the English and Welsh parishes, and were made between 1838 and 1854. Their purpose was to regularise the payment of tithes, and they show and number each field and building. The numbers refer to corresponding tithe schedule books, which describe the land and its rentable value and supply names of owners and occupiers – providing you with a fine written and graphic description of where your ancestors were living. Copies are at **county record offices** and also at the **NA** in classes IR 29 (schedules) and IR 30 (maps).

⊡ Enclosure maps were produced when landowners wished to do away with the medieval open field system with its associated smallholdings and commons, and reallocate the land as hedged fields, often making space too for elegant deer parks or landscaped gardens. Dating from the 17th century onwards, the maps and associated enclosure awards, detailing which landowners were allocated what, can be found at **county record offices** and the NA, while those carried out by Act of Parliament are at the **House of Lords Record Office**.

QUICK REFERENCE

See also main sources in Useful Addresses, page 306

HOUSE OF LORDS RECORD OFFICE
Palace of Westminster
London SW1A 0PW
☎ 020 7219 3074
www.parliament.uk

BOOKS

There are usually several antiquarian county histories for each county, many of which are beautifully illustrated with prints, especially of churches and mansions. G. Ormerod's *The History of the County Palatine of Chester* (George Routledge & Sons, 1882), for example, contains so many prints of old Chester that it is not difficult to imagine walking round the city in the 17th or 18th centuries. Much emphasis is given to landowning families, and very detailed and usually excellently researched pedigrees are a common feature, but they do not by any means exclude normal inhabitants. One of their virtues is that the authors had intimate knowledge of the areas they were writing about and had access to many records that may now have been lost.

ONLINE GAZETEERS

THERE ARE SEVERAL online gazetteers for locating places:
- www.ordnancesurvey.co.uk/oswebsite/freefun/didyouknow
- www.gazeteer.co.uk
- www.digitaldocuments.co.uk/archi/placenames.htm

Also useful are:
- http://tiger.iso.port.ac.uk:7778/pls/nfp/prog.core.home. This site tells you the former poor unions and registration districts for specific places and includes *Bartholemew's Gazeteer of the British Isles* (1887).
- www.genuki.org.uk/big/parloc/search.html locates all churches within a given radius of a given parish.

WHERE TO SEARCH

BOOKS

- Among the topographical dictionaries that are so useful for familyhistory purposes is S. Lewis's *A Topographical Dictionary of England ... and the Islands of Guernsey, Jersey and Man* (S. Lewis & Co., 1831), with similarly titled volumes for Wales (1838), Scotland (1847) and Ireland (1837). They provide excellent snapshot descriptions of the parishes, including details of institutions, churches, agriculture and historical events.

- Many local histories have been published over the last century, and many are still being written. Most are well illustrated with old photographs, so besides finding surprising references to your family, you may even see pictures of them. Wherever your ancestors came from, it is worth studying these books, which can be found through local **libraries** and **museums**, **county record offices** and (for Britain) the British Library's online catalogue: www.blpc.bl.uk.

- The *Victoria History of the Counties of England*, normally called *Victoria County Histories*, are a series of books still being written, with over 200 volumes already in print, detailing the general history and geography of the English counties, followed by histories of the individual parishes, with particular attention to the manorial histories. They are excellent for identifying old records relevant to each parish (which may in turn mention your forebears) and for providing a solid background to the lives of your family, especially in places that have been urbanised or have changed a great deal in other respects.

- Much local printed material can also be identified through Stuart Raymond's county bibliographies (see page 34).

CHAPTER SEVENTEEN
RECORDS OF ELECTIONS

Records of who voted for what, or who was entitled to vote where, can be interesting in their own right, but their main use is in pinning people down to particular places and years, either to gain further genealogical co-ordinates on where they may have originated or to trace long-lost friends or relatives.

ELECTORAL REGISTERS

Electoral registers are of prime importance as they list all those entitled to vote, and have been kept annually since 1832, with the exception of 1916–17 and 1940–44. They were originally arranged alphabetically, changing gradually in the 19th century to a street-by-street arrangement within electoral wards. Bear in mind that they were usually printed about half a year after the information had been collected, so may include people who had died by the date of publication.

These records can be used to pinpoint roughly when families appeared and disappeared from places (and, later, from specific addresses) and they sometimes tell you when events took place within families. When searching the history of a house in Fulham, for example, I found William and Jane Porter appearing under the address in question in 1923. In 1927 a Mabel Porter appears, joined by Olive Porter in 1929 and finally Frederick William Porter in 1930 – in other words, children appearing as they attained their 21st birthdays. This theory was borne out when Olive was found marrying in 1937, aged 30, that is, born about 1907 (she was in fact 'of age' in 1928 but clearly only joined the electoral register the year after).

PARLIAMENTARY ELECTIONS

Originally, only men aged over 20 could vote. Those who owned a freehold worth 40 shillings or more could vote, unless they lived in towns and cities, where qualifications varied: in some cases, only freemen could vote, while in others all householders, known as 'potwallopers', could have their say.

➤ **From 1832,** all men owning land worth £10 or over, and townsmen leasing land worth £10 or over, could vote.

➤ **In 1867** the countryside qualification value was dropped to £5 and the franchise also extended to those paying £50 or more in rent, while in the towns all male householders were allowed to vote.

POLL BOOKS

THESE ARE LISTS of those who had voted in elections, stating parish of residence and for whom they cast their vote. Most poll books date from after 1696, but a few pre-date 1711, the year they started being deposited with Clerks of the Peace. They ceased with the introduction of secret ballots in 1872.

➤**In 1884** this latter qualification was extended to the countryside. Votes for all men over 20 and female householders over 30 came in 1918, with the vote extended to all women aged over 20 in 1928.

➤**Up to 1970** those over 20 were listed, and in the year someone reached the age of 21 the letter 'Y' may appear.

➤**From 1971,** everyone over 17 appears.

LOCAL ELECTIONS

From 1835, voting in local elections was generally open to more than were eligible to vote in Parliamentary elections. All men who paid poor rates could vote from 1835, and women who paid the same rate and owned property of the requisite value could vote from 1869, making local poll books (see box, opposite) of more genealogical use than those for national elections.

On the 7th May you will have the opportunity to elect a Conservative Councillor who is pledged to serve the interests of our local Community.

Jerome Rietchel

△My grandfather's election leaflet, printed a year before his death in 1987.

WHERE TO SEARCH

ELECTORAL RECORDS

⊟ Poll books. are held locally at **libraries**, **county record offices**, the **SoG**, **British Library** and **Institute of Historical Research**.

⊟ Electoral registers are held locally by the **district council office** with previous years at the local **library**. They can also be examined nationally: those for the current year are at the **Office for National Statistics**. The previous year is kept at the **FRC** and the earlier ones are at the **British Library**. The letter 'S' against a name indicates someone serving in the armed forces.

⊟ A guide to electoral registers and poll books is J. Gibson and C. Rogers' *Electoral Registers since 1832 and Burgess Rolls* (FFHS, 1990), although this omits many Scottish ones, which you can find listed in R. H. A. Cheffins' *Parliamentary Constituencies and their Registers since 1832* (British Library, 1998), and there is also a large collection at the **British Library.**

SCOTLAND

⊟ The franchise here was extremely restricted – only 2662 men could vote in Parliamentary elections in 1788. The number began to grow rapidly from 1832, and poll books, detailed in Gibson and Roger's book (above), are mainly at the **NAS** and the **National Library of Scotland.**

IRELAND

⊟ Most Irish poll books for before 1922 were destroyed in the bombing of the Four Courts. Those that survive are included in J. G. Ryan's *Irish Records – Sources for Family and Local History* (Ancestry, 1997).

QUICK REFERENCE

See also main sources in Useful Addresses, page 306

INSTITUTE OF HISTORICAL RESEARCH
Senate House
University of London
Malet Street
London WC1E 7HU
☎ 020 7862 8740
www.ihrinfo.ac.uk

OFFICE FOR NATIONAL STATISTICS
Customer Contact Centre
Room 1.015
Office for National Statistics
Cardiff Road
Newport NP10 8XG
Wales
☎ 0845 601 3034

NATIONAL LIBRARY OF SCOTLAND
George IV Bridge
Edinburgh EH1 1EW
Scotland
☎ 0131 466 2812
www.nls.uk

CHAPTER EIGHTEEN
THE PARISH CHEST

Besides registers, the parishes generated a great deal of other records. Because they were kept with the parish registers in the iron-bound parish chest, these records are often called 'parish chest' material. Survival of records varies greatly from parish to parish.

THE RECORDS

The type of record you might expect to find in a parish chest varies enormously. Outlined here are the main records, starting with vestry minutes and moving on to removal orders and information about parish apprentices, each of which may add colour to your family tree.

VESTRY MINUTES

From the 14th century until they were superseded in 1834 by the Poor Law Guardians and then replaced by parish councils in 1894, parishes were administered by the vestry, a council usually chaired by the resident clergyman. Disputes within the vestry were often resolved by the Justices of the Peace, whose records usually contain much information about parish life.

Vestry minutes can tell you about the administration and maintenance of the parish schools and almshouses, the church, water supply and the care (or otherwise) of the poor.

PARISH RATES

During the 16th and 17th centuries, vestries took over many of the roles previously exercised by manorial courts, and were granted the right to raise rates for looking after bridges (1531), building prisons (1532), caring for the poor (1598) and maintaining roads (1654). These were generally combined with the 'poor rate' from the 18th century. The rate books provide an annual 'census' of heads of household who were not exempt by being paupers, and can be used to determine the spans of their adult lives and observe families' arrivals in and departures from the parish.

SETTLEMENT RECORDS

Probably the most important parish chest material for genealogists are those that record the comings and goings of the poor. From 1601,

LONDON PATENT ATTORNEY Simon Mountenay wanted to trace his ancestry and learn whether he was entitled to use the ancient coat of arms of the de Mounteneys. Many people think there is simply a coat of arms for each family name, but Simon was aware that a coat of arms is granted to a specific individual, and only male-line descendants of the original grantee are entitled, subject to the College of Arms' permission, to use the arms.

In contrast to his own prosperity, Simon's 19th-century ancestors were not at all well-to-do and included some general labourers. I traced the line back to Thomas Mounteney of Southwell, Nottinghamshire, who was baptised in the neighbouring parish of Bleasby in 1785, son of Benjamin and Anne Mounteney. Benjamin and Anne had married there in 1781, but his origins simply could not be found in the registers of Bleasby, or any of the nearby parishes.

The Bleasby parish chest, however, came up trumps. A settlement certificate had survived, dated 24 November 1783, concerning Benjamin Mountney, a tailor, and his wife, Anne, and stating that Benjamin had the right of settlement in Keyworth, Nottinghamshire. He was allowed to stay, the Bleasby vestry having reassured itself that, should Benjamin or his family need financial assistance in the future, it was the Keyworth vestry that would have to come up with the cash.

DELVING BACK YET FURTHER

Keyworth is 14 miles from Bleasby and it would have been impossible to prove his origins there, because his baptism in fact took place close by in Quorndon, over the country border in Leicestershire. He was baptised in 1751, the son of an earlier Benjamin, who was baptised there in 1711, son of an earlier Benjamin still. This earliest Benjamin was not baptised in Quorndon, but again settlement records came to our aid – Benjamin and his wife and family had handed in a settlement certificate stating their legal place of settlement was Atherstone in Warwickshire.

Atherstone was a hamlet in the parish of Mancetter, whose registers show Benjamin's baptism on 10 September 1680, the fifth son of Thomas Mounteney. And after several generations of poor weavers and 'ag. labs' (agricultural labourers) moving from parish to parish, presumably looking for work, we had a great surprise, because Thomas appears in John Nichols' *History and Antiquities of Leicestershire* (vol. 4, pt 2, p. 848) as the third son of George Mountney Esquire, of Newbold Verdon, Leicestershire, whose father's coat of arms was recorded when the Heralds visited Leicestershire in 1619. Benjamin may have been a landed gentleman's grandson, but he was the fifth son of the third son, and clearly there had not been enough money to go around.

Simon discovered his right to bear the ancient arms of de Mountenay, and I gained a splendid example of how some families of labourers really do have blue blood in their veins after all.

While the elderly, sick or widows with young children could still receive outdoor relief, the choice for the able-bodied poor in need of assistance was stark: enter the workhouse, or starve. The Act centralised the system, moving it a step closer to direct state intervention in the lives of individuals and the transfer of responsibility for the poor from the gentry to the government. The introduction of old age pensions in 1908 and unemployment benefits in 1911 was effectively a return to 'outdoor relief', but the workhouses remained until the Poor Law was abolished in 1948. Many ex-workhouses still function as NHS hospitals to this day.

▽ **Inside a workhouse:** *The Westminster School of Industry, Old Pye Street*, **printed by Leighton Brothers (19th century).**

WORKHOUSES

WHERE TO SEARCH

Many of our ancestors spent time in workhouses other than when they were born, married or died and consequently you may not find out about this aspect of their lives unless you find them there in an indexed census, such as those for 1901 or 1881 (see pages 66–72), or specifically look for them. Directories will tell you which Poor Law Union covered their parish of residence.

The post-1834 records of the board of guardians will be at the relevant **county record office**. Of most use are the admission and discharge registers, which will tell you:
- Name
- Age
- Occupation
- Marital status
- Parish of settlement
- Denomination
- Sometimes a physical description
- Why the person needed help

Indoor relief lists were made twice a year and can be much easier to search. There were also:
- Registers of births, baptisms, deaths and burials of inmates, which contain many events omitted from General Registration.
- Records of those receiving outdoor relief.
- Binding of apprentices.
- Registers of offences and punishment of inmates and payments to prevent poor families from costing any further expense by assisting them to emigrate!

Records of workhouse staff are in class MH 9 at the NA. Much correspondence between the guardians and commissioners concerning inmates is in NA class MH 15, but there are no indexes to names or places.

Workhouse records also include records of smallpox vaccination. This was compulsory from 1853 until 1948, and workhouses that administered the system kept registers from 1862, noting children's names, ages and birthplaces. Most records are in the relevant **county record office**. A detailed guide to the whereabouts of all post-1834 records is provided by J. Gibson, C. Rogers and C. Webb's *Poor Law Union Records* (FFHS, 1993/97). A guide to workhouse records is at **www.workhouses.org.uk**.

IRELAND

Irish workhouse records survive (from 1838) in great quantities and are particularly useful in view of the relative lack of parochial records. The records are at **local** and **national archives** and can best be traced through J. G. Ryan's *Irish Records – Sources for Family and Local History* (Ancestry, 1997).

△ *Applicants for Admission to a Casual Ward* by Luke Fildes (1874). How little things have changed!

QUICK REFERENCE

See main sources in Useful Addresses, page 306

SELECTED OCCUPATIONS

Almost all occupations operated records, now covered by indexes, books and so on. Here are some examples.

ACTORS

Actors are problematical as there were very few formal records, especially before the foundation of Equity in 1930. However, the **Theatre Museum** has a vast collection of playbills and programmes. For actors since 1912 you can consult *Who's Who in the Theatre*, which includes some dates of birth and parents' names (and, of course, the parents could themselves have been on the stage).

There were a number of 19th-century journals, starting with *The Era* (founded in 1838), which can also be searched at the **Theatre Museum**.

ARCHITECTS

There are several biographical dictionaries of architects, especially H. A. Colvin's *A Biographical Dictionary of British Architects 1600–1840* (Yale University Press, 1995) and A. Felstead, J. Franklin and L. Pinfield's *Dictionary of British Architects 1834–1900* (Mansel Publishing, 1993).

ARTISTS AND SCULPTORS

There are many biographical dictionaries of artists, mainly focusing on what they exhibited rather than providing much of genealogical use, save (often) places of residence and a date of death, which can lead you to a will. **Westminster Central Reference Library** is one of the best places to research an artist's career. See also my article 'Artists' in *Family History Monthly*, April 2003, no. 91.

CIVIL SERVANTS

Most documentation for civil servants is at the **NA**, in the records of their department. Pension records 1855–1924 are in class PMG 28 and examination records 1876–1962 are in CSC 10. Prior to the 19th century, you may find civil servants mentioned in the records of government such as the State Papers Domestic. Many civil service appointments were announced in the *London Gazette* (see page 144) and appear in the *Civil Service Year Book*, the Foreign Office list and almanacs such as the *Royal Kalendar*.

Records of British civil servants in India to 1947 are at the **India Office Library** as are the records of the East India College, where they were trained. The records include many petitions for employment, accompanied by baptism or birth certificates, pension records, and published lists of civil servants for each of the Indian presidencies.

CLERGYMEN

The following remarks concern clergymen in the Churches of England, Wales, Ireland or the Episcopal Church of Scotland. For others, see page 256.

Until the establishment of theological colleges in the mid-19th century, it was highly unusual for anyone to become a clergyman without having a university degree, so details of most clergymen, including fathers' names, can usually be found in the printed lists of university students (see page 239). Most English and Welsh clergy were therefore graduates of either Oxford or Cambridge, although some had, of course, come from universities further afield.

△ **Rev. Perry Nursey (1799–1867), an alumnus of Sidney College, Cambridge (1819–23) who became an Anglican clergyman.**

Equally, until 1858, the wills of many clergymen were proved at the Prerogative Court of Canterbury (see page 129).

Further information can be found in the *Clerical Guide*, published from 1817, the Clergy List (from 1841) and Crockford's *Clerical Directory* (OUP, since 1858), which will tell you the clergyman's position and parish, previous appointments and details of where he was educated. To supplement this there is J. Foster's *Index Ecclesiasticus* (Parker & Co, 1840 (sic)), covering many clergymen, 1800–40.

Potted biographies of higher-ranking clergy from 1066 to 1854, arranged by diocese, are listed in T.

D. Hardy's *Fasti Ecclesia Anglicanae, or A Calendar of the Principal Ecclesiastical Dignitaries in England & Wales ... From the Earliest Time to the Year 1715* (OUP, 1854), which has since been expanded in a series of volumes, *John Le Neve Fasti Ecclesia Anglicanae* (Institute of Historical Research); online at **www.british-history.ac.uk**.

🖶 The Fawcett card index to many clergymen is at the **SoG**.

🖶 Information about a clergyman's daily work can be found by studying the records of the parish or parishes where he worked. Bear in mind that the writing in the register could be that of the parish clerk.

🖶 In Scotland, details of established church clergymen up to 1638 are in D. E. R. Watt's *Fasti Ecclesiae Scoticanae Medii Aevi ad Annum 1638* (St Andrews & Scottish Record Society, 1969) and from the Reformation onwards in the *Fasti Ecclesiae Scoticanae* series (Oliver & Boyd).

🖶 In Ireland, Church of Ireland clergy are listed in the Almanack and Registry (from 1836), and the Irish Church Directory (from 1862). Irish Catholic priests can be traced through the **Catholic Directory** (from 1837). You can look, too, in bishops' transcripts (see page 114).

COASTGUARDS, CUSTOMS OFFICERS AND EXCISEMEN

🖶 Coastguards' records are in **NA** class ADM, dating from 1822, and described in information leaflet 8. **Mrs E. R. Stage** has an index to over 70,000 coastguards.

🖶 Customs officers were supposed to collect import duties and catch smugglers, while excisemen made

sure duty was paid where due on domestic goods. Until their union in 1909, they were governed by two separate boards. The records are in **NA** class CUST, detailed in leaflet 106 and described in J. Cox and T. Padfield's *Tracing your Ancestors at the PRO* (PRO Publications, 1999).

🖶 **Mrs J. Underwood** has an index to customs officers' superannuation allowances 1831–81. Postings of excisemen start to be recorded from 1695: the entry papers in CUST 116 cover the period 1820–70 and give age, place of birth, marital status and character.

🖶 Scotland had separate customs and excise boards from 1707 to 1829, whose records – including those of the most famous Scottish exciseman of all, Robert Burns – are at the **NAS**.

🖶 Irish customs officers' records from the 17th century to 1922 are at the **NA** in classes CUST 20 and 39.

FIREMEN
🖶 A good source of information is the **London Fire Brigade Museum**.

GYPSIES
🖶 Those with gypsy ancestry should also consult S. Floate's *My Ancestors were Gypsies* (SoG, 1999) and join the Romany and Traveller FHS, whose library is at **Reading University**.

INVENTORS
🖶 Did your ancestor patent an invention? Have a look in B. Woodcroft's *Alphabetical Index of Patentees of Inventions 1617–1852* (Adams & Mackay, 1969). Fuller details, and also details of patents after 1852, are in the **British Library**, printed in annual volumes, though many of these are now indexed on CD-Rom.

QUICK REFERENCE

See also main sources in Useful Addresses, page 306

THEATRE MUSEUM
1E Tavistock Street
London WC2E 7PR
☎ 020 7943 4700
www.theatremuseum.org

WESTMINSTER CENTRAL REFERENCE LIBRARY
35 St Martin's Street
London WC2H 7HP
☎ 020 7641 4636
www.westminster.gov.uk/libraries/westref

INDIA OFFICE LIBRARY
British Library
96 Euston Road
London NW1 2DB
☎ 020 7412 7513
www.bl.uk/collections/orientalandindian.html

MRS E. R. STAGE
150 Fulwell Park Avenue
Twickenham
Middlesex TW2 5HB

MRS J. UNDERWOOD
174A Wendover Road
Weston Turville
Buckinghamshire HP22 5TG

LONDON FIRE BRIGADE MUSEUM
Winchester House
94A Southwark Bridge Road
London SE9 OEG
☎ 020 7587 2894
www.london-fire.gov.uk

READING UNIVERSITY
Whiteknights
PO Box 217
Reading
Berkshire RG6 6AH
☎ 0118 378 8628 (research enquiries)
www.rdg.ac.uk

LAWYERS

The best place to start seeking a lawyer is the Law Lists, which have been published annually since 1775 and can be examined at specialist law or genealogical libraries. The **Law Society Library** holds many useful records and, for a fee, can help you trace the career of a solicitor or attorney ancestor. **Brian Brooks** keeps an index of solicitors, attorneys, notaries public, proctors and conveyancers.

Solicitors specialised in civil cases. From 1728, solicitors had to qualify by becoming articled clerks. They can be traced through the indexed registers of due execution of clerkship (i.e. successful completion of training) in **NA** class KB 170, which cover 1749–1877 (see leaflet 112). These often state fathers' names. Most articled clerks between 1728 and 1774 appear in the **SoG's** Apprentices index (1710–74).

Lawyers in church courts and the Court of Admiralty were either proctors (similar to barristers) or advocates (solicitors). Records of admissions and appointments 1727–1841 are in **NA** class HCA 30. An index to 658 proctors is kept by **John Titford**. Advocates were also doctors of law and belonged to the College of Advocates in Doctors' Commons, whose records are at **Lambeth Palace Library**.

Barristers were lawyers called to practise at the bar through one of the Inns of Court. Many of the admission registers have been printed and will provide a date of admission and name and residence of the father. The four surviving inns – Lincoln's Inn, Gray's Inn, Middle Temple and Inner Temple – have excellent archives for further

△ *The Doctor* by Arthur Miles (c.1860).

research, not least, in some cases, registers of baptisms, marriages and burials of lawyers and their families in their own chapels. The exact location of records is given in D. S. Bland's *A Bibliography of the Inns of Court and Chancery* (Selden Society, 1965).

Some barristers became judges. They are easily traced through E. Foss's *A Biographical Dictionary of the Judges of England, 1066–1870* (John Murray, 1870).

Justices of the Peace, who presided at the Quarter Sessions (see page 232) were seldom trained lawyers. Records of their appointments are indexed in **NA** class C 202 and announcements of their appointment are also in the *London Gazette* (see page 144).

Scottish solicitors were called writers and can be traced through the Scottish Law List (Law Society of Scotland, from 1848). Scottish barristers were called advocates and their details, including in many cases birth, marriage and death details, are in F. J. Grant's *The Faculty of Advocates in Scotland,*

1532–1943, with Genealogical Notes (Scottish Record Society, 1944).

MEDICS

From 1511 until 1775, licences to practise medicine can be found in the records of the bishop's court that issued them, but will tell you little more than names and home parishes. From 1845 medics appeared in the *Medical Directory* and from 1859 in the *Medical Register* – there are good sets at the **SoG**, giving the date the medics qualified and from which institution, which should itself hold further records.

Excellent secondary sources for many doctors, dentists and midwives is P. J. and R. V. Wallis's *Eighteenth-century Medics (Subscriptions, Licences, Apprenticeships)* (Project for Historical Geography Research Series, 1994) and C. H. Talbot and E. A. Hammond's *The Medical Practitioners in Medieval England; A Biographical Register* (Wellcome Historical Medical Library, 1965).

Apothecaries made medicines and those in London were often members of the Grocers' Company. After 1815,

LIFETIMES: TRACED THROUGH A LICENCE

THOMAS ROBINSON appears in White's Suffolk directory in 1844, listed as a surgeon in Haverhill. The 1855 directory does not list him, however, and indeed the Bury and Norwich Post (1 February 1854) confirms that 'On the 24th Inst, aged 49 years, Mr Thos. Robinson, for many years surgeon at Haverhill', died. Unfortunately, he was not in Haverhill for the 1851 census, so his origins proved something of a mystery, until his apothecary's licence was discovered at the Guildhall Library. The alphabetical register of Licentiates (8421/B1) listed five Thomas Robinsons, of which the following was clearly correct.

On Valentine's day, 14 February 1833, Mr Thomas Robinson of full age (i.e. 21 or over), a candidate for a certificate to practise as an apothecary, was examined to see if he was suitable for a licence. The record states that John Bridge provided a testimonial to Thomas's moral character and Thomas himself produced evidence that he had been born on 11 June 1804. He had been apprenticed to Mr Adam Douglas of Kilenaul, Co. Tipperary, for seven years. He had attended anatomical demonstrations and courses in chemistry, 'materia medica', botany, anatomy, physiology and the principles and practice of medicine at Trinity College, Dublin, in 1826. He then spent 12 months at the Richmond Hospital, taking courses in midwifery and clinical medicine. Only one Thomas Robinson who attended Dublin University was of the right age to fit this person:

ROBINSON, THOMAS, Pen. (Mr Martin), Nov. 1, 1819, aged 15, s. of Thomas, generosus [gentleman], b. Waterford.

The registers of Christ Church, Waterford, included:

1804, June 25, Thomas, the son of Capt. Thomas Robinson of the South Cork Regt. of Militia and Mary his wife, born 11th inst.

Problem solved!

QUICK REFERENCE

See also main sources in Useful Addresses, page 306

LAW SOCIETY LIBRARY
113 Chancery Lane
London WC2A IPL
☎ 0870 606 2511
www.library.lawsociety.org.uk

BRIAN BROOKS
Cambria House
37 Pembroke Avenue
Hove
East Sussex BN3 5DB

JOHN TITFORD
Yew Tree Farm
Hallfieldgate
Higham
Derbyshire DE55 6AG

LAMBETH PALACE LIBRARY
Lambeth Palace Road
London SE1 7JU
☎ 020 7898 1400
www.lambethpalacelibrary.org

---

all apothecaries and many physicians and surgeons who wished to practise in England and Wales had to be licensed by the Society of Apothecaries, whose records are kept at the **Guildhall Library**, indexed 1815–40 in *A List of Persons who have Obtained Certificates of their Fitness to Practise as Apothecaries from August 1, 1815 to July 31, 1840* (SoG, 1990).

⊟ Dentistry was originally undertaken by surgeons. Dentists were registered from 1878 and appear in the Dentists' Register at the **SoG**, while licentiates in dental surgery also appear in the back of some medical directories.

⊟ Nurses appear in the records of nursing training schools, attached to many hospitals, from the mid-19th

WHERE TO SEARCH

century. Twentieth-century nurses up to 1973 are indexed in the register of nurses in class DT 11 at the **NA**.

Midwives had to obtain licences to practise from their local bishop's court (see page 231) until the mid-18th century.

Physicians diagnosed and treated ailments. They usually had medical degrees, especially from one of the Scottish universities, though many more attended on an ad hoc basis. the **Royal College of Physicians** holds records of many London and provincial physicians from 1518, and also a number of biographical dictionaries, which may include your ancestor and provide an age and father's name. A useful study of some 17th-century physicians is John H. Raach's *A Dictionary of English Country Physicians 1603–1643* (Dawsons of Pall Mall, 1962), compiled from various sources such as PCC wills.

Surgeons undertook operations. Many used to combine their trade with barbering, and in London they belonged to the Barber-Surgeons' Company, whose records, including freedom admissions from 1522, can be examined at **Guildhall Library**. the **Royal College of Surgeons** was founded in 1800 and holds records of members.

MUSICIANS

These are best studied through *Grove's Dictionary of Music and Musicians* (various eds from 1878).

POLICEMEN

The Metropolitan Police was not formed until 1829. Its records up to the 1930s are in **NA** class MEPO, described in leaflet 53. See also

Metropolitan Police Historical Museum and **www.policeorders. co.uk**.

County police forces started to be formed in 1835 and became compulsory in England, Wales and Scotland by 1857. Records for the county constabularies are held variously by the constabularies or local record offices as detailed in L. A. Waters' *Notes for Family Historians* (Police History Society, 1987). You also can contact the **Police History Society**.

The Irish Constabulary was formed in 1836, added 'Royal' to its name in 1867 and was abolished in 1922. Its service records, giving name, age, denomination, previous trade, country of birth and dates of service are at the **NA** in class HO 184, with indexes there and at the **National Archives of Ireland**. Pension records are in **NA** class PMG 48.

△ *The Postman* by **William Pyne** (1769–1843).

POLITICIANS

The **House of Lords Record Office** holds registers of all who attended Parliament. Careers of peers are given in G. E. Cockayne's *Complete Peerage* (see page 295) and careers of members of the House of Commons are being researched in an on-going project by the History of Parliament, currently covering MPs 1386–1832 and lords 1660–1832.

POSTMEN

Records of high-ranking post office officials date back to 1672 at the **Post Office Archives**, and from 1831 onwards there are appointment books recording all employees. Pension records survive for all staff for the 19th and 20th centuries (indexed to 1921), and these include dates of birth.

Scottish post office records from 1803 to 1910 are at the **NAS**.

TRAIN DRIVERS

Train drivers and other railway workers survive among the records of the 1000 or so railway companies that existed before 1923. That year, most merged into the London & North Eastern, Southern, London, Midland & Scottish and Great Western Railways, and these were nationalised as British Rail in 1948. Most surviving records, including some for Ireland (others for Ireland are at the **PRONI**), are at the **NA** in class RAIL: some records are in **local record offices**.

The best guide to the records, including other sources such as trades union records and staff magazines, is T. Richards' *Was your Grandfather a Railwayman? A Directory of Railway Archive*

LIFETIMES: POLICE RECORDS

IMAGINE A 5' 8" TALL MAN with a florid complexion, dark brown hair and brown eyes, born in 1821 in Whitechapel, London. This was the description given in the Surrey police records of one of its earliest members, Samuel Baxter.

These records also tell us that this colourful cockney, who originally worked as a groom, joined the Metropolitan Police as a constable in 1844 and served for nine years. After a couple of weeks' respite, he joined the two-year-old Surrey constabulary in 1853, starting at Merrow near Guildford as a 4th class constable, rising rapidly to 3rd and then 2nd class. Within a year of joining, he was posted to nearby Great Bookham, near Leatherhead, but on 21 December 1854 he failed to attend a meeting (too much Christmas cheer?), was demoted to 3rd class and packed off to Abinger. Here he regained his composure and won back 2nd class status the following December. May Day 1856 – another public holiday, significantly – he was re-demoted for neglect of duty and transferred, at his own expense, to Thorpe. He won back 2nd class status in November 1856 and, after three and a half years' sustained effort, reached 1st class in June 1860.

In January 1861 he moved to Addlestone, where the census shows him at Crouch Oak Lane with his wife and daughter, and a lodger. December that year saw a move to York Town, Frimley, where, in 1865, after almost a decade of keeping out of trouble, he was demoted to 2nd class for neglecting to visit a pub when ordered. Here he remained, PC (2nd class) Baxter, until he resigned in 1867 with a £50 gratuity out of the superannuation fund. He went back to London, becoming as grocer at 1 Cottage Place, Tottenam Hale, where he remained for the rest of his life.

If Samuel had been just a groom or grocer, little or no such comparable detail would have been recorded about him.

Sources for Family Historians (FFHS, 1995). An index to some railway employees is kept by **J. F. Engert**.

🗗 Searching can be complicated if you do not know the company for which your ancestor worked, because conurbations like Manchester were serviced by hundreds of separate companies. It is therefore worth seeing if the company is named alongside the job description in the **GRO** of the man's marriage or births of his children. If you persist, however, you may find detailed records including the date of birth – it is certainly worth having a go.

QUICK REFERENCE

See also main sources in Useful Addresses, page 306

ROYAL COLLEGE OF PHYSICIANS
Library and Information Services
11 St Andrews Place
London NW1 4LE
☎ 020 7935 1174 x 312
www.rcplondon.ac.uk/college/library

ROYAL COLLEGE OF SURGEONS
35–43 Lincoln's Inn Fields
London WC2A 3PE
☎ 020 7869 6520
www.rcseng.ac.uk

METROPOLITAN POLICE HISTORICAL MUSEUM
Unit 7 Meridian Estate
Bugsby Way
Charlton
London SE7 7SJ
☎ 020 8305 2824
www.met.police.uk/history

POLICE HISTORY SOCIETY
Secretary: Steve Bridge
(no mailing address given)
Email steve@bridge100.fsnet.co.uk
www.policehistorysociety.co.uk

HOUSE OF LORDS RECORD OFFICE
Palace of Westminster
London SW1A 0PW
☎ 020 7219 3074
www.parliament.uk

POST OFFICE ARCHIVES
Freeling House
Phoenix Place
Farringdon Road
London WC1X 0DL
☎ 020 7239 2570
www.royalmail.com

J. F. ENGERT
'Lundy'
31 Tennyson Road
Eastleigh
Hampshire SO50 9FS

LIFETIMES: THE CARPUES

SOMETIMES, APPRENTICESHIP RECORDS can be enough to prove a family tree. In the case of the Carpues of London, who were Catholic and therefore very hard to trace through conventional parish registers, they were essential. Edward Carpue of Serle Street, Lincoln's Inn, was a cordwainer (a superior sort of shoemaker, so-called for the use of fine-quality Cordoban leather) who married Mary Hodgson in 1779 and died in 1792. He was a Catholic so records of a baptism could not be found and his parentage could not be proved. However, the SoG's Apprentices Index showed him being apprenticed to his uncle Joseph Carpue, cordwainer, in 1755. In his will, which was found in the indexes to the Prerogative Court of Canterbury (see page 129), Joseph made his nephew Edward an executor and left £200:

'towards apprenticing or putting out [to trade] such children ... to such respectable and honest trade and employment as [his executors] ... shall think most deserving objects of such authority'.

Joseph recognised the value of apprenticeship doubly, for that was how he had started his career. The Apprentices Index reveals him being apprenticed in 1721 to his elder brother Charles Carpue of St Clement Danes, shoemaker. And Charles is there right at the beginning of the records, apprenticed in 1711 to Robert Mothersall of St Clement's, described as son of Charles Carpue of Missenden, Buckinghamshire, thus identifying Edward's grandfather and revealing the family's rural origins before they became London tradesmen.

▽ A typical apprentice indenture, this time for Henry Keogh, who, with the consent of his guardian Benjamin Humphrey Smart, was apprenticed to Thomas Spooner to become, of all things, a 'table decorator and manufacturer of desert and other ornaments'.

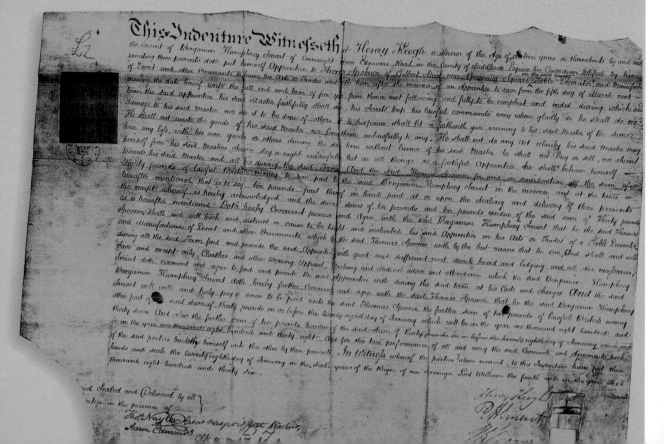

APPRENTICE, MASTER AND FREEMAN

Besides records of people doing jobs, there are also copious records of them being trained – or apprenticed – in trades and occupations. These are often linked to the records of boroughs and cities. They provide a lot of extra detail about people's lives and they often supply those all-important fathers' names as well.

APPRENTICESHIP

What we usually now term as 'vocational training' was in the past covered by apprenticeship, an agreement whereby a child was 'bound' to serve a master who would in turn teach him to follow his trade or profession. Apprenticeship usually started at ten years (or seven years for the navy) and seldom after 18, and lasted seven years or until the age of 21 years. The apprentice was then free, but if he submitted a test-piece, called a 'masterpiece', which passed muster, he qualified to become a master craftsman. It is not uncommon to find yourself descended from both apprentice and master, because a favoured apprentice would often be encouraged to marry his master's daughter, and less scrupulous boys endeavoured to fast-track their careers by marrying the boss's daughter in any case!

FREEMEN OF GUILDS

Many peoples' ancestors were freemen of guilds. In many cases there will be surviving records detailing what they did and who their fathers were. You could become a freeman by one of four ways:
➤**Apprenticeship or servitude**
➤**Honour:** honorary freedoms were occasionally bestowed on men of great distinction.
➤**Patrimony:** being the son of a freeman.
➤**Redemption:** buying your way in, a system abolished in 1835 in everywhere but London.

Guilds mostly flourished in towns and cities. Medieval guilds came in three varieties, religious, merchant and craft. The first were abolished at the Reformation, and the third tended to be absorbed by craft guilds, although in small towns there might be only one craft guild, to which all craftsmen belonged, regardless of their trade. Guilds had many functions, including regulating quality of produced goods, and acting as friendly societies, caring for elderly members and their widows and orphans.

WOMEN'S WORK

MOST PEOPLE THINK THAT, in the past, men went out to work and women stayed at home producing babies. While this was sometimes true, many women did work. At the surface of coalmines were miners' wives and daughters whose job was to clean and sort the newly mined coal, and quaysides reverberated with the songs of fishwives, whose role in life was to sort and clean their husbands' catches. Many working-class women worked in service until they got married (most had to leave once they had husbands) and it is true that many babies born to them resulted from liaisons, voluntary or not, with their employers' families. Once married, women worked as cleaners or took in sewing or laundry, or did more specialised work, such as embroidery or mantua (skirt) making.

Many more acted as unpaid staff in their husbands' businesses, tending the family shop or working alongside the men as potters, framework knitters, bakers and so on. And there were those who defied the odds and, when their husbands died or became incapacitated, took over the business or ran businesses themselves. Dr Sheila Sweetinburgh's work on medieval Hythe has turned up several examples, such as Katherine Peccyng who paid dues to town on the salt fish and shellfish she was selling in 1417, or Alice Heniper who left her fishing nets to her husband.

△ ▷ **My great-grandfather Herman Julius Rietchel and a page from his early employment records at Sun Life. He later rose to become the firm's general manager. Because the record was made before the First World War, it records him under the original spelling 'Rietschel'.**

BUSINESSES

Many businesses were founded by and for families. Their records of appointment of directors and shareholders may therefore reveal names of many relations, male and female, and add a fascinating extra layer to a family history. Equally, many kept records of employees, which can be helpful in tracing family histories.

CLUBS AND SOCIETIES

Besides records to do with work, your ancestors may also appear in documents recording their collaboration for security or advancement.

WHERE TO SEARCH

BUSINESSES

⌗ If the business is still functioning, ask its archivist what information may be available. Many family businesses are very proud of that fact and may have published a company history, containing family history information. Chocolate makers Cadburys, for example, are covered by J. F. Crosfield's *The Cadbury Family Book*, which includes an illustrated family tree of the Cadburys involved with the company.

⌗ Records of extant companies and a selection of papers of companies no longer in business are kept by the Registrar of Companies, which also has a search room at **Companies House**.

⌗ Irish company records can be traced through the **National Archives of Ireland** or the **Companies Registration Office of Northern Ireland**.

⌗ Further business archives may be traced through the **local record offices** and the National Register of Archives on **www.hmc.gov.uk/nra**.

⌗ Businesses are listed in directories and, if you are lucky, your ancestor may even have placed an advertisement in one.

⌗ Formation and dissolution of business partnerships (and bankruptcies) were announced in the *London Gazette* (see page 144). An index of dissolved partnerships is at the **IHGS**. Original records of winding up companies are at the **NA** in the Chancery or Bankruptcy Court records and, from 1890, records of the Companies Court.

CLUBS AND SOCIETIES

FREEMASONS

⌗ Randle Holme's list of Cheshire Freemasons, which dates from about 1665, is almost unique. This, together with other chance references, is published in R. F. Gould's *The History of Freemasonry, Its Antiquities, Symbols, Constitutions, Customs &c* (Caxton, no date).

FREEMASONS

Freemasonry's origins are a not entirely understood 17th-century fusion of stonemasons' craft guilds and esoteric groups studying aspects of mysticism and proto-science that fell outside the pale of the churches. There seems to have been a coherent system of Freemasonry in Britain by the early 17th century, although there are practically no records until the 18th century, after which they became very detailed.

FRIENDLY SOCIETIES

There were many friendly societies, such as the Oddfellows, to which our ancestors belonged, paying small subscriptions in return for financial support in times of need.

TRADES UNIONS

Trades unions started to be established in the mid-19th century. Be aware the early trades unions – and friendly societies – often used banners and regalia based on Freemasonic designs, so don't judge from first appearances.

After the establishment of Grand Lodge in 1717 records improve greatly. Records of deceased Freemasons can be sought by contacting the Grand Secretary at the **United Grand Lodge of England**.

From 1799 onwards, lists of members of Freemasonic lodges had to be enrolled in the Quarter Sessions (see page 232). A guide to available records is given in P. Lewis's *My Ancestor was a Freemason* (SoG, 1999).

For Scottish Freemasons, you can write to the **Grand Secretary** at the Freemasons' Hall, Edinburgh.

For Irish Freemasons, write to the **Grand Secretary** at the Freemasons' Hall, Dublin.

FRIENDLY SOCIETIES

Most records are still with local branches, or **county record offices**.

TRADES UNIONS

Branch records are the best ones to use, as they may provide details of your ancestor in terms of joining, transfer from one branch to another, payment of benefits such as sick pay, funeral benefits and benefits for widows and orphans. The records can be sought through the **union** itself or at the relevant **county record office**. Many are listed in J. Bennett, A. Tough and R. Storey's *Trade Union & Related Records* (University of Warwick, 1991).

QUICK REFERENCE

See also main sources in Useful Addresses, page 306

COMPANIES HOUSE
21 Bloomsbury Street
London WC1B 3XD
☎ 0870 3333 636
www.companieshouse.gov.uk

COMPANIES REGISTRATION OFFICE OF NORTHERN IRELAND
1st Floor Waterfront Plaza
8 Laganbank Road
Belfast BT1 3LX
Northern Ireland
☎ 0845 604 8888
www.companiesregistry-ni.gov.uk

UNITED GRAND LODGE OF ENGLAND
The Grand Secretary
Freemasons' Hall
Great Queen Street
London WC2B 5AZ
☎ 020 7831 9811
www.ugle.org.uk

THE GRAND SECRETARY
Freemasons' Hall
96 George Street
Edinburgh EH2 3DH
Scotland
☎ 0131 225 5304

THE GRAND SECRETARY
Freemasons' Hall
17 Molesworth Street
Dublin 2
Eire
☎ 00 351 1 676 1337
www.irish-freemasons.org

CHAPTER TWENTY-ONE
FIGHTING FORBEARS

The information in this chapter is divided as follows: the army is covered on pages 190–201; the Royal Navy on pages 202–6; the Merchant Navy on pages 207–9; the Royal Marines on page 210 and the Royal Airforce on page 211.

One way or another, war, conquest or the prospect of either, played a substantial role in our forbears' lives. From the bloody trenches of the Somme back to the pitched chaos of Flodden and Agincourt, not to mention the raging seas of Trafalgar and, more recently, the turbulent skies over southern England, ancestors of ours have been skewering and exploding each other with gusto throughout British history.

From the 17th century onwards, the scale of warfare increased with the creation of a large standing army and the constant expansion of the British Empire. With this came almost continual conflict from the monumental conflicts with France, America and Germany, to hundreds of lesser campaigns throughout Africa and the East.

Almost all our ancestors were caught up in these, and many served as soldiers, more so than most of us realise. Many of us have forbears who appear in parish registers being baptised and then, in an orderly fashion, being married and having their children. A surprising number of these men would, in fact, have filled at least part of the intervening periods far from home, kitted up in uniform and serving as Tommys or Tars in the farthest-flung reaches of the Empire. Looking for your ancestors' service records is always a good idea, as they will often tell you a great deal about your forbears, what they did and maybe what they looked like, how they behaved, and even what sexually transmitted diseases they carried. All excellent grist to the mill of family history.

THE ARMY

Army records can provide splendid details for genealogists, especially ages and places of birth, while they can also expand family histories with information about campaigns, conduct and even physical descriptions of ancestors. When we were making the pilot of *Extraordinary Ancestors* I found myself in Chester, showing Albert Charlotte the army service papers of his great-grandfather, John Edward Charlotte. John was 5' 4½'' tall, without scars, with a fair

△ **My great-great-uncle Ernst Otto Rietschel, MC, who was killed in the First World War fighting on the British side.**

◁ Battle of Agincourt, 25 October 1415. An exhausted force of 9000 soldiers, mainly foot-soldiers and archers, scored a collosal defeat of the French cavalry. Sadly, few non-noble participants' names were ever recorded.

△ Filming the story of Albert Charlotte's soldier ancestor John Edward Charlotte for *Extraordinary Ancestors* at Chester Castle, October 1999 (see left).

complexion, grey eyes and light brown hair. I realised that Albert was about that height, and had grey eyes – but so too was his hair. Without prompting, however, Albert answered my unspoken question, 'My hair used to be light brown too!'

For the show, Albert and I also tried on the uniform John would have worn, with its heavy red felt coat and roughly sewn canvas trousers. But all this, including having most of our normal clothes underneath, was no protection against the cold October wind blowing across from Snowdonia as we stood in the shadow of Chester Castle. Yet this was also the uniform John would have worn when he was sent to serve in the sweltering climate of Greece, when he was part of the force installing Prince Philip's ancestor on the Greek throne.

THE ARMY

GENERAL RECORDS

There are many detailed guides to using army records, particularly S. Fowler's *Army Records for Family Historians* (PRO Publications, 1998, revised by W. Spencer); M. J. and C. Watts' *My Ancestor was in the British Army: How Can I Find out More About Him?* (SoG, 1995); S. Fowler's *Tracing your First World War Ancestor* (Countryside Books, 2003) and S. Fowler's *Tracing your Second World War Ancestor* (Countryside Books, 2005).

MILITIA RECORDS

The earliest records of men at arms are the militia records. In times of emergency, able-bodied men were summoned to serve in the local militias. The whereabouts of muster rolls of all those liable for service, together with details either of their income or what arms they were supposed to provide, is given in given in W. Spencer's *Records of the Militia and Volunteer Forces* (PRO Publications, 1997). The earliest survive from the 16th century, particularly for the years 1522, 1539, 1542, 1569 and 1624, in the NA and **county record offices**.

The **NA** also holds records of militia men in WO 13 (1780–1878) and WO 68 (1859–1925) and there are a few birth and baptism records of serving militia men's children in WO 32 and WO 68. The latter also contains some marriage records and other information on militia men's physical appearance, places of birth, casualties, courts martials and so on. Pensions 1817–1927 are in PMG 13.

Most Welsh musters are at the National Library of Wales and are covered by a series of books *The History of the Welsh Militia and Volunteer Corps* (Palace Books).

Scottish records are at the **NAS**, both for before the Act of Union (1707) and after the re-creation of the Scottish militia in 1797.

Most Irish militia lists (1793–1876) are at the **NA** in class WO 13.

Most Channel Island militia lists are held on their respective islands although lists for Jersey and Guernsey 1843–52 are at the **NA** in class WO 13.

On the Isle of Man, the lists of the Manx Fencibles are at the **Manx Museum**.

The fear of French invasion, which lasted from the French Revolution to the fall of Napoleon (1793–1815), generated further militia-style forces. Posse Comitatus lists, covering able-bodied men aged 15–60 who were not already in the militia, were made in 1798 and a similar *Levée en Masse* list of able-bodied men aged 17–55 was

FROM 1758 TO 1831, lists were made of all men aged 18–50 (or 18–45 after 1762). Militia men were then chosen from the lists by ballot. They had to attend a military camp for a week a year for three years, but during times of war they could be in service for the full three years, stationed anywhere in the British Isles (but not abroad). It is worth bearing this in mind if an ancestor crops up a long way from home. Those who did not want to serve could pay for someone else to be trained instead. Men with disabilities were also noted. From 1802 the number of children each man had was recorded and, from 1806, the mens' ages as well.

made in 1803. Some survive and have been printed, particularly I. F. W. Beckett's *The Buckinghamshire Posse Comitatus 1798* (Bucks Record Society, 1985).

Other militia-style forces from this period were the fencible infantry, fencible cavalry and yeomanry cavalry. Yeomanry regiments continued to be raised to deal with civil unrest during the 19th century, becoming the Territorial Army in 1921. Most records are at the **NA** and **county record offices** and are also detailed in J. Gibson and M. Medlycott's *Militia Lists and Musters 1757–1876: A Directory of Holdings in the British Isles* (FFHS, 1994).

PUBLISHED LISTS OF SOLDIERS

Some records of those who fought in famous conflicts have been published. For 1066 and all that, see A. J. Camp's *My Ancestor came over with the Conqueror: Those who Did, and Some of Those who Probably Did Not* (SoG, 1988).

Later, we have A. Livingstone, C. Aikman and B. Hart's *Muster Roll of Prince Charles Edward Stuart's Army 1745–6* (Aberdeen University Press, 1984), which attempts to trace the fate of each man, and *The Waterloo Roll Call* (Arms and Armour Press, 1978), which covers commissioned and non-commissioned officers.

THE CIVIL WAR

The officers and some soldiers on both sides of the Civil War appear in paylists and musters in **NA** class E 315, but the best resources are published. Sir C. Firth and G. Davies' *The Regimental History of Cromwell's Army* (Clarendon Press, 1940) and E. Peacock's *The Army Lists of the Roundheads and Cavaliers* (Chatto & Windus, 1874) cover both sides well. There is also the 1663 list of Indigent Officers, detailing the claims made by former Royalist officers to the £60,000 bounty, which Charles II made available for their relief. This has been published and indexed, with some supplementary information from the Royalist news sheet **Mercurius Aulicus**, the State Papers and other sources, in S. Reid's *Officers and Regiments of the Royalist Army* (Partizan Press, no date). Those whom Cromwell's Parliament fined for having fought for Charles I are well documented in Green's *Calendar of the Proceedings of the Committee for Advance of Money, 1642–1656* and *Calendar of the Proceedings of the Committee for Compounding, 1643–1660* (HMSO, 1888–92). Many, officers and men, appear in the printed calendars to the Domestic, Thurloe and Clarendon State Papers, which you can find in major **libraries**.

◁ **18th-century soldiers on parade outside St James's Palace. Note the multi-racial mix even then, with black bandsmen and white soldiers.**

QUICK REFERENCE

See main sources in Useful Addresses, page 306

For Channel Islands and the Isle of Man, see page 311

WHERE TO SEARCH

THE ARMY'S REGIMENTS

THE ARMY has its roots in the troops Charles II employed full-time after his Restoration (1660), whose numbers were dramatically expanded by James II (1685-8). Officers aside, though, few records exist until the 18th century. The army comprised regiments of foot soldiers (regiments of infantry-men and footguards) and mounted cavalry (regiments of hussars, dragoons, dragoon guards, lancers, lifeguards and royal horseguards), supple-mented by special regiments such as the Royal Artillery, Royal Horse Artillery and Royal Engineers. In 1881 the infantry was reorganised and most regiments were linked to a county. An online guide to regimental histories and engagements is at **www.army.mod.uk.unitsandorgs**.

THE STANDING ARMY

C. Dalton's *English Army Lists and Commission Registers 1661–1714* (Francis Edwards, 1960) and *George the First's Army 1714–1727* (Eyre & Spottiswoode, 1910–12) outline officers' careers, after which you can turn to Army Lists (see page 196).

For publications concerning the First World War, see page 198.

MUSEUMS

Many regiments have published regimental histories and maintain regimental museums. Even if they do not have specific records to do with your ancestors, they can provide a wealth of information on what your soldier ancestors wore, wielded and worried about. **The Army Museum Ogilby Trust** can put you in touch.

The **Imperial War Museum**, which is concerned with events since 1914, and the **National Army Museum** both hold splendid collections. Most useful records are kept at the **NA** in class WO (War Office), and are mainly arranged by regiment.

MEDALS

The Battle of Waterloo (1815) was the first campaign for which soldiers were awarded special medals, recorded in medal rolls. Those up to 1919 are in the **NA** (WO 100). Many have been published and can be studied at the **NA** or **SoG**. For example, Waterloo recipients are in **NA** class MINT 16/112, published in *The Waterloo Medal Roll*, compiled from the Muster Rolls (Naval & Military Press, 1992)

Medals awarded for gallantry, such as the Victoria Cross, Military Cross and so on, with citations, were printed in the *London Gazette* (see page 144), and the **NA** has indexes to gazetted awards of certain medals

Medal rolls for the First World War are referred to on page 198. For medal awards after 1919, write to the **Army Medals Office**.

The more prestigious the medal, the more information is likely to have been recorded about an ancestor. The Victoria Cross has a splendid website, **www.chapter-one.com/vc** giving biographical details.

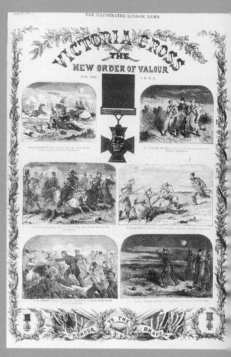

△ **The Victoria Cross awards for the army, 1857.**

QUICK REFERENCE

See also main sources in Useful Addresses, page 306

ARMY MUSEUM OGILBY TRUST
58 The Close
Salisbury SP1 2EX
☎ 01722 332188
www.armymuseums.org.uk

IMPERIAL WAR MUSEUM
Lambeth Road
London SE1 6HZ
☎ 020 7416 5320
www.iwm.org.uk

NATIONAL ARMY MUSEUM
Royal Hospital Road
Chelsea
London SW3 4HT
☎ 020 7730 0717
www.national-army-museum.ac.uk

ARMY MEDALS OFFICE
Government Office Buildings
Worcester Road, Droitwich
Worcestershire WR9 8AU
☎ 01905 772323
www.army.mod.uk

△ *The Battle of Isandhlwana* during the Zulu War by Charles Edwin Fripp (1854–1906).

LIFETIMES: WILLIAM ALLEN

FOR *ANTIQUES GHOSTSHOW* I visited the regimental museum of the Welsh Borderers, in Brecon, to learn about William Allen (1844–90), one of the men who was awarded the Victoria Cross for his bravery at Rourke's Drift, when a Zulu army attacked a weakly garrisoned hospital station on 22–3 January 1879. His citation (in the NA – WO 32/7390) stated that he and his friend Frederick Hitch,

> 'must also be mentioned. It was chiefly due to their courageous conduct that communication with the Hospital was kept up at all – holding together at all costs a most dangerous post, raked in reverse by the enemy's fire from the hill, they were both severaly wounded, but their determined conduct enabled patients to be withdrawn from the Hospital, & when incapacitated by their wounds from fighting themselves, they continued, as soon as their wounds had been contained, to serve out ammunition to their comrades during the night.'

The museum was a delight, including vivid models of the battle, showing the red-coated British soldiers battling it out with the almost completely skinned but viciously armed Zulu warriors. I was shown Allen's pocket watch, a pin cushion he had made from scraps of material found after the battle, and a picture of him having the VC pinned to his chest by the Queen herself. I was allowed to hold the very medal, which is worth about £200,000, and that of his commanding officer, Lieutenant Bromhead – the one who Michael Caine played in the film *Zulu* – worth a cool quarter of a million!

The museum gave me four pages of notes on Allen, and showed me the notice of his military funeral, published in the local paper. It transpired that although he was a hero under pressure, Allen was in fact a teacher, who spent many years teaching basic writing and arithmetic to his fellow soldiers and, after returning to Wales from South Africa, taught musketry. We know from his descendants that the events of that terrible night traumatised him deeply. I left, therefore, with a much fuller picture of the man behind the medal than I could possibly have got elsewhere.

OFFICERS

Until the 20th century, officers were almost exclusively drawn from the middle and upper classes. The main ranks were general, colonel, lieutenant colonel, major, captain and lieutenant.

The **Royal Military College**, originally the Royal Military Academy at Woolwich, founded in 1741, holds records of cadets, often including baptism certificates, from 1790.

Officers' regiments can be discovered easily from Army Lists, which have been published from 1740 and are usually well indexed. Besides identifying the regiment, they will also tell you a bit about the officer, such as which medals he had been awarded, where he had fought, dates of promotion and whether he had been mentioned in the *London Gazette* (see page 144). Most good genealogical libraries have collections, and the **NA** also has manuscript lists from 1702 (WO 64–5). There are also published lists as outlined below.

The main **NA** holdings are services of officers on the active list (WO 25 and 76, partially indexed), dating back to 1829 and in some cases to 1764.

In the **NA**, WO 25 also includes various returns of officers made in 1809/10, 1829 and 1870–2, and retired officers 1828 and 1847. Once you have found the date of the officer's commission, you can seek the officer's letters applying to buy or sell it in the commander-in-chiefs' memoranda (1793–1870) in class WO 31. Announcements of promotion or retirement are in the *London Gazette*.

Before pensions were introduced in 1871, retiring officers received 'half-pay', recorded from 1730 at the **NA** in WO 23–5 and in the Paymaster General's records (PMG 3–14), which should provide a date of death, and details of where the retired officer subsequently lived. Pensions for wounded officers are in WO 23 and pension applications by widows of officers killed in active service, 1760–1818, are in WO 25, and 1815–92 in WO 23, with further widows' pension applications, sometimes including details of birth, baptism, marriage and death, in 'miscellaneous certificates', in WO 2.

OTHER RANKS

Until the 20th century, these were almost exclusively lower-class men. The minimum age to sign up was 18, though many boys lied about their ages to get in earlier. They would join for life, but in reality they usually served for 21 years (12 years from 1871).

Soldiers are well recorded, but up to 1873 almost everything is arranged by regiment. The **NA** catalogue indexes soldiers 1760–1854, giving regiments. Soldiers after then may be identified by uniforms shown in pictures, or medals. Alternatively, you may find the regiment recorded on a birth or marriage certificate, in wills, parish registers or elsewhere. In frustrating cases, the occupation will simply say 'soldier' (or, if he had retired, 'pensioner'), in which case you will have to keep searching further records.

If you find a record, such as a census, showing that a soldier had a child born somewhere unexpected, in Britain or abroad, you can find

out which regiments were stationed there from the monthly returns of regiments in **NA** classes WO 17 and 73 or the *United Service Journal & Naval and Military Magazine*, later called *Colburn's United Service Magazine* (which also details officers' promotions).

You may also find soldier ancestors in the Registrar General's Indexes to Regimental Returns of Births and Baptisms of Soldiers' Children (1761–1924) (see page 57): the indexes should cover all the regiments and the records most certainly do specify the regiments.

Muster rolls and pay lists

At the **NA**, class WO 12 covers 1878–98 and class WO 15 covers 1760–1872, with a few stragglers going back to 1708. Those records for artillery, engineers and others are in class WO 10, 11, 14 and 15. They were compiled quarterly.

Description books

These cover the period 1795–1900, with a few dating back to 1756, and are in the **NA** classes WO 25 and 67, arranged by regiment and then by initial letter of the surname.

Discharge and pensions

Until the late 19th century, pensions were paid through the Royal Hospitals at Kilmainham, Dublin, founded by Charles II (1679) and Chelsea, opened in the reign of William and Mary (1692). Those resident there are called Kilmainham or Chelsea Pensioners, while all other non-officers in receipt of a pension for disability or completion of their term of service were called Kilmainham or Chelsea Out-pensioners.

Discharge documents of pensioners 1782–1854 for Chelsea (in the **NA**, WO 121) have been indexed on-line in **www.catalogue.nationalarchives. gov.uk**. They complement WO 97 and are particularly useful for tracing 18th- and early 19th-century soldiers.

Soldiers discharged in Ireland were paid via Kilmainham, regardless of where they subsequently lived. There are many records relating to pensions. In-pensioners are recorded in the **NA**, class WO 23.

Kilmainham In- and Out-pensioners admission registers are in the **NA**, class WO 118 (1704–1922).

Chelsea long-service admissions are at the **NA** in WO 116 1823–1920 and disability pensions WO 118 1715–1913. In-pensioners' regimental registers are in WO 120 (from 1715).

Regimental returns

The returns of soldiers who were discharged to pension are in the **NA**, class WO 120, covering 1715–1843 (with a second series going up to 1857), arranged chronologically. They are also partially indexed by J. D. Beckett's *An Index to the Regimental Registers of the Royal Hospital, Chelsea, 1806–1838* (Manchester and Lancs FHS, 1993).

From 1842, pensions were paid through a series of local pension offices throughout the British Isles. If you know where your ancestor lived, you can examine the registers of the most local office at the **NA** in WO 22.

Attestation and discharge papers

Records of men who paid to leave before their term of service was over for the period 1817–70 are in the **NA**,

△ **British troops leaving for France, 1915.**

class WO 25, arranged by regiment. However, the best records are in WO 97, with some others in WO 121, 122 and 131. They cover soldiers who were discharged to pension, who completed their term of engagement or paid to leave early, in the period 1760–1913. From 1883 there is one single alphabetical series, with a supplementary one covering entries that were misfiled. Fortunately, these records are now included in **www.catalogue. nationalarchives. gov.uk** for the period 1760–1854.

A **Soldiers Index** for 1855–72 is held, and can be searched for a fee, by Ms S. Davis.

CASUALTIES AND DESERTERS

Casualties and deserters are listed at the **NA** in class WO 25 in several categories covering 1797–1817 and 1809–1910.

Casualty rolls for specific wars between 1857 and 1898, published

and unpublished, are listed in S. Fowler's *Army Records for Family Historians* (PRO Publications, 1998).

DESERTERS AND COURTS MARTIAL

The **NA** class WO 25 contains records of deserters 1799–1852. Those caught and disciplined for desertion – or for a host of other intriguing offences – appear in records of military courts, dating from 1688 and catalogued in WO 71–2 and 81–93, with officers (1806–1904) in WO 93/1B. Deserters are also listed in the *Police Gazette*

△ The British Cavalry passing Albert Cathedral during the First World War.

and *Hue and Cry*, copies of which are at the **NA**.

PRISONERS OF WAR

Records from 1793 are at the **NA**. Those for the First World War are detailed in **NA** information leaflet 72 and those for the Second World War are in leaflet 111. WO 345 is a card index of 57,000 of those captured by the Japanese.

The **International Welfare Department of the British Red Cross** can deal with humanitarian enquiries, but not those made purely for family history purposes.

THE FIRST WORLD WAR

Some 6 million men served in the 'Great War', mostly after the introduction of conscription in 1916. The records of 15% of officers were destroyed in Second World War bombing but a supplementary series of records of varying degrees of completeness – about 85% - survives divided between WO 339 and WO 374 (searchable in the **NA** catalogue) with an index at the NA in WO 338 and searchable online at **www. catalogue.nationalarchives.gov.uk**.

If you do not find what you are looking, for the officer may have served beyond 1922, so contact the MoD at Kentigern House.

Many non-officer's records were destroyed in the same bombing but about 2 million of the latter still survive at the **NA**, covering men who died or were discharged between 1914 and 1920, arranged in approximate alphabetical order. These are the misleadingly named 'burnt' documents (WO 363).

Be aware that between 1914 and 1920 each regiment numbered its own soldiers, and so men in different regiments ended up with the same number. Furthermore, when battalions and regiments were partially or almost entirely annihilated, the survivors were assimilated into others so a long-serving soldier might have served with several regiments by the end of the war.

There are also unburnt documents, at the **NA**, such as WO 364 covering non-commissioned officers and other ranks that claimed pensions for war services from 1914 to 1920.

There are supplementary files at the **NA** for 140,000 officers in WO 339, arranged numerically (an index to find an officer's number is in WO 338), and WO 374, concerning some 80,000 Territorial Army soldiers. The files vary in detail from full service papers to just date of death. You can also consult pension records 1914– 20 in PMG 4, 9, 42–7 and PIN 26.

9000 surviving service records of the Women's Army Auxiliary Corps are in the **NA** in WO 398.

Where service records do not survive, the medal rolls (c. 1914–22) will at least tell you the campaigns in which your ancestor fought, and Officers' War Diaries may mention their acts of heroism, or at least provide some background to their service. All the former and some of the latter are on **www.nationalarchives.gov.uk/ documentsonline/default.asp**.

For identifying First World War soldiers' regiments also use N. Holding's *More Sources for World War I Army Ancestry* (FFHS, 1991).

The Great War Section of the **Veterans Agency** may also be able to provide details of a soldier's regiment. Electoral registers (see page 164) for autumn 1918 and spring 1919, for the soldier's home, include most men waiting to be demobilised, and name their regiment.

First World War armed forces deaths are at the **FRC**. However the most accessible source is the **Commonwealth War Graves Commission** website, covering 25,600 First and Second World War memorials and cemeteries all over the world, with about 1.8 million names (see box, right).

⊟ Soldiers whose deaths were registered by the Belgian and French authorities are at the **NA** in RG 33/45–69, arranged alphabetically by first letter of surname.

⊟ Many soldiers' names appear alphabetically by battalion in *Soldiers Died in the Great War* (Naval and Military Press, 1989), and a similar work for officers (1919), available in good **genealogical libraries**. There are 81 of the volumes on a CD-Rom version, which has a name-search facility.

⊟ Many names appear on local war memorials and in rolls of honour, which were produced by localities and institutions, all listed in N. Holding's *The Location of British Army Records*,

THIS IS A TYPICAL entry from the Commonwealth War Graves Commission's excellent website, **www.cwgc.org.uk**.

Debt of Honour Register
In Memory of ADOLPHUS OLATUNJI OSUN
Lance Corporal,
NA/87476
Nigeria Regiment, R.W.A.F.F.
who died on Sunday 15 April 1945.

CEMETERY: ENUGU MILITARY CEMETERY, Nigeria
GRAVE OR REFERENCE PANEL NUMBER: African Mohd. Plot. Row E. Grave 4.
LOCATION: Enugu, the capital of the Eastern Region, is 193 kilometres north of Port Harcourt on the main railway line to Kaduna and Kano. The Military Cemetery is situated on the left of the main road to Onitsha, just below Milliken Hill, and is 2 kilometres from the railway station.
HISTORICAL INFORMATION: The cemetery contains 90 Commonwealth burials of the 1939–1945 War, 1 of whom is unidentified. There are also 24 post-war graves. The cemetery is circular and is divided by radial paths into separate plots. A Cross of Sacrifice has been erected near the centre. The three United Kingdom soldiers are buried in the European plot on the southern perimeter of the cemetery. The war graves of the African soldiers are in denominational plots.

COMMONWEALTH WAR GRAVES COMMISSION

A National Directory of World War I Sources (FFHS, 1999). Of particular note are the *National Roll of the Great War 1914–1918* (National Publishing Company, 1918–21 - available on CD), compiled with information on about 150,000 men, alive or dead, mostly supplied by their families. The Marquis de Ruvigny's *The Roll of Honour, a Biographical Record of Members of His Majesty's Naval and Military Forces who Fell in the Great War 1914–1918* (LSE, 1987) covers about 25,000 deceased soldiers, including names of fathers and sometimes of mothers. Many entries are accompanied by a photograph.

There is also a useful website, **www.great-war-casualties.com**, and an index to many soldiers who died in the First World War kept by **Robert Base**, giving battalion number, places of birth and enrolment, residence, service number, rank, and date and place of death.

The best sources for general information about conditions, battles and so on are the archives and associated publications of the **Imperial War Museum**. At the **NA** in class WO 95 are war diaries for each infantry battalion. Men mentioned tend to be officers, but the relevant diary will still tell you exactly what your ancestor's battalion was doing, and when. Some soldiers, especially officers, kept their own diaries. MH 106 contains about a tenth of the soldiers' hospital records that survived.

RECORDS AFTER 1926

Soldiers' records after 1926 are held at the **Army Records Centre.** They are not open for public searching, but you can apply for a service record of a deceased forebear, so long as you can prove they are deceased and you are the next of kin. On application, you will be sent a form to fill in and you must also pay £20 for a search and send your evidence.

The **FRC** holds army deaths and the Commonwealth War Graves Commission website **www.cwgc.org** includes British soldiers who have died in wars since 1918. See also **www.great-war-2-casualties.com**.

THE SECOND WORLD WAR

For the Second World War there are rolls of honour, including place of birth and normal address, at Westminster Abbey and the **NA**, also available on CD-Rom from the Naval and Military Press.

Second World War war diaries are in NA classes WO 165–79, 215, 218 and 257. The **Army Medals Office** holds records of medals awarded for Second World War service.

Other NA sources are outlined in J. D. Cantwell's *The Second World War: A Guide to Documents at the PRO* (PRO Publications, 1998).

HOME GUARD

Records of the real life 'dads' army', the Home Guard, are in **NA** classes WO 199, 166 and also in PREM 3.

SCOTSMEN

Scots in the British army appear in military records after the Act of Union (1707). Prior to then (and aside from Scots who happened to fight in English regiments) the records of the ad hoc Scottish armies are sparse, and what survives in terms of musters are at the **NAS** and listed in J. Gibson and A. Dell's *Tudor and Stuart Muster Rolls: A Directory of Holdings in the British Isles* (FFHS, 1991). A fine secondary source is C. Dalton's *The Scots Army 1661–1688* (Naval and Military Press, 1989).

THE ARMY OVERSEAS

AUSTRALIA

First World War army records for Australia are at the Australian Archives.

INDIA

The Honorable East India Company (HEIC) maintained armies in each of the three Indian presidencies, comprising regiments of Indians, called Sepoys, led by British officers, and also regiments of British soldiers. In 1861 some of these troops were amalgamated into the British Army (records at **NA**) and the rest were formed into the Indian Army (records at the **India Office Library**, except officers' commissions, which are at NA in HO 51; WO 25/1–88 and WO 31), under the direct control of the Viceroy. Most records relating to these soldiers are also in the India Office Library. The records include HEIC court minutes, including indexed cadet papers (1789–1860), which usually include a birth or baptism

LIFETIMES: A HARD-WORKING SUBADAR

THE JALIL FAMILY who live in the Midlands knew that their immediate forebear was born in Bihar and that his father, Saiyid Mohammod Jalil, born in 1905, was the son of Abdul Majeed Mugurjalil Cahman, a doctor in the Indian Army. Many Indians living in the 19th century do not appear in records, but because of his involvement with the British, there was a good chance that Abdul would appear in the records of the India Office Library, part of the British Library, in London. And indeed he did.

In the 1910 Indian Army List, under 'Medical Services: Indian Subordinate Medical Department (Bengal)', we find listed Abdul Majid, born on 1 April 1882, who entered the service, proficient in English, to serve in the 19th Punjab Regiment, on 2 April 1903 – in other words, immediately after his 21st birthday. He became a 3rd class hospital assistant on 2 April 1908 and subsequent directories show his steady rise, no doubt through extremely hard work, to become a sub-assistant surgeon, 1st class, serving with the 125th Rifles, by the outbreak of the First World War.

Later directories show that, for his service in the war, he won the Indian Distinguished Service Medal. In 1926 he was 'specially promoted' to the rank of 'subadar', which was the equivalent to the rank of captain within the hierarchy of Indian warrant officers. Had he been white, he would no doubt have become a high-ranking surgeon – but this was as far as the British were prepared to promote Indians. Yet at least he was recorded in such a way that we can find this much about him.

certificate and all providing parents' names.
⊟ Records of the British officers serving under the HEIC 1796–1841, with some records relating to officers' and soldiers' pensions, are at the **NA** in classes WO 23 and 25. The **National Army Museum** has a card index to them, and both the **India Office Library** and **SoG** have army lists and biographical dictionaries detailing their promotions, where they served and usually when and where they died. The SoG also holds its own collection of material relating to the British in India.

NEW ZEALAND
⊟ Militia and army records for New Zealand are at the **National Archives** in Wellington.

THE ROYAL NAVY

As a great maritime power, Britain has two navies, the Royal Navy and a great fleet of privately owned ships known as the Merchant Navy (see page 208). Many people's ancestors served in one or the other, or sometimes both. Some families' histories are closely bound up with the navy: very few will have had no involvement with it at all. Naval service was one of the few sources of employment open to black and Asian people in Britain in the 18th and 19th centuries.

FIRST FIND YOUR SHIP

GENERALLY, OFFICERS are easier to trace than non-commissioned sailors. Apart from the exceptions outlined below, you will not get very far seeking records of ordinary sailors without knowing the name of at least one of the ships on which they served. General Registration records, parish registers, medal rolls, wills and other records mentioned in this book may mention a ship's name. The GRO index to births and deaths at sea from 1837 may also reveal entries relevant to a sailor's family, and certificates will tell you the ship's name.

The fully indexed 1881 census, and the indexed 1861 census of people on ships will lead you directly to the right ship, wherever it was on the globe. The indexed Trinity House petitions (see page 206) provide another short-cut means of getting a hook on many seamen. For the Royal Navy there is class ADM 7–8 at the NA, which can help you find out which ships were where at specific times. If you know where an ancestor was, you can find out which ships were there at the same time, and then search their musters or pay books for your man. Remember that many ordinary sailors wrote wills: many records of those who died abroad or at sea before 1858 are in the Perogative Court of Canterbury (see page 129), usually annotated 'pts', meaning 'foreign parts', while others may be found in country record offices.

▽ A Gosport sailor's letter of administration, naming the ship on which he died.

△ ▷Naval records relating to Thomas Potter, a fatherless boy from a Greenwich orphanage who went to sea but was killed tragically young in the West Indies. His subsequent unexpected reappearance in Greenwich is related in 'A Greenwich Ghost Story' by me, in *Bygone Kent* (19, no.11 November 1998).

THE ROYAL NAVY

GENERAL

Henry VIII made the navy the responsibility of the Lord Admiral in 1546. Naval records up to 1660 are scattered among the State Papers (Domestic), Privy Council, Exchequer and Admiralty, but, if you are lucky, you will find mention of ancestors who served as officers.

From the Restoration in 1660 and until 1832, records are mainly in the Navy Board and Admiralty records at the **NA** and exclusively in the Admiralty records (ADM) for 1833–1926.

The very best guide to the NA's holdings is B. Pappalardo's *Tracing Your Naval Ancestors* (TNA, 2003). After 1926, if you can prove you are the next of kin of a deceased sailor, you can apply for their records to the **Naval Personnel Records Office**.

Naval museums will give you a true flavour of what life was like for your nautical forebears. The main one for naval history (Royal and Merchant) is the **National Maritime Museum** and there is also the **Royal Naval Museum**. Both have complete sets of the Navy Lists from 1797.

OFFICERS

The main ranks of commissioned officers were admiral, rear admiral, commodore, commander, captain and lieutenant. Below them came warrant officers, who were in charge of functional aspects of the ship, such as master, engineer, sailmaker, gunner, boatswain, surgeon and carpenter.

Commissioned officers serving 1660–1814 are outlined in D. Syrett

and R. L. DiNardo's *The Commissioned Sea Officers of the Royal Navy 1660–1815* (Naval Records Society, 1994), which draws on a wide variety of sources and includes details of officers commissioned by 1815 but whose careers continued long after.

Also worth checking is J. Charnock's *Biographia Navalis, Or Impartial Memoirs of the Lives and Characters of Officers of the Navy of Great Britain from 1660 to the Present Time* (R. Faulder, 1794–8). N. Hurst's *Naval Chronicle 1799–1818: Index to Births, Marriages and Deaths* (N. Hurst, 1989) is useful for the Napoleonic period. Coming forwards to 1835 is J. Marshall's *Royal Naval Biography, Or Memoirs of the Services of all the Flag-officers ... whose Names Appeared on the Admiralty List of Sea Officers at the Commencement of the Present Year [1823], or who have Since been Promoted* (Longman, 1823–35).

Finally, there is W. R. O'Byrne's *A Naval Biographical Dictionary; Comprising the Life and Services of every Living Officer in Her Majesty's Navy, from the Rank of Admiral of the Fleet to that of Lieutenant* (John Murray, 1861). This details the careers of officers often including correspondence between author and subject, detailing officers living in 1845 and also 600 who died in that year. In many cases the father's name and residence is given, making this particularly useful to genealogists.

Most First World War officers will appear in the *Naval Who's Who* (1917). There are also lists of officers published occasionally from 1700 and consistently as Navy

Lists from 1782. These include warrant officers. They are available at the **NA** and **SoG**, and will enable you to build up a picture of your ancestor's career.

Useful original sources at the **NA** include classes C 215/6, oaths of allegiance to Charles II taken by officers and men, and a similar list for oaths made to William III in 1696, is in C 213. Lieutenants' passing certificates, 1691–1902 (ADM 6, 13 and 107), arranged alphabetically, include baptism and later birth certificates, with a similar series for warrant officers.

Commissioned and warrant officers' service records, c.1840–1920, some of which include dates of birth, marriage and death, are at the **NA** in ADM 196. Chronological registers of commissions are in ADM 6 (1695–mid-19th century). Records of commissioned and warrant officers on full pay are mainly in ADM 24 (1795–1872) and half-pay in ADM 25 (1693–1926); the latter may record the officer's residential address.

Class ADM also contains records of courts martial, wounded officers' pensions, widows' pensions (including letters of application, proof of marriage and baptism of children) and so on, all detailed in N. A. M. Rodger's *Naval Records for Genealogists* (PRO Publications, 1998).

RATINGS

Before 1853, ordinary sailors (ratings) were discharged after each voyage and could (and did) serve on merchant ships, so can be very difficult to find in records. Sailors who served from 1853 onwards can be easily traced

y certify that my son, *Thos Potter* , has my full consent

(& himself willing) to enter Her Majesty's Navy for a period of Ten Years'

...ous and General Service, from the age of 18, in addition to whatever period

..e necessary until he attain that age, agreeably to Her Majesty's Order in

..., dated 1st April, '53, and the Admiralty Regulations of the 14 June, '53,

...g thereto.

Witness our hands at *Woolwich*

10 day of *December*   186 *8*

Date of Boy's Birth, *October 2. 1849. Baptised a Roman Catholic.*

Parent's Signature, { or, if dead, .) *A Potter* (nearest relative)

Boy's Signature of consent, and who further declares that he is not

Indentured as an apprentice. *Thomas Potter A Potter*

◁ **Thomas Potter's continuous service agreement. Note that Thomas's mother got confused and wrote her name where his should have been.**

THE NATIONAL ARCHIVES has a new database of resources for the Battle of Trafalgar (1805) at **www.nationalarchives. gov.uk/ trafalgardatabase**.

🗐 Pensions for 1802–94 may be found at the NA in ADM 29, for which there is an index. Remember that after 1853 sailors who had served for 20 years could leave and receive a pension even if they carried on working outside the navy for decades to come.

🗐 The hospital at Greenwich was established in 1695 to care for naval pensioners and their families. Records of its admissions and discharges (1704–1869) are in at the NA in ADM 73. N. A. M. Rodger's *Naval Records for Genealogists* (PRO Publications, 1998) outlines the hospital's many other records, including that of its school for sailors' children.

through the indexed continuous service engagement books at the NA in ADM 139 (1853–72) and ADM 188 (1873–1923), fully indexed in ADM 188/245–67.

🗐 Once you find a ship on which your ancestor served, you can examine its muster rolls at the NA in ADM 36–9 (1740–1808, with some for the period 1688–1739). Your ancestor's first and last musters on a ship should tell you the previous vessel on which he had served, and the one to which he was transferring, or whether he was being discharged, or had died. With luck, therefore, you should be able to track his whole naval career.

Pay books

🗐 Pay books covering 1691–1856 are in the NA, classes ADM 31–5. They can be used to substitute gaps in the musters and may also name next of kin, such as the sailor's wife or parents who received the pay on the sailor's behalf.

Ships' logs

🗐 Some of these survive from the 17th century. They are in classes ADM 50–5 at the NA and will provide much useful background. They may even mention your ancestor, especially if he had an accident or was killed.

Seamen's effects papers

🗐 These are at the NA in class ADM 44 (1800–60). Other wills may be found in ADM 48 (indexed in ADM 142). In ADM 171 are medal rolls for all ranks covering 1793–1972, arranged by ship and not indexed. Description books are in ADM 38.

Pensions

🗐 The Chatham Chest (in the NA, ADM 82) was a fund set up in 1590 to pay pensions to wounded sailors or the families of sailors killed in action. Registers survive for 1653–7 and 1675–1799 (indexed from 1695). From 1803, these pensions were paid through the Royal Naval Hospital at Greenwich.

QUICK REFERENCE

See also main sources in Useful Addresses, page 306

NAVAL PERSONNEL RECORDS OFFICE
Ministry of Defence
CS(RM)2 Navy Search
Bourne Avenue
Hayes
Middlesex UB3 1RF
☎ 020 8573 3831
www.mod.uk

NATIONAL MARITIME MUSEUM
Park Row
Greenwich
London SE10 9NF
☎ 020 8858 4422
www.nmm.ac.uk

ROYAL NAVAL MUSEUM
Buildings 1–7, College Road
HM Naval Base
Portsmouth
Hampshire PO1 3NH
☎ 023 9272 7562
www.royalnavalmuseum.org

△ Shipyards, from the Clyde to Chatham, provided employment for many from the Middle Ages but especially in the 19th and early 20th centuries.

WHERE TO SEARCH

Courts martial

Courts martial 1680–1913 are at the **NA** in class ADM 1.

RESERVE SAILORS

Some peoples' ancestors became reserve sailors, such as the Sea Fencibles, raised to help defend the country against France between 1798 and 1813, and many Merchant Navy sailors were also members of the Royal Naval Reserve (RNR), created in 1859. The records of members of the RNR who served in the First World War are in the **NA** in class ADM 337.

DOCKYARDS

The main naval dockyards in Britain were at Portsmouth, Woolwich, Deptford, Chatham, Sheerness and Plymouth. If you discover a record of the baptism or marriage of an ancestor in one of these places, he could well have had naval connections and, if you loose sight of him, look in the parish records of other dockyard towns. It may be worth considering the other British dockyards abroad at Halifax, Nova Scotia; Port Royal, Jamaica and Gibraltar.

Many men worked in the dockyards as clerks or tradesmen. Their records are in the ADM series too at the **NA**, particularly paybooks 1660–1857 (ADM 42, 32, 36 and 37) and books containing physical descriptions of tradesmen between 1748 and 1830 (ADM 106).

The **National Maritime Museum** has a card index compiled from its own holdings and records at the **NA**, especially classes ADM 6 and ADM 11, covering all types of dockyard officers employed in naval dockyards both in this country and abroad for the 17th–19th centuries. The information given is generally confined to periods of employment in a specific job, though if someone died in service the date of death may appear. A project to index the dockyards' letterbooks (ADM 106) is underway and will include names and positions held.

TRINITY HOUSE PETITIONS

Trinity House issued pensions to retired seamen or their widows and orphans between 1514 and 1854. From 1727 there are registers at Guildhall Library giving the names and ages of recipients, together with where they were and why they needed help.

Petitions, including details of the hardships being suffered, often accompanied by certificates proving baptisms, marriages, apprenticeships and so on, survive from 1787. These are at **Guildhall Library** with copies on film at the **SoG**, and indexed in A. J. Camp's *The Trinity House Petitions: A Calendar of the Records of the Corporation of Trinity House, London, in the Library of the SoG* (SoG, 1987).

QUICK REFERENCE

See also main sources in Useful Addresses, page 306

NATIONAL MARITIME MUSEUM
Park Row
Greenwich
London SE10 9NF
☎ 020 8858 4422
www.nmm.ac.uk

JAMES GALLOWAY'S Trinity House petition (see opposite), dated 13 February 1817, shows that he was aged 57 and residing in Marske (Yorkshire) where he had lived for over 20 years as a seaman, and was currently renting a house and working as a day labourer. He went to sea at 17 in a vessel out of the nearby port of Whitby, and served as an 'apprentice to William Maler in the coasting and Baltic trade, latterly in the situation of mate on board the Ship Palion, Captain Livingston, Master, in the Coasting Trade, of which ship John Goodchild Esq. was owner, and in that capacity served for thirty or more voyages'. Galloway's wife was Jane, aged 49, and they had two children under 12, David and Shemelds, and another (unnamed) under 13 who, through infirmity, James could not look after. When the form asked for his property and income, the person filling it in for James (probably Captain Goodchild) wrote '£0-0-0'.

At the foot of the petition is written in bold writing:

'NB. The above named James Galloway was in ye voyage wrecked on the coast of Norfolk and the cold he suffered at the time has continued.'

Attached to the petition is a genealogist's dream – original notes signed by parish clergymen confirming James's marriage to Jane Shemelds, by banns, on 10 January 1792 at Whitby, the baptisms of the children, of the wife Jane and of James himself:

BAPTISM 1759
August 12 James son of George Galloway. This is a copy of the above Baptism as taken from the parish register of baptisms for the parish of Dunferling in the County of Fife. Richard Thompson, minister, William McKintosh, Eld[er], John Dickison, Eld[er].

The only place with a name similar to this in Fife was Dunfermline, but none of the registers in Dunfermline contained a record of his baptism, nor had any of them ever had a minister with such a name, and nor could elders of the names mentioned be traced. After finding so much fascinating and true information about James, the trail ended with the fake certificate he had probably used to join the merchant navy as an under-age boy. His authentic origins have never been established.

THE MERCHANT NAVY

While the Royal Navy gets most of the press, the majority of Britain's shipping activities were undertaken for trade – by the Merchant Navy. Although not always as glamorous, records of Merchant Navy service can be equally enlightening and make a worthy addition to any family history.

THE MERCHANT NAVY

GENERAL

⊟ The best guide to Merchant Navy records is C. and M. Watts' *My Ancestor was a Merchant Seaman* (3rd edition, SoG, 2004).

⊟ Many boys and men were trained for the Merchant Navy by the Marine Society, whose indexed registers 1772–1950 are at the **National Maritime Museum**. Many poor boys were apprenticed to the Merchant Navy by their parish (see page 185). Apprentices' indentures were issued from 1824 and are indexed at the **NA** in class BT 150. They include ages and the ship on which the boys sailed.

⊟ From 1747 onwards, muster rolls (at the **NA**, class BT 98) were kept, listing the crew of each Merchant Navy ship. Until 1834, they gave each man's home address, date of joining and date of leaving the previous ship. Unfortunately, these musters were deposited at the ports where the ships happened to be, and only those for Shields (1747), Dartmouth (1770), Plymouth (1761) and Liverpool (1772) pre-date the 19th century. Thereafter many more survive and can be searched, provided you have an idea where and when your ancestor set sail, but beware – the records for larger ports may take you a very long time to search.

⊟ For the period 1835–57, prospects of finding what you want perk up considerably. In 1835, all merchant vessels came under the control of the Board of Trade, whose records are in class BT at the NA. The period 1835–57 is covered by indexed registers of seamen in classes BT 120 (1835–6), 112 and 119 (1835–44), and BT 114

(1845–53), which can lead you straight to the crew lists described above. BT 114 can also be used to look up seamen's tickets (1845–53) in BT 113. There is also an alphabetical register of seamen covering 1853–7 at the NA in class BT 116.

⊟ After 1857, searching reverts to being as difficult as it was before 1835, until 1913–41, which is covered by a Central Register of Shipping and Seamen at the **NA** on **www.catalogue.nationalarchives.gov.uk**. BT 350 (1918–21) and 348–9 (1921–41) include places of birth and some photographs.

CREW LISTS AND AGREEMENTS

⊟ These span the period 1835–60 and are at the **NA** in BT 98. They outline the course of the proposed voyage of a ship and give specific information about each sailor. They are arranged by voyages, so are only easily searched between 1835 and 1857.

⊟ The **NA** also holds the crew lists up to 1861, after which most (up to 1976) have gone to an unusual home – the **Maritime History Archive** in Canada. They offer a search service at $35 (Canadian) per hour. Their collection is indexed for the period 1863–1938. The rest of the records are divided between the **NA**, **National Maritime Museum** and **county record offices** (for which the Newfoundland archive has also produced a single index) and (for the period 1939–50) are with the **Registrar General of Shipping and Seamen**.

DIED AT SEA

⊟ If your sailor ancestor died at sea between 1852 and 1889, you can find details of the death, wages due and date and place of joining

the ship at the **NA** in BT 15, indexed in BT 154.

SECOND WORLD WAR

⊟ Medals awarded to merchant seamen who served in the Second World War – some 100,000 of them – are now searchable online at **www.documentsonline.nationalarchives.gov.uk.**

LOG BOOKS

⊟ These can provide much information about your ancestors' voyages, but survival is patchy and they are divided between the **NA** (BT 165), **National Maritime Museum** and the **Maritime History Archive**. They include details of births, marriages and deaths abroad with a register compiled by the Registrar General of Shipping and Seamen for 1854–87, 1883 and 1890 respectively (BT 158).

CERTIFICATES OF COMPETENCY

⊟ Merchant Navy captains were usually referred to as masters, and second-in-commands as mates. From 1845 new masters and mates could – and from 1850 had to – obtain a certificate of competency. These included year and place of birth, and are in registers at the **NA** in classes BT 112 and 123–6, with an index in BT 127. There is also an alphabetical register of masters (1845–55) in BT 115.

⊟ Engineers' certificates of competency from 1862 are in the **NA** in BT 139 and 142 (indexed in BT 141). Those to colonial masters and mates are in BT 128, indexed in BT 127, with colonial engineers in BT 140, indexed in BT 141.

⊟ Skippers and mates of fishing boats needed certificates from 1883 and these are at the **NA** in BT 129–30, indexed in BT 138.

△ *Merchant Ships under Sail and at Anchor off a Town*
by William Anderson (1757–1837).

BT 317, 318 and 320 cover certificates for masters and mates 1917–68, examination registers for masters, mates and engineers 1913–35 and engineers 1919–29. Masters are also recorded between 1868 and 1947 in Lloyd's Marine Collection at the **Guildhall Library**.

SHIPS

Lloyd's Marine Collection also contains much information about the ships themselves, as does **Lloyd's Register of Shipping**.

SHIP OWNERS

Many people's ancestors were ship owners. This was not always as grand as it sounds, as most ships were divided into 64 shares of ownership, some held by investors and others by craftsmen on the ships, all of whom expected a share of the profit accrued by the voyage. Some records from the 17th century may be in the **county record office** covering the ship's home port.

From 1786 to 1854, registers for ships over 15 tons, listing the ship owners and their home addresses, are in **NA** class BT 107. For 1855 to 1889, see BT 108. An index to the ships in both is in BT 111. Records after 1889 are in BT 110.

EAST INDIA COMPANY

Records of the Honourable East India Company's fleet of merchant and warships (the latter was known as the 'Bombay Marine' and later the Indian Navy) are in the **India Office Library**, including information about captains, masters and mates, and logs of voyages covering 1605–1856. You are unlikely to find records of East India seamen listed before the mid-19th century.

QUICK REFERENCE

See also main sources in Useful Addresses, page 306

NATIONAL MARITIME MUSEUM
Park Row
Greenwich
London SE10 9NF
☎ 020 8858 4422
www.nmm.ac.uk

MARITIME HISTORY ARCHIVE
Memorial University of New Foundland
St John's
Newfoundland A1C 5S7
Canada
☎ 00 1 709737 8428
www.mun.ca/mha/about.html

REGISTRAR GENERAL OF SHIPPING AND SEAMEN
Anchor House
Cheviot Close
Parc Ty Glas
Llanishen
Cardiff CF14 5JA
☎ 029 2044 8800

LLOYD'S REGISTER OF SHIPPING
71 Fenchurch Street
London EC3M 4BS
☎ 020 7709 9166
www.lr.org

INDIA OFFICE LIBRARY
British Library
96 Euston Road
London NW1 2DB
☎ 020 7412 7513
www.bl.uk/collections/orientalandindian.html

THE ROYAL MARINES

Charles II created the Marines in 1665 to serve as soldiers on board Royal Navy ships, acting as sentries and additional labour in peacetime and providing musket fire in sea battles. The force was disbanded in the early 18th century and reformed in 1755: they were known as 'Royal' from 1802.

WHERE TO SEARCH

THE ROYAL MARINES

⊟ Records of Marines are arranged by three divisions: Chatham, Plymouth and Portsmouth. The records, which are in most respects identical to those of the army, are at the **NA** in the Admiralty records (class ADM). The NA has a card index to many (but not all) attestation forms (ADM 157/1–659) in the Research Enquiries Room and has several information leaflets, especially no. 46, 'How to find a division', to guide you through the records.

⊟ Lists of marine officers 1757–1850 and 1760–1886 are at the **NA** in ADM 118/230–336 and ADM 192 respectively, fully indexed from 1770. Marine officers are listed in the Navy Lists. Further information may be obtained, especially concerning officers who were appointed after 1926, from the Commandant General at the **Royal Marines** and the **Royal Marines Museum**, which details the whereabouts of service records before and after 1926.

⊟ Like army and navy records, post-1926 service records are confidential but can be applied for by proven descendants from **Royal Marines Historical Records and Medals**. The best book on Marines is G.Thomas' *Records of Royal Marines* (PRO Publications, 1994).

QUICK REFERENCE

See also main sources in Useful Addresses, page 306

ROYAL MARINES
Commandant General
Ministry of Defence (Navy)
Whitehall
London SW1
☎ 0870 607 4455
www.royalnavy.mod.uk

ROYAL MARINES MUSEUM
Eastney Barracks
Southsea
Hampshire PO4 9PX
☎ 0239 281 9385
www.royalmarinesmuseum.co.uk

ROYAL MARINES HISTORICAL
RECORDS AND MEDALS
HRORM
Room 038
Centurion Building
Grange Road
Gosport
Hampshire PO13 9XA
☎ 023 9270 2126
www.mod.uk

◁ 'Captain, Flag Officer and Commander' from *Costume of the Royal Navy and Marines*, engraved by L. and E. Mansion (19th century).

THE ROYAL AIR FORCE (RAF)

The army founded the Royal Flying Corps (RFC) in 1912, only nine years after the first powered flight, followed two years later by the Royal Navy's Royal Naval Air Service (RNAS). The two were unified as a third branch of the military in 1918. The force then numbered 291,000 officers, rising to a million men and women during the Second World War.

THE ROYAL AIR FORCE

▢ Records up to 1918/20 are at the **NA** in classes WO 363, 364 and ADM 273, with further records in WO 339 and 374 (RFC officers who left before 1918) and other ranks in WO 363 and 364.

▢ Records of RNAS officers who left before 1918 are at the **NA** in class ADM 273 and other ranks in ADM 188. RAF officers who left by 1926 are in AIR 76 and some airmen for the same period are in AIR 79, indexed in AIR 78.

▢ Women's RAF records for the First World War are at the **NA** in AIR 80.

▢ After 1926, the same confidentiality rules apply as to army and navy records. If you can prove you are the next of kin of a deceased serviceman you can contact the **RAF Personnel and Training Command**. Those for the Fleet Air Arm are at the **Ministry of Defence**. W. R. Chorley's *Royal Air Force Bomber Command Losses of the Second World War* (Midland Counties Publications, 1992-3) is also worth searching.

▢ Officers were included in the published Army and Navy Lists until the formation of the RAF, which subsequently published its own Airforce Lists. W. Spencer's *Air Force Records for Family Historians* (PRO, 2002) is a useful guide to discovering more about the airforce careers of members of your family. The **RAF Museum** has a useful website.

QUICK REFERENCE

See also main sources in Useful Addresses, page 306

RAF PERSONNEL AND TRAINING COMMAND
Branch PG 5a(2) (for officers) and P Man 2b(1) (for non-officers)
RAF Innsworth
Gloucestershire GL3 1EZ
☎ 01452 712612
www.mod.uk

MINISTRY OF DEFENCE
CS(R)2
Bourne Avenue
Hayes
Middlesex UB3 1FR
☎ 0870 607 4455
www.mod.uk

RAF MUSEUM
Grahame Park Way
Hendon
London NW9 5LL
☎ 020 8205 2266
www.rafmuseum.org.uk

WHERE TO SEARCH

◁ RAF flyers in England during the Second World War.

CHAPTER TWENTY-TWO
TAX & OTHER FINANCIAL MATTERS

Since the Norman Conquest, the state has been ruthless in its efforts, efficient or otherwise, to tax us. But what was bad for our ancestors is good for us, because not only were vast amounts of taxes raised but detailed records of them were made and still survive today.

For the 12th and 13th centuries, tax records indicate how surnames were spelled, at the very period in which they were becoming hereditary, and therefore help us to work out what they originally meant. For the period before parish registers (up to 1538), they provide one of the best sources for determining who was alive, and when. They do not tell you how people were related, but the disappearance of one person from a series of tax lists and his replacement by another with the same surname can indicate a possible father–son relationship.

Tax records add a little colour to family history, indicating how much people's houses or landholdings were worth, how many windows and fireplaces they had, and so on. They can also be invaluable if you do not know where an ancestor came from. A county tax list for the period when the ancestor was likely to have been born can provide a list of parishes where people of the same surname lived, and thus where your ancestor may have been born.

QUICK REFERENCE

See main sources in Useful Addresses, page 306

WHERE TO SEARCH

TAX RECORDS AND GENEALOGY

Some **county record offices** have card indexes to many of their tax lists, including lay subsidies, hearth tax, window tax and so on. Many sections of tax lists have been published, especially by **county record societies**, as listed in E. L. C. Mullins' *Texts and Calendars: an Analytical Guide to Serial Publications* (RHS, 1958 and 1983).

M. Jurkowski, C. L. Smith and D. Crook's *Lay Taxes in England and Wales 1188–1689* (PRO Publications, 1998) is a comprehensive survey of national taxes, ranging from poll tax to land tax, subsidies and forced loans, many of which survive in class E 179 at the **NA**. The same text is on **www.nationalarchives.gov.uk/e179/**. Be aware that these are not transcriptions or indexes of the lists themselves – they still need to be searched manually.

THE MAIN TAX LAWS

The main taxes you are likely to encounter, and which you should be able to use yourself for tracing your family tree, are as follows.

LAY SUBSIDIES

These were taxes chargeable on movable goods. The clergy were exempt – hence the term 'lay' – as were the poor, and some goods, such as knights' armour, were not taxable. Lay subsidies list names from the late

12th century, although in practice few survive from before 1327. From 1334 only the places and sums raised were recorded. In 1523, with Henry VIII's Great Subsidy, names of all those aged 16 or more with land or goods worth £2, or annual income of £1 or more, were recorded. Lay subsidies continued to be raised periodically until the end of the 17th century.

POLL TAX (1377–1703)

Centuries before Margaret Thatcher, poll taxes were causing misery and unrest throughout England and Wales. They were raised in 1377, 1379 and 1381(resulting in the Peasants' Revolt), then in 1641, and 18 times between 1660 and 1703. All men aged 16 or over who were not paupers were liable to pay a set amount.

SHEEP TAX (1549)

This was a tax raised by Edward VI on flocks of sheep. Ewes kept on enclosed land were changed at 3d a head, shear-sheep on such land 2d a head and shear-sheep on commons 3½d. Even though sheep owners only had to pay if the amount assessed exceeded what they had paid in a subsidy on goods earlier that year, the tax caused great

SHEEP TAX

THERE ARE A FEW surviving returns listing flock-holders' names at the NA in E 179 listed under 'poll tax on sheep'. See my article in *Ancestors* (the NA's magazine), August 2004, pp. 50–5 and note on returns for newly-found Breconshire returns in *Ancestors*, October 2004 edition, page 7.

QUICK REFERENCE

See main sources in Useful Addresses, page 306

WHERE TO SEARCH

THE MAIN TAX LAWS

LAY SUBSIDIES

⊟ Some records are in **county record offices**, but most are at the NA in class E 179, listed in S. Colwell's *Family Roots; Discovering the Past in the PRO* (Weidenfeld & Nicolson, 1991). Many have been published by **county record societies**. E 179 also contains other Tudor taxes, such as assessments for forced loans of 1522–3, which were raised from men aged 16 or over.

⊟ These records are particularly useful when they pre-date the registers of the parish where your ancestors lived. If you are lucky, you will find surviving tax lists for every couple of years, showing people with your surname, indicating who earlier generations may have been.

⊟ Some Irish subsidy rolls survive, particularly for Northern Ireland, at the **PRONI**.

POLL TAX

⊟ The 13th- century returns are in **NA** class E 179 and sometimes provide not just names but also occupations and relationships. They are being published: vol. 1 is C. Fenwick's *The Poll Taxes of 1377, 1379 and 1381* (OUP for the British Academy, 1998). The 17th- and 18th-century lists survive only patchily. The 1641 survivals are listed in J. Gibson and A. Dell's *The Protestation Returns 1641–42 and other Contemporary Listings* (FFHS, 1995) and those from 1660 are in J. Gibson's *The Hearth Tax, and other Later Stuart Tax Lists and the Association Rolls* (FFHS, 1996).

⊟ Scottish poll tax records 1693–99 are at the **NAS** and listed in Gibson, and some for Northern Ireland are at the **PRONI**.

A FEW YEARS AGO, I successfully traced the Chard family back through a number of parishes on the Devon–Somerset border, to Thomas Chard of Hemyock, whose children, Elizabeth, William, Oliver, Edward and Cornelius, had been baptised there between 1692 and 1705. Thomas himself was baptised in Hemyock in 1667, son of a John Chard, but the registers of that parish showed no sign of his baptism, or indeed any other Chards. It seemed likely, therefore, that the family had come from somewhere else. To establish where this might have been, we examined the printed 1582 Lay Subsidy returns. These gave three references to the surname:

St Mary Church	John Charde	goods	5d
Clayhidon	John Charde	goods	12d
Crediton	Walter Charde	goods	3d

Clayhidon adjoined Hemyock, and in the Clayhidon registers were records of the following baptisms:

1648, 18 December,	Anne d. of John Chard
1642, 20 May,	Oliver Chard s. of John Chard jnr
1639, 13 March	John s. of John Chard jnr

The occurrence of the name Oliver here was pretty conclusive and this, coupled with the absence of a burial for John, indicated that the boy baptised in 1639 was the person who later settled in Hemyock.

John junior's baptism does not appear in the registers, but they only started in 1634. A few years' worth of bishops' transcripts survived, however (see page 114), and these indicated other children of John senior, including Grace (1626), Richard (year unspecified) and William (1620). John senior appears as a churchwarden of Clayhidon in 1640/1, and is listed in the Protestation returns of 1641.

Earlier, there is a Richard Chard listed in the 1569 muster roll (see page 208) for Clayhidon as an 'harquebusier' – an arquebus was a large and rather clumsy gun – and he was, in turn, son of the John who paid his taxes in 1581. This earlier John also appeared in the muster roll, recorded as having to provide an 'almain rivet', two bows, two sheafs of arrows, two steel caps and a bill, in case of Spanish invasion. There are even earlier tax lists, such as the 1332 Devonshire Lay Subsidies, which list three Chardes, Walter and John in Broadwoodwidger and Richard in 'Athens' St Mary, and even a John de Charde in Otterton – possible forebears of the Chardes of Hemyock.

resentment and contributed to rebellion that summer. It was repealed in November.

SHIP MONEY (1634–40)

Charles I's raising of ship money – a tax ostensibly for the navy, which he could raise without Parliament's agreement – was a major cause of the argument between the King and Parliament that led to the Civil War.

CONTRIBUTIONS FOR IRELAND (1642)

In autumn 1641, a Catholic rebellion broke out in Ireland, and in February 1642 the King and Parliament agreed to send an army out to protect the Protestant settlers. To raise funds for the army, the wealthy were asked to lend money at 8% interest, while all men were invited to make 'gifts' of money via the overseers of the poor and churchwardens, and this was done between June and the following April. Some of the resulting lists of contributors survive.

△ *Charles I in Three Positions*, painting by Carlo Maratta after Van Dyke (1625–1713).

COMMITTEES FOR ADVANCE OF MONEY AND COMPOUNDING (1642–60)

From 1642 onwards, a Parliamentarian committee forced people, Royalist and Parliamentarian alike, to loan money to the Commonwealth. From 1646, only defeated Royalists had to make these loans although, to be fair to Parliament, efforts were made to pay the money back with interest.

From 1643 onwards, a Parliamentarian committee called the Committee for the Sequestration of Delinquents' Estates sat in judgement on landowners who had supported the King, and seized their land. The Committee for Compounding, which was not wound up until the Restoration, then gave the land back in return for an oath of loyalty to the Commonwealth and a hefty fine.

FREE AND VOLUNTARY PRESENT (1661)

This pseudo-tax, which was theoretically voluntary, although the well-to-do were expected to pay, was raised for the newly restored – and heavily indebted – Charles II in 1661.

WHERE TO SEARCH

SHIP MONEY

Surviving returns for the period 1634–40 are in **NA** class SP 16 and SP 17.

FREE AND VOLUNTARY PRESENT

Lists of some 130,000 names, usually with occupations, are in **NA** class E 179.

QUICK REFERENCE

See main sources in Useful Addresses, page 306

SPINNING WHEEL PREMIUMS

IN THE NAPOLEONIC WARS, the Navy needed much linen. The flax needed to make linen made heavy demands on the soil, so farmers were reluctant to grow it. The Government introduced an incentive scheme in the north of Ireland whereby farmers growing flax received a spinning wheel for every quarter acre or a loom for a full acre. The lists, especially for 1796, survive at the National Archives, PRONI and Mormon Family History Library.

△ *The Quillwinder* by John Harden (1772–1847).

HEARTH TAX RETURNS (1662–89)

The hearth tax was one of the Restoration government's chief methods of raising extra income. Assessments of how many fireplaces were in each house in the realm were made by constables, and enrolled at the Quarter Sessions, and the householders taxed at 1s per six months per hearth. Those occupying property worth less than 20s in yearly rent, or had less than £10 worth of movable goods, or were receiving poor relief or alms, were let off, as were charitable institutions, alehouses, kilns and furnaces and blowing houses. After May 1664, those with two hearths or more had to pay regardless.

Because the law empowered constables to enter houses to search for hearths, the tax was rightly detested as an unwarranted intrusion on Englishmen's 'castles' and was repealed in 1689.

LAND TAX (1693–1963)

Land tax replaced earlier, random taxes, particularly hearth tax and subsidies. It was levied from 1693 to 1963, but most records survive from between 1780 and 1832. They are arranged by parish within hundreds and list all landholders with property worth 20s or more and (from 1772) tenants, although if more than one tenant lived in a building, only one will be listed. The property may also be described briefly.

MARRIAGE DUTY ACT (1695–1706)

This Act, introduced in May 1695 to fund one of our many wars with France, taxed all births, marriages and burials – and just to be fair, it also taxed widows without children and bachelors aged over 25! Paupers were let off.

WINDOW TAX (1696–1851)

This tax was introduced in 1696 and, despite being very unpopular, was not repealed until 1851. Paupers were exempt (not many paupers' cottages had windows anyway), but when records survive most other ancestors appear in the records – mostly at county record offices.

OTHER FINANCIAL RECORDS

Taxes record the removal of our ancestors' money, but there are some happier records showing what they did with their remaining pennies. For the more nosy-minded among us, there is nothing more fascinating than finding out exactly how many pennies our ancestors (or, indeed, other people's) actually had.

COMMITTEES FOR ADVANCE OF MONEY AND COMPOUNDING

The records of the committee's highly intrusive activities from 1642 have been indexed and calendared in Mary Anne Everett Green's *Calendar of the Proceedings of the Committee for Advance of Money, 1642–1656, Preserved in the State Paper Office of Her Majesty's Public Record Office* (1888).

The original records for the Committee for Compounding, called Royalist composition papers, are in **NA** class SP 23 and have been calendared and indexed in Mary Anne Everett Green's *Calendar of the Proceedings of the Committee for Compounding, etc, 1643–1660* (1889–92).

HEARTH TAX RETURNS

Generally, the parish assessments give names, sometimes with the inclusion of 'senior', 'junior', 'widow' and so on, and the number of hearths, annotated with what was actually paid. Those exempt are sometimes listed. Most records at the **NA** are for 1662–6 and 1669–74. To find what has survived, you can search on **www.nationalarchives.gov.uk/e179/**.

Also check J. Gibson's *The Hearth Tax, and other Later Stuart Tax Lists and the Association Rolls* (FFHS, 1996), which will indicate what is in **county record offices** and what has been published. Their main use is in finding out in which parish people of your surname lived just after the end of the Civil War, complementing Protestation Returns and Covenant Records (see page 220), which show who was where when the disruption started.

Scottish hearth taxes survive for 1661–95 and are at the **NAS**.

Those for Ireland, called hearth money rolls, have survived in places, as listed in J. G. Ryan's *Irish Records – Sources for Family and Local History* (Ancestry, 1997). Those for Dublin are at **www.irishfamilyresearch.co.uk.**

LAND TAX

Returns mainly survive for the countryside and are in Quarter Session records (see page 232). An almost complete record for England and Wales for 1798 is in **NA** class IR 23. After 1798, the tax could be commuted by a lump-sum payment equivalent to 16 years' tax. Records of those 'exonerated' are in IR 22. Whereabouts of records is in J. Gibson, M. Medlycott and D. Mills' *Land and Window Tax Assessments* (FFHS, 1998).

MARRIAGE DUTY

The **county record offices** hold those relatively few assessments which have survived – details are in J. Gibson's *The Hearth Tax, and other Later Stuart Tax Lists and the Association Rolls* (FFHS, 1996). Where they do survive – mainly borough records and a handful of Wiltshire parishes – they will tell you who the householders in the parish were.

WINDOW TAX

The records are mostly at **county record offices**. Details of surviving records are in J. Gibson, M. Medlycott and D. Mills' *Land and Window Tax Assessments* (FFHS, 1998). The assessments state name, address, number of windows and amount payable – an interesting side-light on a family history. Many old houses still have windows, which were bricked up to lessen the amount of tax due.

Scottish returns, at the **NAS**, are mainly for 1748–98, and provide occupiers' names. The series is almost complete and includes records of the properties not liable to tax.

▽ **A hearth tax return from 1664.**

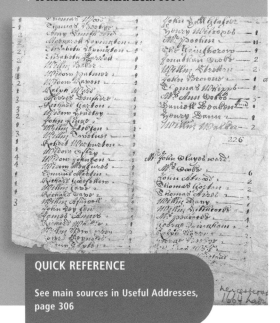

QUICK REFERENCE

See main sources in Useful Addresses, page 306

TITHE APPLOTMENT BOOKS & GRIFFITH'S VALUATION

TWO IMPORTANT SOURCES for Irish research are the Tithe Applotment Books and Griffith's Primary Valuation. The tithe records date from 1823 to 1837 and record, parish by parish, the occupiers of all agricultural land, the name of the land, the landlord and the amount of tithes deemed to be payable. The original records are at the National Archives of Ireland and those for Northern Ireland at the PRONI.

The primary valuation of Irish landholdings was overseen by Sir Richard Griffith, a civil engineer who served as Commissioner of Valuation in Ireland from 1828 to 1868, whose work created a resource of immense value to family historians. Griffith's task was to record all those liable to pay the poor rate and assess how much they should pay. To this end, his team worked throughout the Irish counties from 1847 to 1865, recording the landlords and occupiers of all buildings and land, noting the nature of the holding, with precise size and rateable value within each poor law union. The original records are at the National Archives of Ireland, with some copies at locations such as the SoG and IHGS, and full, indexed copies on CD-Rom, produced by Heritage World and the Genealogical Publishing Co. Inc. It is also searchable online at **www.genuki.org/big/ir** and more recently at **www.irishorigins.com**.

Besides the obvious fascination of seeing exactly what land and buildings your ancestors tenanted, Griffith's valuation is an excellent way of locating families. Say your ancestor James Crowley turned up in Liverpool in the 1870s, but you have no idea where he came from. At best you might find him through the index, tenanting his smallholding in the 1860s. Even if he is not listed himself (only heads of households were listed), you can learn where in Ireland the majority of Crowleys lived, and then you can look for heads of households with the same Christian name, giving you a good idea as to which parish registers to search for your James.

Maps showing the location of the properties in Griffith's valuation are at the Valuation Office. The Valuation Office at 6 Ealy Place, Dublin, also has the surveyors' notebooks, which sometimes provide extra information about the individuals recorded in the valuation, later valuations, made in 1865 and 1968, and books recording changes in ownership and occupation since the original valuation was made.

For landowners, you can also search in *A Return of Owners of Land of One Acre and Upwards* (HMSO, 1876), which contains 32,000 people, listed alphabetically by county.

OTHER FINANCIAL RECORDS

BANK ACCOUNTS

A surprising amount of records have survived for ancestors' bank accounts. The best are in the **Bank of England Archives**.

During the 17th and 18th centuries, many small banks were established, most of which either folded or were swallowed up to create the present big high-street names. Records of small local banks can sometimes be found in the local **county record offices**.

FIRE INSURANCE

Was your ancestor prudent enough to insure their property against fire? From 1696 onwards, records exist, many among the papers of the Sun Fire Office (papers at **Guildhall Library**, indexed 1816-24 at **www.a2a.org.uk**), whose 'sun' plaques are still to be seen on many old buildings. There are some records in county record offices but, because most insurance firms were based in the City, many are at Guildhall Library, which has indexes to some of the 18th-century records. The records will usually tell you your ancestor's occupation, the address of the property being insured and, of course, the amount.

TONTINES AND ANNUITIES

Public annuities were established by the state as a means of raising capital. People were encouraged to pay a lump sum in return for which a nominated person (who could be the person who made the payment or a dependent) would receive a guaranteed annual income for life. Similar schemes were tontines, whereby a group of people invested money into a scheme and shared the income: as they died, the survivors got a greater share of the income. Tontines were especially popular in Ireland and amongst Huguenots.

Various schemes were organised between 1693 and 1789 and records of these are at the **NA** in classes NDO 1–3 and E 401, 403 and 406–7. See also F. Leeson's *A Guide to the Records of the British State Tontines and Life Annuities of the 17th and 18th Centuries* (Pinhorns, 1968). There is an index to participants in some of the 18th-century schemes is in F. Leeson's *Index to the British State Tontine and Annuities 1745–1779* (SoG microfiche, 1994).

LOTTERIES

Records of the Million Lottery, established in 1694, is in **NA** class C 46.

TAXING THE RICH

THIS IS NOT a modern Socialist idea, but one deeply embedded in Hanoverian policy. Taxes devised to raise money from the middle and upper classes included:

- Carriages: 1747–82
- Silver plate: 1756–77
- Male servants: 1777–1852 (except those working in farming, trade or industry)

The SoG has an index to the employers listed in the 1780 returns.

- Game: 1784–1807
- Horses used for transport: 1784–1874
- Female servants: 1785–92
- Coats of arms: 1793–1882
- Hair powder: 1795–1861
- Dogs: 1796–1882
- Empty houses: 1851–1924
- Income: (for the very wealthy only) 1789, 1803–16 and 1842–present

The only surviving pre-1842 records are of those who failed to pay.

Surviving records, listing the tax payers only – and the survival is very patchy – are in NA classes E 182 and T 47, but many more will be found in county record offices and are always worth a search. The NAS hold many comparable lists.

CRIMINAL COURTS

GENERAL

⊟ The most detailed information on searching for criminal trials and their consequences is D. T. Hawkings' *Criminal Ancestors: A Guide to Historical Criminal Records in England & Wales* (Sutton, 1992).

⊟ Besides records of the trials themselves, there are also some useful records of payments to sheriffs made by the Treasury for their expenses in catching criminals, which name many people accused of felony. These are indexed in the NA in class T 53 (1721–1805) and T 54 (1806–27).

EYRE

⊟ Derived from the Latin *iter*, meaning journey, this term describes the visitations of the King's judges to administer justice in the counties between the 12th and 14th centuries. The records, covering 1194–1348, cover a vast range of criminal and civil matters and are mostly in NA class JUST 1-4 and many have been translated and published and listed in E. L. C. Mullins' *Texts and Calendars: an Analytical Guide to Serial Publications* (RHS, 1958 and 1983).

ASSIZES

⊟ These replaced the Eyres and continued until superseded in turn by Crown Courts in 1971. Surviving records are in NA classes JUST and ASSI 1–54 (England) and 57–76 (Wales), except for those for London and Middlesex, and those which have been lost.

⊟ The judges operated either under royal commissions of 'oyer and terminer' (meaning they could hear felony cases in the provinces rather than in London), or 'gaol delivery' – hearing cases against prisoners awaiting trial in local gaols. Records include calendars of indictments, describing the accused and giving residence and alleged crime; gaol books detailing those in prison and their charges; and gaol delivery calendars giving the barest details of the trial.

⊟ Middlesex and the City of London's criminal justice system was administered by the Lord Mayor, recorder and aldermen sitting at the Old Bailey. Brief records, detailing the accused and their offence survive from 1684, with verdicts and sentences from 1791. Trial records concerning the City of London are at the **Corporation of London Records Office** and those to do with Middlesex at the **London Metropolitan Archives**.

⊟ In 1834, this system was replaced by the Central Criminal Court, which sat at the Old Bailey and whose records are in NA class CRIM. Some have been published and indexed in J. Cordy Jeaffreson's *Middlesex County Records* (GLC, 1975).

⊟ Searching for Old Bailey trials has recently become a lot easier with the launch of **www.oldbaileyonline.org**, which contains more than 100,000 trials for the period 1674–1834.

WELSH COURTS

⊟ From its conquest by England in 1282, Welsh justice was administered by county courts called Great Sessions, and the Welsh marches were covered by courts held by the Marcher lords. Following the abolition of the Welsh marches in 1540, the whole of Wales was covered by a Court of Great Sessions which visited each county twice a year, and Justices of the Peace. Its records are at the **National Library of Wales**.

⊟ In 1830, the Welsh counties were incorporated into the English system of assizes, with its own circuit, which was then split into two, for North and South Wales, in 1876. The post-1830 records are at the NA in class ASSI 57–77.

SCOTTISH COURTS

⊟ Serious crime, such as murder, arson, rape and robbery, were dealt with by the King's Justiciar and his assistant justiciars and by the High Court of Justiciary, which sat in Edinburgh then, from 1708, travelled around the country hearing cases in different towns and cities. Its records, at the NAS, survive in part from 1572 and are partially indexed.

⊟ Less serious cases tended to be heard in sheriff courts, with minor ones appearing in the burgh and franchise courts and those of the Justices of the Peace, but few of these records are indexed and searching for cases is tough going. Full details of what is available is given in C Sinclair's *Tracing your Scottish Ancestors: A Guide to Ancestry Research in the Scottish Record Office* (HMSO, 1997).

IRISH COURTS

⊟ The bombing of the Four Courts in 1922 destroyed most Irish legal records. What little survived is in the **National Archives of Ireland**, which also holds vast collections of solicitors' papers.

As with England, however, cases are easier and better reported in newspapers and law reports. Butterworth have produced several hundred volumes of the *Irish Reports*, starting in 1838 and working forwards towards the present. There are also plenty of legal records at the **NA** concerning Ireland, such as the Court of Chancery of Ireland, which are in class C 79.

FORFEITED ESTATES (1715)

The Forfeited Estates Commission was established to punish those who had supported the 1715 rebellion and its records are in the **NAS**, while those for English and Welsh rebels are at the **NA** in FEC1 and 2, indexed by name in *The Records of the Forfeited Estates Commission* (HMSO, 1968).

▽ The bombing of the Four Courts in Dublin in 1922 destroyed most Irish court records, wills and many Protestant parish registers. However, some records survived – and they are still available to be searched!

QUICK REFERENCE

See also main sources in Useful Addresses, page 306

CORPORATION OF LONDON RECORD OFFICE
c/o London Metropolitan Archives
40 Northampton Road
London EC1R 0HB
☎ 020 7332 3820
www.cityoflondon.gov.uk

LONDON METROPOLITAN ARCHIVES
40 Northampton Road
London EC1R 0HB
☎ 020 7332 3820
www.cityoflondon.gov.uk

CIVIL COURTS

The civil courts do not record criminal behaviour. Instead, they record the quarrels and disputes that raged among our ancestors. The records bring out an extraordinary range of ways in which human beings can fall out with each other, and provide many useful genealogical details into the bargain.

CIVIL COURTS

CHANCERY RECORDS

The Court of Chancery, whose records date from the late 14th century, provided merciful justice that was not constrained by the severe rules of the common law courts. In 1875 the Court of Chancery became the Chancery Division of the High Court, and still exists today. The records are at the **NA**, chiefly in class C, and some in class J. They concern disputes over money and land, often between relations, and can therefore provide a cornucopia of family history information.

The records are usually filed per category, so pleadings, evidence and decisions (see box, opposite) are seldom found together, and unfortunately the records are very far from comprehensively indexed. Remember that many cases dragged on for years (sometimes bankrupting either or both parties) and many never ended. Therefore, you may find a complete set of records for a case involving your ancestor, or you may simply be lucky enough to find a reference to an ancestor in an index to one of the foregoing categories of records, and thus learn something more about them than you knew already.

The best finding aids to Chancery cases are the **NA**'s new online index **www.catalogue.nationalarchives. gov.uk**, now covering 15th and early 16th century cases, with cases from 1558 not yet so well covered.

There is also the Bernau Index, compiled by Charles Bernau, which covers over 4 million parties and witnesses up to and including the 18th century, and which can be searched in microfilm at the **SoG** and **Mormon Family History Centres**. Bear in mind, though, that this only scratches the surface of what is available in the original records.

A comprehensive list of Chancery records and available finding aids is given in M. Herber's *Ancestral Trails* (Sutton Publishing and SoG, 2000).

EXCHEQUER RECORDS

Exchequer records seldom pre-date 1558, by which time the court, originally for disputes between the Crown and its subjects over money, had taken on a role very similar to that of the Court of Chancery. Indeed, in 1841, the two were amalgamated. The records are in **NA** class E. The cases generally take the form of pleadings – with production of evidence and witnesses' statements, which include age, address and occupation – and decisions.

Many of the records are indexed in the Bernau Index at the **SoG** (including all deponents and defendants in E 134, though the index is not thought to be complete). **www.catalogue.nationalarchives.gov.uk** indexes class E 134, covering plaintiffs, defendants and subjects but not deponents (nor does it cover London or any cases not involving depositions). **NA** information leaflet 19 covers this in detail.

KING'S COUNCIL

This was known in Latin as *Curia regis* and the records, kept in rolls, survive for the 12th and 13th centuries and are in **NA** class KB 26. Some have been printed and are listed in E. L. C. Mullins' *Texts and Calendars: An Analytical Guide to Serial Publications* (RHS, 1958 and 1983).

COURT OF COMMON PLEAS

This mainly dealt with land and money. Records 1194–1875 (after which it became part of the Common Pleas division of the High Court of Justice) are in class CP at the **NA**.

PLEA ROLLS

These record common law actions in the courts of Common Pleas, King's Bench, Exchequer and others. Most are at the **NA**: the City of London's, at **Guildhall Library**, have been translated and published from their original Latin and French in volumes covering 1298–1482, including A. H. Thomas' *Calendar of Plea and Memoranda Rolls Preserved among the Archives of the Corporation of the City of London at the Guildhall a.d.1413–1437* (CUP, 1943).

THE RECORDS generally take the form of:

Pleadings: a bill of complaint, in which the aggrieved party stated their case, and the defendant's answer, followed by any replications and rejoinders by the two parties.

Evidence: depositions taken from witnesses including their ages, residences and occupations.

Court decisions: the cases were then generally reviewed by the Masters in Chancery, or the six Chief Clerks on their behalf, who gave their view on who was right and who was wrong, and an order could be given stating the outcome of the case.

QUICK REFERENCE

See main sources in Useful Addresses, page 306

COURT OF KING'S BENCH

Court of King's Bench (class KB) contains such things as writs of *habeus corpus*. There are some indexes to defendants (London and Middlesex, 1673–1845) and provincial defendants 1638–1704, 1765–1843) in **NA** in class IND 1.

COURT OF REQUESTS

This dealt mainly with disputes over money and land of the poor 1493–1642, for which the **NA** has indexes in class REQ.

STAR CHAMBER

This court, presided over by the monarchs and privy counsellors, sat in a chamber whose ceiling was painted with stars, from 1487 to 1641. Despite being infamous for its trials of nobles and others for treason, heresy and rebellion, it also heard appeals from common people seeking justice that they felt unable to obtain in other courts. Surviving records are in **NA** class STAC and some have been printed in E. L. C. Mullins' *Texts and Calendars, An Analytical Guide to Serial Publications* (RHS 1958 and 1983).

PALATINE COURTS

Cheshire, Durham and Lancashire were each run entirely separately from the rest of the country, as palatines, with their own courts for chancery, equity and criminal cases. Almost all records are at the **NA** in classes CHES, DURH and PL respectively. There was also a court for the Royal Duchy of Lancaster, which heard disputes over land within the duchy, whose records are in class DL.

COURT OF WARDS AND LIVERIES

This existed from 1541 to 1660 and is in the **NA** in class WARD. It oversaw the rights of children under 21 who were orphaned heirs to land held direct by franchise from the Crown.

HIGH COURT OF ADMIRALTY

Set up in the 14th century, this dealt with maritime matters, from piracy to sailors' claims for prize money – their share of the profits from captured enemy ships. Vice-admiralty courts were also established to deal with similar affairs in coastal counties and colonies abroad. Their records are in the **NA** in class HCA and are described in C. T. Watts and M. J. Watts' *My Ancestor was a Merchant Seaman: How can I find out more about him?* (SoG, 1991).

PALACE COURT

This operated from 1630 to 1849 for small debt claims within 12 miles of Westminster and records are in the **NA** in class PALA.

COURT OF DIVORCE & CAUSES

See page 95.

COURTS AFTER 1875

HOUSE OF LORDS

The Upper House could hear appeals from the Court of Appeal, especially in matters relating to divorce and probate between 1858 and 1875. These are chronicled along with all other business of the House, in the *House of Lords Journal*, which is held with the rest of the Upper Houses's records in the **House of Lords Record Office**.

PRIVY COUNCIL

The Privy Council grew out of the King's Council in the 14th century and comprised the monarch's chief ministers, household officials and bishops. The main records are in **NA** class PC 2 covering 1540 onwards. These have been printed in facsimile form 1631–45 and printed and indexed in *Acts of the Privy Council 1542–1631*. The Privy Council dealt with affairs of state but also heard appeals and petitions on all sorts of matters involving ordinary people. Scottish Privy Council papers 1545–1691 have been published as listed in E. L. C. Mullins' *Texts and Calendars: An Analytical Guide to Serial Publications, Vol. 1* (RHS, 1958).

COUNTY COURTS

Established in 1846 to deal with civil matters, their records are in **county record offices**.

COURT OF AUGMENTATIONS

This sat between 1536 and 1554 and dealt with Henry VIII's dissolution of the monasteries. Records include receipts of rent from monastic tenants while the land was in Crown hands. Records are in **NA** class SC and there are some in Exchequer records (see page 226).

CIVIC COURTS

Many cities and boroughs had their own courts, whose records are in **county record offices**. The City of London's courts, including the Court of Hustings and Mayor's Court, whose records go back to the 14th century, are at the **Corporation of London Record Office** and some early records have been published. The Fire Court was established in 1666, for which see P. E. Jones's *The Fire Court: Calendar to the Judgements and Decrees of the Court of Judicature Appointed to Determine Differences between Landlords and Tenants as to Rebuilding after the Great Fire* (William Clowes & Sons, 1966–70).

SCOTTISH COURTS

The records are at the **NAS** but are hard to search if you do not know exactly where a case was heard. Civil cases were generally heard in the Court of Session, whose minute books date from 1557 and are printed and indexed annually from 1782. These, in turn, can lead you to a court's acts and decrees, providing further details of the case.

However, civil cases could also be heard by the Scottish Privy Council (until 1707), the Courts of Exchequer, which had jurisdiction over cases involving revenue 1708–1859 and the Admiralty Court, which oversaw maritime cases. Many more civil cases were heard at the sheriff courts, though their records tend to be patchy until the late 18th century.

Burgh courts, known as Bailies, are worth considering for civil and criminal matters, though during the 18th century their use declined greatly and the **NAS**'s holdings are sparse. The same applies to franchise courts, such as Barony and Regality Courts, which were courts held by landowners by franchise from the Crown.

QUICK REFERENCE

See also main sources in Useful Addresses, page 306

HOUSE OF LORDS RECORD OFFICE
Palace of Westminster
London SW1A 0PW
☎ 020 7219 3074
www.parliament.uk

CORPORATION OF LONDON RECORD OFFICE
c/o London Metropolitan Archives
40 Northampton Road
London EC1R 0HB
☎ 020 7332 3820
www.cityoflondon.gov.uk

COURTS AFTER 1875

In 1875 the judicial system was reformed and amalgamated into the Supreme Court of Judicature, divided into the High Court of Justice and Court of Appeal, and then into divisions to cover Chancery, probate, common pleas and so on. There are full details in the *Guide to the Contents of the Public Record Office* (HMSO, 1963 and 1968).

▽ *House of Lords* by T. Rowlandson (1756–1827) and A. C. Pugin (1762–1832), the most senior Court of Appeal until 1875.

BANKRUPTCY IS THE official winding up of the affairs of people unable to meet their debts. Initially it was available to those in trade or business: many insolvent gents, therefore, would describe themselves as tradesmen, usually chapmen, in order to qualify. In 1861, bankruptcy was available to all. The Lord Chancellor dealt with bankruptcy from 1571 until 1831, when the Court of Bankruptcy was formed. This established district courts, whose work was transferred to county courts in 1861, and the Court of Bankruptcy became the High Court of Justice in Bankruptcy in 1883.

Records from the 18th century are in NA class B, but the *London Gazette* and local newspapers make much easier and often more detailed reading. Details of sales of some 3000 bankrupt Irish estates 1848–80 whose cases passed through the Encumbered Estates Court are at the NA.

BANKRUPTCY

LIFETIMES: PERRY NURSEY GOES BANKRUPT

PERRY NURSEY was a Suffolk landscape artist whose expensive tastes led to him collecting more of other peoples' paintings than selling his own. This, and the severe slump in the agricultural economy which decimated the income from his small estate, ruined him. This is the harrowing process that followed, all described in minute detail in a succession of reports in his local newspaper, the *Ipswich Journal*, whence they were extracted at the Suffolk Record Office in Ipswich.

Towards the end of 1833, Perry's creditors made an affidavit before one of the Masters of Chancery, pleading that he was so much in debt he should be made bankrupt. The Lord Chancellor agreed, granting a commission of bankruptcy on 21 December – just in time to ruin Perry's Christmas – and appointing five commissioners, who in turn appointed two solicitors to handle the affair. The announcement appeared in the local paper and the *London Gazette* at the beginning of the next year. Perry, as the contemporary expression had it, had been 'gazetted'. Because bankruptcy was only available to tradesmen, Perry, who formerly described himself as 'Esquire', was now termed an 'architect, builder, dealer and chapman'.

SALE OF POSSESSIONS

On 14 January Perry 'surrendered' himself to the solicitors and his creditors, by pre-advertised arrangement, at a local hotel. Both sides produced their relevant accounts and the creditors appointed three assignees of their number to oversee the sale of Perry's possessions, using the proceeds to repay the debts and also make Perry an allowance of 5% of the value raised to a value not exceeding £300, a small mercy available to all but gamblers. Several subsequent meetings were held to decide whether to sell or retain the leases of two of his farms, to regain another from the landlord, Lord Bristol, who had himself repossessed it, and decide whether Perry was eligible for his certificate of bankruptcy.

In the meantime, starting on 14 February, a series of auctions were held to dispose of his goods and other leases, each item meticulously described in the paper and in specially printed and widely circulated catalogues. His art collection was auctioned in April, with advertisements circulated in London to attract the best dealers. Ironically, having neglected to sell many of his own paintings over the years, his creditors now did an excellent job marketing him, so as to raise the highest prices: even unfinished works were sold off.

STARTING OVER AGAIN

By May, Perry was free from claims by any further creditors. That December, the assignees paid the creditors 2s 4d for each pound originally owed. Perry himself was left with his clothes, the tools of his trade, including his paintbrushes and the ability to contract new debts, should anyone be ill-advised enough to lend him money or supply goods on credit. A friend lent him a cottage and he started a new life, as an art teacher, though age, financial worries and probably a great sense of failure contributed to his death a mere seven years later.

It is a sad story, but the detailed lists of his belongings, musical instruments, books and paintings was fascinating and would never have been made had he not been a bankrupt. Posterity, ultimately, was better served by Perry having been bankrupt than had he remained solvent.

ECCLESIASTICAL COURTS

Church courts dealt with practical matters relating to the church, such as tithe payments or drunken priests; religion, such as heresy and witchcraft; and morality. In fact the courts dealt mainly with sexual misconduct in all its many and varied forms, and for this reason they were known as the 'bawdy courts'. Sadly, the records are in Latin and few have been published – the county record office staff can tell you if anything relevant to your searches is in print. For all that, the original records are still worth searching for a chance mention of your ancestor as a last resort if you are stuck, or if you have plenty of time, in the hope of finding some salacious tales to embellish your family history.

Cases were usually heard in the archdeaconry courts, with appeals being made to the bishop's court. The lawyers who practised in these were proctors and advocates.

Cases were usually opened following a presentment by the churchwardens of a parish, often made during the annual archdeacon's visitation of the parishes, or the triennial bishop's visitations. Cases took the form of civil action between two individuals, called instance cases, and actions by the church against individuals, called office cases. Evidence might be heard orally, in which case few records will survive, or by written evidence, and these can result in detailed records.

The records can provide useful information for genealogists, such as ages and places of birth of witnesses, and how long they had lived in the parish. They may also describe relationships (especially in cases of adultery, illegitimacy and so on) and religious denomination – many cases were brought against non-conformists for non-attendance at church or refusal to pay tithes.

ECCLESIASTICAL COURTS

The organisation of church courts, the location of their records, their role in proving wills and dealing with subsequent disputes over them, is explained above.

🗗 Appeals against sentences could be made to the Court of Arches (with records at **Lambeth Palace Library**, indexed in J. Houston's *Cases in the Court of Arches 1660–1913* (BRS, vol. 85, 1972)), and the Chancery Court of York (records at the **Borthwick Institute**), depending on the province in which your ancestor lived.

🗗 Final appeals were made to the Pope and, after the Reformation, to the High Court of Delegates (mostly indexed in **NA** class DEL 11).

A. TARVER'S *Church Court Records: An Introduction for Family and Local Historians* (Phillimore, 1995) provides many salacious (and not unfamiliar) examples of our ancestors' sex lives.

Mr St John Haynes, for example, was horrified when his servants told him his wife Mary had been having sex with Dr Joseph Berrington in the small parlour next to the kitchen in their house in Willoughby, Warwickshire. He sent her away to a boarding house in Chelmsford, under the strict chaperoning of a servant, Mary Webb. This measure did not quell Mrs Haynes' libido, however, and before long Mary Webb, finding black hairs in the bed of her blonde mistress, realised more hanky-panky was afoot. Mr Haynes obtained a separation from his wife, but neither she nor he, despite being the wronged party, were permitted to remarry while the other one lived.

QUARTER SESSIONS

Quarter Sessions dealt with a vast amount of business, criminal and civil, that, indirectly or not, touched the lives of most of our ancestors. They are a fabulous resource for family history, and the only reason they are not much more widely used is that, on the whole, they tend not to have been transcribed or indexed. I imagine this will change over next few decades.

Quarter Sessions were courts held from 1361 to 1971 in each county four times a year, and on other occasions called 'divisions', when they were petty sessions. They were presided over by Justices of the Peace (JPs), also called magistrates, who still deal with cases in Magistrates' courts. Like them, quarter sessions tended to deal with less serious crimes than the assizes (see page 224), such as theft and poaching, and were also concerned with many matters of local government, especially licensing inns; prosecuting Catholics; enforcing the poor law; taking of oaths; overseeing matters relating to apprenticeship and qualification of craftsmen; policing local militias; maintenance of roads and bridges; and overseeing tax collection.

THE RECORDS USUALLY COMPRISE THE FOLLOWING:

➤**Books** (or, earlier, rolls) for orders detailing the JPs' decisions and orders; minutes or processes, recording what happened at each sitting.
➤**Indictments with details of criminal charges** and information about the accused in terms of residence, alleged offence and perhaps some information about the victim.
➤**Other documentation brought to or issued by the hearings,** such as sworn statements; lists of prisoners, jurors, people born abroad (from 1792), voters and freemasons; licences for the likes of alehouse keepers, itinerant traders and gamekeepers; bonds and sureties; tax returns; enclosure awards; and lists of householders liable for paying county rates.

CRIMINALS

Once people were found guilty in court — whether they were really guilty or not – they generated a new set of records, which can tell you about their lives as convicted criminals.

PRISONERS

The fate of many of our criminal ancestors was either branding and flogging, execution or transportation. Public execution, usually by hanging, was a commonplace event, a cheap form of entertainment in

WHERE TO SEARCH

QUARTER SESSIONS

The records were kept by the Clerk of the Peace and are in **county record offices**, and those for Scotland are in the **NAS**. They are detailed in J. Gibson's *Quarter Sessions Records for Family Historians: A Select List* (FFHS, 1995), which also notes the relatively little that has been published on the subject.

You may be able to work out when an ancestor was likely to appear in the records (if he was an alehouse keeper, for example), or you may wish to approach the records simply as a 'lucky dip' and see if you run across any forebears by chance. If you do, you will most likely open up new windows on their lives offering riches you could never have anticipated.

QUICK REFERENCE

See main sources in Useful Addresses, page 306

▽ *Execution of John Thurtell at Hertford Jail* in 1824 (anon).

IT WAS KNOWN that William Seal was transported to America in 1747 and a published compilation of sources, *English Convicts in Colonial America*, cited the Middlesex Sessions of Gaol Delivery, at Greater London Record Office, as the source. The original record told us:

> *'That William Seal late of the parish of Enfield in the County of Middlesex Labourer ... on the 8th Nov in the 21st year of the reign of our sovereign Lord George ... and with force & arms at the parish aforesaid ... one Plough Chain of the value of 2 shillings and one Iron Bolt of the value of sixpence of the goods & chattels of one Samuel Wyburn then & there being found feloniously did steal take and carry away against the peace of our said Lord the King ... his dignity.*

This got us back to Enfield. Although William's baptism was not found in the registers of Enfield, Essex, the IGI revealed that there was a baptism in the neighbouring Hertfordshire parish of Cheshunt, for William and Thomas, twin children of Robert Seale, baptised on 4 July 1726 – what an appropriate date for someone later sent to America.

the days before television, and many hangings were recorded in souvenir pamphlets and prints. It was abolished in 1868, by which time the death penalty was rarely applied for offences other than murder.

In the Middle Ages, prisons were generally used for those awaiting trial, and it was only in the 16th century that Houses of Correction started to be built to hold criminals (and other 'wrongdoers', like vagrants and pregnant women) for punishment. But with so many hanged or transported for the most minor of thieving offences, prisons of the sort we know today did not really come into being until during the 19th century.

△ Interior of the Debtors' Prison, Whitecross Street in the 1830s.

TRANSPORTEES

Many people who were not executed for their misdemeanours were transported to British colonies. Indeed, many early settlers in America and the Caribbean were transportees and once the American War of Independence put paid to this, prisoners were sent to Australia instead.

CRIMINALS

PRISONERS

From 1823, records relating to prisons often appear in Quarter Session records while gaolers' journals, usually providing names and dates of admission and discharge, and what the offence was, will be found in **county record offices**.

Criminal registers arranged year by year, county by county, for England and Wales 1805–92, with date and place of trial and details of the verdict and punishment are at the **NA** in HO 26–7. These are partially indexed on disk by S. Tamblin's *Criminal Register Index, 1805–40*, which can be viewed at **www.fhindexes.co.uk**. The registers for London and Middlesex go back to 1791 and those to 1802 give place of birth and a physical description as well.

Different categories of calendars of prisoners, some dating from as early as 1774, can give you the age and occupation of the prisoner, as well as details of the alleged crime. At the **NA** (in HO 7, 8, 9, 23 and 24, and PCOM 2, ADM 6, KB 32, T 1, T 38 and WO 25) and also the **county record offices** are many prison registers, which provide name, birthplace, age, details of the crime and punishment, and often a physical description. From the mid-19th century you may even find a photograph. If your ancestor was imprisoned on a hulk – old navy ships used as prisons – or petitioned for pardon, their records may also be found at the **NA**. Full details of the NA and county record office holdings are given in D. T. Hawkings' *Criminal Ancestors: A Guide to Historical Criminal Records in England & Wales* (Sutton, 1992). Criminals' petitions 1819–39 are in HO 17.

A useful site for British prisons and their records (and many other institutions such as orphanages, hospitals and prisons) is **www.institutions.org.uk**.

Scottish prisoners' records are at the **NAS**, though few survive from before the mid-19th century.

TRANSPORTEES

The main sources for pre-Australian transportation have been collated and indexed in P. W. Coldham's *The Complete Book of Emigrants in Bondage, 1614–1775* (GCP, 1990), but there are many others. Those in print include J. C. Hotten's modestly titled *The Original Lists of Persons of Quality, Emigrants, Religious Exiles, Political Rebels, Serving Men Sold for a Term of Years, Apprentices, Children Stolen, Maidens Pressed and Others who went from Great Britain to the American Plantations 1660–1700 from MSS Preserved in the State Paper Department at the PRO* (GCP, 1962) and W. M. Wingfield's *The Monmouth Rebels 1685* (Somerset Record Society, 1985), which lists the men caught and sentenced to transportation (as opposed to execution under Judge Jeffries) after the Monmouth rebellion in 1685.

Hawkings' *Criminal Ancestors* (see left) lists the **NA** sources for those sent to Australia; the main one being the registers of convict transportation 1787–1867 in HO 11, which are sadly unindexed.

Most records of transportees will tell you where they were convicted, but not where they originated. If you are lucky, though, their place of conviction will be near their place of origin, enabling you at least to narrow your search to a particular geographic region. Of great interest for people with Scottish ancestry are the uprisings of 1715, in favour of the exiled prince James Stuart, and 1745, in favour of his son, Bonnie Prince Charlie. Much information appears in the calendared and indexed State Papers (Domestic) and (Scotland) series at the **NA**, while records of trials of rebels are in the King's Bench records, KB 8. Other cases appear in assize, palatine and treasury papers listed in NA information leaflet 4.

QUICK REFERENCE

See main sources in Useful Addresses, page 306

OVERSEAS STUDENTS

SOME BRITISH STUDENTS went abroad, particularly to Leyden or Heidelberg University if they were Protestants, but there were other destinations. *Family Tree Magazine* (July 2003) contains J. Titford's transcript of British students at Franeker University in Friesland, 1585–1811 and 1816–44.

Catholics went, whenever they could, to Catholic universities on the Continent, such as those in Spain, Portugal, France and Italy. Much material covering these has been published by the Catholic Record Society (see page 258).

compulsory, although some exemptions were made for children over ten. Free secondary education, for children up to about 18, existed in some places from 1880 but did not become normal until after 1902.

For these reasons, many people could not read or write. But it is important not to think of everyone below the middle class as a herd of illiterates: many children were taught a lot at home, or by members of the gentry or clergy. Sometimes, I hear people saying, 'But great-grandfather was so well educated: his parents couldn't have been labourers.' The truth, though, is that bright children could learn a great deal at even the smallest village schools, enabling them to rise from labouring backgrounds to join the middle class.

UNIVERSITIES

The only two universities in England before the establishment of Durham University in 1832 were those of Oxford and Cambridge. Registers of those who attended Oxford and Cambridge – including most of the Anglican clergy – have been published. Later universities, such as Durham and London (founded in 1836) also have published registers and all universities have archivists who can be consulted.

WHERE TO SEARCH

SCHOOLS

⊟ School records, such as reports, team photographs and leaving certificates, are often found in family papers. School archives may also contain information about your ancestors, such as admission books, records of clubs, log books, school magazines and much else.

⊟ If you know the name of the school, you may find it is still there and in possession of its own archives, or if not, the records may be in the local **studies library** or **county record office**. You can work out where your ancestor may have been educated by consulting contemporary directories (see page 82). Registers of many public schools have been published and will usually give you age or date of birth and father's occupation and residence. They may include team photographs and information about what the pupil did later in life. Remember to look up not just your ancestor, but anyone else of the same name, as many families tended to use the same school generation after generation. There are good collections of printed registers at the **SoG**.

⊟ An excellent source of background information is C. R. Chapman's *The Growth of British Education and its Records* (Lochin Publishing, 1992).

⊟ Scottish schools were generally maintained by burghs and parishes, and many were founded by the Society in Scotland for Propagating Christian Knowledge, whose records are at the **NAS**. School boards were established in 1872, with records variously at the **NAS**, **regional record offices** or **local council archives**.

⊟ There are some published records of Irish grammar schools dating back to the 17th century. Irish primary education started in 1831, and registers can provide names and ages of pupils, with their fathers' addresses, occupations and denomination, mainly held by the schools themselves. Most for Northern Ireland are at the **PRONI**.

QUICK REFERENCE

See main sources in Useful Addresses, page 306

WHERE TO SEARCH

UNIVERSITIES

⊟ Cambridge is covered by J and J. A.Venn's *Alumni Cantabrigiensis: A Biographical List of all known Students, Graduates and Holders of Office at the University of Cambridge from the Earliest Times to 1900* (CUP, 1922–7 and 1940–54), with sometimes quite detailed biographical notes about the graduate's subsequent career.

⊟ The period before 1500 is supplemented by A. B. Emden's *A Biographical Register of the University of Cambridge to 1500* (CUP, 1963).

⊟ Oxford is covered by J. Foster's *Alumni Oxoniensis: The Members of the University of Oxford 1500–1714; their Parentage, Birthplace, and Year of Birth, with a Record of their Degrees* … (James Parker & Co., 1891) and *Alumni Oxoniensis: The Members of the University of Oxford 1715–1886* (James Parker & Co., 1888–91), supplemented for the 16th and previous centuries by A. B. Emden's *A Biographical Register of the University of Oxford to AD 1500* (OUP, 1957) and another volume *1501–1540* (OUP, 1974).

⊟ By the Reformation, Scotland had four universities, St Andrew's, Aberdeen, Glasgow and Edinburgh, all of whose matriculation lists have been published. The universities hold many further records.

⊟ The only university in Ireland was Trinity College, Dublin, whose registers have been published in G. D. Burtchaell and T. U. Sadlier's *Alumni Dublinenses: A Register of the Students, Graduates, Professors, and Provosts of Trinity College, in the University of Dublin* (Williams and Norgate, 1924).

▷ My great-great-grandfather, Rev. Patrick Henry Kilduff, a clergyman in Tottenham, who trained at Trinity College, Dublin.

CHAPTER TWENTY-SIX
IMMIGRATION & EMIGRATION

It was with good reason that Eddie Izzard called his recent series on the origins of the British people *Mongrel Nation*. Although the British derive from three clear racial groups, the 'original' Bronze Age people, and the later immigrant waves of Celts and Saxons, there have been countless other lesser immigrations which have added to the rich soup of the British gene-pool.

DEATH ON OR AFTER 1st JANUARY, 1898.

BE IT KNOWN that *Heinrich Julius Rietschel of 16*

The Avenue Hornsey in the County of Middlesex

died on the *12th* day of *February* 19*13*

at *9 Fore Street Avenue in the City of London*

intestate

△ Grant of administration of the estate of Heinrich Julius Rietschel to his widow Caroline, 1913. Although born English, Caroline had to live with the stigma of having been married to a German right through the First World War and subsequently Anglicised her surname to Rietchel in the 1920s (see page 242).

▷ Heinrich Julius Rietschel, an immigrant Saxon lamp salesman, whose sudden death in 1913 saved him from the ignomy of being interred as an enemy alien in the First World War.

AND BE IT FURTHER KNOWN that at the date hereunder written Letters of Administration of all the Estate which by law devolves to and vests in the personal representative of the said intestate were granted by His Majesty's High Court of Justice at the Principal Probate Registry thereof to

Caroline Ellen Rietschel of 16 The Avenue

Widow and Relict

The Phoenicians, sea-going merchants from North Africa, traded extensively with the inhabitants of Cornwall and southern Wales in the centuries leading up to the Roman Invasion, Rome in turn sent tens of thousands of soldiers here from all over the empire, many of whom left their genes behind in the form of illegitimate children, or simply settled here and had families. Today there are families living in ancestral farms built on the site of forts along Hadrian's Wall who have persistent, and probably true, stories of being descended from the last Roman captain to have been stationed there. Equally, a family called Jelly in Staffordshire, who believed they were of Roman stock, found astonishing confirmation when the tomb of a Roman centurion was unearthed on their land, complete with his inscribed name – Gellus!

Subsequently, besides the Saxons, came Vikings, the Normans and their many Flemish and French associates, and many later waves of French Huguenot, people from German Palatine, Sephardic and Ashkenazi Jews and, more recently, the countless Chinese, Indian, African and Caribbean incomers of the mid- to late 20th century. And, in among these well-documented mass immigrations, there are the vast amount of miscellaneous others, like my German ancestors who slipped in unnoticed 170 years ago, and all the rest besides.

Needless to say, the British have been actively leaving as fast as immigrants have been coming in, mainly due to the expansion of the Empire, but elsewhere, too, for more surreptitious and varied reasons. The Scots, for example, created thriving communities in Scandinavia, France, Russia and Holland (for this last, see Where to Search, below).

BOUNDARY CHANGES

BEAR IN MIND with foreign research that national boundaries change with time, so an ancestor who came from 'India' might turn out to have originated in what is now Bangladesh, just as ancestral villages in old 'Austria' or 'Russia' could now be in Hungary, or Romania, Poland or Armenia.

QUICK REFERENCE

See also main sources in Useful Addresses, page 306

CALEDONIAN SOCIETY
c/o Roelof Vennik
Burg v.Slijpelaan 45
Rotterdam, 3077AD
The Netherlands

WHERE TO SEARCH

FAMILY OVERSEAS

⊟ Much foreign material, especially for Europe, has been microfilmed by the Mormons and can be ordered on film through your local **Mormon Family History Centre**. There is also a substantial collection of foreign records, such as copies of parish registers and wills, at the **SoG**.

⊟ Detailed guides to research abroad include T. F. Beard with D. Demong's *How to Find your Family Roots* (McGraw-Hill Book Company, 1977) and A. Baxter's *In Search of your European Roots: A Complete Guide to Tracing your Ancestors in Every Country in Europe* (GCP, 1986).

⊟ This is an area where the Internet comes into its own. Foreign archives and researchers can be sought through the search engines, and an excellent central point of enquiry is **www.cyndislist.com**. The *Genealogical Services Directory* provides contact details for archives and societies all over the world. See its website **www.genealogical.co.uk**.

⊟ So many Scottish people settled in Holland that there exists a **Caledonian Society** for Dutch people with Scots ancestry. Its genealogical advisor, Roelof Vennik has produced a number of indexes to the Scots names that fill the Rotterdam records.

INCOMERS

We all have ancestors who were born outside Britain. Tracing back to the original immigrant is usually reasonably straightforward, but then the big question arises: 'Where did that person come from?' Fortunately, British bureaucracy, the bane of modern incomers, generated a great series of records, which can be a godsend to researchers.

NATURALISATION AND DENIZATION

Anyone living in Britain but who was born abroad was regarded as an alien and lacked rights, such as the bequeathing of property, until they had become naturalised or 'denizised'. Not everyone who arrived in Britain became naturalised, however, for the simple reason that the process was expensive and unnecessary if they had no property to bequeath, and also in many cases because the immigrant had no long-term plans to stay in the country.

▽ My great-great-grandmother Caroline Ellen Rietchel née Smart, pictured here in 1945 aged 88 years.

Children of immigrants born here automatically became British subjects, as did the wives of those who did become naturalised. By the same token, British women who married aliens themselves became aliens. This happened to my great-great-grandmother Caroline Smart, who married a young lamp salesman, Heinrich Rietschel, an immigrant from Saxony. Her husband dropped dead mere months before the First World War broke out. This saved him from being interred as an enemy alien – but his poor wife found herself classified throughout the war as a German widow! Needless to say, Caroline's successful application for naturalisation as a British subject was duly filed in 1919, giving useful genealogical details about her late husband's place of origin.

Many found it prudent or desirable to become a British subject. Denization made the person a British subject by a grant from the Crown, either by letters patent under the Great Seal or by Royal Charter, while naturalisation made someone a British subject – not just from the date of the grant but retrospectively – for their entire lives by private Act of Parliament. In practice, the two amounted to pretty much the same thing, although until the 19th century naturalisation required the taking of Anglican communion, making denization preferable to Jews and Catholics. From 1844, naturalisation could also be conferred by a certificate from the Home Secretary.

"A"

HE RIGHT HONORABLE
HER MAJESTY'S SECRETARY OF STATE
FOR THE HOME DEPARTMENT.

Naturalization.

2.—Memorial.

RLOW & SONS
LIMITED,
on Wall, London.

The Humble Memorial of *Leonard Reibold*
of *12 Bury Street, St James's*
London S.W.
in the County of *Middlesex*
an Alien

heweth—

1.—That your Memorialist is a Subject of *the Grand Duchy of Hesse Darmstadt, Germany* having been born at *Siedelsbrunn, Hesse Darmstadt* in the Empire of *Germany* on the *20th* day of *May* 18*24* and that the Names and Nationalities of my parents are *Adam Reibold, Hesse Darmstadt Germany Mary Reibold Hesse Darmstadt Germany*

2.—That your Memorialist is of the age of *sixty five* years and is *a courier and now steward or caretaker of Her Majesty's Estates at Aix-les-Bains, France*

3.—That your Memorialist is *a married* man and has *one daughter, aged seven years, named Helene Leopoldine Mary Reibold*

4.—That your Memorialist's settled place of business is at *12 Bury St, St James's, London S.W. England*

FROM THE volumes of the Huguenot Society (see page 244).

NATURALISATIONS

14 Car II 1663–4: a group including 55-year-old Peter de Cou from Dau, Lille, Flanders, and his 32-year-old son Peter born in 'Bosnerd, Bulloign, Picardy': *'within Thorny Fenns and Ramsey Fenns in the Isle of Ely and Counties of Cambridge and Huntingdon they have peaceably settled themselves and dwelt for divers yeares past, being husbandmen and farmers of divers grounds in the same Fenns.'*

27 June 1661: *'Anna Ferrers, wife of John Ferrers of Tamworth Castle in the County of Warwick, Esq., born at the Hague in Holland, daughter of Sir Dudley Carleton Knt, Resident for his late Majesty in Holland, and Margaret his wife.'*

DENIZATIONS

18 Feb 1615–16: *'Robert Trotter, born in Scotland, farrier to the Prince.'*

18 June 1615: *'Paul Tymerman, a subject of the King of Poland, born in the city of Riga in Livonia'* (on condition that he would not build a sugar house in or near London lest he should prejudice the London refiners).

March 1637–8: *'Sir Anthony Vandyke, Kt and to his heirs, born in foreign parts.'*

NATURALISATION AND DENIZATION

⊞ The records normally tell you where the migrant came from. Up to the 19th century, it is worth noting the names of other people who became subjects at the same time – migrants often moved, and acted, in groups. From the 19th century onwards, the records can provide date of birth, details of spouse and children, residence, occupation, how long the migrant had been in the country and sometimes even reasons for migrating.

▽ **Naturalisation documents of David Kahn, known as 'David Carr', 1929.**

⊞ Looking for these records is joyfully simple. Those from 1509 to 1800 have been published in three volumes by the **Huguenot Society of Great Britain and Ireland**; Vol 8, W. Page's (ed.) *Letters of Denization and Acts of Naturalization for Aliens in England, 1509–1603* (1893); Vol. 18, W. A. Shaw's (ed.) *Letters of Denization and Acts of Naturalization in England and Ireland, 1603–1700* (1911) and Vol. 27, W. A. Shaw's (ed.) *Letters of Denization and Acts of Naturalization in England and Ireland, 1701–1800* (1923).

⊞ Denizations from 1801 to 1900, Parliamentary naturalisations 180–1947 (the original records for Parliamentary naturalisations are at the **House of Lords Record Office**) and Home Secretary's certificates (HO334) 1844–71, are all indexed in HO 1 at the **NA** and **FRC**, whilst all Home Secretary's certificates are indexed in HO 409/vols 1–11, 1800–1980, though from 1962 the indexes are by year. Correspondence relating to naturalisations and denizations are in HO 1 1789–1871, HO 45 184–1878 and HO 144 1879–1934 at the NA . The periods 1844–71 (from HO 1) and 1925–30 (HO 104) are indexed in the NA catalogue. Thereafter, 1934–48 can be searched by surname in HO 405: surnames for that period from O to Z will be released in 2007. Files dating after 1923 are closed, but you can ask to inspect them under the Freedom of Information Act by pressing the 'Request review' button in the catalogue.

⊞ From 1935, naturalisations are closed to public inspection but House of Commons Sessions papers to 1962, arranged annually, give name, date of oath of allegiance, place of residence and country of origin.

ALIENS

⊞ In the First and Second World Wars, those 'enemy aliens' who did not voluntarily return home were interned in special camps but the lists of internees are kept by the Red Cross and cannot be searched, though there is very slight coverage in the **NA** classes WO 900/45–6 (First World War) and HO 214/5 (Second World War) and an index to some lists held by the Anglo-German Family History Society. Some, such as doctors, were allowed alien registration certificates, many of which are at the **West Midlands Police Museum**.

🗐 Whether or not an ancestor became naturalised or denizised in Britain, you can also search in the **NA** for your immigrant ancestor registering with a JP under the Aliens' Act of 1792, giving their name, rank, occupation and address. At the NA, class HO 1 contains a collection of passes granted to 'aliens' between 1793 and 1836, detailing the immigrant's name, nationality, religion, occupation, where they had been and where they were going. The new Aliens' Act of 1836 generated certificates (HO 2) noting the arrival of each immigrant giving name, occupation, port of entry and, of course, date of arrival; these are indexed up to 1849 in HO 5/25–32. Correspondence relating to the arrival of immigrants are in the entry books 1794–1909, in HO 5.

🗐 After the First World War, the county police forces kept records of immigrants. These are held by the **county police archive** or the **county record office**. They tell you where immigrants came from, where they lived on arrival and their occupation, together with a photograph.

SHIPPING LISTS

🗐 Ships' passenger lists for immigrants from outside Europe are at the **NA** in BT 26 for 1878–1960. They give age, occupation and intended place of residence, but they are arranged by port, year and ship, so without a very good idea of when and where your ancestor stepped onto British soil your search could be very lengthy. Between 1836 and 1869 there are some ships' lists of alien arrivals, in HO 3. If you find such a record, you can then use *Lloyd's Register* at **Guildhall Library** to find out where the ship sailed from. **Len Metzner** has compiled an index to these records, from 1853 to 1869.

BRITISH NATIONALITY ACT

THE BRITISH NATIONALITY ACT came into force in 1949. Those born in British colonies that became independent states before 1949 automatically became citizens of that state. Those born in colonies not yet independent become British Subjects without Citizenship. If the country then became independent after 1949, people born there could became Citizens of the United Kingdom and Colonies. From 1989, anyone can apply to become a British Citizen provided they can prove at least one grandparent was born in Britain (Eire operates a similar policy). For further information contact the Home Office.

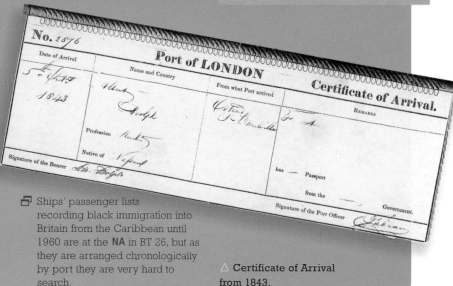

🗐 Ships' passenger lists recording black immigration into Britain from the Caribbean until 1960 are at the **NA** in BT 26, but as they are arranged chronologically by port they are very hard to search.

△ **Certificate of Arrival** from 1843.

LOOKING EAST

FOR COUNTRIES FURTHER EAST, quality of archives tends to decrease, and research into non-noble gentile families in the old Russian and Ottoman empires can be virtually impossible due to lack of records – although it is always worth making enquiries.

WHERE TO SEARCH

EUROPEAN ANCESTRY

⊟ The Mormons have made great inroads in microfilming and indexing many European baptism and marriage records in the IGI (see page 110), while websites for research in all countries are proliferating on the Internet and accessible through **www.cindyslist.org**.

⊟ In Britain there are family history societies for people with ancestors from some European countries, which produce helpful indexes and research guides, such as the Anglo German Family History Society. All are accessible via the **Federation of Family History Societies**.

⊟ For European Jewish ancestry, see page 270.

QUICK REFERENCE

See main sources in Useful Addresses, page 306

EUROPEAN ANCESTRY

Most European countries had parish registers broadly similar to our own, and these will be with the local churches or in local archives. Britain is unusual in having such centralised records. For most European research you will need to contact the nearest big town to the place where your ancestor lived, or use a source such as **www.cyndislist.com** to hire a local record searcher or genealogist to search for you. Most records you will need will be at the local mayor's office – called the *mairie* in France and the *Rathaus* in Germany. Bear in mind that countries such as Germany and Italy were only unified during the 19th century and previously consisted of many tiny states, each with its own entirely separate records.

In general, where war has not devastated everything, the records of most western European countries are very good. Those for some Italian towns and fortified villages can go back for well over a millennium. Many records in France (as in Italy) were generated by notaries (lawyers) and many records over 125 years old are deposited at departmental archives. In areas that Napoleon conquered – most of Western Europe – a detailed, if short-lived, system of civil registration was introduced, which provides excellent detail, for example, providing parents' names in records of death.

In 19th- and early 20th-century Germany, a fascination with ancestry combined with latent anti-Semitism led to the researching and publication of many pedigrees, called *Stammbäume*, accessible through local archives and libraries. Under Hitler, members of the Nazi party had to prove their non-Jewish lineage with Arnheim passes, resulting in an archive of some 30 million documents, providing family trees deposited at the German Federal Archives.

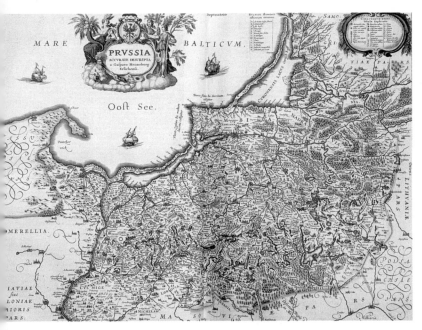

△ Map of East Prussia, 1645, whence came many migrants, gentile and Jews alike.

NON-EUROPEAN ANCESTRY

RECORDS VARY in quality from country to country. Generally, those for Asia and Africa are poor and in many cases non-existent. When talking about this to an Indian historian a few years ago, I asked why, given India's ancient culture, there was relatively so little in the way of surviving records. His answer was simple: 'termites!' You may be surprised, though, and by making detailed enquiries in your ancestor's place of origin you may find surviving documents, as we found in the case of Ari Alibhai (see page 236).

Although public archives may be thin on the ground, families themselves may provide rich mines of written information. In the case of Shilpa Mehta (see overleaf), her own family back in India was able to come up with a great deal of information from its own sources. Alternatively, there may be nothing in writing at all, but if an oral tradition survives, you can still triumph, sometimes learning more in terms of generations than you could expect in most cases in well-documented Europe, as illustrated by the case of Benhilda Chisveto (see page 15).

FINDING AN ANCESTOR'S PLACE OF ORIGIN

✉ POST 1837, look for the migrant marrying after arrival – the certificate will give you the name and occupation of the father back home.

✉ For the late 19th century onwards, find out what name they gave their house. It will invariably be the name of their home town.

✉ Look for their place of origin in 19th-century census returns (see page 66).

✉ Look for a will (see page 124). Wills of migrants will often include bequests to relatives, such as siblings, nieces or nephews, in the country of origin.

✉ Look for a record of naturalisation or denization.

✉ Look for aliens' registration certificates, police records and ships' passenger lists.

✉ Failing these, use localisation techniques, analysing the origins of the surname, and using international telephone directories (see page 84) or Internet searches to pin down the name to a country or geographical area, where you can then conduct searches. Occupations can sometimes provide clues – a 19th-century tailor in an industrial town could well have been Jewish, and a silk dyer in London, Norwich, Southampton or Canterbury would probably have Huguenot ancestry.

SHILPA MEHTA was the co-presenter of our Channel 4 series *Extraordinary Ancestors*. Not surprisingly, she became interested in her own family, and I helped her find out more from her father and cousins in America and India.

△ Shilpa's great-grandfather, Laxmilal Mehta (centre), in charge of a construction site near Bombay.

Twenty years ago, there was a terrible flood in the city of Bhavnagar, in Gujerat. Among the damage done was the destruction of a venerable house, known as the House of Pilewala in the street called Diwanpara. On the wall of the house was a great family tree, drawn in European style, as a tree, containing all the names of the Pilewala family, who were also known by their nickname, derived from their centuries-old occupation (see below) – Mehta. After the waters receded, the tree was found to have been washed away.

Had this disaster occurred in Europe, the loss of the family tree would probably have meant the loss of all family knowledge. What the waters could not wash away, however, were the excellent memories of the Mehta family, which were already used to holding a considerable amount of family knowledge. And so, the family tree of the Mehtas came to Europe in the form of oral history, and then here, to the printed page.

THE NAGAR BRAHMINS

Within Gujerat, the most prestigious of the Hindu castes were the Nagar Brahmins. They were Brahmins, although some simply styled themselves Nagars to indicate that they were not priests. They were generally landowners or high-ranking state officials, and from their number come many of the high-ranking literary figures of modern Gujerat.

It was from among the Nagars living in the city of Bhavnagar that the Maharajah of Bhavnagar picked his political administrators, called 'mehtas'. More interested in their hedonistic lifestyles and in spending, rather than raising, taxes, the Maharajahs relied heavily on their mehtas, particularly those drawn from the House of Pielwala. Indeed, so many of the men in the family served as mehtas that Mehta became a substitute surname for the family, and that is how they became known.

Memories of the family tree go back to the end of the 17th century, to Bhanji Mehta, born in about 1690. From him, a clear line comes down to the present day, as shown overleaf. One famous Mehta who does not appear on the family tree, but who could be related to Shilpa's ancestors, was Narsingh Mehta. He lived 500 years ago, in Junagadh (about 100 miles from Bhavnagar). Having fulfilled his duties as a husband and father, he retired to study, meditate and compose hymns and poems. So highly regarded was his mysticism that he became regarded as a holy man – a saint.

THE FAMILY BACKGROUND

In the 18th century, Bhavnagar was a proud independent state, surrounded by plenty of other proud, independent states, constantly at war with each other, with a strong army including Rajputs and Arabs, with Indo-Portuguese men from the south manning the city's formidable batteries of artillery.
S. M. Edwardes' *Ruling Princes of India: Bhavnagar* (Bombay, 1909) tells us that when the British arrived in 1807–8 all this started to change under Colonel Walker. Thereafter, British interference in Bhavnagar was extensive, holding back attempts at internal reorganisation. From 1863, however, Colonel Keatinge introduced the police of British non-interference in the region and the port of Bhavnagar was placed solely in the state's hands.

Now that the state was not held back by external interference, the Maharajah's prime minister, or Diwan, Azam Gavrishankar Oza, started an energetic programme of reforms – roads and harbours were built, land was reclaimed from the sea, mass education and vaccination was encouraged, laws were codified, prisons built and a proper police force was instituted. Azam Gavrishankar (Azam was a title) was aided by a council of seven administrators, including Shilpa's 4x great-grandfather Azam Vajeshankar Gulabrai Desai, who became deputy administrator, and who is shown in an old photograph, and also Savilal Somji Mehta, Shilpa's 3x great-grandfather, who was Karbhari in charge of the state's political department.

Thus, Bhavnagar became the most orderly and progressive state in the region, working closely with but not dominated by the British, and Shilpa's ancestors had a great deal to do with it.

Subsequent Diwans included Azam Samaldas Parmanandas Mehta and Vithaldas Samaldas Mehta, who belonged to an extended branch of Shilpa's family, while

△ Shilpa's maternal grandfather, Damodar Thakker, and his teacher, Atre Acharya, striding off to meet Ghandi on his famous march against salt tax.

◁ Laxmilal Mehta overseeing the construction of a railway.

LIFETIMES: SHILPA MEHTA/1

Azam Harilal Savailal Mehta, who was Shilpa's 3x great-uncle, was a deputy prime minister, shown in white seated on his own and in the group photograph seated immediately to the left of the Diwan (who is in the centre, in white).

MOVING ON

Shilpa's great-grandfather Laxmilal Mehta, born in 1877, broke the mould and trained as a consulting civil engineer. Continuing the Mehtas' policy of modernisation, however, he built the port of Bhavnagar under the Maharajahs. It is from Laxmilal's son Krishnavadan Mehta, born in 1909, that Shilpa may derive

△ Shilpa with her brother and father, in Zambia, where their father was temporarily stationed.

some of her flare as a presenter. In the days before film and television, he loved the theatre and directed numerous plays, including the first three-act play ever performed in Gujerat, in 1935. His work as an engineer for the Indian Hume Pipe Company took him away from Bhavnagar, to places as far-flung as Delhi, Karachi, Mumbai and Chinnai. His work also took him to Porbunder, where his son Shailendra Mehta, Shilpa's father, was born in 1931.

Porbunder was also the birth place of Mahatma Ghandi and, having spent several centuries working with the British, many members of the Mehta family joined Ghandi's struggle for Indian freedom. Several were imprisoned for civil obedience, most notably Shilpa's great aunt Akhileshwari and her husband, but in the end their cause was won and India achieved independence in 1947.

Ironically, when Shilpa went to Gujerat to film Ari Alibhai's family for *Extraordinary Ancestors* (see page 236) her journey took her to within minutes' walk of the house where her father was born. By the time the Mehtas settled there, Ari's family had migrated to East Africa, but relatives of his would almost certainly have known the Mehtas.

SHILPA'S MATERNAL ANCESTRY

In 1955, eight years after Indian Independence, Shilpa's father settled in England where he worked for 40 years as a specialist advisor, essentially performing the same task for the British government as his forebears had done for the Maharajahs.

Shilpa and her brother Shayur Mehta were both born here. Shayur, who played Prince Jhoti in *The Far Pavilions* and Crown Prince Chululongkom in *The King and I*, and Shilpa have also inherited strong artistic genes from their mother, Nivedida Thakkar, who is an actress, a radio artist and an Indian classical dancer. Nivedida's mother was Vidushi Kumair Omkarnand, an early Indian feminist. Besides being Principal of the Baroda Women's College, she was also an ardent disciple of Swami Vivekananda, whose cult she promoted in southern Africa in the 1920s, travelling there by dhow. Her husband, Shilpa's grandfather, was Damoder Thakker, a leading light of Nehru's Congress Party in Thane, Mumbai, while his grandfather, Shilpa's

△ 'British Indian Passport' of Shilpa's grandmother, Miss Vidushi Kumari Omkarnand.

maternal great-great-grandfather, was Valji Thakker, a botanist and agriculturalist in Kutch, Gujerat, whose portrait is said to hang in the main entrance of the agricultural college at Puhna.

The thing about Shilpa's ancestry that I find most remarkable is that so much is still known within the family, despite the flood and the fact that they now live thousands of miles away from India.

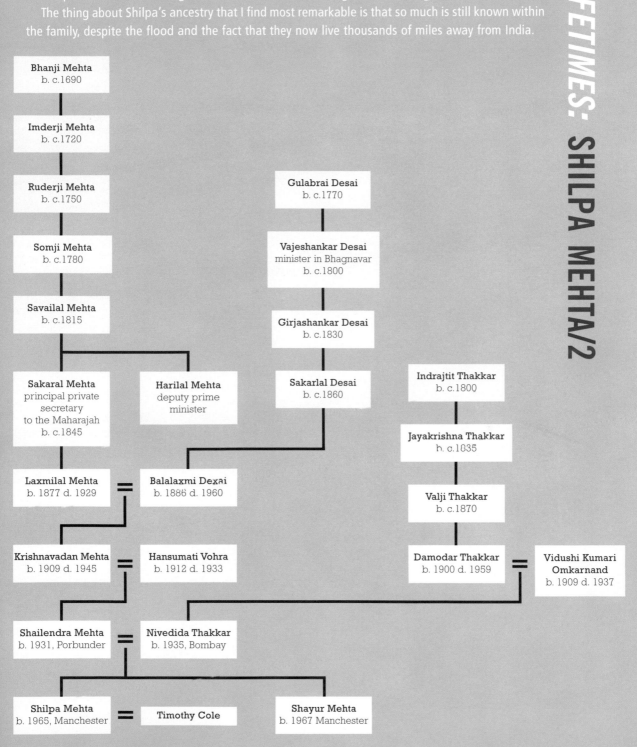

EMIGRANTS

Many people migrated from Britain, mainly to inhabit new colonies, either voluntarily as settlers or involuntarily as convicts. Generally, emigration from Britain was poorly recorded, though many countries of arrival kept records of incomers, such as the Ellis Island records of immigrants to New York, which can be accessed at **www.ellisisland.com**.

EMIGRANTS

▯ Many towns and cities founded by emigrants have excellent archives including memoirs of settlers, describing how they got there and where they came from, and often the most useful of these will have been published. Such a book may not mention your ancestor, but it may still help if it indicates where most original settlers started their journeys – always bear in mind that people preferred to travel in groups with people (often relatives) already known to them. It is also worth looking for obituary notices, especially from the late 19th century onwards. Even if the obituary is of the grandchild of an emigrant, it may give some information on the family's origins – or reputed origins – in Britain or Europe (see page 144).

▯ At the **NA** in class T 1 are Treasury Board records 1557–1920, calendared 1557–1775, containing many references to emigrants to the colonies. Passenger lists of ships leaving Britain generally survive only from the 1890s and are in BT 27 (see also page 255). You will need to know from where and have pretty good idea of when someone left to make the search feasible – and they will only give name, age, occupation and place of destination- not place of birth.

▯ Some 16th- and 17th-century travellers applied for licences to pass 'beyond the seas': these can be sought in **NA** classes E 157 and CO 1. Applications for and issue of passports 1794–1948, including details of where the applicant wanted to go, are in FO 610, in date order but partially indexed for the periods 1851–62 and 1874–1916 in FO 611, now indexed 1851–1903 at **www.nationalarchivist.com**. However, passports were not compulsory, and therefore very few were issued, before the start of the First World War.

▯ At the **NA**, the Colonial Papers (CO 1) and Board of Trade Minutes 1675–1704 (CO 391) have been calendared and indexed by HMSO, and you may also find references to migrant ancestors or relatives in the *Calendar of State Papers Colonial, America and West Indies 1574–1738* – a lucky dip, but relatively easy to search at the **NA**, **British Library** and many other major **libraries**.

▯ From 1890, the Board of Trade kept passenger lists for people leaving for destinations outside Europe (**NA** class BT 27), including names, ages and occupation and usually last place of residence – but they are arranged by port and ships and are virtually unsearchable.

▯ Records of assisted emigration of the poor, who had their passage paid for them in return for agreeing to work as indentured servants for a term of years after their arrival, are at the **NA** and **Guildhall Library**, and many such records have been printed in P. W. Coldham's *The Complete Book of Emigrants in Bondage, 1614–1775* (GCP, 1988). Other details of emigrants whose dispatch to the colonies was considered less irksome than supporting them at home are in parish vestry minutes (see page 166) and, after 1834, in Poor Law Union records (both at **county record offices**), while lists of many who emigrated under the latter system are in **NA** class MH 12.

▯ Once they had arrived in their new homes, migrants started keeping records, which are generally still in those countries. However, many Anglican communities abroad sent their original registers, or copies of bishops' transcripts, to the Archbishop of Canterbury and Bishop of London, and these are now divided between **Lambeth Palace Library**, **Guildhall Library** and the **NA**. Holdings are listed in G. Yeo's *The British Overseas: A Guide to Records of their Baptisms, Births, Marriages, Deaths and Burials available in the United Kingdom* (Guildhall Library, 1994). The NA holds a substantial collection of miscellaneous foreign returns, from all over the world, in classes RG 32–6 and RG 43, dating back to the 17th century but mainly for the 19th century. Copies of RG 43 are at the **FRC**.

▯ The NA also holds many Foreign Office records of baptisms, births and so on, some but not all of which are included in the GRO

▷ Migrants to America. *In the Land of Promise* by Charles Frederic Ulrich (1858–1908).

consular returns. If the entry you want is not there, you might yet find it in the unindexed returns in the FO papers at the NA. A search in **www.catalogue.nationalarchives.gov. uk** under the city or country where you think the event took place should tell you if returns for the right period are available.

www.theshipslist.com is a website of previously unpublished resources, including passenger records; contemporary immigration reports; newspaper records; ship wreck information and ship pictures.

POPULAR DESTINATIONS FOR EMIGRATION

THE AMERICAS

Emigration was also a favoured way of dealing with orphans or children of paupers. Many were sent to Virginia from the 17th century onwards by Christ's Hospital in London, and are listed in P. W. Coldham's *Child Apprentices in America from Christ's Hospital, London, 1617–1778* (GPC, 1990). Parish Guardians of the Poor were permitted to dispatch orphans and poor children to the colonies from 1850, and many charities like Dr Barnardo's did so as well, Canada being one of the most popular destinations. P. Bean and J. Melville's *Lost Children of the Empire* (Unwin Hyman, 1989) provides further information for those with such children in their family tree.

Also worth mentioning is NA class T 47/9–12, a detailed and unique register of emigrants from Britain to the Americas 1773–6 containing name, age, occupation, last place of residence and dates of departure and destination.

A formidable compilation of records relating to migrating to the Americas is given in P. W. Coldham's *The Complete Book of Emigrants* (GPC, 1987–93), also available on CD-Rom.

Assisted emigration to Australia, North America and the West Indies was also encouraged by free passage and grants of land to willing settlers, by the Colonial Land and Emigration Office, which was founded in 1833. It became the Colonial Commission of Land and Emigration and its records, to 1896,

are at the **NA** in CO 384, with further records in CO 386 (emigration entry books) and CO 327–8 (North American emigrants registers 1850–68). Many Australian records of assisted immigrants have been indexed, and are accessible through the relevant **state archive office**.

QUICK REFERENCE

See also main sources in Useful Addresses, page 306

LAMBETH PALACE LIBRARY
Lambeth Palace Road
London SE1 7JU
☎ 020 7898 1400
www.lambethpalacelibrary.org

△ *A Government Jail Gang in Sydney* by Augustus Earle (1793–1838).

WHERE TO SEARCH

AUSTRALIA

Australia was discovered by Captain Cook in 1770, and a penal colony was established by the First Fleet, which arrived in (what was to become) New South Wales in January 1788, followed by a second fleet in 1790 and a third in 1791.

Most of the original colonists, who are now regarded as highly desirable ancestors, have been researched in biographical dictionaries, such as M. Gillen's *The Founders of Australia: A Biographical Dictionary of the First Fleet* (Library of Australian History, 1989).

Between the first and second fleets was a single ship, the *Lady Juliana*, which bore a shipment of female convicts to provide breeding stock for the new colony, whose voyage and experiences are vividly described in Sîan Rees's *The Floating Brothel* (Review, 2001).

Transportation – orders for which are in British court records (see page 235) – stopped in 1869. Records of wives petitioning the government to be able to join their husbands are in **NA** classes PC 1 and HO 12 and early correspondence concerning the New South Wales colony is in CO 201.

Australia remained a collection of separate colonies until they were formed into a federation in 1901, by which time over a million people had emigrated there. The most detailed account of Australia's archives and records is N. Vine Hall's *Tracing your Family History in Australia: A Guide to Sources* (N. Vine Hall, 1994).

CANADA

See A. Baxter's *In Search of your Canadian roots: Tracing your Family Tree in Canada* (Macmillan of Canada, 1989). Canada was first colonised by the French, followed soon after by settlements established by the Hudson's Bay Company (whose records are on microfilm at the **NA**).

The whole of eastern Canada was controlled by the British after the end of the Seven Years' War (1763). After the British lost the American War of Independence, many Americans, black and white, who had fought for the Crown were given land in Canada. The ten provinces and two territories, which were all fully united as Canada in 1949, have separate records, so it is important to know (or use telephone directories to guess) where to look.

An excellent website for emigrants to Canada is **www.ist.uwaterloo.ca/~marj/genealogy/thevoyage.html**. See too P. Horne's 'The emigration of pauper children to Canada' in *Genealogists' Magazine*, 25, no. 10, June 1997.

NEW ZEALAND

White settlers started appearing in New Zealand from the 1790s, and in 1840 the islands became a Crown colony, independent of New South Wales, whence many of its settlers had come. Until 1875, it was divided into provinces, each of which kept their own records of arrivals. A guide to New Zealand records is A. Bromell's *Tracing Family History in New Zealand* (Government Printing Office Publishing, 1988).

SIERRA LEONE

In 1787 a fleet of three ships set sail from London carrying the first settlers. Most were black men, either freed or escaped slaves and servants, or soldiers who had fought for the British in the American War of Independence, drawn from the ten or twenty thousand black people then in London. With them went some black women, and a not inconsiderable number of black men and women were accompanied by their white spouses. Those who survived the depredations of the voyage founded Granville Town, later redeveloped as Freetown.

The records of the Committee for the Relief of the Black Poor, which organised the assemblage of people for the original voyage, are in **NA** class T 1/631–8, 641–7. The original ships' passenger lists are in NA class T 1/643, Reg. no. 487, 27/2/1787 and fully transcribed and indexed by myself in 'The founders of Sierra Leone', *Ancestors' Magazine*, October/November 2003.

Records of black refugees from the American War of Independence compiled in New York in 1783 before they were settled in Nova Scotia are in the

'Book of Negroes', **NA** 30/55/100, no. 10427: an index by G. C. Branch was published by the United Empire Loyalists' Association of Canada.

Records of claims for compensation for losses of loyalists are at the **NA** in T 50 and T 79 and AO 12–13. The subsequent records of black loyalists from Nova Scotia who went to Sierra Leone in 1791 are in CO 217/63, ff. 361–6.

SOUTH AFRICA

South Africa, the first Dutch colony in southern Africa, was founded at Cape Town in the 18th century. The British annexed South Africa in 1806 and colonists started arriving in numbers, displacing many of the original Dutch settlers to the Orange Free State and Transvaal, both of which were subsumed following the bloody Boer War into the Union of South Africa in 1910.

Most useful records are in the **government archives** in Pretoria and the **provincial archive depots** of Johannesburg, Bloemfontein, Cape Town, Pretoria and Pietermaritzburg, and described, along with the records of Zimbabwe (Rhodesia) and Namibia, in R. T. Lombard's *Handbook for Genealogical Research in South Africa* (Institute for Historical Research, Human Sciences Council, 1984). Unfortunately, due mainly to chronic underfunding, South African archivists have become increasingly unable to respond to genealogical enquiries, making research in the country a slow and frustrating process.

QUICK REFERENCE

See main sources in Useful Addresses, page 306

AMERICA

PASSENGER LISTS for those going to America are an immensely useful source for those tracing the origins of American settlers because, although they will seldom tell you where the migrant came from, they will at least indicate how many people of the same surname made the journey across the Atlantic, and from which port or ports they left. If a migrant left from Bristol, it would not be unreasonable to assume they came from the southwest of England or southern Wales as opposed, say, to Scotland, although of course there were always exceptions.

In general, although a great many names of pre-19th-century migrants appear in ships' passenger lists, the majority of those who travelled to America by sea were not recorded by name. From 1820, masters of ships arriving with passengers had to file lists of their passengers, giving name, age, occupation and country of origin, and these can be studied at the National Archives in Washington. The Library of Congress, SoG and IHGS hold many published passenger lists and indexes compiled from them, of which the most substantial is P. W. Filby and M. K. Meyer's *Passenger and Immigration Index* (Gale Research Co., 1981) with annual supplements to 2000 and now also on CD-Rom (to 1999). This should be your first port of call for trying to locate a migrant to America. Do not forget the Ellis Island records of immigrants to New York, now easily accessible at **www.ellisisland.com**.

AUSTRALIA

Lists of non-convict ships' passengers to Australia tend not to survive from before 1890, but thereafter tend to provide name, age, place of birth and occupation – and many are indexed. The best place to start looking is **www.cyndislist.com/austnz.htm#Ships**.

CANADA

Many ships' passenger lists for Canada – and bear in mind that many immigrants arrived by sea from America – are at the National Archives of Canada.

CHAPTER TWENTY-SEVEN
RELIGIOUS DENOMINATIONS IN BRITAIN

Before Henry VIII's Reformation of 1534, virtually everyone in England belonged to the Catholic Church. From 1534 onwards, divisions occurred, first between the Protestant Anglicans and those who clung tenaciously to Catholicism, and from the 16th century onwards between different types of Protestant denomination. While the Church of England doubled up as a form of state registry of baptism, marriage and burial until 1837, the fact is that many non-Anglicans do not appear in its records, thus posing problems for family historians.

△ King Henry VIII, instigator of the Reformation in England and Wales.

CATHOLICS

In the decades following the Reformation, many families abandoned Catholicism, while the remainder formed a small, cohesive social group, often tacitly left alone by local officials who were, in many cases, their not-too-distant relations. The main Catholic areas were the north, especially Lancashire, with sizeable pockets in Essex, Sussex and Wiltshire and London, where they tended to live around Holborn and St Pancras.

Records of Catholic persecution tend to date from the 1559 Acts of Supremacy and Uniformity, which forbade Catholic mass, and imposed a fine of 12d a week to be levied by the Churchwardens for Catholics who refused to attend church on Sundays and Holy Days or for 'misliking' or grumbling about having to do so.

After the Restoration (1660) the 'Clarendon Codes' ushered in further fierce anti-Catholic legislation, forcing all teachers and ministers to use the Book of Common Prayer and office holders to take Anglican Communion and deny transubstantiation. The Codes also forbade non-Anglican ministers from going within five miles of a town or hold religious or political meetings of more than five people.

Most anti-Catholic laws were lifted by the Catholic Relief Acts of 1778 and 1791, with almost full civil rights granted by the 1829 Catholic Emancipation Act, after which many Catholic chapels were opened and registers became universal. Catholic schools also sprang up, starting with those relocated here from the Continent due to the French

Revolution. The Catholic hierarchy was officially restored in 1851 and urban Catholic churches proliferated, especially in London, Glasgow and Liverpool.

▷ Baptism certificate showing an entry extracted from the registers of the Catholic chapel at Kelvedon Hatch, Essex, and subsequently kept at St Helen's, Brentwood, of Michael [Lawrence] Mason, baptised on 7 March 1793.

△ The baptism certificate of his brother George Mason, baptised on 9 November 1791.

▷ Old family photographs, taken from a glass negative, showing two great-great-great-great-aunts of mine, Margaret and Rosina Mason, who were nuns at New Hall, Essex, under the names Aloysius Stanislaus and Ignatius Francis.

SEMINARY PRIESTS

FROM 1574, English priests trained in Continental seminaries started infiltrating the country. Because their records often include parents' names, they can tell us a lot about the Catholic families from which they came. The best sources are:

▷ G. Anstruther's *The Seminary Priests, St Edmund's College, Ware and Ushaw College*, Durham, Vol. 1 (Elizabethan) and Vol. 2 (Early Stuarts 1603–59) (Mayhew-McCrimmon, 1975); Vol. 3 (1660–1715) (Mayhew-McCrimmon, 1976); and Vol. 4 (1716–1800) (Mayhew-McCrimmon, 1977)

▷ A. Bellinger's *English and Welsh Priests 1558–1800* (Downside Abbey, 1984); C. Fitzgerald-Lombard's *English and Welsh Priests 1801–1914* (Downside Abbey, 1993)

▷ C. Johnson's *Scottish Catholic Secular Clergy 1879–1989* (John Donaldson Publishers Ltd, 1991)

▷ G. Holt's *The English Jesuits 1650-1829: A Biographical Dictionary* (CRS, vol. 70, 1984)

CATHOLICS

GENERAL

⊡ Catholics are generally well recorded both in their own records and in state records of their persecution. Much of both have been published by the **Catholic Record Society (CRS)**, and a good collection is at the **Catholic Central Library**. There is also an excellent **Catholic Family History Society**.

⊡ A good source for London and London-area marriages of Catholics is Fr Godfrey Anstruther OP's *Catholic Marriage Index*, which I have written about fully in *Family History*, New series 105, at present looked after by the **IHGS**. It covers some 30,000 marriages from the late 19th century back as far as the registers go (in some cases to the 18th century). One of its great virtues is that its compiler added many notes from his personal knowledge, and its arrangement also facilitates searching through all marriages under a surname looking for others with the same parents. Its corresponding Converts index is described in *Family History*, New series 114.

⊡ The whereabouts of the main records described here can be found through M. Gandy's *Catholic Family History: Bibliography of Local Sources* (M. Gandy, 1996) and D. Steel's 'Sources for Jewish and Catholic Family History', *National Index of Parish Registers*, Vol. 3. Another useful reference work for Catholic ancestry is J. Gillow's *A Literary and Biographical History, or Bibliographical Dictionary of the English Catholics; from the breach with Rome in 1534 to the present time* (Burns & Oates, 1885–1902). **www.catholic-genealogy.com** is a portal for British Catholic ancestry.

16TH AND 17TH-CENTURY CATHOLICISM

⊡ Annual returns of resulting fines, levied under 16th and 17th-centuries anti Catholic legistration. The Recusant Rolls, are in **NA** class E 367 and 377 (1592–1691), though in practice these tend only to record the well-to-do. In the early years of the Restoration the fines for non-attendance at church were fairly strictly enforced: transcripts of surviving records are given in J. Gillow and J. S. Hansom's 'A List of Convicted Recusants in the Reign of Charles II' in Vol. 6 of the **Catholic Record Society**'s publications.

⊡ Persecution records include those fined £100 under the Act of 1606 which compelled everyone to have their children baptised as Anglicans: documentation is sometimes found in Ecclesiastical Courts (see page 231).

⊡ The Protestation Returns of 1641 (see page 220) and 1643 Covenant contain many Catholics, as do the Royalist Composition Papers and records of the Committee for the Advance of Money (see page 215) generated by the Civil War.

⊡ Many Catholics joined James II in his exile at Saint-Germain-en-Laye near Paris in 1689. Many later returned, but not before they had married or had children baptised there – your 'missing ancestors', perhaps. The best sources are C. E. Lart's *Saint-Germain-en-Laye: The Parochial Registers: Jacobite Extracts 1689–1720* (St Catherine's, 1910) and the Marquis de Ruvigny's *The Jacobite Peerage* (Charles Skilton, 1974).

⊡ The 1715 rebellion in favour of James II's son generated some very useful records when the state ordered the registration of well-off

Papists' estates and wills. Original records are in Close Rolls of the Chancery courts (**NA**, C 54) and Recovery Rolls of the Court of Common Pleas (CP 43), listed in a series of articles in *The Genealogist*, new series, vols. 1–3, and Quarter Sessions (those for Lancashire are indexed at the Lancashire Record Office). Printed records are in E. E. Estcourt and J. O. Payne's *The English Catholic Nonjurors of 1715* and Payne's *Records of the English Catholics of 1715* (1889) and *'Cosin's List'– The Names of the Roman Catholic Nonjurors and others, who Refus'd to take the OATHS to His Late Majesty King George* (J. Robinson, 1862).

⊡ The 1767 national census of Catholics has been published as E. S. Worrall's *Returns of Papists 1767: Diocese of Chester* (CRS, 1980) and *Dioceses of England and Wales except Chester* (CRS, 1989).

⊡ Because of death penalties, priests went about incognito and only a handful of registers survive for the 17th and 18th centuries, but the Catholic embassies in London and chapels of the Vicars Apostolic kept registers which contain names of many English Catholics. Most surviving material has been published by the **CRS**.

⊡ After Hardwicke's Marriage Act (1754, see page 99), Catholics had to marry in the Church of England, although they also conducted separate Catholic marriages of their own. Because enforcement of penal legislation had become negligible, priests now started keeping registers of baptisms. Most Catholic registers are still with the parishes which created them: an essential tool is M. Gandy's *Catholic Missions and*

Registers 1700–1880 (M. Gandy, 1993) and his *Catholic Parishes in England, Wales and Scotland: An Atlas* (M. Gandy, 1993). Although some Catholic priests kept notes of members of their congregation who had died, burial registers were rare until the 19th century. Most Catholics were buried at night in parish churchyards (which had, after all, been consecrated before the Reformation) but without the Anglican burial service. Records of such burials may nevertheless be found in Anglican burial registers.

From 1768 English Catholics were served by the Laity's Directory, which included many death announcements, succeeded by the Catholic Directory in 1837, copies of which can be seen at the **Catholic Central Library**.

19TH-CENTURY CATHOLICISM

The 'Oxford Movement' of the 1830s saw a wave of conversions to Catholicism, and waning Catholic numbers were vastly increased by the Irish who migrated here due to the potato famine of 1847. **Crook's Liverpool Marriage Index** aims to identify all Irish marriages that took place there, and includes many other foreign marriages of Spaniards, Genoese, Chinese, Polish, French and so on.

SCOTLAND

In Scotland, Catholicism was made illegal in 1560, but it remained a small but potent force north of the border, as was demonstrated by the risings of 1715 and 1745, which contained strong Catholic elements. Both rebellions caused severe repercussions for Catholics, the latter continuing until 1793. Most of the surviving pre-1855 Catholic registers are at the **NAS**, and those kept subsequently are with the churches.

IRELAND

Irish Catholicism is covered on pages 178–9.

Irish Catholicism is covered on pages 178–9.

QUICK REFERENCE

See also main resources in Useful Addresses, page 306

CATHOLIC RECORD SOCIETY (CRS)
c/o 12 Melbourne Place
Wolsingham
Co. Durham DL13 3EH
☎ 01388 527747
www.catholic-history.org.uk/crs

CATHOLIC CENTRAL LIBRARY
New address not available at time of going to print
☎ 020 7732 8379
www.catholic-library.org.uk

CATHOLIC FAMILY HISTORY SOCIETY
The Secretaries
45 Gates Green Road
West Wickham
Bromley
Kent BR4 9DE

CROOK'S LIVERPOOL MARRIAGE INDEX
25 Gerneth Road
Speke
Liverpool L24 1UN

▽ *Landscape in Spring, with a Nun Walking among Daffodils* by John Sowerby (1876–1914). Many Catholic girls became nuns; an index to these is being compiled by the Catholic Family History Society.

IN 1742 THE BAPTISTS, Presbyterians and Independents formed a General Register of the births of children of Protestant Dissenters of the three Denominations at Dr William's Library – an idea copied by the Methodists in 1818. The Dr William entries, which are generally considered to be very accurate, are mainly for Londoners but there are many entries from all over the country and abroad. They provide the full names of both parties, father's residence and occupation, and the mother's and father's name and residence. They run from January 1743 to June 1837 – a total of 48,975 births, mainly concentrated in the late 18th and early 19th centuries. They take the form of a duplicate parchment certificate signed by the parents and witnesses, one copy of which was lodged at the library and the contents copied into a register, and the other returned with a note affirming that the information has been registered. From 1768 onwards, baptisms were recorded as well, not least because some Anglican clergy refused burial when proof of baptism could not be produced. The Library entries are now indexed in the VRI.

From 1837 legally recognised marriages could be performed in Catholic churches with a registrar present, but in some cases the practice of a double marriage, one in a Catholic church one in an Anglican one (or now in a registrar's office) continued until Catholic priests could themselves be licensed to perform legally binding marriages in 1898. It was not until 1926, however, that it ceased to be technically illegal for a Catholic clergyman to wear a habit in public.

PROTESTANT NON-CONFORMISTS

Protestant non-conformity arose through groups splitting off from the Church of England. The 'three denominations' of Congregationalists, Baptists and Presbyterians trace their roots to the Elizabethan Puritans within the Church of England, who broke away completely after the failure of the Savoy Conference in 1661. Quakerism was founded by George Fox in the 1640s and, in the 18th century, Unitarianism broke off from the three denominations and Wesleyan Methodism split away from the Anglican church. Because people often changed denomination, sometimes leaving the Church of England, at other times returning to it, you can never predict what you will find in your ancestry. Among the most useful guides to this subject is D. J. Steel's *Sources for Non-conformist Genealogy and Family History* (Phillimore for the SoG, 1973).

CONGREGATIONALISTS, BAPTISTS AND PRESBYTERIANS

During the 17th century, Protestant non-conformists were most likely to be recorded in records of persecution, especially in Quarter Sessions (see page 232) and church courts. This is especially so following the 1662 Act of Uniformity, which excluded all non-Anglican clergy, schoolmasters and fellows of colleges from practising, and the 1664 Conventicle Act, which imposed first fines and then imprisonment and transportation on people attending non-Anglican religious assemblies numbering over five. In 1672 the Declaration of Indulgence allowed non-conformist teachers and ministers holding assemblies ('conventicles') to apply for licences – 1061 ministers did so.

The Toleration Act of 1689 guaranteed religious freedom to Protestant non-conformists. Thousands of meeting houses, mainly of Independents, were built for the now legal conventicles, licences being granted by the Quarter Sessions. Baptist congregations proliferated, mainly in towns. The subsequent rifts and reunions of the various denominations and their sub-sects are too complicated to detail here, but in general terms they succeeded at the expense of the Church of

LIFELINES: LOUISA JENKINS

FOR *EXTRAORDINARY ANCESTORS*, I was asked to find the original name of Louisa Jenkins' ancestor, Mark Brown. Louisa knew he came from Italy, and that he had changed his name to avoid the prevalent anti-Italian feeling in Edinburgh at the time. But what had it been before? The first surprise was when his daughter Theresa's 1876 Edinburgh marriage record was obtained, giving the father as Stack Brown, a figure maker. The censuses indicated he was born in Italy, and that he had a son Charles born in 1855. This was the annus mirabilis for Scottish genealogy because of the wealth of information contained on certificates made in that year alone. Charles's birth record told us that Stack Brown was born in Milan and that he married Theresa Brady (from Dublin) in 1839 in Edinburgh. An Italian marrying an Irish girl called Theresa pointed clearly to Catholicism, and Catholic registers of Edinburgh rewarded us with the marriage record of Theresa Brady and Eustachio Bruni.

Directories (see page 82) showed there were several Italian figure makers in Edinburgh at the time: the *figuristi di gesso* like Eustachio made the beautiful plaster statues that ornament many of Edinburgh's grandest houses and public buildings.

The photographs here are of Eustachio Bruni and Theresa Brady's descendents, down the female line, through their daughter Theresa Turnbull (née Brown), Eliza Mackenzie (née Turnbull), to Louisa Jenkins (née Mackenzie).

△ (top) Louisa's Aunt Anna, sister of Eliza Mackenzie, daughter of Theresa Turnbull.
△ (above) Aunt Julia and Uncle Jim Turnbull, Louisa's mother's brother.
▷ (right) Eliza Mackenzie (née Turnbull), mother of Louisa Jenkins, with her son William and daughter Eliza.
▷ (far right) Louisa Jenkins (née Mackenzie), daughter of Eliza Mackenzie, daughter of Theresa Turnbull.

LIFETIMES: THANK GOODNESS FOR DR WILLIAM

IN THE MONTHS leading up to the introduction of General Registration, John and Mary Burbage were clearly worried that their children had no formal Anglican baptism to verify their ages. Accordingly, on 24 February 1837, they made the short journey from their house at Tyso Street to Redcross Street with three friends, Henry Whitmore, a surgeon of Colcath Square, Ann Colbey of 25 Graser Street, spinster, and Ann Yereysnor of 21 Hertford Street, both cousins of either John or Mary.

At Dr William's Library they registered the births of Jonas, 25 August 1815, at 6 Pinder Street, St Pancras; John, born on 21 November 1816 at Lucas Street, St Pancras; and William, born at 15 Gough Street, St Pancras, on 13 November 1821.

In each entry John stated that he was a cabinet maker of Clerkenwell and that Mary was daughter of Jonas Jeffries of Wood Mills, Shropshire, a miller.

WHERE TO SEARCH

CONGREGATIONALISTS, BAPTISTS AND PRESBYTERIANS

⊟ Details of licences to hold assemblies in 1672 have been published in G. Lyon Turner's *Original Records of Early Non-conformity under Persecution and Indulgence (1911–14)*. The best source for non-conformist ministers up to 1689 is A. G. Matthews' *Calamy Revised* (1934).

⊟ Anglican churchwardens' presentments from 1660–89 record those presented to the Quarter Sessions for not attending Anglican communion. The subsequent fines or other punishments are recorded in the quarter session records themselves. Numbers (but not names) of non-conformists in each parish can be found in the various episcopal returns of the late 17th and 18th centuries, especially the 1676 Religious Census, the 'Compton census', covering southern England, at **Lambeth Palace Library**. Recusant rolls contain many Protestant non-conformists as well as Catholics.

⊟ The **United Reformed Church** holds many records relating to what were once a proliferation of groups.

⊟ Whatever their denomination, your Protestant ancestors' marriages will generally be in Anglican registers, especially after Hardwicke's 1754 Marriage Act (see page 99) (the only non-Anglican marriage registers kept thereafter were by Quakers, Jews and Catholics). Despite the fact that Anglican baptisms remained a prerequisite for proof of age for all government posts, even down to employment in dockyards, non-conformists' baptisms tend not to appear in Anglican registers, although births were sometimes recorded, especially after 1680.

⊟ Almost all burials were in Anglican graveyards (and thus registers) because there was seldom anywhere else to bury bodies. Some non-conformist burial grounds were opened in the late 17th and 18th centuries, though records of these seldom survive. Monumental inscriptions often provide a useful substitute for missing or non-existent records in burial registers.

⊟ In general, if your ancestors' marriages and burials but not baptisms are in the parish registers, they were probably non-conformists, and you should seek their baptisms in those surviving non-conformist registers that cover the area around the parish.

England: if you have Yorkshire ancestors from the 1850s, there is a 50% chance they were Protestant non-conformists. In recent years there has been a tendency to reunification, culminating in 1972 with the Congregationalists and Presbyterians combining into the United Reform Church.

Because of persecution (or fear of it) few Protestant non-conformist chapel registers save those of the Walloons (see page 268) pre-date 1700 and none go back further than 1644. Many surviving Protestant non-conformist registers were deposited with the Registrar General in 1837, and are held in **NA** class RG 4. This has a comprehensive catalogue and its entries have been indexed in the **IGI**. Many more are now in county record offices and indexed in the Vital Records index, searchable on **www.familysearch.org**.

Once they came into existence (generally after 1689), registers often cover wide geographical areas, and sometimes more than one chapel. Some were even moved from one county to another. Because baptisms sometimes had to wait for the minister to arrive in an isolated area, you cannot assume that all entries relate to small babies.

Much documentation generated by congregations has been deposited at **county record offices** (and remember, your ancestors may have used a chapel situated across a county border), but many records are still with the church or chapel.

Minute books contain much useful information about congregations and their members, including disciplinary measures: they often pre-date registers and some contain notes of baptisms, marriages and burials. There is a large collection of these at **Dr William's Library** (see box on page 260).

Church rolls list members, their residence, date of joining and leaving a congregation. They often record deaths and also note changes of surname when women married. There are many of these at the **United Reformed Church History Society Library**.

Trust deeds include names of at least a dozen original trustees drawn from the congregation and their successors over time. From 1736 many of these are enrolled in Chancery records at the **NA**.

Most denominations had magazines and yearbooks, such as the *Congregational Year Book and Baptist Handbook*, including birth, marriage and death announcements, and often very detailed obituaries of ministers. These are best sought at the relevant denomination's headquarters.

In Scotland, Knox introduced Presbyterianism as the most widespread form of Christianity in the 1560s. In 1637, in defiance of Anglican England, the Scots signed a covenant, agreeing to defend Presbyterianism against all comers and made it their national church, and so it remained, save for the period 1660–87. Therefore, the *Scottish parochial registers* (see page 105) are Presbyterian.

QUICK REFERENCE

See also main sources in Useful Addresses, page 306

LAMBETH PALACE LIBRARY
Lambeth Palace Road
London SE1 7JU
☎ 020 7898 1400
www.lambethpalacelibrary.org

UNITED REFORMED CHURCH
Church House
86 Tavistock Place
London WC1H 9RT
☎ 020 7916 2020
www.urc.org.uk

DR WILLIAM'S LIBRARY
14 Gordon Square
London WC1H 0AR
☎ 020 7387 3727
www.dwlib.co.uk

UNITED REFORMED CHURCH HISTORY SOCIETY LIBRARY
Westminster College
Madingley Road
Cambridge CB3 0AA
☎ 01223 741300
www.urc.org.uk

QUAKERS

The Civil War spawned many sects, including Muggletonians, Ranters, Seekers, Familists and Fifth Monarchy Men, and the Society of Friends, known as the Quakers, founded in the 1640s by George Fox. The Quakers' refusal to take oaths made them a particular subject of state

SPOTTING A QUAKER ANCESTOR

△ George Fox

QUAKERS REFUSED to use the names of days and months, as they were derived from paganism. Thus they called Sunday 'first day' and March the 'first month' (even though the new year did not begin technically until 25 March) until 1752 when the calendar changed and January became the 'first month' of the year.

Occasionally, Quaker births and marriages were recorded in Anglican registers – they were often misdescribed as 'anabaptists' – but most were not: Some Quakers were buried on the north sides of churchyards, without an Anglican burial service. The registers often refer to these events disparagingly as 'hurl'd into ye ground'. Not surprisingly, most Quakers preferred to be buried in orchards, or in Quaker burial grounds. Monumental Inscriptions were expressly forbidden.

△ George Fox surveys the ruins of London after the Great Fire in 1666.

hostility and the Quaker Act of 1662 represented a failed attempt to obliterate the movement. Persecution declined in the 18th century but, unlike the many who had settled in Pennsylvania, the English Quakers began to fall away, many converting to less exacting denominations, meaning that many people with non-conformist ancestry may have unsuspected lines of descent from Quakers.

The Society of Friends was run by a hierarchy of meetings (or actually two heirarchies, as women and men met separately), starting with local 'particular' meetings, several of which would meet periodically at 'preparative' meetings and send representatives to monthly meetings of several constituent congregations. In turn, representatives would attended quarterly meetings, roughly equivalent to a diocese, all of which were governed by the yearly meeting of Friends in London, which included representatives from Scotland and Wales.

Because they set themselves outside the parish system, the Quakers had their own highly organised and strictly observed system of settlement certificates and examinations, to ensure that poor Quakers would receive poor relief from the correct monthly meeting, and not become falsely chargeable on the wrong monthly meeting.

QUAKERS

An excellent guide to Quaker sources is E. H. Milligan and M. J. Thomas's *My Ancestors were Quakers: How Can I Find Out More About Them?* (SoG, 1989).

Quaker registers of birth, marriage and burial were kept either by the local or monthly meetings, and tended to be very detailed, especially after the system was reorganised in 1776, from which date copies were also sent to the quarterly meeting. Almost all registers were surrendered to the Registrar General in 1837 and are now in **NA** classes RG 6 and 8.

Before they were surrendered, though, the Quakers copied all their records into two digests, one for the relevant quarterly meeting (most of which are now in **county record offices**) and one for the Quaker headquarters in London, which can be searched at the **Friends' House**. Here, guidance is given on how to use the records and also how to cross-reference them with the original and somewhat more detailed registers at the **NA**. The digests can also be seen on film at the **SoG**. Furthermore, there is a single alphabetical index at the Friends' House to all birth, marriage and death entries, right up to 1959. There are omissions, of course: many marriages were registered only if both parties were Quakers, and the births of children of mixed marriages tended to be ignored too. The death records are considered to be relatively complete.

Quakers kept many other records, including membership records, 'sufferings' books and minute books. These are mostly at **county record offices**, with a central catalogue at the **Friends' House**. Minute books contain, among other things, detailed records of enquiries made to ensure that parties wishing to marry had the consent of parents or other living relatives, that they were free to marry, practising Quakers and not closely related. All these records make excellent additions to a family history.

In addition, most marriage and death announcements appear in *The Friend*, which was first published in 1843, with births announced from 1850. Many births appear in

The Friend that do not appear in Quaker registers. The Friends' Library at **Friends' House** also has an archive including letters, diaries and biographical information. In **county record offices**, the churchwardens' accounts and Quarter Sessions records (see page 232) are also valuable sources for records of Quakers being persecuted.

SCOTLAND

Most registers of Scottish Quakers are either with their churches or deposited at the **NAS**, although many records are also at the **Friends' House**.

IRELAND

Quakers were established in Ireland in 1654 and their records, which do date back that far, albeit in an incomplete state, are at the **Religious Society of Friends** with many of those for Northern Ireland at the **PRONI**. Irish Quaker births and marriages 1850-75 are on the BVRI section of **www.familysearch.org**.

QUICK REFERENCE

See also main sources in Useful Addresses, page 306

FRIENDS' HOUSE
173–177 Euston Road
London NW1 2BJ
☎ 020 7663 1135
www.quaker.org.uk/library

RELIGIOUS SOCIETY OF FRIENDS
Swanbrook House
Bloomfield Avenue
Morehampton Road
Donnybrook
Dublin 4
Eire
☎ 00 353 1 668 3684
www.quakers-in-ireland.org

TITUS CLOSE COLLIER'S baptism was recorded in the Wesleyan Methodist Registry: it tells us he was born on 24 July 1835 at 'Sheet', Hampshire, and baptised at Guildford, Surrey, on 25 October that year, the son of John Collier and Eliza, daughter of John and Ann Adams. John was a Methodist minister – listed as a 'Westleyan' minister in the 1851 census of Axminster, Devon, born in Little Houghton, Northamptonshire. Further details of his career were found in Rev. W. Hill's *An Alphabetical Arrangement of all the Wesleyan-Methodist Ministers, and Preachers on Trial, in Connection with the British and Irish Conferences; with Several of the Affiliated Conferences, Showing Circuits and Stations* (Wesleyan Conference Office, 1869).

His impressive list of postings started in 1829 at Brixham, Devon, moving on almost each year to posts from Cornwall to Manchester and the Isle of Man: he was indeed posted to Axminster 1850–52 and, interestingly, in 1835 he was stationed not at Guildford but relatively nearby at Petersfield, Hampshire – another two-year posting, perhaps to allow Mrs Collier to recover from the birth.

There is also an obituary for him in the 1870 Minutes of the Methodist Conference, kept at the John Rylands Library. In a list of ministers who had died since the last conference is John, 'born at Little Houghton in the Northampton Circuit, in the year 1803. Through the tender care of a pious mother he became early in life a regular attendant at the Wesleyan-Methodist chapel…'– sadly, that is all it says about his origins, and does not even name the 'pious mother'.

◁ Titus Close Collier

MORAVIANS

Founded in Bohemia and originally aimed at reforming the Lutheran church from within but eventually becoming a denomination in its own right, a branch of the Moravian church was established in London in the 1730s and enjoyed short-lived popularity, especially in Yorkshire.

METHODISTS

The Moravians were the chief inspiration for John Wesley, an Anglican clergyman who, with his brother Charles and George Whitfield, founded Methodism as an evangelical preaching movement within the Anglican church in the late 1730s. As with so many other similar groups, it soon split from the Church of England and became an independent denomination by the 1770s. Splinter groups from Methodism included the Methodist New Connexion, the Countess of Huntingdon's Connection, Primitive Methodists, United Methodist Free Churches and Bible Christians. Some were absorbed into Congregationalism, while most were reabsorbed to form the United Methodist Church in 1857 and the Methodist Church in 1932. A detailed account of Methodism's byzantine

△ *John Wesley outside Swathmore Hall* **by John Jewel (1835–95).**

WHERE TO SEARCH

MORAVIANS

⊟ Most registers were deposited in the **NA** in class RG 4 at the and are therefore indexed on the IGI but the original registers are often much more detailed than those of any other denomination.

⊟ Other sources for Moravian ancestry are congregation books and diaries, elders' minutes and memoirs. Records are with the congregations, if still extant, or at **Moravian Church House**.

METHODISTS

⊟ A useful guide is W. Leary's *My Ancestors were Methodists: How Can I Find Out More About Them?* (SoG, 1999).

⊟ Few 18th-century registers survive: those that do were mostly deposited with the Registrar General in 1837 and are in **NA** class RG 4 and in the IGI. Post-1837 registers (and some undeposited pre-1837 ones) may by in **county record offices** but many were never given up by the minister who made them and were lost, or have become private family heirlooms.

⊟ Circuit records also include minutes of meetings, and various membership rolls and pew rents. These may be with surviving chapels or at county record offices. It is important to remember the potentially wide area covered by a circuit: the best way to find out which places were covered by which circuit (so you can tell which one might have covered your ancestor's home) are local histories and also the **Methodist Archives and Research Centre**. The library also holds Methodist newspapers such as the *Watchman and Methodist Magazine*, particularly useful for ministers' obituaries.

⊟ The Metropolitan Wesleyan Registry was established to record births and baptisms of Methodists from 1818, but with some retrospective entries dating back to 1777. It stopped in 1838 and was deposited in class RG 4 at the **NA**, but it is not in the IGI.

QUICK REFERENCE

See also main sources in Useful Addresses, page 306

MORAVIAN CHURCH HOUSE
5 Muswell Hill
London N10 3TJ
☎ 020 8883 3409
www.moravian.org

METHODIST ARCHIVES AND RESEARCH CENTRE
John Rylands Library
University of Manchester
Oxford Road
Manchester M13 9PP
☎ 0161 275 3764
www.rylibweb.man.ac.uk

LIFELINES: BORN BEYOND THE SEAS

AN EXCELLENT PRINTED source for Huguenots and Walloons, and many others from abroad, is Irene Scouloudi's *Returns of Strangers in the Metropolis 1593, 1627, 1635, 1639: A Study of an Active Minority* (Huguenot Society of London, 1985). The first list (1593) is compiled from three manuscript sources including one by Sir William Dugdale, and the latter three from the Domestic State Papers.

I wonder how many Drakes claiming kinship with Sir Francis are actually descended from Mr Cornelius Drak who appears in the 1635 returns as having been born at Gorcum in Holland, listed with his wife Anna, from Vermeer's home town of Delft. Cornelius had been in England for 50 years and had two sons and two daughters, all born in England. He lived in St Dionis Backchurch and rented a house worth £16, but he only paid £12. In the same return was Robert Moore, a Scottish tailor in the household of Thomas Dipper; Sir Kenelm Digby's three unnamed French servants; Francis Deynes, a French-born weaver in Spitalfields; Anthony Dolivar, Lord Stanhope's Italian secretary; Diego Perera Dorta, a Parisian-born merchant – and so on.

history is given in D. J. Steel's 'Sources for Non-conformist Genealogy and Family History', *National Index of Parish Registers*, Vol. 2 (Phillimore, 1973).

Methodism was organised by chapels at the centre of large circuits, around which ministers would travel to preach, hold services and perform baptisms and, in a few cases before 1753, marriages. Burials were generally in Anglican graveyards, and listed in Anglican registers, but when Methodist burial grounds were opened, registers were kept at the chapels.

OTHER DENOMINATIONS

Some of the many smaller sects and denominations to which your ancestors may have belonged are described in Vol. 2 of the *National Index of Parish Registers*. These sects include Cambellites, Inghamites, New Church (Swedenborgians or New Jerusalemites), Universalists, Plymouth Brethren, the Catholic Apostolic Church (or Irvingites and Sandemanians). The main ones were:

MORMONS

The Church of Jesus Christ of Latter-day Saints was founded in New York in 1830. By 1851 there were 30,000 converts in Britain, and many more joined. Most British Mormons eventually emigrated to Utah.

SALVATION ARMY

Founded in 1865 by William Booth, a Methodist preacher, this denomination's records, including dedication of children (akin to baptisms) and commissioning of officers, can be found at local Army centres (see opposite).

WALLOONS AND HUGUENOTS

Walloons were Flemish Protestants who came to England to escape Catholic persecution in the 16th century. They were followed after the St Bartholemew's Day Massacre of 1572, and especially after the Revocation of the Edict of Nantes in 1685, by many French Protestants, called Huguenots, who came here for the same reason. These asylum-seekers were generally welcomed, for they were mostly hard-working tradesmen, merchants or moneyed nobles with valuable business-skills, which made them valued taxpayers. They were encouraged to settle in certain towns and cities, particularly Canterbury, Southampton, Norwich, Bristol, and Spitalfields and Bethnal Green in London.

OTHER DENOMINATIONS

MORMONS

Their records, kept in branch membership books, are, needless to say, excellent. Start by contacting your local **Mormon Family History Centre.**

SALVATION ARMY

To find out about local Army centres contact the **Salvation Army** or its **International Heritage Centre.**

WALLOONS AND HUGUENOTS

They kept detailed registers, mostly deposited in RG 4 at the **NA** and thus indexed in the **IGI**, and almost all transcribed and published by the **Huguenot Society of Great Britain and Ireland**.

Their warm reception often led to rapid integration with the Anglican community, so many Huguenot entries are often Anglicised, e.g. John Chamberlain instead of Jean Chamberlayne, and thus unrecognisable as such, in Anglican registers.

Huguenots kept other records, especially of charities supporting those with proven Huguenot ancestry. The **Huguenot Society** (HS) publishes many of these, e.g. those of the French hospital, La Providence, dating back to 1747. Applicants for treatment had to prove their Huguenot connections, so this a gold mine of detail. Sets of publications are at the HS's Library or the **SoG**. Huguenots also appear extensively in other records (many are also published by the HS) such as naturalisations and denizations (see page 242).

The *National Index of Parish Registers*, Vol. 2 (Phillimore, 1973), also provides guidance on the location of Protestant records in France. A splendid guide is N. Currer-Briggs and R. Gambier's *Huguenot Ancestry* (Phillimore, 1985).

Many Huguenots settled in Ireland, especially in Dublin. Many of the surviving records have been published by the **Huguenot Society**.

PALATINES

German Protestant refugees in the 17th and 18th century. Many went to Ireland. See **www.irishpalatines.org**.

◁ *The Salvation Army* by Jean Francois Raffaelli (1850–1924).

JEWS

Following their brutal suppression and expulsion by Edward I, there was no official Jewish presence in England until the 1650s. Thereafter, Sephardic Jews immigrated from Spain, Portugal and the Spanish Netherlands, followed in the 18th century by the generally much poorer Ashkenazi Jews from Germany and Eastern Europe. Over the centuries, many immigrants became Christian, so that many people with Christian ancestry may well have Jewish forbears.

In the 1930s and '40s, numbers increased from some 250,000 to 650,000 due to refugees from Nazi Germany and its neighbours. Records of the latter can be sought through World Jewish Relief with many records deposited at the Wiener Library.

Sephardic Jews tended to have their own hereditary surnames, such as Pereira and Rodrigues from Spain and Portugal, and Montefiore and Disraeli from Italy. Ashkenazi Jews, however, tended to use patronymics, such as Isaac ben (son of) Moses or just plain Isaac Moses. Ashkenazis also used nicknames, such as Mordecai Hamburger (Mordecai from Hamburg) and, when dealing with the outside world, might adopt a 'surname' that sounded perfectly English, and Anglicise their forename too. That sounds confusing, and the unfortunate truth is that it can be difficult working out that Michael Lawrence was one and the same as Moses ben Levy. The answer, as with so many other genealogical problems, is to keep on seeking further co-ordinates on your ancestors until you have found the evidence you need to prove who was who.

▽ **An illuminated page from *Exodus* from a Hebrew Bible, 1299.**

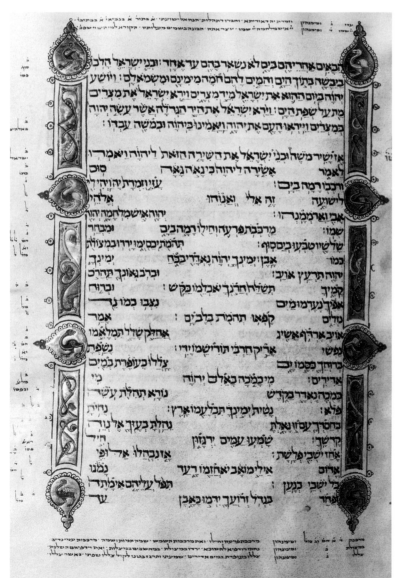

IN 1992, THE *DAILY MAIL* asked me, at very short notice, to trace the ancestry of Commander Timothy Lawrence, fiancé of Princess Anne. Normally, a line of ancestry simply cannot be traced back in a matter of hours – but it can if the ancestors went to university.

The *Daily Mail* was able to tell me that the Queen's son-in-law-to-be was the grandson of Henry Hamilton Laurence, a barrister born in 1864, and his wife Mary Butler. Most barristers then would have been to university, and at that stage Oxford and Cambridge were still the most popular: both have published lists of alumnis. Alumni Oxonienses (see page 239) lists the following:

Laurence, Henry Hamilton, 5s [5th son of] Percival, of East Claydon, Bucks, cler[ic]. NEW COLL[ege], matric. 12 Oct. 1883, aged 19; elected scholar of HERTFORD COLL. 1882, scholar of NEW COLL. 1883, BA 1887.

As Henry's father was a clergyman, he was highly likely to have attended Oxford or Cambridge. It turned out to be the latter: Alumni Cantabrigienses, which often goes into much more detail than its Oxford counterpart, lists Percival Laurence, educated at Trinity College, who went on to become a clergyman at, among other places, East Claydon. It states that he married Isabella Sarah, daughter of Capt. William Scarth Moorson, late 52nd Regiment, on 13 April 1853 and that he died on 6 June 1913 at Walesby Rectory. And it also states that he was born on 29 December 1829, son of Joseph Laurence, formerly Levi, and Penelope, daughter of John Jackson, of West Rainton Hall, Durham.

Joseph did not appear in University lists. 'Levi' appears as a Christian surname, but also as a Jewish one, and it was not at all unusual in the 19th century for prosperous Jewish families to become Anglican and adopt English sounding names. A good source for wealthy Jewish families is *Anglo Jewish Notabilities* and I was extremely lucky that this listed a grant of arms, made by the College of Arms on 11 December 1813, to Zaccaria Levy of Walthamstowe, Essex and the City of London, merchant, of 'the arms used by his ancestors seated at Venice not being recorded and having become a Free denizen of this country'. The memorial was signed by his son Joseph Levy for Zaccaria Levy and a note states that Zaccaria Levy of Bury Court, London and Regency Square, Brighton was born in 1751 in Venice and died in 1828, having married an aunt of Sir Moses Montefiore, and that his children took the name Lawrence.

Later, the *Genealogist's Magazine* (September 1993) published a descent of Commander Lawrence's paternal grandmother Mary Butler through her grandfather Capt John Butler of Ramsbury, Wiltshire, back through the Davidson, Musgrave, Wharton and Clifford families from Lady Margaret Percy, 3 x great-granddaughter of John of Gaunt, son of Edward III.

LIFELINES: COMMANDER TIMOTHY LAWRENCE

LIFELINES: RUBY WAX

WHEN I WAS TRACING Ruby Wax's ancestry, for her BBC 1 show, *Ruby*, I came across a number of references to people called Wachs in the area of Eastern Europe where she knew her family originated. Included among the recorded memories of survivors of the Holocaust was the following (www.jewishgen.org/yizkor/ Lezajsk/lez167.html). I do not know if this was a member of Ruby's family, but from the way she was behaving I would not be at all surprised if it was:

The Rebbetzin, the wife of Rabbi Yechezkel, was from the well-known Wachs family, which was renowned for its riches and piety. They were landowners … and they enabled the rabbi to turn his home into a place where guests would be received on a constant basis. [There were] many guests from all parts of Poland, who came to prostrate themselves at the grave of Rabbi Elimelech of holy blessed memory. Amongst them were needy people who lacked money for food. Such people knew the address of the rabbi … and approximately twenty people would eat at his table every day, receiving their meals as if they were members of the household. It is said that once a guest arrived late after everyone had finished eating, and was turned away by the Rebbetzin with the comment,

'There is nothing to eat, Mr tardy Jew'.

However, as he left, she changed her mind,

'Why is he guilty that twenty people came before him?'

She immediately asked him to return, and told him that she did not have any meat left, but that nobody starves [in her house], and she gave him other food to eat. When he left, he said to her,

'Rebbetzin, you should know that I have eaten a Simchat Torah feast here'.

△ The Jewish cemetery in Worms, Germany.

JEWS

⊡ The main records are those of the synagogues and are in Hebrew, so it is advisable to hire a researcher with knowledge of that language. You can expect to find birth registers, and middle-class Jews sometimes paid to have their children's births registered in parish registers too.

⊡ Boys were usually circumcised eight days after birth and records of circumcision (*brit milah*) were kept by surgeons, but can be very hard to locate.

⊡ Marriage contracts (kethubot) are in synagogue records and many were announced in the *Jewish Chronicle*, published (with a gap June 1842–September 1844) from November 1841.

⊡ Synagogues also recorded deaths, and many were announced in the *Jewish Chronicle*.

⊡ Many prosperous Jews' births, marriages and deaths were also announced in *The Times* and *Gentleman's Magazine*, and many of these were copied in the Collyer-Fergusson manuscripts (at the **SoG**), which also includes will abstracts. A useful list of Jewish wills in the PCC (see page 129), references to obituaries and facsimiles of Jewish bookplates (mainly for the Sephardic community) are in Anglo-Jewish notabilities (see below).

⊡ Synagogues may also have other records such as offering books, listing donations made by all males save the very poor, commemoration books recording charitable bequests from wills, synagogue membership lists. A full list of pre-1837 Jewish synagogue registers is given in D. Steel's 'Sources for Jewish and Catholic Family History', *National Index of Parish Registers Series*, Vol. 3. Many London records are now at the United Synagogue Record Room and the Court of the Chief Rabbi, although most have been moved to the Archive Office of the Chief Rabbi, where public access is no longer possible.

⊡ A useful guide to the records is I. Mordy's *My Ancestors Were Jewish: How Can I Find More About Them?* (SoG, 1995) and A. Kurzweil's *From Generation to Generation: How to trace your Jewish Genealogy and Family History*, reissued 2004 by Jossey-Bass (Wiley). For the better-off sort, there is also *Anglo–Jewish Notabilities* (Jewish Historical Society of England, 5709/1949), which covers *London Magazine* notices of Jewish births, marriages and deaths 1732–85, Anglo–Jewish wills and administrations in the PCC, Anglo–Jewish coats of arms, including many facsimile bookplates and a collection of biographical references.

⊡ There are few areas of genealogy in which the Internet has had such a revolutionary impact as Jewish research. **www.cyndislist.com** contains a formidable array of Jewish resources. Useful too is the index to the Poor Jews Temporary Shelter at Leman Street, Whitechapel, containing 43,000 names at **www.chrysalis.its.uct.ac.za/shelter/shelter**. There is also **www.jgsgb.org.uk/info1.shtml**, which provides a gateway to many British and foreign Jewish and general research websites, but foremost is **www.jewishgen.org**, which includes a discussion group, a database of 300,000 surnames and towns, the 'Family Tree of the Jewish People' with over 2 million people and 'ShtetLinks' for over 200 communities. Many Jewish communities were destroyed by the Holocaust, but survivors wrote memoirs of their own experiences and recorded as much as they could about their original communities and family history. Harrowing though they can be to read, they are a magnificent historical and genealogical resource.

QUICK REFERENCE

See main sources in Useful Addresses, page 306

PART FOUR

Family history has many intriguing byeways. Do you belong to a clan? Have you a coat of arms? What does your surname mean? Can DNA tests or even psychics help you learn yet more about your family's past? This section tells you how to find out.

CHAPTER TWENTY-EIGHT
GENETICS

We all inherit our appearance from our ancestors. Sometimes all you need to do is look at someone and, by studying their hair, eye or skin colour and facial features, you can make a few reasonable assumptions about where they may or may not have originated.

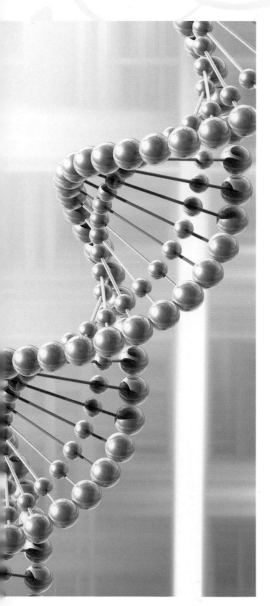

HOW GENES OPERATE

Eye and hair colour are determined by combinations of both parents' genes and work rather like mixing watercolour paints – the darker colour being dominant over the paler. So, if one partner is dark-eyed and the other pale eyed, then their children are likely to be dark-eyed – but not necessarily. Each child inherits an eye-colour gene from each parent, and it is up to the laws of chance which one will be passed on to their children. The dark-eyed partner might, therefore, have inherited a dominant dark-eyed gene from one parent and a hidden, pale-eyed gene from the other. If they, in turn, pass on their pale-eye gene to their child, and this matches with a pale-eyed gene from the other partner, then the child will have pale eyes. However, if you put it the other way around, a couple who both have pale eyes, such as blue or grey, cannot be carrying a 'hidden' dark-eyed gene, because, logically, if one of them had such a gene, they would have dark, not pale, eyes. Thus, such a couple are highly likely to produce only pale-eyed children.

Similar principles apply to hair colour – blonde mixed with brown or black tends to make paler brown or black, or sometimes red, while the fairer both parties' hair, the fairer the children's are likely to be. Red and red almost always produce red. Curly or wavy hair tends to dominate over straight. Among black people, very curly hair tends to be dominant. In Caucasian–African unions this usually results in at least half of the resulting offspring having curly hair. Thick lips and large ear lobes, likewise, dominate over thin ones. But these are only generalisations.

GENES FOR DNA TESTS

One of the most exciting things about tracing family history at the beginning of the 21st century is the advent of DNA technology. Up to the

◁ Until quite recently, the double helix of DNA was an impenetrable scientific mystery. Now it is a dynamic genealogical tool.

last decades of the 20th century, genealogy had remained relatively unchanged for centuries. Records had become much easier to access, and computer indexing had had a major impact, but genealogy was still based on what people could remember, or upon written records. Then, suddenly, DNA technology became accessible to genealogists, providing an entirely new way of adding to or detracting from the burden of proof in family trees – not by historical records – but by the very stuff of which our bodies are composed.

DNA is deoxyribonucleic acid, a major constituent of our chromosomes and carrier of the genetic information that makes us what we are. There are two sorts of DNA test. One is to see if your DNA matches someone else's, thus helping to prove or disprove a presumed genealogical connection. The other is to see how your DNA matches (or is similar to) samples already taken from populations around the world, helping you pinpoint where in a country or on the globe your distant genetic roots lie.

THE LIMITATIONS OF DNA

Exciting though DNA testing sounds (see box, overleaf), there are some big limitations. First, you can't test for relationships with simply anyone in your family tree. At present, tests are only possible with direct male-to-male or female-to female lines, and thus with people with whom you have, or suspect, a male-to-male (A) or female-to-female line link (B). In other words, you can have a comparative test with someone who you think is your father's father's brother's son (A), but there is no point having a comparative test with your father's father's sister's son (C), because his father's Y chromosome will have come from a different source to yours in any case.

The reason for these limitations is that the only DNA on which the test is practical is the 'Y' chromosome, which is passed from fathers to sons (but not daughters), and the mitochondrial DNA within the 'X' chromosome, which is passed from mother to both her sons and daughters, but then only from the daughters, not the sons, to their own offspring. Thus, men can have their direct male and female line DNA tested, but women can only have their female line DNA tested. If a woman wants to know about her male-line ancestry, she must secure a DNA sample from a brother, father or other direct male-line male relation (D).

➤**If two people who fit these criteria have their DNA tested and find it matches exactly, they can be sure they are related.**

A

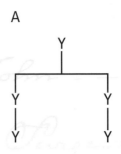

B

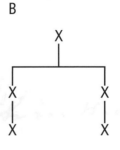

C

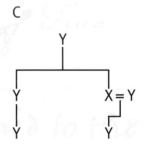

D

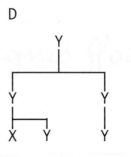

Key
Y = male
X = female

TAKING A DNA TEST

DNA TESTS are simple and generally cost around £100–£150 per person. There are several firms in Britain and America (I find www.FamilyTreeDNA.com the best). They will send you a kit, including a little brush which you use to rub off a small skin sample from the inside of your cheek and post back to them. The firm then performs their test (make sure the firm you use has a rigorous privacy policy) and produces a table giving numerical figures for the number of times certain 'markers' within the chromosome are repeated. Because DNA mutates very slightly over long periods of time, the closer the markers in two people's DNA are, the more likely they are to be related. The testing firm can also compare your results with other people in their database to see if close relatives of yours have already been tested, or see how you match up with existing population data, or compare your DNA to one or more specific people to whom you think you may be related. For paternity testing see www.lgc.co.uk/ paternity.

> If there are only small discrepancies between their results, they can assume they are related, but through a more distant connection.

But 'How far back?' is a question geneticists cannot answer. If DNA matches perfectly, there is a 50% chance that the most recent common ancestor lived within the last seven generations, but a 50% chance that the ancestor they share in common lived up to 30 generations ago, while slight discrepancies tend to indicate cousinship through ancestors living even further back.

So, if two people trace their family tree and think they are descended, male-to-male, from a set of brothers born in the 1650s, a positive 'Y' chromosome match will confirm that they are related. But it won't confirm that their genealogy is accurate – the relationship may actually have come through any two other male members of the same family, possibly hundred of years before or after 1650. However, if the genealogical link is pretty certain, and the DNA test comes back positive, then it is an excellent piece of circumstantial evidence that the tree is correct.

Equally, DNA cannot be used to prove a family tree is wrong. If our two researchers find their DNA is completely dissimilar, their record-based genealogical research might be completely accurate but, at some point in the history of either line, an undisclosed fostering, adoption or illegitimacy might have occurred to alter the biological link.

SOME TEST CASES

I have seen DNA tests used in a number of highly effective ways. A group of people with a fairly unusual Irish surname (let's call it O'Boru) had spent decades trying to match oral traditions with the decidedly patchy records of early 19th-century Donegal to work out their family tree, but nothing tied in properly. I suggested DNA testing and a dozen O'Borus took one. On a 12-marker test of their 'Y' chromosomes, four matched exactly and four others fell into a group with only slight dissimilarities, indicating that the first four had a 50% chance of being related within the last seven generations and were definitely related within the last 30. They were more distantly connected (that is, almost certainly more than seven generations ago) to the second four. Everyone matched closely enough to show that their branches had split *away* after the surname had arisen – in other words, after Boru himself had lived. That's a bit hazy still, I know, but it introduced a great deal more clarity than before, when nobody knew for certain how closely or not anyone was to any of the others.

◁ A typical Norwegian port, from where the Vikings set sail.

MUCH WORK has also been done on Viking DNA. When a Mr Jones from Cardiff approached *Extraordinary Ancestors* and said he thought he had Viking blood on the basis that he believed he looked a bit like some Scandanavians he had met, I was extremely sceptical, but we commissioned a DNA test to see what the results would be. By taking extensive samples from modern Scandanavians, geneticists have been able to establish a profile of what Viking DNA would have been like, and then see if it matched people living in the areas settled by Vikings – northeastern England, Iceland, Dublin and, as it turns out, Cardiff. It transpired that Mr Jones was right and I was wrong. While his male-line ancestors had acquired a Welsh surname, probably in the last couple of hundred years, his 'Y' chromosomes were indeed a positive testimony to his remoter Norse forbears. Conversely, when geneticists tested the Icelandic population, which was supposedly pure Viking, they found a quarter of the population was originally of Irish descent!

Another case is that of Nicholas Betts-Green Esq., formerly Nicholas Green. His persistent family tradition was of an illegitimate Green fathered by 'the lord of the manor'. Research suggested that the culprit could have been a 19th-century army major, George Betts of Wortham Hall, but there were no documents to prove this for certain. Poor Mr Green might have spent the rest of his life wondering, but a test on his 'Y' chromosomes and those of a co-operative legitimate descendant of Major Betts showed that they matched, adding a vast weight of circumstantial evidence to the genealogical findings and prompting Mr Green, very properly I think, to add 'Betts' to his surname.

CHARTING INTER-RELATED GROUPS

The other sort of DNA test is for racial roots. Just as families have genetic similarities, so too, to a lesser degree, do larger, inter-related

THE BEST GUIDE TO DNA testing is C. Pomery's *DNA and Family History: How genetic testing can advance your genealogical research* (TNA, 2004), with a supporting website **www.dnaandfamilyhistory.com**. It includes links to other sites on which DNA test results can be analysed.

LIFETIMES: HEMOPHILIAC HERITAGE

SOMETIMES, DNA CAN THROW an established family tree into question. Queen Victoria's family's hemophilia is a case in point. Before DNA was understood, her carrying of hemophilia was regarded as simple bad luck, but now we know that, whilst it can arise as a birth-defect it is, in most cases, genetically inherited. This suggests that instead of the Duke of Kent, who was not a carrier of hemophilia, Victoria's real father might have been a passing and, as yet, unidentified hemophiliac (and yes, hemophiliacs could produce children – Victoria's son Leopold did, and thus passed the affliction on to his daughter Alice). This does not mean that Victoria was illegitimate – she was born within wedlock and was thus the legal heir of her mother's husband – but it does mean that her genetic roots might not have been what we once thought they were. If such genetic discoveries then lead to proven academic research into her true genetic origins, then all well and good.

◁ Queen Victoria, seen here with her mother, passed hemophilia on to some of her descendants, but neither her mother nor her supposed father had a history of it in their families.

groups. The more people whose DNA is tested, the better able geneticists become to map racial groups and then see where displaced people's DNA best matches. This has been done recently, by a number of TV programmes including *Extraordinary Ancestors* (2000) and *Motherland* (2003), for descendants of black slaves who had absolutely no other way of finding out where in Africa their forebears lived.

For *Extraordinary Ancestors,* we found a match between a nurse from Bristol and a member of the Kikuyu tribe in Kenya, and *Motherland* contained several examples, linking one woman with a tribe on an island off the Gold Coast and another man, who had dark skin, with Germany. This indicated that his male-line ancestors were European, not African (because slave women often bore children to their white slave owners, many mixed-race families of West Indian descent have European male-line ancestry).

BEWARE CONJECTURE

Most DNA testers are very reliable. Some, however, have developed some rather far-fetched schemes whereby they conjecture how many thousands of years ago certain genetic mutations in DNA might have taken place, set a date for an 'ancestor', give her a name and then make up an entirely hypothetical scenario about what her life might have been like. I suspect that several hours exposed to nuclear radiation could clock up many millennia's-worth of such genetic mutations. Such so-called 'ancestors' are not worth the money being charged to 'trace' them.

EXHUMATION

More realistic is the possibility of making a comparative DNA test between someone living and a deceased ancestor's (or supposed ancestor's) DNA, using surviving hair, dried blood or even exhumed bones. The mitochondrial DNA within 'X' chromosomes usually survives much better than 'Y' chromosomes, but exhuming a body (if that's what it takes) requires permission from the legal heir both of the deceased and the original grave-owner, the burial authority and a permissive licence from the Home Secretary. The total cost can be vast, but it can be worth it. The technique was used to identify the presumed body of the murdered Tsarina Alexandra when it was exhumed at Ekaterinburg in 1991, by comparing her mitochondrial DNA with that of Prince Philip, whose mother's mother was Alexandra's sister. The DNA in the remains did indeed match Prince Philip – the identification was thus positive.

△ The Tsarina Alexandra, a granddaughter of Queen Victoria, who passed hemophilia on to her son, the Tsarevich Alexei.

CHAPTER TWENTY-NINE
WHAT'S IN A NAME?

Both forenames and surnames can tell us a lot about the ancestry and cultural origins of their bearers, both of which are discussed in this chapter.

△ Winston Churchill, whose popularity spawned a generation of boys called Winston.

△ *The Blacksmith* from *Le Livre des Echecs Moralises* by Jacques de Cessoles. Many medieval blacksmiths' children ended up surnamed 'Smith'.

FORENAMES

Forenames, called Christian names in Christian countries, can be chosen randomly, as they often are now in the Western world. They can tell us a little about the parents' tastes – my mother, for example, is a devout Catholic with a particular devotion to St Anthony. Many parents choose names of the moment: children called Kylie and Elvis hint strongly at their parents' musical tastes, and in centuries to come genealogists may be able to guess that an ancestor called Kylie was unlikely to have been born before the mid-1980s, when Kylie Minogue first appeared in *Neighbours*. Equally, names like Winston and Horatio reflect our ancestors' admiration for earlier wartime heroes, and again help us to set the earliest likely date when children so named would have been born. Monarchs and their spouses have always been a source of inspiration for naming children. There were very few Victorias in Britain before 1837 and not too many Alberts before the queen married her beloved consort in 1840.

Going back only a few generations, however, we find that families tended to have had a more regimented system for giving names to children. The presence of people called Ignatius in a family usually suggests Catholicism, as do names like Timothy, Ambrose, Stanislaus and Theresa. Old Testament names like Aaron, Joshua and Rachel suggest Protestant non-conformist links. Catholic names can often suggest Irish connections, while names like Mungo, Murdoch and Christian (for a female) suggest Scottish or Protestant Northern Irish roots.

Outside Europe, most cultures have customs governing how names are chosen for children. Many children are named after ancestors, especially grandparents, not least among Hindus, for whom the new-born child may be regarded as the living incarnation of an earlier generation. Children are often given similar names to their fathers, such as a name with the same prefix or suffix. Other Indian names are chosen from gods, places, professions, plants or animals, or words with positive connotations.

△ Krishna Mehta with his sons Dhairendra and Shailendra. The surname Mehta is Hindu, meaning political administrator: his forename was chosen to venerate the Hindu god Krishna.

THE MEANINGS OF NAMES

➤**European forenames** all mean something. Some are Anglo-Saxon (Edmund, Edward, Alfred and so on) in origin and others are French or German (like Robert and Ludwig) or Greek (like Anthony). However, the majority of European forenames come from the Bible, and don't you think it extraordinary, on reflection, that the bulk of the indigenous population of Western Europe are walking about using names derived from a tiny tribe who lived in the Middle East over 2000 years ago, and from whom most are not descended? The actual meaning of the names now, however, seldom has any relevance for their bearers. George means 'farmer' in Greek, but I doubt anybody giving that name to their child in the last two millennia has done so because they were agriculturalists.

➤**Many Hindu names** are derived from Sanskrit and are taken from gods, especially those whose stories are told in the Bhagavad Gita (such as Krishna and Arjun) and the Ramayana, such as Sita, Janaki, Lakshman and Rama. In many cases, the choice of names is dictated by caste too – hence names connoting spirituality for the Bhahmins, power for the Ksatriyas (warriors), wealth for the Vaisyas (merchants) and servitiude for the Sudras (labourers and peasants).

➤**Buddhist names,** because of their Sanskrit roots, are not always easily distinguished from Hindu ones. Some popular ones, however, are Tara (the name of a Mahayan godess), Mani and Padma, derived from the tantric mantra *om mani padme hum* – 'the jewel is in the lotus'.

➤**Islamic names** are mostly derived from vocabulary words still in use: as Mona Baker wrote in P. Hanks and F. Hodge's *A Dictionary of Christian Names* (OUP, 1990) – and without any apparent hint of irony – 'Arabs

IN CATHOLIC FAMILIES, a child's name was often that of their same-sex godparent. My German Catholic ancestors followed this practice to an absurd degree when a forebear of mine was given the names of both godparents, his cousin William Adolph and his uncle Adolph Fischer. They called him William Adolph Adolph.

Scottish Presbyterian families usually named the eldest son after his paternal grandfather, the second son after the maternal grandfather and the third after the father. They would name the eldest daughter after the maternal grandmother, the second daughter after the paternal grandmother and the third after the mother. If you have a complete list of a Scottish Presbytarian couple's children, therefore, you can make a pretty good guess at what the couples' parents were called.

△ A page from a copy of the Koran printed in Arabic, 1537, from San Michele in Isola, Venice.

more often than not know what their names mean. If they do not, they can look them up in an ordinary dictionary, like any other vocabulary word. This may well have contributed to the apparent lack of interest in the study of names in the Arab world'!

Mohammed (under its many different spellings), and also Ahmad, come from the Arabic *hamida*, 'to praise'. Many other names start with 'Abd, meaning 'servant of', followed by Allah or one of His 99 attributes, such as 'Aziz ('beloved') and Rahīm. Some popular names, such as Hasan, Husayn, 'Ali and 'Umar (for boys) and Khadija, 'A'isha and Zaynab (for girls), come from members of Mohamed's family, and from military leaders, such as Tariq and Khalid. Some, too, come from the stories which appear both in the bible and in the Koran, such as Ibrahim for Abraham and Maryam for Mary.

SURNAMES

Unless it was acquired by adoption, a surname can suggest where a family line may have originated, or tell us something else about a remote ancestor, such as what they did or what they looked like. Knowing where surnames arose can be helpful in family history research as they can at least suggest the part of the country (or world) in which you should be looking.

LIFETIMES: SUPRISE!

SOMETIMES, SURNAMES that appear to have been hereditary for centuries are in reality not. I wrote recently to a Mr Deane asking him if he was related to some other Deanes I was researching. He replied, 'No, we actually changed our name from Deane to Drain'. Equally, another family of Deans I have encountered while researching *Meet the Descendants* changed their name in the 1920s. Previously, their surname was Mohamed and they were descended from Sake Dean Mohamed, a late 18th-century immigrant to Britain who opened the first ever Indian restaurant here.

The surname Foster was sometimes bestowed to a foster child (see page 88), and foster children sometimes received the name of the place they were found (Bridge, Porch and so on) or the name of the saint after whom the parish church was named.

There are broadly two types of surname. One is used during all or part of a person's life. The original John Smith was John the Smith: before he became a smith he would have been known differently (perhaps Smithson, if his father was a smith – but it could have been anything). If he stopped being a smith his surname might then have changed too.

The other type is a fixed or hereditary surname, one which arises as I have just described but which becomes fixed at a random point and then gets passed down generation to generation. In some countries, hereditary surnames are not used. Icelanders still use their father's name as their surname, and thus family surnames change each generation.

In many countries, surnames became hereditary, often because the state wanted to identify people within families so they could be taxed more efficiently. In England, hereditary surnames came in during the 12th and 13th centuries, although there was a degree of fluidity up to the Tudor period. In Scotland, hereditary surnames started being adopted as Norman influence spread north of the border but did not really become entrenched in the Highlands until the 18th century. In Wales, where the same system as Iceland operated, the process started in the 16th century but it is only in the last two centuries that most families have adopted a particular surname and stuck to it.

△ **My great-great-great-grandfather James Paterson (d. 1887) as a young, ambitious station master, before he founded the great haulage firm of Carter Paterson. 'Paterson' is a Scottish surname meaning 'son of Patrick'.**

TYPES OF SURNAME

Wherever you are in the world, there are generally five types of surname.

Patronymic or matronymic surnames

These are derived from the father's or mother's forename. They are the most common form of surname in Wales, where *(m)ap* or *(m)ab*, meaning 'son of' (or *verch*, *ferch* or *ach*, 'daughter of,' in the case of women) was often added, hence Thomas ap Howell was Thomas son of Howell, often contracted to Powell. Sometimes, to tell apart people with the same name and father's name, several generations were added on – Thomas ap Howell ap Edward, for example (a mini family tree, there for the taking!). The surname Tudor means 'ap Tudor' and became a fixed surname earlier than most when Henry VII's grandfather moved out of Wales and into the English court, thus adopting English surname customs.

Most such names come from fathers, but sometimes women wore the trousers, hence names such as Margison ('son of Margaret'). Very occasionally, people were best known by their brother-in-law. Hickmott

LIFETIMES: THE PUDWELL FAMILY

THE BEST CASE of alterations I have encountered is that of a Brazillian family called Pudwell. The surname sounds completely English, but the family knew their ancestor migrated to South America from Germany. There are indeed Pudwells and Pudwills in Germany, and over the Polish border there are Budwills, and heraldic records confirm that the Budwills belonged to the Sulima family group (somewhat akin to a Scottish clan) and were well established in eastern Germany. The older version was Budywil, derived from the Slavic *budi* meaning 'awaken, inspire', a word derived directly from the self-same Sanskrit word which gave the epithet 'enlightened one' to the 5th-century BC Prince Gautama Siddhartha – the Buddha himself!

and Watmough mean brother-in-law of Richard ('Hick') and Walter ('Watt') respectively.

The parents' name sometimes appeared as just that, hence 'Thomas' meant 'son of Thomas'. But in many cases, especially in the north, where there was a greater Scandanavian influence, it was suffixed 'son', sometimes shortened to '-s', thus Sanderson and Saunders both meant 'son of Alexander'. In the case of Norman names, 'fitz' was added as a prefix for 'son of', so Fitzgerald means 'son of Gerald'.

Sometimes, the original forename was modified before it became a surname. Now, to be familiar, we often shorten a name and by adding a 'y' to it, so Thomas becomes Tommy. Our medieval ancestors tended to use 'cock' and 'kin' (both perhaps due to Dutch influence), thus Tomkin, which might then become someone's surname. Metathesis is when two letters in a word are swapped around. I was very taken when I came across John Giblet of St George's, Hanover Square, in 1765 working – of all things – as a butcher. It turns out that his gorily appropriate surname meant 'son of Giblet', a metathesised version of Gilbert!

Occupational or metonymic surnames

This group of surnames is derived from peoples' occupations. If surnames were still fluid, we would have plenty of people surnamed Enginedriver, Typist and Programmer. As it is, British occupational surnames tend to reflect what people were doing here in the Middle Ages. Some, such as Smith, Farmer and Serjeant are obvious. Others, such as Fletcher and Fuller, require more detailed knowledge of old occupations – these two examples mean 'arrow maker' and 'cloth bleacher' respectively.

Locative surnames

These derive from the place someone lived in or came from. They are the most popular type of surname in England. Originally, they were often prepositioned 'de', so John de Prescot was John of or from Prescot: he may have owned the place, or simply lived at Prescot – or he may even have come from Prescot and only acquired the surname once he had moved elsewhere.

Some feudal lords who had several different landholdings used different surnames according to where they were. If John de Prescot owned Prescot and Redwood, he might call himself John de Prescot whilst in residence at Prescot and John de Redwood whilst in residence at Redwood. Confusing, but unavoidable.

Topographical surnames

These arose from a geographical feature that distinguished the person's home. Originally, they often were often prepositioned 'atte' or 'at', so Clement who lived in or by a meadow would have been Clement atte Lee. The prepositions were usually shed by the 14th century but, where they were not, surnames such as Atlee arose.

Working out what surnames means often involves some knowledge of Saxon, Norse and so on – *lee* is a Saxon word. Others are more obvious because words have not changed – Wood, Church, Brook and so on are as clear now as they were almost a thousand years ago when they described where ancestors of ours lived.

Sobriquets or nicknames

Such surnames describe someone's dominant characteristic, often starting, as in school playgrounds to this day, as a jest or taunt. Black, Redhead; Wiseman and Little are all examples, but remember that nicknames were sometimes used ironically – Robin Hood's chum Little John was absolutely enormous!

EVOLVING LANGUAGE

One factor to be aware of when studying surnames is the way they can change over time through pronunciation or translation, or simply be written down in an unusual way, such as Rebecca Oldfield in the example on page 169.

Surnames do not have 'correct' and 'incorrect' spellings. They have changed over time and will probably continue to do so despite mass

CLAN LOYALTIES

TARTANS AROSE through regional variations in weaving patterns and, despite claims to the contrary, only became distinctive to specific clans in the late 18th century. Use of tartan is not bound by any official rules, though proper use of it is recorded by Lord Lyon. For more information, see Roddy Martine's *Scottish Clan and Family Names: Their Arms, Origins and Tartans* (Mainstream Publishing, 1992); G. Way and R. Squire's *Collins' Scottish Clan and Family Encyclopaedia* (HarperCollins, 1994) and F. Adam's *The Clans, Septs and Regiments of the Scottish Highlands* (revised by Sir Thomas Innes of Learny, Johnson & Bacon, 1984). Contact the Scottish Tartan Society at www.scottish-tartans-society.co.uk. Useful clan maps are at www.scotroots.com.

literacy. People who say 'that person called John Chamberlain cannot possibly be an ancestor of mine because we have always spelt our surname "Chamberlayne"' are buffoons for various reasons. The surname might have been written down on that occasion by someone who did not know how the name should be spelt and it also presupposes John cared or even knew about spelling. My reply is usually, 'If I gave you a cheque for a million pounds and spelt your surname "Chamberlain" you wouldn't throw it away, would you?'

Sometimes, people deliberately adopted unusual spellings to stand out from the crowd. Charles Whyllyames Burton is one of the most

GAELIC SURNAMES

GAELIC SURNAMES were often changed by being Anglicised, such as Ó Blathmhaic becoming Blawick, and then further changes sometimes took place to make them more familiar, such as Blawick to Blake. Similarly, some Ó Maoláins became De Moleyn, although there was no ancestral connection with the original Norman family of that name. This can cause great confusion, and the jury is still out in the case of the Dennings of Co. Cavan. Denning derives from the Old English denu which became dean, meaning 'valley'. The Irish Dennings may therefore have come from England, perhaps as planters to the northern Irish counties in the 17th century. However, Denning might be an Anglicised version of O'Dinneen or O'Duinnin, from the Gaelic donn meaning 'brown'. Perhaps only a DNA test would clear up the matter for good.

In Scotland, many Gaelic surnames were Anglicised after Culloden to avoid hostility from the English authorities. MacLevy went to Livington, MacDonald to Donald and so on. Equally, many names of Irish immigrants were Caldonianised, such as O'Toole to Doyle and McGrimes to Graham.

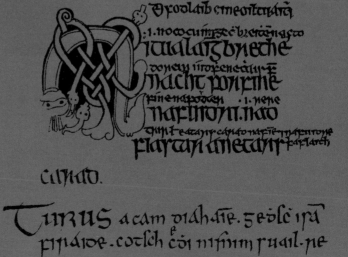

extreme I have encountered. When tracing your family tree, always look out for variant spellings and never be daft enough to reject an entry on the grounds that the parish clerk simply wrote the name down in his own particular way.

Most Indian people have several names, such as a personal name, a patronymic name, a village name and (if Hindu) a caste name: customs vary according to religion and locality and it is not always obvious, on first sight, which is the personal name and which the surname. The Gujerati ancestors of the Alibhai-Brown family, for example, descend from Alibhai Lalji Kanji in the 19th century. Lalji was the caste name, Alibhai was his personal name and Kanji his father's name. His son then took Alibhai as his surname, at which point the family moved to the West and the surname stuck as an hereditary one. In southern India, many people have three surnames – the village name, the father's name and finally the personal name. Westernisation has sometimes caused such patterns to alter, and many Indian families coming to the West will, just like the Welsh coming to England in the Middle Ages, fix their patronymic name as an hereditary surname.

Sikhs usually have three: a personal name; a name to proclaim his identity, usually Singh; and a third name for the particular clan or sect or, if a woman, the name Kaur, which simply denotes female gender.

Surnames are studied by seeking the earliest possible references to them in records, such as tax lists. By seeing how they were written down around the time when they were first used, it is easier to work out what they really meant. It is not obvious what Atlee, as in my example above, might mean, but the early medieval references to 'at Lee' is much clearer. Similarly, it is a way of avoiding pitfalls. Lucy might seem to mean 'son of Lucy', but early references show it to have been 'de Luci', Luci being a place in Normandy.

WHERE TO SEARCH

NAMES

Useful guides to surnames include: P. H. Reaney and R. M. Wilson's *A Dictionary of English Surnames* (Routledge,1958); J. Rowlands's *Welsh Family History; A Guide to Research* (Association of Family History Societies for Wales, 1997); G. F. Black's *The Surnames of Scotland, Their Origin, Meaning, and History* (New York Public Library, 1946); E. MacLysaght's *The Surnames of Ireland* (Irish Academic Press, 1985); and *Irish Families and More Irish Families* (Irish Academic Press, 1985)

To understand the meaning of place names that became surnames, see E. Ekwall's *The Concise Oxford Dictionary of English Place-names* (Clarendon Press, 1960) and the English place name series, published county by county by Leopard's Head Press.

A FINAL WORD OF WARNING

MOST COMPUTER PROGRAMS that print certificates showing you the origin of your 'ancient and distinguished name' are copied straight out of surname dictionaries, usually, it seems, by people with very little understanding of the subject and very low powers of concentration. They mostly contain misleading statements or plain old mistakes.

CHAPTER THIRTY
ROYALTY, NOBILITY & LANDED GENTRY

Some people hope to find distinguished connections because they enjoy the thought of having such an ancestor, but others are delighted when they do so because finding such a link enables you to tap into a vast amount of very well-recorded family trees.

You may not know whether your Smith, Jones or Williams ancestors fought at the battle of Hastings, but if you have also traced a royal descent, it's quite comforting to know that your ancestor William the Conqueror won it.

ROYALTY

If you are very fortunate in your research, you may discover that you are descended from a member of the landed gentry, a titled aristocrat or even from a member of the royal family. Some people hope very much that they will because they hope to inherit a title themselves. There have been cases of people discovering a direct link back to a now extinct title, and successfully claiming it for themselves. But the number of cases amount to a mere handful over the centuries and the chances of this happening to you are less than winning the National Lottery.

The quest sends some people, quite literally, mad. A few years ago I was contacted by an American (I'll call him Alexander Murdoch) who lived in a trailer park in Arkansas. He had cobbled together a spurious family tree, linking him back to a Scottish noble family who were, in turn, descended from the royal family. Fabricated it may have been, but he clearly believed it. Not only that, he also thought that, because he was descended from a king, he must actually be one himself. Enclosed with his family tree were copies of letters he had written, under the name Prince Alexander Murdoch, to parts of the British establishment, making his claim for the throne, and the replies he had received. The Speaker of the House of Commons had replied: 'Dear Mr Murdoch', she went on to explain that she could not involve herself in such constitutional affairs as deciding who should and should not occupy the British throne. The Queen herself had replied, through one of her ladies-in-waiting, starting: 'Dear Alexander', and politely acknowledging his interesting information and wishing him well for

▽ **Achievement of arms of the House of Hanover as Kings of Great Britain.**

the future. I must say, I was less courteous in my response, and received a rather threatening letter telling me that, once he had made good his claim and was ensconced on the British throne, I had better watch out. I await my just desserts.

INTER-CONNECTIONS

There is, in fact, another reason why many genealogists hope to find aristocratic connections, and that is because the pedigrees of everyone from landed gentry upwards have, generally speaking, been carefully traced and published, especially by Burke's publishing house. So, once you have made a connection, you can benefit from a vast amount of pedigree work that has already been completed.

And, if you do, you are unlikely to connect back to just one pedigree. Landed gentry tended to marry among themselves, but sometimes a well-to-do landed gentleman might make a good match for the daughter of a slightly faded aristocrat, whose own ancestors, in better times, may have made a fine match for the daughter of one of the vast brood of Plantagenet princes, who all descended from Edward I. So, rather than finding just one family tree, you may be able to connect back to many, and discover that you are related to most of the aristocracy and the royal family, with ancestry derived through the dynastic marriages of the Plantagenets and Normans from all over Europe. Indeed, there is even a line, which Sir Anthony Wagner published in his *Pedigree and Progress: Essays in the Genealogical Interpretation of History* (Phillimore, 1975), going back through the intermarriages of Western and European royalty and of the latter with Armenian princesses whose family was an offshoot of the ancient rulers of Parthia (Mesopotamia).Tentative lines go further, perhaps even to Alexander the Great himself.

That line of descent from the ancient world is unique, but there are further, indirect connections to antiquity. Wagner and, later, Charles Mosley demonstrated links from the English monarchy back to Gundioc, King of the Burgundians in the 5th century. His brother-in-law Ricimer was married to the daughter of the Roman Emperor Anthemius, who was, in turn, related to Basilina, daughter-in-law of Emperor Constantinus – and so the links go back, to Julius Caesar and beyond. The reasons why such connections arose are obvious. Families that gained power either did so by marrying the heiresses of the previous dynasty or, having gained power by force, sought a veneer of legitimacy by marrying the daughters of the men they had ousted.

△ **A tabard, worn by Officers-at-Arms on all ceremonial occasions.**

▽ **Many lines of descent from royalty appear in Burke's *Royal Descents*.**

FINDING AN ANCESTOR with aristocratic forbears is a wonderful thing. They are called gateway ancestors and are much sought after in America. There, a good number of early settlers were the younger sons of the landed gentry with family links back to the numerous progeny of Edward III. Because subsequent waves of immigrants married into established families (descended from the original migrants), the blood of such gateway ancestors is flowing through the veins of a large proportion of modern Americans. There is even a society for people who can prove descent from the Emperor Charlemagne (an ancestor of our Edward I). Membership is substantial and carries genuine social weight, which is one of the reasons why America was once notorious for the number of bogus pedigrees, like that of my Mr Murdoch (see page 290), that it produced. I am glad to say that things have improved considerably over the last couple of decades.

ROYAL ANCESTRY

A vast number of Americans have aristocratic or even royal ancestry, including all but a couple of the American presidents (Bush is distantly related to the Queen several times over). The same applies to vast numbers of people in Britain and of British descent elsewhere in the world. Many mixed-race Caribbean people are descended from plantation owners of whom a not inconsiderable number were gateway ancestors (see box, left) as well.

Quite how many descendants Edward I has is an open question, but at the beginning of the 20th century the Marquis of Ruvigny and Raineval attempted to trace all the legitimate descendants he could from Edward's grandson Edward III using published sources, especially the pedigrees published by the Burkes. His *The Blood Royal of Great Britain, Being a Roll of the Living Descendants of Edward IV and Henry VII* (T. E. Jack, 1903) and *The Plantagenet Roll of the Blood Royal, Being a Complete Table of all the Descendants now Living of Edward III, King of England* listed some 20,000 living people. But this was only scraping the surface, not least because *Burke's Peerage* seldom goes into any detail over younger branches of families. One estimate I have read of the number of royal descendants in Britain now is 4 million, but I suspect that the true number is a very great deal higher. Indeed, the chance of anyone with British ancestry not being descended from Edward III in one way or another seems fairly slight.

Besides being able to link in to these well-established pedigrees, I think there is a genuine value in knowing your own connection to some of the great figures in our history and indeed to the present head of state. The Queen is, after all, more than a mere figurehead. Her office evolved out of the ancient tribal leaders who were literally the heads of their families, and it makes a considerable amount of sense to think of Elizabeth II not just as a head of state, but as the head of the vast, extended, inter-related web of families that inhabit the British Isles.

NOBILITY

In Britain, the 'nobility' is taken to mean those who have been granted titles by the Crown. Nobody else but the monarch can grant titles in Britain, and only legitimate, ruling sovereigns elsewhere in the world can grant titles in their own dominions. All those many characters on the Internet claiming to be able to grant titles for a fee on the grounds that they are the exiled Archimandrake of Timbucktoo, Prince of Potty, or whatever, best ignored.

△ Royal descents exercise such a magnetic attraction that some genealogists simply make them up. This 19th-century family pedigree, proudly updated in the 20th century, includes an entirely spurious descent from the Duke of Somerset, brother of Henry VIII's wife Jane Seymour.

WHERE TO SEARCH

ROYAL CONNECTIONS

There are numerous published works on royal families. One of the grandest and most detailed is James Anderson's *Royal Genealogies, Or the Genealogical Tables of Emperors, Kings and Princes, from Adam to These Times*. (Charles Davis, 1736). More detailed and accurate is the British royal pedigree at the beginning of the 1965 edition of *Burke's Peerage*. Some of the very many known descendants of the royal family appear in *Burke's Royal Descents*, which has been published on the Internet at **www.peterwestern.19.co.uk/burke1/Royal%Descents**.

Among modern works on European royalty (and their heraldry) is J. Louda and M. Maclagan's *Lines of Succession: Heraldry of the Royal Families of Europe* (Little, Brown & Company, 1999), which provides pedigrees of the European royal houses, with illustrations of their arms. Stretching its reach even further afield is Sir Iain Moncrieffe of that Ilk's *Royal Highness: Ancestry of the Royal Child* (Hamish Hamilton, 1982) and C. Mosley's *Blood Royal* (Smith's Peerage, 2002).

A source of great snobbery in Britain used to be the claim that an ancestor came over with William the Conqueror. The best book to consult on that subject is A. J. Camp's *My Ancestor Came over with the Conqueror: Those who Did, and Some of Those who Probably Did Not* (SoG, 1988).

LIFETIMES: JAMES CHALMERS

BESIDES THOSE who can find lines of descent from royalty, there are also those many more who discover indirect links. The numerous descendants of James Chalmers (1741–1810) may be proud that their ancestor was proprietor and editor of the *Aberdeen Journal*, founder of the *Aberdeen Almanac*. He was a drinking companion of Robbie Burns, too ('A facetious fellow,' Burns called him), but Bishop Skinner, also present at their meeting in 1787, wrote, 'We adjourned for a dram, and though our time was short, we had fifty auld songs through hand, and spent an hour or so most agreeably.'

But there is more – one of James's daughters, Jean, married James Littlejohn, whose grandson David had a daughter Ruth, wife of William Gill. Their daughter Ruth married Lord Fermoy, whose daughter Frances married Earl Spencer. Their daughter was Diana – oh yes! And in fact, illustrative of the point that many more people have royal ancestry than may be suspected, we can also take a line back from James's wife, Margaret Forbes, to her great-grandmother Lady Grizel Stewart, a great-granddaughter of James V of Scotland. This therefore makes the descendants of James Chalmers distant cousins of Prince William, and also more distant cousins of the Queen herself.

△ Through his Chalmers ancestry, Prince William has many close, 'commoner' cousins.

The British nobility is structured as follows. At the top of the pile and nearest in dignity to the Crown are dukes, followed by the ranks of marquis, earl, viscount and baron. Barons were originally those who held substantial amounts of land from the Crown, and subsequently were summoned to sit in the House of Lords, the earliest writs creating hereditary baronies dating back to Edward I.

NOBLES

⌸ Among the best works on the peerage are G. E.Cockayne's 13-volume *The Complete Peerage* (Alan Sutton, 1987), known as *'GEC'*, and P. W. Hammond's *The Complete Peerage, Vol 1* (Sutton, 1998), which brings *GEC* up to 1995. These volumes describe the descent of each title, providing great scholarly detail about the bearers and their wives, offices held, places of birth, death and burial, extent and value of their estates, with amusing or enlightening anecdotes given in footnotes. They do not provide details of offspring who did not inherit titles.

⌸ For this you will need *Burke's Peerage*, which has been published periodically from 1826: the latest edition is C. Mosley's (ed.) *Burkes' Peerage, Baronetage and Knightage*, Burke's Peerage and Gentry (2003). This includes an index to the living but, excitingly, it can be searched under names, places, dates, schools – whatever you want – at a subscription website **www.burkes-peerage-baronetage.net** In Burke's you can see holders of ancient titles such as the Duchy of Norfolk and Barony of Camoys rubbing shoulders with the likes of Jeffrey Archer and Margaret Thatcher.

⌸ If a title has become extinct, you will usually find it (besides in *GEC*) in J. B. Burke's *A Genealogical History of the Dormant, Forfeited and Extinct Peerages of the British Empire* (Burke's Peerage, 1964), and L. G. Pine's *The New Extinct Peerage 1884–1971* (Heraldry Today, 1972) or J. Burke's *A Genealogical and Heraldic History of the Extinct and Dormant Baronetcies of England, Ireland and Scotland* (1841).

⌸ There are many published works concerning non-British nobility, such as the *Almanach de Gotha*, which you might describe as the Holy Roman Empire equivalent of *Burke's Peerage.* An excellent guide is F. R. Pryce's *A Guide to European Genealogies Exclusive of the British Isles: With an Historical Survey of the Principal Genealogical Writers* (University Microfilms Limited, 1965).

⌸ All the families in the Burke's publications are covered by a useful little book, *Burke's Family Index* (Burke's Peerage, 1976). For wider coverage of pedigree sources, see the bibliographies of Whitmore, Marshall and colleagues listed on page 33.

BURKE'S PEERAGE has two virtues over *GEC.* It traces peers' family lines as far back as they are known (regardless of when the title was granted) and includes details of younger sons, and daughters. However, *Burke's Peerage* has two great failings.

First, it does not always include details of all younger sons, and sometimes omits daughters altogether, so the absence of someone from Burke's does not mean they did not exist: the best means of checking is to seek a record of the father's will.

Second, broadly speaking, family pedigrees were printed as submitted by the families themselves, and therefore contain mistakes, inaccuracies, deliberate omissions of family members regarded at the time as black sheep (handicapped children, suicides, daughters who ran off with grooms, and so on), and downright lies, such as claims of descent from non-existent companions of William the Conqueror. These have been weeded out of the modern versions of the book, but not for nothing were the old versions of *Burke's Peerage* described as the greatest work of fiction in the English language after the complete works of Shakespeare!

Peerages created before 1707 were either English or Scottish; peers of Great Britain are those created between 1707 and 1801; Irish peers are all those created before 1801: after 1801, all peers created were – and remain – peers of the United Kingdom. Most peerages pass strictly down to each successive senior male representative of the family in the male line. Some old Medieval titles can be inherited by a woman and passed on to her senior heir, but these are unusual. The recent invention of life peerages means that the majority of titles granted now are for the holder only, and are not hereditary.

ALL KNIGHTS, with their date and place of knighthood, are listed in W.A.Shaw's *The Knights of England* (1906). A good source for 17th-century ones is Le Neve's *Pedigrees of Knights [made] by King Charles II*, edited by George Marshall and published as volume 8 of the Harleian Society.

NON-NOBLES

Below the nobility come baronetcies, which are hereditary knighthoods, allowing the bearers to be styled 'Sir', and their wives 'Dame' or 'Lady'. Baronetcies were dreamed up in 1611 by James I and his lover the Duke of Buckingham as a means of raising much needed funds and establish new colonies to boot. The King stung some of his wealthiest, non-titled subjects for £1095 each, ostensibly to pay for 30 soldiers to protect the Protestant settlers of Ulster for three years, in return for which he gave them an hereditary knighthood: these were Irish baronetcies. In 1625, Charles I started creating baronets of Nova Scotia, who paid £116-13s-4d towards the establishment of that colony in what is now Canada. Scottish baronetcies were replaced with baronetcies of Great Britain after 1707. Irish baronetcies ceased to be created in 1800, after which anyone who became a baronet became one of the United Kingdom.

Below baronets come the ranks of the landed gentry, manorial lords or 'squires' and similar.

THE GOSSIP FAMILY HANDBOOK

WHEN FAMILIES are well recorded, it becomes easier to seek out the complex inter-connections that bind them together. A fascinating exercise in this is Andrew Barrow's *The Gossip Family Handbook* (Hamish Hamilton, n.d.). The book is nothing more than a great sprawling web of links between well-known people, to which many unknown people may be able to make a connection. From Marx Brother Zeppo's wife Barbara, who was also married to Frank Sinatra (whose wife Mia Farrow was also married to André Previn), you can go to Frank (and also Mickey Rooney's) other wife Ava Gardner, to her husband Artie Shaw, to his wife Evelyn Keyes, to her husband John Huston (father of both Angelica and Tony), whose wife Lady Margaret Cholmondeley was sister of Lady Caroline, wife of Roo d'Erlanger, husband of Sarah Giles, whose father Frank Giles was married to Lady Kitty Giles, daughter of Earl de la Warr, whose wife Sylvia Harrison was sister of actor Rex Harrison, who was married to Elizabeth Harris, who was also married to Peter Aitken, son of the Hon. Peter Aitken, son of Lord Beaverbrook (whose brother Joseph was grandfather of ex-MP Jonathan Aitken and also of Maria, whose husband Mark Aiden-Smith was brother of Judith Chalmers' husband Neil). And from Lord Beaverbrook you can go to his sister Janet, who married Hon. Drogo Montagu, who was also married to Tanis Guiness, sister of Lionel Guiness, at which point you can either go to his wife Gloria, who was also married to Ahmed Fakhry, son of Princess Fawkieh, sister of King Farouk of Egypt and himself brother-in-law of the Shah of Iran, or you can go to Lionel's other wife, Princess Joan Aly Khan, who was also married to Prince Aly Khan, whose wife Rita Hayworth was also married to Orson Welles!

NON-NOBLES

⊟ The most detailed work on the holders of baronetcies up to 1800 is G. E. Cockayne's *The Complete Baronetage* (Alan Sutton, 1987), while Burke's Peerage includes baronets. Extinct baronetcies are also in J. B. Burke's *A Genealogical and Heraldic History of the Extinct and Dormant Baronetcies of England, Ireland and Scotland* (Burke's Peerage, 1964).

⊟ Other excellent works on the baronetage include Sir W. Betham's *The Baronetage of England, or the History of the English Baronets, and such Baronets of Scotland as are of English Families, with Genealogical Tables and Engravings of their Armorial Bearings* (William Miller, 1801–4).

⊟ Anyone with a big house and a bit of land, or whose family used to have these, could say they were landed gentry and submit their pedigree to the equally unofficial *Burke's Landed Gentry*, which is officially called *A Genealogical and Heraldic History of the Commoners of Great Britain and Ireland (1833–7)*, reprinted in a fully indexed version 1842–48 and then updated (but not indexed) in many subsequent editions up to 1972 as Burke's *Landed Gentry of Great Britain and Ireland*.

⊟ Also worth mentioning is J. B. Burke's *A Genealogical and Heraldic History of the Colonial Gentry* (Heraldry Today, 1970), which is fully indexed.

⊟ If you are descended from the Jamaican plantocracy, obtain a copy of Donald Lindo's CD-Rom of Jamaican planter families via **www.discoverjamaica.com**.

⊟ Many Irish families appear in the books mentioned above under nobility and non-nobility, but special in Irish research are J. B. Burke's *Burke's Irish Family Records* (Burke's Peerage, 1976), previously published as *Burke's Landed Gentry of Ireland (1899–1958)*, and J. O'Hart's *Irish Pedigrees, Or the Origins and Stem of the Irish Nation* (James Duffy & Co., 1892). This covers the old tribal lords and the ancient royal families of Ireland, stretching far back into antiquity and legend, and also contains much valuable material concerning the planter families and the Protestant establishment.

⊟ A good manuscript source for Irish lineage is the 42-volume Carew MSS at **Lambeth Palace Library**. MS 599 consists of '636 Pedigrees wherein most of the descendants whether of the mere Irish or the English families in Ireland are mentioned; and 626 Pedigrees of most of the Lords and Gentlemen of the Irish Nation', with a calendar to the collection.

WHERE TO SEARCH

HERE·LYETH·INTERRD·THE·BODY·OF
THOMAS·HAWKINS·ESQ·WHO·AFTER
HAVING·HAD 5·CHILDREN·3·SONS·
AND·2·DAWGHTERS·DEPARTED·THIS
LIFE·IN·THE·YEAR·OF·OVR·LORD 1678
THE·19ᵀᴴ·DAY·OF·DECEMBER·IN·THE·31
YEAR·OF·HIS·AGE·TO·WHOSE·DEAR
MEMORY·HIS·BELOVED·WIFE·LAID THIS
STONE·IN·THE·YEAR·OE·OVR·LORD·168
This Stone was laid by Catherine the Daugh
f Walter Giffard Efq of Chillington, who v
indered at ÿ Revolution & forced into Fran

◁ Church memorial to my forebear Thomas Hawkins, Esq., Lord of the Manor, at Boughton-under-Blean, Kent.

CHAPTER THIRTY-ONE
HERALDRY

Heraldry is the use of distinctively painted shields that are passed down within families from father to son. Because of its strictly hereditary nature, heraldry and its records are therefore intimately connected with genealogy.

▽ Arms of my forebears, the Colegrave-Manbys of Cann Hall, Essex, showing an impressive 20 quarterings.

HISTORY OF HERALDRY

It is 14 October 1066. The invading Norman army has succeeded in luring the Saxons down from the heights of Senlac Hill and the pitched battle could go either way. Suddenly, dismay spreads among the Normans – Duke William has been slain! Among those hearing the dismal news is William himself, perfectly unharmed, yet thoroughly alarmed at the wavering courage of his men. He waves his chainmailed arms about and shouts, but to no avail. Then, desperately risking arrow-shot and axe-blow alike, he pulls up his helmet with its wide nosepiece, revealing his distinctive face. Seeing him alive, his men take courage and throw themselves back into the fray.

William won the day, but the solution of how to identify knights on the battlefield eluded both him and his children for 61 years. It was not until 1127 that his son Henry I invested his own son-in-law Geoffrey of Anjou with a blue shield decorated with golden lions, the first recorded coat of arms. The fact that the same arms appear on the tomb of Geoffrey's grandson William Longespee (d. 1226) indicate that the arms were not only personal, but hereditary in the male line. With this, the first recorded hereditary coat of arms, heraldry was born.

◁ Jousting knights from Sir Thomas Holmes' book (English School, 15th century).

COATS OF MANY COLOURS

Over the next three centuries, armoured knights galloped onto battlefields arrayed in ever-more elaborate regalia. Their coats of arms were painted brightly on their shields and embroidered on their banners. Their surcoats, the mantling draped over their massive helms and, of course, the liveries of their squires, matched the principal colour and 'metal' (gold or silver) of the shield. On top of their helms, tied on by a wreath of the main colour and metal twisted together in a 'tort', sat the impressive crest, often the head of the beast calculated to be most intimidating to the enemy. And on a finger, hidden beneath their armoured gloves, was a signet ring also engraved with the arms. By pressing this into wax, they could indicate their assent to legal agreements and letters because, despite all their chivalric splendour, precious few of them could even sign their own names.

Towards the end of the 15th century, when gunpowder enabled common artillerymen to fell their betters, heraldry was already retreating from the battlefield to the libraries of the new gentry who had made their money by selling armaments, gunpowder and provisions to the aristocracy during the Wars of the Roses. Very soon, crests sprung onto paper, which could never have balanced on top of helmets and the simple mantling which stopped the Crusaders' helms from boiling their heads flourished over printed pages in ever more luxuriant arabesques. This was paper heraldry.

During the 16th century, an even more extraordinary development was taking place. From Henry I's time, power to grant arms was clearly vested in the sovereign, and the practice of inheriting arms through the male line alone became enshrined in the Laws of Arms. Monarchs delegated the granting of arms to the Kings of Arms who in turn delegated some of the work designing them, and recording lines of descent, to the heralds. To the heralds too fell the job of picking through dismembered corpses on battle fields and identifying the slain from their bright heraldry. The Kings of Arms and heralds were incorporated into the College of Arms by Richard III in 1484. From 1555 they have occupied the same site, rebuilt as it is now after the Great Fire in 1666.

However, despite the heralds' presence, some members of the nouveaux riches had the temerity to start making up their own coats of arms or – which was possibly worse – to lay claim to those of older families to whom they could not even begin to prove a genealogical connection.

Between 1530 and 1686, the heralds fought back by visiting the English and Welsh shires, enquiring after all those using arms and demanding to know by what right they were being used. Those families using arms legitimately had their pedigrees recorded in the visitation records. Those making improper use of arms were in some cases quietly encouraged to pay for a new grant. Others, either belligerent or simply unfortunate, were publicly disclaimed and suffered the humiliation of witnessing their bogus heraldry being trampled into the filth of the market place. Some heralds, such as the great antiquarian Sir William Dugdale, tore through churches like avenging angels, defacing unauthorised heraldry on funery monuments and tearing down the diamond-shaped, black-grounded hatchments depicting the arms of deceased pseudo-armigers.

By the 18th century, exhausted by the Civil War and Glorious Revolution, the heralds pretty much gave up. Retreating to their

△ Heraldic lion from the roof of the Great Hall, Stirling Castle, Scotland.

△ A coat of arms of the town of Gouda, Holland, supported by two worthy burghers' wives.

HOW HERALDRY WORKS

△ Coat of arms of Sir Christopher Wren (1632–1723).

ONLY MALE-LINE descendants of the original grantee can use a coat of arms – there is no such thing as a 'coat of arms for a surname'. The senior descendent can use the arms as they were originally granted, while the younger sons and their descendants can use the arms with the addition of small symbols to distinguish them from the head of the family. However, even if families know for sure they are descended from a grantee, they must still register their up-to-date pedigrees with the College of Arms before using the arms.

Until 1997, women scarcely existed in the world of heraldry. A woman would be represented by a diamond-shaped lozenge, bearing the arms of her father, if she was unmarried, or of her husband if she was. If she married an 'armigerous' husband, the two coats of arms would be 'impaled', the husband's appearing on the left of the shield and the wife's father's on the right. If she had no brothers, her arms could be inherited by her son provided his father already had a coat of arms. The son could 'quarter' his father's arms (in the top left and bottom right of the shield) with his mother's father's arms (in the top right and bottom left). If the process was repeated and another heraldic heiress married into the family, the coats of arms could be reorganised and some families ended up with many more than four 'quarters'. Being able to identify quarterings is an effective way of finding out which families married into each other – such quartered coats of arms are, in fact, a form of pedigree in themselves.

The year 1997, however, was the year of heraldic women's lib. Women may now bear arms in their own right. Unmarried women bear their paternal arms on a lozenge; a married woman can bear her husband's arms impaled by her paternal arms on a shield, or simply bear her paternal arms or husband's arms alone, on a shield 'differenced' by a small escutcheon (shield) at the top of the shield. But if she has no paternal arms of her own, she bears her husband's by courtesy only. Widows can bear arms likewise, but on a lozenge.

respective homes, they administered the system more or less for the benefit of those paying customers whose conscience and sense of history spurred them either to seek a new grant or to update an existing pedigree.

CREST CONNOTATIONS

Heraldic bookplates and stationery had superseded chivalric battledresses, but heraldry was far from declining. In an age when most employment and marriage agreements were dependent on perceived social status, the appearance of a crest – real or bogus – on one's dinner invitations could tip a very real balance between prosperity and poverty. The heraldic stationers or 'bucket shops' of Doctors' Commons were always happy to oblige, looking up the surname (or even a vaguely similar one) in one of the many armorials on the popular market and supplying a coat of arms for a fraction of the cost of a grant of arms from the College of Arms around the corner.

Except in Scotland, where Lord Lyon was and still is a High Court judge, the heralds could do little to curtail such travesties taking place, literally, under their noses. Indeed, some, such as Bernard Burke, cashed in on the growing market, producing the first edition of *The General Armory of England, Scotland, Ireland and Wales, Comprising a Registry of Armorial Bearings from the Earliest to the Present Time* in 1842. The most complete version is Harrison & Sons' 1884 edition (repr. Burke's Peerage, 1961) and updated by *General Armory Two: Alfred Morant's Additions and Corrections to Burke's General Armory* (Tabard Press, 1973).

The egalitarianism of the 20th century saw a mass disappearance of heraldry from letterheads and monuments alike, to be replaced instead by a plethora of commercial logos. Yet despite everything, the heralds still remain part of the Royal Household. Although their theoretical powers to inflict the death sentence on misusers of heraldry were only removed at the end of the century, their control of the Laws of Arms remain intact to this day.

And so heraldry has survived, partially because of its intimate connection with genealogy, but also in its own right, and arms continue to be granted. In December 2002, Paul McCartney was granted a coat of arms showing four black half-flaunches, symbolising the backs of four beetles, two circles alluding to records and CDs, lines for guitar strings and the crest of a 'Liver bird' holding a guitar. You can't get more up to date than that!

WHERE TO SEARCH

HERALDRY

⊟ The best overall guide to the subject is A. Fox Davies' *A Complete Guide to Heraldry* (J. P. Brooke-Little, 1969).

⊟ The **College of Arms** records, which can be searched for you by the heralds for a fee, are mainly:
➲ About 10,000 grants and confirmations of arms by the heralds in the 15th–17th centuries, with evidence such as patents, blazons and sketches.
➲ Pedigrees and sketches of arms from the heralds' visitations, 1530–1687.
➲ Funeral certificates for the 16th–17th centuries.
➲ Collections of pedigrees voluntarily submitted from the ending of the visitations to the present day.
➲ Special pedigree collections such as those of Ralph Bigland.
➲ Full texts of all grants from 1673.
➲ Earl Marshal's books, including royal warrants.

⊟ The pedigrees recorded in the visitations (see above) are mainly at the **College of Arms** and **British Library** (**www.catalogue.bl.uk**) and many have been published (with or without scholarly notes and additions) by the Harleian Society and indexed in Whitmore and Marshall (see page 33) and C. R. Humphery-Smith's *Armigerous Ancestors and Those who Weren't: A Catalogue of Visitation Records Together with an Index of Pedigrees, Arms* and *Disclaimers* (IHGS, 1997). These pedigrees form the basis for many of those that appear in the Burke's publications (see page 295), but of course they also include the pedigrees of many families whose money had dissipated by the time *Burke's Landed Gentry* started to be published, so these records contain the forebears of very many families of tradesmen and labourers.

For crests, look at *Fairbairn's Crests of the Families of Great Britain and Ireland* (New Orchard editions, 1986). Inaccurately computerised and widely syndicated, *Burke's Peerage*, and sometimes *Fairbairn's Crests* too, form the basis for the modern 'coat of arms for your surname' booths that clutter modern shopping arcades and seaside piers.

If you want to identify a coat of arms, you can use J. W. Papworth and A. W. Morant's *An Alphabetical Dictionary of Arms belonging to Families of Great Britain and Ireland Forming an Extensive Ordinary of British Armorials* (T. Richards, 1874), reprinted as *Papworth's Ordinary of British Armorials* (Tabard Publications, 1961). If the arms are European, consult J. van Helmont's *Dictionnaire de Renesse* (Uitgeverij-Editions, 1992).

SCOTLAND

Scottish heraldry is regulated, fairly strictly, by Lord Lyon King of Arms and his or her heralds, who operate from the **Registrar General of Scotland**. The Lyon Court has maintained a 'register of all arms and bearings in Scotland' since 1672, in which all those using arms are supposed to register. Details of all arms granted and/or registered up to 1972 are published in Sir J. Balfour Paul's *An Ordinary of Arms* contained in the *Public Register of all Arms and Bearings in Scotland* (William Green and Sons, 1903) and *An Ordinary of Arms, Vol. 2* (1977).

IRELAND

Under British rule, Irish heraldry was regulated by the Ulster King of Arms. Northern Irish heraldry remains under the jurisdiction of the **College of Arms**, while Eire established its own Office of Arms in Ireland, operating from the **Genealogical Office**, whose grants, visitation pedigrees and funeral certificates can be inspected either there or on microfilm at the **National Archives of Ireland** or at **Mormon Family History Centres**.

△ The crest used, with very dubious authority, by my Hammond ancestors. Not all coats of arms and crests are genuine!

QUICK REFERENCE

See also main resources in Useful Addresses, page 306

COLLEGE OF ARMS
Queen Victoria Street
London EC4V 4BT
☎ 020 7248 2762
www.college-of-arms.gov.uk

REGISTRAR GENERAL OF SCOTLAND
New Register House
Charlotte Square
Edinburgh EH1 3YT
☎ 0131 334 0380
www.gro-scotland.gov.uk

GENEALOGICAL OFFICE
2–3 Kildare Street
Dublin 2
Eire
☎ 00 353 1 603 0200
www.nli.ie

CHAPTER THIRTY-TWO
PSYCHICS

Some people are repelled by the idea of psychics, or object to them on theological grounds, while many more are intrigued by them and believe them wholeheartedly. There are many cases of people seeking direction from psychics for family history research. After all, if it is true that psychics can ask questions of deceased ancestors then, presupposing the ancestors want to assist, you will get help direct from the horse's mouth.

❝I cannot say that psychics can paint accurate portraits of the past. But the evidence I've seen through my television work is certainly pretty good.❞

PSYHIC INVESTIGATIONS

I had the opportunity of investigating whether psychic investigation could be of genuine use to genealogists when I worked with psychic Derek Acorah for Living TV's *Antiques Ghostshow* in 2002 and 2003. Derek believes he can communicate directly with those who have 'passed into the world of spirits' and also that their energy is still closely connected to their living descendants, and with objects they owned and cherished. By handling family heirlooms, he can then form a picture of who past owners were, and provide some details about them including, sometimes, names, dates, places and occupations – exactly what genealogists want to know.

For the series, we introduced Derek to a succession of people, each of whom had brought a family heirloom for him to 'psychometrise'. Without having met or spoken to them before, Derek gave a series of readings and it was then my job to verify or disprove the details he had given. His results were impressive. For a 1930s clock, which was owned by one of our guest's grandmothers, Derek spoke of a very kindly woman (as opposed to a man), while for a First World War medal he described a stern-hearted man who would kill – and it turned out the owner was so hard-hearted he had even pushed his own mother down the stairs.

In most cases Derek would come up with just a Christian name, which might have been associated either with the original owner or the intervening generations, but in many cases, despite having studied the family trees of the guests in advance, I could not place the name. There were cases, however, when he managed to come up with surnames too. A watch owned by James Simpson Dinnie, who was Scottish, elicited 'Jamie Simpson' and, later, 'the Dinnie crowd'.

One of the most impressive cases was an old, dirty oil painting of a Victorian man in normal gentleman's clothing. Derek worked his way through, 'Big tomes' to putting something on his head which was white but not a hat, to the cry 'Justice!' and then, 'Not a solicitor but a barrister', and, 'But not a judge', 'Robert', 'North and south', 'I see water', and, 'The Thames.' We knew that the painting depicted a Victorian lawyer called Robert Wilbraham Jones, who became a barrister at the Temple (which is on the Thames) but did not become a judge, and whose family home was at Bridge House, Chester, overlooking the River Dee. Had the owner not known who the painting depicted, therefore, Derek's reading would have suggested that it was of a barrister called Robert, which would have brought researchers much closer to a positive identification.

FIRST IMPRESSIONS

Besides offering what I believe would have been some useful pointers to genealogical research, Derek also provided something more. The bulk of his readings comprised not so much precise details of names, dates or places, but more of impressions of what the people were like. When giving a reading on a picture of William Buckley, who had been transported to Australia as a petty criminal but ended up as a revered Aboriginal chief (none of which Derek knew beforehand), he spoke passionately of a man in a distant land. The man, Derek said, was proud of his accomplishments, not desiring to return to his native land but longing nonetheless for the people he had left behind to see and approve of what he had achieved. Even if William had left behind memoirs or letters, he might not have been so honest about his feelings as in the raw emotions that Derek recreated. Similarly, a Burnley blacksmith who had enjoyed wrestling shire horses came back to life before our eyes as Derek, having handled a cobbler's last that the blacksmith had owned, started miming the act of shire horse wrestling, much to our amusement and his bemusement.

I do not know if we witnessed authentic reappearances of ancestors and their personalities, thoughts, dreams and fears, but it certainly seemed like it. In so far as I was able to investigate the ancestors concerned, they fitted with what Derek re-enacted for us. It seems possible, therefore, that a good psychic may be able to offer at least some clues about ancestors, which can be followed up through original records. It may even be that psychics may be able to tell us more about ancestors' inner personalities than even the most insightful memories of our elderly relatives, or the most detailed of written records, ever could.

△ The *Antiques Ghostshow* team – Chris Gower (standing, right), Derek Acorah (sitting) and me (standing, left) – on location at Gilston Hall, Essex, in Spring 2003.

USEFUL ADDRESSES

These addresses are divided into main sources (below) and then general addresses, which start opposite. In the main body of the book, the quick reference panels contain the pertinent general addresses, but as the main sources recur so frequently, they only appear in the quick references panels on their first mention. Thereafter the reader is guided to these pages.

All addresses are in alphabetical order and those for Ireland, Scotland, the Isle of Man and the Channel Islands are on the follow pages:

⮿ Ireland – see page 310

⮿ Scotland – see page 311

⮿ Channel Islands – see page 311

⮿ Isle of Man – see page 311

MAIN SOURCES

ASSOCIATION OF GENEALOGISTS AND RECORD AGENTS (AGRA)
29 Badgers Close
Horsham
West Sussex RH12 5RU
Website www.agra.org.uk

BRITISH LIBRARY
96 Euston Road
London NW1 2DB
☎ 020 7412 7676
http://blpc.bl.uk

FAMILY RECORDS CENTRE (FRC)
1 Myddleton Street
London EC1R 1UW
☎ 020 8392 5300
www.familyrecords.gov.uk/frc

FEDERATION OF FAMILY HISTORY SOCIETIES (FFHS)
PO Box 2425
Coventry CV5 6YX
☎ 024 7667 7798
www.ffhs.org.uk

GENERAL REGISTER OFFICE (GRO)
Smedley Hydro
Trafalgar Road
Southport PR8 2HH
☎ 0870 243 7788
www.gro.gov.uk

GUILDHALL LIBRARY
Aldermanbury
London EC2P 2EJ
☎ 020 7332 1868
www.cityoflondon.gov.uk

HISTORIC MANUSCRIPTS COMMISSION (HMC)
See National Archives
www.archon.nationalarchives.gov.uk/
hmc/

INSTITUTE OF HERALDIC AND GENEALOGICAL STUDIES (IHGS)
79–82 Northgate
Canterbury
Kent CT1 1BA
☎ 01227 768664
www.ihgs.ac.uk

MORMON FAMILY HISTORY CENTRES
Locations can be found on
www.familysearch.org or in your local
phone book. The main one is:
Hyde Park Family History Centre
64/68 Exhibition Road
South Kensington
London SW7 2PA
☎ 020 7589 8561
www.familysearch.org

NATIONAL ARCHIVES (NA) (INCORPORATING HISTORIC MANUSCRIPTS COMMISSION)
Ruskin Avenue
Kew
Richmond
Surrey TW9 4DU
☎ 020 8876 3444
www.nationalarchives.gov.uk

NATIONAL LIBRARY OF WALES (LLYFRGELL GENEDLAETHOL CYMRU)
Panglais
Aberystwyth
Ceredigion SY23 3BU
☎ 01970 632800
www.llgc.org.uk

SOCIETY OF GENEALOGISTS (SoG)
14 Charterhouse Buildings
Goswell Road
London EC1M 7BA
☎ 020 7251 8799
www.sog.org.uk

IRELAND

NATIONAL ARCHIVES OF IRELAND
Bishop Street
Dublin 8
☎ 00 353 1 407 2300
www.nationalarchives.ie.

PUBLIC RECORD OFFICE OF NORTHERN IRELAND (PRONI)
66 Balmoral Avenue
Belfast BT9 6NY
☎ 028 9025 5905
http://proni.nics.gov.uk

SCOTLAND

NATIONAL ARCHIVES OF SCOTLAND (NAS)
HM General Register House
2 Princes Street
Edinburgh EH1 3YY
☎ 0131 535 1334
www.nas.gov.uk

GENERAL

A

ADOPTION CONTACT REGISTER (England and Wales)
Smedley Hydro, Trafalgar Road,
Southport, Merseyside PR8 2HH
☎ 0151 471 4830
www.statistics.gov.uk/registration

ARMY MEDALS OFFICE
Government Office Buildings,
Worcester Road, Droitwich,
Worcestershire WR9 8AU
☎ 01905 772323
www.army.mod.uk

ARMY MUSEUM OGILBY TRUST
58 The Close, Salisbury SP1 2EX
☎ 01722 332188
www.armymuseums.org.uk

ARMY RECORDS CENTRE
Ministry of Defence,
Historical Disclosure, Mail Point 400,
Kentigern House, 65 Brown Street,
Glasgow G2 8EX
☎ 0141 224 3030
www.mod.uk

B

BANK OF ENGLAND ARCHIVES
Threadneedle Street,
London EC2R 8AH
☎ 020 7601 5096
www.bankofengland.co.uk/archive.htm

BARNARDO'S AFTER-CARE DEPARTMENT
Barnardo's, Tanners Lane, Barkingside,
Essex IG6 1QG
☎ 020 8550 8822
www.barnardos.org.uk/whatwedo/after
care

BORTHWICK INSTITUTE FOR ARCHIVES
University of York, Heslington,
York YO10 5DD
☎ 01904 321166
www.york.ac.uk/inst/bihr

BRITISH AGENCIES FOR ADOPTION & FOSTERING (BAAF)
Skyline House, 200 Union Street,
London SE1 0LX
☎ 020 7593 2000
www.baaf.org.uk

BRITISH LIBRARY NEWSPAPER LIBRARY
Colindale Avenue, London NW9 5HE
☎ 020 7412 7353
www.bl.uk/collections/newspapers.html

BRITISH LIBRARY, ORIENTAL AND INDIA OFFICE COLLECTIONS
96 Euston Road, London NW1 2DB
☎ 020 7412 7873
www.bl.uk/collections/orientalandindian.
html

BRITISH TELECOM ARCHIVES
3rd Floor, Holborn Telephone Exchange,
268–270 High Holborn,
London WC1V 7EE
☎ 020 7492 8792
www.btplc.com/archives

C

CAMDEN LOCAL STUDIES & ARCHIVE CENTRE
Holborn Library, 32 Theobalds Road,
London WC1X 8PA
☎ 020 7974 6342
www.camden.gov.uk/localstudies

CAMDEN PUBLIC LIBRARY
88 Avenue Road, London NW3 3HA
☎ 020 7974 6522
www.camden.gov.uk

CATHOLIC CENTRAL LIBRARY
New address not available at time of
going to print
☎ 020 7732 8379
www.catholic-library.org.uk

CATHOLIC FAMILY HISTORY SOCIETY
The Secretaries,
45 Gates Green Road, West Wickham,
Bromley, Kent BR4 9DE

CATHOLIC RECORD SOCIETY
c/o 12 Melbourne Place,
Wolsingham, Co. Durham DL13 3EH
☎ 01388 527747
www.catholic-history.org.uk/crs

CHILDREN'S SOCIETY
Post Adoption and Care Project,
91–3 Queen's Road, Peckham,
London SE15 2EZ
☎ 020 7732 9089
www.the-childrens-society.org.uk

CITY OF WESTMINSTER ARCHIVES CENTRE
10 St Ann's Street, London SW1P 2DE
☎ 020 7641 5180
www.westminster.gov.uk/libraries/archives

COLLEGE OF ARMS
Queen Victoria Street, London EC4V 4BT
☎ 020 7248 2762
www.college-of-arms.gov.uk

COMMONWEALTH WAR GRAVES COMMISSION
2 Marlow Road, Maidenhead,
Berkshire SL6 7DX
☎ 01628 634221
www.cwgc.org

COMPANIES HOUSE
21 Bloomsbury Street, London WC1B 3XD
☎ 0870 333 3636
www.companieshouse.gov.uk

COMPANIES HOUSE
Crown Way, Maindy, Cardiff CF14 3UZ
☎ 0870 333 3636
www.companieshouse.gov.uk

CORPORATION OF LONDON RECORD
c/o London Metropolitan Archives,
40 Northampton Road,
London EC1R 0HB
☎ 020 7332 3820
wwwcityoflondon.gov.uk

COURT OF THE CHIEF RABBI
London Beth Din, Adler House,
735 High Road, London N12 0US
☎ 020 8343 6270
info@chiefrabbi.org
www.chiefrabbi.org

CREMATION SOCIETY OF GREAT BRITAIN
Brecon House, 16 Albion Place,
Maidstone, Kent ME14 5DZ
☎ 01622 688292
www.cremation.org.uk

CROOK'S LIVERPOOL MARRIAGE INDEX
25 Gerneth Road,
Speke, Liverpool L24 1UN

D

DR WILLIAM'S LIBRARY
14 Gordon Square,
London WC1H 0AR
☎ 020 7387 3727
www.dwlib.co.uk

F

FAMILY HISTORY LIBRARY
64/68 Exhibition Road,
South Kensington, London SW7 2PA
☎ 020 7589 8561
www.familysearch.org

FRANCIS FRITH COLLECTION
Frith's Barn, Teffont,
Salisbury, Wiltshire SP3 5QP
☎ 01722 716376
www.francisfrith.co.uk

FRIENDS' HOUSE
173–177 Euston Road,
London NW1 2BJ
☎ 020 7663 1135
www.quaker.org.uk/library

G

GUILD OF ONE-NAME STUDIES
C/o Society of Genealogists,
Box G, 14 Charterhouse Buildings,
Goswell Road, London EC1M 7BA
www.one-name.org

H

HER MAJESTY'S STATIONERY OFFICE (NOW THE STATIONERY OFFICE LTD)
St Crispins, Duke Street,
Norwich, Norfolk NR3 1PD
☎ 01603 622211
www.thestationeryoffice.com

HISTORY OF PARLIAMENT
Wedgwood House,
15 Woburn Square,
London WC1H 0NS
☎ 020 7862 8800
www.ihrinfo.ac.uk/hop/

HM LAND REGISTRY
32 Lincoln's Inn Fields,
London WC2A 3PH
☎ 020 7917 8888
www.landreg.gov.uk

HOME OFFICE NATURALISATION OFFICE
3rd Floor, India Building,
Water Street, Liverpool L2 0QN
☎ 0151 237 5200
www.ind.homeoffice.gov.uk

HOUSE OF LORDS RECORD OFFICE
Palace of Westminster,
London SW1A 0PW
☎ 020 7219 3074
www.parliament.uk

HUGUENOT SOCIETY OF GREAT BRITAIN AND IRELAND
University College Library,
Gower Street, London WC1E 6BT
☎ 020 7679 5199
www.ucl.ac.uk/library/huguenot.htm

HULTON GETTY COLLECTION
Unique House, 21–31 Woodfield Road,
London W9 2BA
☎ 020 7579 5777
www.hultongetty.com

I

IMPERIAL WAR MUSEUM
Lambeth Road, London SE1 6HZ
☎ 020 7416 5320
www.iwm.org.uk

INDIA OFFICE LIBRARY
British Library, 96 Euston Road,
London NW1 2DB
☎ 020 7412 7513
www.bl.uk/collections/orientalandindian
.html

INSTITUTE OF HISTORICAL RESEARCH
Senate House, University of London,
Malet Street, London WC1E 7HU
☎ 020 7862 8740
www.ihrinfo.ac.uk

INTERNATIONAL WELFARE DEPARTMENT OF THE BRITISH RED CROSS
9 Grosvenor Crescent,
London SW1X 7EJ
☎ 020 7201 5153
www.redcross.org.uk

L

LAMBETH PALACE LIBRARY
Lambeth Palace Road, London SE1 7JU
☎ 020 7898 1400
www.lambethpalacelibrary.org

LAW SOCIETY LIBRARY
113 Chancery Lane, London WC2A 1PL
☎ 0870 606 2511
www.library.lawsociety.org.uk

LLOYD'S REGISTER OF SHIPPING
71 Fenchurch Street, London EC3M 4BS
☎ 020 7709 9166
www.lr.org

LONDON FIRE BRIGADE MUSEUM
Winchester House,
94A Southwark Bridge Road,
London SE9 0EG
☎ 020 7587 2894
www.london-fire.gov.uk

LONDON METROPOLITAN ARCHIVES
40 Northampton Road,
London EC1R 0HB
☎ 020 7332 3820
www.cityoflondon.gov.uk

M

MANORIAL SOCIETY OF GREAT BRITAIN
104 Kennington Road, London SE11 6RE
☎ 020 7735 6633
www.msgb.co.uk

MARITIME HISTORY ARCHIVE
Memorial University of New Foundland,
St John's, New Foundland A1C 5S7,
Canada
☎ 00 1 709 737 8428
www.mun.ca/mha/index.php

METHODIST ARCHIVES AND RESEARCH CENTRE
John Rylands Library, University of
Manchester, Oxford Road,
Manchester M13 9PP
☎ 0161 275 3764
www.rylibweb.man.ac.uk

METROPOLITAN POLICE HISTORICAL MUSEUM
Unit 7 Meridian Estate, Bugsby Way,
Charlton, London SE7 7SJ
☎ 020 8305 2824
www.met.police.uk/history

MINISTRY OF DEFENCE
Bourne Avenue, Hayes,
Middlesex UB3 1FR
☎ 0870 607 4455
www.mod.uk

MORAVIAN CHURCH HOUSE
5 Muswell Hill, London N10 3TJ
☎ 020 8883 3409
www.moravian.org

N
NATIONAL ARMY MUSEUM
Royal Hospital Road, Chelsea,
London SW3 4HT
☎ 020 7730 0717
www.national-army-museum.ac.uk

NATIONAL ART LIBRARY
Victoria and Albert Museum,
Cromwell Road, London SW7 2RL
☎ 020 7938 8315
www.nal.vam.ac.uk

NATIONAL MARITIME MUSEUM
Park Row, Greenwich,
London SE10 9NF
☎ 020 8858 4422
www.nmm.ac.uk

NATIONAL MONUMENTS RECORD CENTRE
Kemble Drive, Churchland, Swindon
☎ 01793 414600
www.swindon.gov.uk/nmro

NATIONAL PORTRAIT GALLERY
St Martin's Place,
London WC2H 0HE
☎ 0207 306 0055
www.npg.org.uk/search

NATURAL PARENTS' NETWORK
Garden Suburb, Oldham,
Lancashire OL8 3AY
☎ 01273 307597
www.n-p-n.fsnet.co.uk

NAVAL PERSONNEL RECORDS OFFICE
Ministry of Defence,
CS(RM)2 Navy Search,
Bourne Avenue, Hayes,
Middlesex UB3 1RF
☎ 020 8573 3831
www.mod.uk.

NORCAP
112 Church Road, Wheatley,
Oxford OX33 1LU
☎ 01865 875000
www.norcap.org.uk

O
OFFICE FOR NATIONAL STATISTICS
Customer Contact Centre,
Room 1.015,
Office for National Statistics,
Cardiff Road, Newport NP10 8XG
☎ 0845 601 3034

OFFICE FOR NATIONAL STATISTICS LIBRARY
1 Drummond Gate,
London SW1V 2QQ
www.statistics.gov.uk

P
POLICE HISTORY SOCIETY
Secretary: Steve Bridge
(no mailing address given)
Email steve@bridge100.fsnet.co.uk
www.policehistorysociety.co.uk

POST OFFICE ARCHIVES
Freeling House, Phoenix Place,
London WC1X 0DL
☎ 020 7239 2570
www.royalmail.com

POSTAL SEARCHES AND COPIES DEPARTMENT FOR WILLS AFTER 1858
The Probate Registry,
Castle Chambers, Clifford Street,
York YO1 9RG
☎ 01904 666777

PRINCIPAL REGISTRY OF THE FAMILY DIVISION
First Avenue House,
42–49 High Holborn,
London WC1V 6NP
☎ 020 7947 6980
www.courtservice.gov.uk

R
RAF MUSEUM
Grahame Park Way,
Hendon, London NW9 5LL
☎ 020 8205 2266
www.rafmuseum.org.uk

RAF PERSONNEL AND TRAINING COMMAND
Branch PG 5a(2) (for officers) and P,
Man 2b(1) (for non-officers),
RAF Innsworth,

Gloucestershire GL3 1EZ
☎ 01452 712612
www.mod.uk

REGISTRAR GENERAL
(Adoption Section),
Smedley Hydro, Trafalgar Road,
Southport, Merseyside PR8 2HH
☎ 0151 471 4830
www.statistics.gov.uk/registration/
adoptions.asp

REGISTRAR GENERAL OF SHIPPING AND SEAMEN
Anchor House, Cheviot Close,
Parc Ty Glas, Llanishen,
Cardiff CF14 5JA
☎ 029 2044 8800

ROYAL MARINES
Commandant General,
Ministry of Defence (Navy),
Whitehall, London SW1
☎ 0870 607 4455
www.royalnavy.mod.uk

ROYAL MARINES HISTORICAL RECORDS AND MEDALS
HRORM,
Room 038, Centurion Building,
Grange Road, Gosport,
Hampshire PO13 9XA
☎ 023 9270 2126
www.mod.uk

ROYAL MARINES MUSEUM
Eastney Barracks,
Southsea, Hampshire PO4 9PX
☎ 023 9281 9385
www.royalmarinesmuseum.co.uk

ROYAL MILITARY COLLEGE
Sandhurst, Camberley GU15 4PQ
☎ 01276 63344
www.atra.mod.uk/atra/rmas

ROYAL NAVAL MUSEUM
Buildings 1–7, College Road,
HM Naval Base, Portsmouth,
Hampshire PO1 3NH
☎ 023 9272 7562
www.royalnavalmuseum.org

ROYAL NAVAL PERSONNEL RECORDS OFFICE
Ministry of Defence,
CS(RM)2, Navy Search,
Bourne Avenue, Hayes,
Middlesex UB3 1RF
☎ 020 8573 3831
www.mod.uk

S

SALVATION ARMY
101 Newington Causeway,
London SE1 6BN
☎ 0845 634 0101
www.salvationarmy.org.uk

SALVATION ARMY
Social Work Department,
101 Newington Causeway,
London SE1 6BN
☎ 0845 634 0101
www.salvationarmy.org.uk

SALVATION ARMY FAMILY TRACING SERVICE
101 Newington Causeway,
London SE1 6BN
☎ 0845 634 0101
www.salvationarmy.org.uk

SALVATION ARMY INTERNATIONAL HERITAGE CENTRE
101 Queen Victoria Street,
London EC4P 4EP
☎ 020 7332 0101
www.salvationarmy.org/heritage.nsf

T

THEATRE MUSEUM
1E Tavistock Street, London WC2E 7PR
☎ 020 7943 4700
www.theatremuseum.org

U

UNITED GRAND LODGE OF ENGLAND
The Grand Secretary, Freemasons' Hall,
60 Great Queen Street,
London WC2B 5AZ
☎ 020 7831 9811
www.ugle.org.uk

UNITED REFORMED CHURCH
Church House, 86 Tavistock Place,
London WC1H 9RT
☎ 020 7916 2020
www.urc.org.uk

UNITED REFORMED CHURCH HISTORY SOCIETY LIBRARY
Westminster College, Madingley Road,
Cambridge CB3 0AA
☎ 01223 741300
www.urc.org.uk

V

VETERANS AGENCY
Norcross, Blackpool,
Lancashire FY5 3WP
☎ 0800 169 2277
www.veteransagency.mod.uk

W

WEST MIDLANDS POLICE MUSEUM
Sparkhill Police Station,
639 Stratford Road, Birmingham B11 4EA
☎ 0845 113 5000
www.birminghamheritage.org.uk/
police.htm

WESTMINSTER CENTRAL REFERENCE LIBRARY
35 St Martin's Street,
London WC2H 7HP
☎ 020 7641 4636
www.westminster.gov.uk/
libraries/westref

WIENER LIBRARY
4 Devonshire Street, London W1W 5BH
☎ 020 7636 7247
www.wienerlibrary.co.uk

WORLD JEWISH RELIEF
The Forum, 74/80 Camden Street,
London NW1 0EG
☎ 020 7691 1771
www.wjr.org.uk

IRELAND

EIRE
ADOPTION BOARD
Shelbourne House, Shelbourne Road,
Ballsbridge, Dublin 4
☎ 00 353 1 667 1392
www.adoptionboard.ie

DEEDS REGISTRY
Kings Inn, Henrietta Street, Dublin 7
☎ 00 353 1 804 8412
www.landregistry.ie

FEDERATION OF SERVICES FOR UNMARRIED PARENTS AND THEIR CHILDREN
The Adopted Peoples Association,
27 Templeview Green,
Clare Hall, Dublin 13
☎ 00 353 1 868 3020
www.adoptionireland.com

GENEALOGICAL OFFICE
2–3 Kildare Street, Dublin 2
☎ 00 353 1 603 0200
www.nli.ie

GENERAL REGISTER OFFICE
Joyce House, 8–11 Lombard Street East,
Dublin 2
☎ 00 353 1 635 4000
www.groireland.ie

THE GRAND SECRETARY
Freemasons' Hall,
17 Molesworth Street, Dublin 2
☎ 00 353 1 676 1337
www.irish-freemasons.org

IRISH FAMILY HISTORY SOCIETY
PO Box 36, Naas, Co Kildare
www.irish-roots.net

IRISH GENEALOGICAL RESEARCH SOCIETY
The Irish Club, 82 Eaton Square,
London SW1 9AJ
☎ 020 7235 4164
wwww.irelandseye.com

NATIONAL ARCHIVES OF IRELAND
See main sources, page 306

NATIONAL LIBRARY OF IRELAND
Kildare Street, Dublin 2
☎ 00 353 1 603 0200
www.nli.ie

REGISTRAR GENERAL
Joyce House, 8–11 Lombard Street,
Dublin 2, Eire
☎ 00 353 1 635 4000
www.groireland.ie

RELIGIOUS SOCIETY OF FRIENDS
Swanbrook House, Bloomfield Avenue,

Morehampton Road, Donnybrook
Dublin 4, Eire
☎ 00 353 1 668 3684
www.quakers-in-ireland.org

REPRESENTATIVE CHURCH BODY LIBRARY

Braemor Park, Rathgar,
Dublin
☎ 00 353 1 492 3979
www.ireland.anglican.org/library

TRINITY COLLEGE

Trinity College Library,
College Street, Dublin 2
☎ 00 353 1 677 2941
www.tcd.ie/library

VALUATION OFFICE

6 Ely Place, Dublin 2
☎ 00 353 1 817 1000
www.youririshroots.com/valoffice.htm

NORTHERN IRELAND
ADOPTION CONTACT REGISTER

General Register Office,
Oxford House, 49–55 Chichester Street,
Belfast BT1 4HL
☎ 028 9025 2000
www.groni.gov.uk

COMPANIES REGISTRATION OFFICE OF NORTHERN IRELAND

1st Floor Waterfront Plaza,
8 Laganbank Road, Belfast BT1 3LX
☎ 0845 604 8888
www.companiesregistry-ni.gov.uk

PUBLIC RECORD OFFICE OF NORTHERN IRELAND (PRONI)

See main sources, page 306

REGISTRAR GENERAL OF NORTHERN IRELAND

Oxford House,
49–55 Chichester Street,
Belfast BT1 4HL
☎ 028 9025 2000
www.groni.gov.uk

ULSTER HISTORICAL FOUNDATION

Balmoral Buildings,
12 College Square East,
Belfast BT1 6DD
☎ 028 9033 2288
www.ancestryireland.co.uk

SCOTLAND

BIRTHLINK

21 Castle Street, Edinburgh EH2 3DN
☎ 0131 225 6441
www.birthlink.org.uk

COMPANIES HOUSE

37 Castle Terrace, Edinburgh EH1 2EB
☎ 0131 535 5800
www.companieshouse.gov.uk

COURT OF THE LORD LYON

HM New Register House,
Edinburgh EH1 3YT
☎ 0131 556 7255

THE GRAND SECRETARY

Freemasons' Hall, 96 George Street,
Edinburgh EH2 3DH
☎ 0131 225 5304

NATIONAL ARCHIVES OF SCOTLAND (NAS)

See main sources, page 306

NATIONAL LIBRARY OF SCOTLAND

George IV Bridge,
Edinburgh EH1 1EW
☎ 0131 466 2812
www.nls.uk

REGISTERS OF SCOTLAND EXECUTIVE AGENCY

Erskine House, 68 Queen Street,
Edinburgh EH2 4NF
☎ 0845 607 0161
www.ros.gov.uk

REGISTRAR GENERAL OF SCOTLAND

New Register House, Charlotte Square,
Edinburgh EH1 3YT
☎ 0131 334 0380
www.gro-scotland.gov.uk

SCOTTISH GENEALOGICAL SOCIETY

15 Victoria Terrace, Edinburgh EH1 2JL
☎ 0131 220 3677
www.scotsgenealogy.com

CHANNEL ISLANDS

ALDERNEY
CLERK OF THE COURT

Queen Elizabeth Street,
Alderney GY9 3AA
☎ 01481 822817
www.alderney.gov.gg

GUERNSEY
HER MAJESTY'S GREFFIER

General Register Office,
Royal Court House,
St Peter Port GY1 2PD
☎ 01481 725277
www.gov.gg

PRIAULX LIBRARY

Candie Road, St Peter Port GY1 1UG
☎ 01481 721998
www.gov.gg/priaulx

JERSEY
JERSEY LIBRARY

Halkett Place, St Helier JE2 4WH
☎ 01534 759992
www.jsylib.gov.je

JUDICIAL GREFFE

Burrand House, Don Street,
St Helier JE2 4TR
☎ 01534 502300
www.judicialgreffe.gov.je

SOCIÉTÉ JERSIAISE AND LORD COUTANCHE LIBRARY

9 Pier Road, St Helier JE2 4UW
☎ 01534 730538
www.societe-jersiaise.org

SUPERINTENDENT REGISTRAR

10 Royal Square, St Helier JE2 4WA
☎ 01534 502335

SARK
GENERAL REGISTRAR

La Valette, Sark

ISLE OF MAN

CHIEF REGISTRAR

The General Registry, Deemster's Walk,
Bucks Road, Douglas IM1 3AR
☎ 01624 687039
www.gov.im/registeries

HOUSE OF KEYS AND REGISTRY OFFICE

Deemsters Walk, Douglas IM1 3AR
☎ 01624 687039
www.gov.im

MANX MUSEUM

Kingswood Grove, Douglas
☎ 01624 648000
www.gov.im/mnh/manxmuseum.asp

INDEX

Page numbers in italics = photographs of documents

PICTURE CREDITS

The publishers wish to thank the following people for use of the following pictures in this book. The other pictures are from the collections of Anthony Adolph and of those listed in paragraph two, overleaf. Where only a picture credit is given, identification details can be found in the caption to the illustration. **BAL** = Bridgeman Art Library; **LMA** = London Metropolitan Archive

Cecilia Doidge-Ripper at the NA in the FRC and Rhys Griffith at the LMA; **12-13** *Portrait of a Family: The Birthday of the Mother* by J. Dastine © Archivo Iconografico, S.A./CORBIS; **26 below** National Gallery, London/BAL; **27 left** *Prosperous Victorian family, three generations united in a garden setting.* Photograph, c.1880. © Bettmann/CORBIS; **27 right** Old portrait of a family. © Andy Washnik/COR-BIS; **28** Public Record Office Building in Kew. © London Aerial Photo Library/CORBIS; **34** © Simonpietri Christian/CORBIS SYGMA; **39** Archivio di Stato, Siena, Italy/Alinari/BAL; **41** Cott Nero DIV f.139, British Library, London/BAL; **47** Office of National Statistics; **51** Christopher Wood Gallery, London/BAL; **52** *Gin Lane*, 1751, by William Hogarth/Bibliothèque Nationale, Paris, France, Lauros/Giraudon/BAL; **54** The Edge of Sherwood Forest, 1878 by Andrew MacCallum/Phillips, The International Fine Art Auctioneers, UK/BAL; **63** LMA; **65** Office of National Statistics; **67** Musée des Beaux-Arts, Arras, France, Giraudon / BAL; **68** FRC (Public Record Office); **76** Census in 1949. © Hulton-Deutsch Collection/CORBIS; **84** Phone directory of the United Telephone Company, 1885; **85** Mary Evans Picture Library; **86** Guildhall Art Gallery, Corporation of London/BAL; **87** Musée de l'Assistance Publique, Hopitaux de Paris, France/BAL; **88** LMA; **92** LMA; **94** LMA; **96** York Museums Trust (York Art Gallery), UK/BAL; **97** *Lord Cromwell, Wearing the Order of St George* by Hans Holbein (school of)/The Trustees of the Weston Park Foundation/BAL; **102** Christie's Images, London/BAL; **103 above** *Racquets at the Fleet Prison*, illustration from *London Life*, pub. 1809, English School (19th century)/Private Collection, photo: Wingfield Sporting Gallery, London/BAL; **108** Phillimore Publishers; **114** Society of Genealogists; **116-17** *View of New Amsterdam*, 1650–3, Dutch School (17th century)/Museum of the City of New York/BAL; **118** Yale Center for British Art, Paul Mellon Fund, USA/BAL; **119** Great Bealings Manorial Court Book 1746–1803. Suffolk Record Office, Ipswich. Ref 51/2/32/2 p.84; **121** The Berger Collection at the Denver Art Museum, USA/BAL; **122** Fol.10v Biblioteca Marciana, Venice, Italy, photo: Roger-Viollet, Paris/BAL; **124** Fol.195v from *Justiniani in Fortiatum*, French School (14th century)/Biblioteca Monasterio del Escorial, Madrid, Spain, Giraudon/BAL; **125** Hampshire Record Office; **142-143** Sir Arthur Conan Doyle and his Family, 1922. © Bettmann/CORBIS; **154** LMA; **156** Private Collection, photo: The Stapleton Collection/BAL; **157** Private Collection, photo: Michael Graham-Stewart/BAL; **158** Musée des Arts d'Afrique et d'Océanie, Paris, France, photo: Archives Charmet/BAL; **159** © New-York Historical Society, New York/BAL; **160** Detail from Camberwell and Stockwell map, reproduced from the 1913 Ordnance Survey Map; **161 above** Private Collection/BAL; **161 below** Lancashire Record Office; **168** Suffolk Record Office, Ipswich; **170** Hampshire Record Office; **172** Guildhall Library, Corporation of London/BAL; **174** City of Westminster Archive Centre, London/BAL; **175** Royal Holloway, University of London/BAL; **176** Private Collection/BAL; **177** National Gallery, London/BAL; **180** The Maas Gallery, London/BAL; **182** The Postman from *Costume of Great Britain*, 1805, by William Henry Pyne/Guildhall Library, Corporation of London/BAL; **191 left** © Stapleton Collection/CORBIS; **192-3** © Historical Picture Archive/COR-BIS; **194** © CORBIS; **195** *The Battle of Isandhlwana*, 1879, by Charles Edwin Fripp/National Army Museum, London/BAL; **197** © Hulton-Deutsch Collection/CORBIS; **198** © Hulton-Deutsch Collection/CORBIS; **199** Unveiling of the Royal Artillery War Memorial, London in 1925. © Hulton-Deutsch Collection/CORBIS; **203** NA (Public Record Office) ADM 38; **205** NA (Public Record Office) ADM 188; **206** NA (Public Records Office) ADM 192; **206** © Hulton-Deutsch Collection/CORBIS; **209** Private Collection, photo: Royal Exchange Art Gallery at Cork Street, London/BAL; **210** Private Collection, photo: The Stapleton Collection/BAL; **211** © Hulton-Deutsch Collection/CORBIS; **215** The Trustees of the Weston Park Foundation/BAL; **216** Abbot Hall Art Gallery, Kendal, Cumbria/BAL; **217** NA (Public Record Office) E 179; **223** An Execution of Witches in England, English School (17th century)/Private Collection, photo: The Stapleton Collection/BAL; **225** © Bettmann/CORBIS; **229** House of Lords from Ackermann's *Microcosm of London* by T. Rowlandson & A.C. Pugin/Private Collection/BAL; **233** *Execution of John Thurtell at Hertford Jail in 1824*, Anonymous/Guildhall Library, Corporation of London/BAL; **234** Guildhall Art Gallery, Corporation of London/ BAL; **239** NA (Public Record Office) HO 144; **247** Map of East Prussia. from *Le Theatre du Monde* or *Nouvel Atlas*, 1645, by Joan Blaeu/ Bibliotheque des Arts Decoratifs, Paris, France, photo: Archives Charmet/BAL; **253** *In the Land of Promise* by Charles Frederic Ulrich/ Corcoran Gallery of Art, Washington DC/BAL; **254** *A Government Jail Gang, Sydney, New South Wales*, 19th century by Augustus Earle/ Private Collection/BAL; **256** Private Collection, photo: Philip Mould, Historical Portraits Ltd, London/BAL; **259** Mallett & Son Antiques Ltd, London, UK/BAL; **264 left** *Portrait of George Fox*, engraving after Painting by Chinn. © Bettmann/CORBIS; **264 right** © Bettmann/CORBIS; **267** *Swarthmore Hall* by John Jewell Penstone/Newport Museum and Art Gallery, . South Wales/BAL; **269** Private Collection, photo: Christie's Images/BAL; **270** © Archivo Iconografico, S.A./CORBIS; **271** © CORBIS SYGMA; **272** © Mike Laye/CORBIS; **273** © Lee Snider/CORBIS; **274–5** Smiling Young Family on doorstep. © Leland Bobbé/CORBIS; **276** © Digital Art/CORBIS; **279** Boats moored along fishing village, Iceland. © Layne Kennedy/CORBIS; **280** *Victoria at age two, with her mother, the duchess of Kent*, 1821, by Sir William Beechey. Mary Evans Picture Library; **281** © Bettmann/CORBIS; **282 above** © Hulton-Deutsch Collection/CORBIS; **282 below** Ms.3066 fol.42 v Bibliotheque Municipale, Rouen, France/BAL; **284** San Michele in Isola, Venice, Italy/BAL; **287** *Clans of Scotland* by W. Eagle, no date (c.1850); **288** Sign at St. Patrick's Quay, Cork. © Richard Cummins/CORBIS; **290** Private Collection, photo: The Stapleton Collection/BAL; **291** Lord Lyon's Office, Edinburgh, Scotland, photo: Mark Fiennes/BAL; **294** © Tim Graham/CORBIS; **299** Harley 4205 f.37 British Library, London/BAL; **300 above** Stirling Castle, Scotland/BAL; **301** © Royal Hospital Chelsea, London/BAL.

ACKNOWLEDGEMENTS

AUTHOR'S THANKS

This book could not have been written without the help of many people – the expertise I have picked up over the years from a host of genealogists, professional and amateur, or the many clients and TV volunteers whose research cases first alerted me to some of the examples I have used in the text. My thanks go out to all of them in proportion to the kindness they have shown me. I would particularly like to thank those colleagues in the profession who have been of direct help in providing facts used in the text: Marie Louise Backhurst, Judith Batchelor, Mrs Nancy Bedwell, Sarah Bulson, Mark Bonthrone, Rosemary Byatt, Philip Coverdale, Veronica Craig Mair, Patric Dickinson (Richmond Herald), Essex Record Office, Norman Fairfax, Simon Fowler (to whom especial thanks are due for his help with the chapter on armed forces), Michael Gandy, Joanna Guariglia, Mrs Josephine Harwood-Little, Reg Havers, Peter Horne, Mrs Dora Kneebone, Daphne Knott, Richard Lloyd-Roberts, Justin Martin, Sue Mendel, Peter Nutt, Jeremy Palmer, Tinka Paterson, Mark Pearsall, Dr Peter Pohl, Chris Schofield, Diana Spelman, Steve Thomas, Gerry Toop, Charles Tucker, Basil Twigg and Michael Watts. Especial thanks, too, go to my esteemed fellow writer James Essinger who gave me enormously valuable encouragement at the outset of my writing career; my agent, Michael Alcock of Johnson & Alcock Ltd, who calmly created the opportunity for me to write this book; Denise Bates of Collins, who had the wonderful prescience to conceive and commission it in the first place; Emma Callery for managing the project, Brian DeLeeuw for his help with the initial stages, Ruth Prentice for her handsome design, and Kate Parker for her meticulous proofreading.

My thanks also go to those who gave me their kind permission to use their stories in this book, including those that space did not, ultimately, permit us to use: Mrs Deorwyn Baker; Mrs Lorna Barbour; J. Blain Esq.; Mrs Claudia Brannback; I. Burns-Thompson Esq.; Mark Curtis Esq.; W. H.Galleway Esq.; Louisa Jenkins; Dr Terry Lacy; T. J. Lewis Esq.; P.Lingen-Stallard Esq.; P. J. Littlemore Esq.; M. A. Lowry Esq.; Messrs M. S. and U. Mehta; Major P. Mercer; Simon Mountenay Esq., W. C. Nichols Esq; Major R. D. Seals; D. P. Stewart Esq.; F. J. Tourlamain Esq.; R. V. Upton Esq.; Vice Admiral D. B. H.Wildish CB; L. A. Wilmshurst Esq.; M. Wilson Esq.; to Ms Petra Barberini; Ms Benhilda Chisveto and Ms Naomi Jalil, whom I was unable to locate, I send my thanks for alerting me to their wonderful family stories through *Extraordinary Ancestors*.

It has been commonplace to say that we live in a dislocated society, in which people do not feel they belong, and do not understand where they come from. Yet, thanks to genealogy (amongst other things), we are becoming much better informed. More and more people tracing family trees means more and more people are aware of the plethora of connections that bind us together and which make nonsense of religious and ethnic divides. If society is becoming a little fairer, less prejudiced and more cohesive, then genealogy can take its share of the credit and, the more popular it becomes, the greater too – I hope – will be its positive effects. But, above all, enjoy it.

To Dad

Happy Birthday

love

Sooney.